Losing Our Minds:
Gifted Children Left Behind

Deborah L. Ruf, Ph.D.

Great Potential Press
www.giftedbooks.com

Losing Our Minds: Gifted Children Left Behind

Cover design: MW Velgos Design
Cover photo: Scott Baxter/Getty Images
Interior design: Lisa Liddy, The Printed Page
Edited by: Jennifer Ault Rosso

Published by Great Potential Press, Inc.
P.O. Box 5057
Scottsdale, AZ 85261

Printed on recycled paper

© 2005 by Great Potential Press

09 08 07 06 05   5 4 3 2 1

Library of Congress Cataloging-in-Publication Data

Ruf, Deborah L.
  Losing our minds : gifted children left behind / Deborah L. Ruf.
      p. cm.
  Includes bibliographical references and index.
  ISBN 0-910707-70-7 (pbk.)
  1. Gifted children—Education—United States. 2. Gifted
children—Identification. I. Title.
  LC3993.9.R84 2005
  371.95—dc22
                                          2005008779

Acknowledgments

My children inspired me to learn about giftedness and to write this book. I only wish I'd known about giftedness sooner so they could have benefited more while they were still children.

Just as this book would never have happened without what I learned as a parent, my husband, too, deserves considerable credit for giving me a way to get it done. He edited, cajoled, cooked, and listened. I couldn't ask for more.

I am grateful to my extended family for their existence, their struggles, and the examples they've given me with their own lives. Knowing them has enriched me and helped to inform my work.

I also acknowledge the tremendous contributions made by the parents of the children in this book. Many of them wrote extensively as they shared their experiences with me. We learned from each other. I am forever grateful to them for their willingness to take so much time to share their stories so that other parents could learn from them.

And finally, I thank my editors Janet Gore, Jim Webb, and Jen Ault Rosso, because they took my words and ideas and made them better, and Great Potential Press for publishing this book.

Contents

Tables and Charts

Preface

When I became the parent of three highly intelligent children, I assumed that the schools—public or private—would know how to treat them. I was wrong. I didn't know how to treat them myself, nor did I know what changes to insist be made by their schools. There were times when I was so totally frustrated that I wanted to scream—or maybe cry. I knew my children and what they could do. Why were the schools insisting that they repeat skills that they had known for a long time? I was incredulous that the schools didn't recognize that my children needed a more advanced level and a faster pace of learning. I tried home schooling for one year and was successful but was unable for personal reasons to continue. So for most of their school years, I managed to negotiate at least some modifications for my children within the school structure that already existed.

As I learned more about high intelligence and schools over the years, I realized that there can never be a "perfect" school situation for a highly or profoundly gifted child. There must always be compromises. Fortunately, I learned how to choose schools that would best meet my children's needs, how to negotiate for important modifications, and how to let go of the idea that everything needed to be perfect. Thankfully, my children are now all grown, out of the nest, and thriving.

My efforts to advocate for my children led me, in time, to enroll in graduate school to study high intelligence. For the past 24 years, I have specialized in consulting with families of highly intelligent children, in which I guide parents through an understanding of various kinds of tests and testing procedures, gifted program approaches, and the options available to them and their children. I help family members and school systems understand and accept what is normal for different levels of intelligence found in gifted children. I give parents my "Crash Course in Giftedness."

This book provides much of the same information I give to parents. Making this information widely available is particularly important, because there are many, many more of these highly intelligent children in our world than most people think. In the book, I explain the reasons for this.

I hope my book will raise some concern about how we, as a society, fail to both recognize and respect highly intelligent children and, consequently, fail to help them develop their potential. If my book fosters a new awareness, if it helps parents accept their children's differences, if it helps schools understand how highly intelligent children grow and learn, if it prompts schools to use more flexible approaches than the current strict grade-level education, then my efforts will be rewarded.

I hope you enjoy the book.

~ Deborah Ruf

Introduction

This is a book about gifted children, their parents, and how our nation's schools currently respond to children with high intelligence—particularly those in the highest levels. It describes how schools often fail to recognize varying intellectual levels and profiles, making it difficult—if not impossible—to meet the social, emotional, and academic needs of large numbers of our nation's brightest students. Wouldn't a rational person believe that a nation should notice and nurture those who have exceptionally high intelligence? The answer seems obvious. But in practice, America is leaving many of its brightest children behind.

We are a nation of many individuals with a multitude of different abilities and talents. We are a democracy. We want everyone to have the opportunity to learn at an optimal level. Yet we are neglecting our brightest children. Rather than implementing strategies to maximize potential in *all* children, schools currently accentuate programs for those who struggle to learn. This emphasis on slower students is important, but it should not deprive those who are able to learn at the highest levels.

Many exceptionally bright children live in homes and learn in classrooms where the adults responsible for them don't know, don't realize, or don't fully understand their true intellectual potential. These bright children languish in classrooms designed to meet the needs of children far slower at learning. Some of these children are mistakenly labeled with behavior problems when in fact it is their frustration that causes them to act out.

The learning differences and needs of children with very high intelligence are described in this book. Data from 50 families with 78 different gifted children provide specific information about the characteristics, behaviors, abilities, and problems that often occur. These children are highly intelligent at different levels, and they each have different strengths, weaknesses, inner drives, and personalities. Their stories illustrate ways in which children at the high end of the ability spectrum differ significantly from average children and even from each other. Five chapters of this book show the progression of intellectual expression, from birth to teen years, for children at five different levels of giftedness, ranging from those who are simply bright to those who are intellectually astonishing.

This book is for parents of gifted children—those whose intellectual levels have been previously estimated primarily by IQ test scores. It is also for those professionals—educators and/or psychologists—who work with the families of these children.

A principal goal of the book is to help readers understand that there is a large range among gifted individuals, that there are different *levels of giftedness*, and that high intelligence is not an "either-or" concept—intelligence exists along an outward-moving continuum. There is no magic line between *gifted* and *not gifted*, nor is there a stationary or fixed line between different levels of intelligence.

A secondary goal of this book is to emphasize the surprising frequency of very high levels of intelligence. Most people don't realize that there are far more potential geniuses—children who are remarkably intellectually different from their same-age classmates—than the oft-repeated "one in a thousand" or "one in a million" statistics would suggest.

The chapters containing information about the five levels of giftedness will show—in clear, factual, conceptual, and anecdotal terms—what gifted people at different, defined levels of high intelligence act like at various stages of their young lives. These descriptions will help readers recognize different levels of giftedness in children they know. The first-person accounts from parents convey a true picture of these subjects as people, which is different from the traditional clinical style of ticking off lists of benchmark behaviors. This illustrates the often-disruptive effect that a child at higher levels—Levels Three through Five—can have on a family, and it allows readers to put their own experiences into perspective.

To some, the term "gifted" implies that unusual intelligence is altogether a blessing, a "gift." The vignettes of real individuals reveals the reality of gifted children—the ways in which the charming, the problematic, and the quirky are all part of the normal range of behaviors among them.

Real people who come from real families are this book's contributors. Though their names are changed, their stories are genuine and sincere. These anonymous collaborators want their experiences to inform and assist others in finding social and emotional connections and balance. They have shared their experiences, feelings, worries, frustrations, angers, joys, and pains as they learned about how high levels of intelligence create special needs and considerations.

It is important to understand, too, that, although giftedness runs in families, not all siblings are necessarily similar to one another or to their parents in intellectual ability. Most of the families highlighted in this book exhibit a range of intelligence and talents, a reality that creates a variety of parenting dilemmas and choices. For example, just as treating all children the same in a classroom is a poor educational practice, treating all children identically within a family is a poor parenting practice. Both can lead to problems.

Intellectual level is a significant aspect of our personality, our drives, our interests, and the ways in which we interpret, cope with, and react to circumstances in our lives. When a child's intellectual level is radically different from others, he or she needs help learning how to handle that difference. The information and stories presented in this book will guide those efforts.

Part I:

What Does it Mean to Be Gifted?

A n abundance of definitions and descriptions exist for the term "gifted." Most people accept that it implies being smarter than the majority of the population. But what exactly does that mean?

Intelligence is an intangible concept that defies being distilled into a checklist of learning or thinking traits. Many behaviors besides intelligence are also associated with giftedness, and the more gifted the child, the more clearly these behaviors are present. The range of behaviors and traits varies enormously within the highly intelligent population. While lists of characteristics are helpful, they are only a starting point for parents trying to figure out whether or not their child is gifted—and to what degree.

Level of intelligence greatly affects how people learn, of course, and there is more to giftedness than just how they perform in school. Intellectual level influences our desire to learn complex material and also our ability to feel connected to and comfortable with those around us. An unusual intellectual level can actually be at the root of many problems for both children and their families.

People who are within the average range of intelligence constitute the majority of the population. Although a bell-shaped curve does not perfectly describe the intellectual distribution of people, we do know that the majority of people—people clustered in the average ability range—are not significantly different from one another in their learning abilities. For these people in the middle, it is fairly easy to find others who share interests and abilities. But those who are not part of the mid-range mainstream have an intellectual level that is likely quite different from those with whom they spend most of their time—especially during their elementary school years—and the differences can make gifted children feel out-of-place, unwelcome, or even unacceptable.

As adults, gifted individuals are usually able to follow their interests and abilities and find people similar to themselves. But during the early school years, it is age, rather than ability or interests, that locks children into classrooms where the number of like-minded classmates is small. The learning environment at school becomes less and less appropriate for the child who is far out on the high end of the intelligence continuum. Keeping this in mind helps parents analyze what each of their children needs in order to thrive.

Parents of unusually intelligent children are typically surprised by their children's behaviors, and they find that the available parenting books don't address many of their concerns. They then begin an ongoing pursuit of information and solutions to meet the needs of their very bright children. To help readers understand what high intelligence is and how it affects individuals and families, Part I of this book offers general definitions of giftedness and high intelligence. It also describes one family's experience with an unusually gifted child. This particular child is at the highest level of giftedness, sometimes called profoundly gifted, and readers should not be misled into thinking that he represents all gifted children. He is, however, a dramatic example—although his story has much in common with the stories of the 78 other children in this book. Vignettes from their parents confirm that these children and their experiences are definitely more common than standard ability and percentile scores would lead us to believe.

Chapter 1
One Family's Story

Just after my middle son, Rick, turned three, he was watching *Sesame Street* and saw basketball player Julius Irving make 20 baskets in a row. Although this was simply a visual demonstration to teach young children to count, my son took it as a challenge to make 20 baskets in a row himself. He had gone to college basketball games with his father from the time he was two years old, and he always amazed others seated nearby with his accurate ability to keep score and focus on the game for hours. Because of his high interest, I taped a child's basketball hoop to our recreation room wall downstairs. Probably about three feet tall at the time, this little boy immediately began his quest to "make 20 baskets in a row like Dr. J."

Rick was definitely intense, and from the kitchen upstairs, I heard him dribbling his little basketball around on the hard basement carpet—he was already quite the ball handler. I heard him counting to the sound of the ball hitting the wood paneled wall and then, "Oh, rats!" before the dribbling started over again. He slowly counted upwards as he made one basket after another and then, "Oh, rats!" again, as he missed and started over again. Since he was prone to mini-tantrums when he got frustrated, I intervened just enough to explain cutaway photography and film editing to him. I was worried that he was going to be bitterly disappointed at his inability to do something that very few could do anyway. I told him that even Dr. J had trouble shooting 20 baskets in a row.

Still, he persisted. He was determined to do it. Not quite three hours later, my little boy emerged from the basement victorious, beaming, arms in the air, exclaiming, "I did it!" I believe that he did do it, too. He has always had the incredible determination it takes to practice and master difficult tasks.

Rick was the same child who, at his preschool screening a year later, was recommended for medical attention due to distractibility and a poor attention span. He had become obsessed with books on natural and manmade disasters and worried incessantly for months about flash floods that could wash our house away. His mind and his will were frequently way ahead of his experience and knowledge of the world. By kindergarten, he was often somber, and he expressed that he wasn't sure there was really any point to living. Other parents called to tell me that they'd heard him say he wished he were dead. Experts I consulted didn't believe me. They said children that young don't think seriously about such things.

Although I figured out years later that my little boy was simply expressing his existential concerns about the value and meaning of life—his own, in particular—I was worried about his mental and emotional health throughout his kindergarten year. He came to me one day and earnestly asked, "What's the worst disease?" Not wanting to give a simplified black-and-white answer, I told him that it was hard to decide because there are so many horrible and tragic diseases. I was also concerned—given his frequent talk about death—that he might want to catch whatever the "worst" disease was in order to end his own life quickly. So I asked him why he wanted to know.

He said, "I figured that if I knew the worst disease, I could find a cure for it, and then my life would have some reason for existing." You can see why I worried about him; he was so serious about life at such a young age.

While still a five-year-old, Rick was trying to decide how to make his mark and find his place in the world. Because inventing something might be as good as curing a disease, he asked, "Mom, what can I invent?" To personally feel that his life mattered, he needed to find a reason for being. Imagine the pressure he felt. Imagine the pressure for both of us. But there was humor in it, too, as I told him, "Rick, if I knew what to invent, I would do it myself." He smiled.

A Family Affair

When Rick was 1½ years old and his older brother Chuck was 3½, I joined a women's bowling league and took the boys with me while I bowled. Rick liked to climb onto a bench by the nursery window to watch us. When my team finished bowling, I was ready to go home, and Chuck was ready to go with me, but not Rick. He wouldn't leave the bowling alley until every last ball had been thrown. He wasn't trying to be naughty; he just wanted to see how all of the games turned out.

Despite his many unusually adult-like behaviors, Rick also had plenty of kid-like tendencies, although he could be unusually intense and strong-willed in exhibiting them. He was very difficult, stubborn, and temperamental. When he was about one year old, he nearly fell out of his father's arms reaching for me and clearly stating, "No! I want *Mom* to do it." He also went through a phase of throwing tantrums. Even after the tantrums subsided, I frequently heard criticism from both sets of grandparents about what a badly behaving child Rick was—and that my lax parenting was causing the problem. They thought that I let him get away with too much. They much preferred Chuck, a darling and well-behaved boy, and accused me of favoring Rick, whom they thought was terribly spoiled. It didn't seem to me that I was spoiling Rick or giving in to him, so these criticisms stung.

By the time Rick was not quite four and his older brother Chuck was five, they could play adult board games without help. *Life* (which is labeled for children ages eight and up) was one of their favorites. It uses game tokens, a number spinner, money, and spaces on the "road of life" that tell players what to do next. Both boys could read the directions, but Chuck figured out early that Rick should be the banker because Rick already had a very good grasp of numbers, money, place value, and making change. He already understood how to multiply by 10s, 100s, and 1,000s.

When Rick was 4½ and Chuck was six, Bill was born. Each child was very different, and although the new baby required a great deal of attention, Rick continued to be the most demanding and difficult. As I took care of the baby, the two older boys spent more time playing with each other. Video games were new, and *Space Invaders* was one the boys enjoyed. When Rick came to me and asked me how to read the large number scores, I wrote out 15 digits, with commas in the correct places, and then wrote above each digit what the "place" was called. Then I pointed and said, "Numbers in this space are the 1s; these are the 10s; these are the 100s. Then this whole group is 1000s, and you start over with 1s, 10s, and 100,000s. Then the millions category…." It took 10 minutes, and he was done learning those concepts. Forever. No additional rehearsals necessary. When I told my mother over the phone about this amazing feat, she responded, "That's nice, dear. Do you have any other children?"

Everyone thought that I should talk equally about my children, and yet I was so often worried or amazed by Rick that it was hard not to talk about what he had learned or done. In addition, I wanted others' perspectives and hoped they could give me advice and support. Most had none to give. Maybe they thought I was making it all up. Or perhaps they just didn't want to hear it, thinking I was shamelessly bragging and preferring one child over the others. My need to talk wasn't just about his abilities; it was about his intensity and his temper. I really didn't know how to handle them. My other two children, both gifted as well, were much easier to deal with.

Chuck and Rick both preferred each other's company to that of other children, which was good, at least for the two of them. My husband and I discovered early that our children did not socialize well with other families, and it hurt a number of our friendships with other couples, neighbors, and relatives. When compared with others, our children were talkative and "bossy," preferred to be with older children or adults, and clearly had knowledge and skills beyond that of children their own ages. I think others saw them as pushy and odd, and they assumed it was our fault. They thought that their intensity—some said the boys were "hyper"—was due to the way we were raising them, rather than because these children were inherently different.

I participated in a babysitting co-op—a group of mothers who exchanged child-care hours. People liked bringing their children to me, probably because their children had a good time at our house. But when it was time for me to take my children to someone else's house, word got out quickly that they were a handful. Several times when I arrived to pick them up, they already had their coats and hats on and were by the door. It seemed that the babysitting mother couldn't wait to get rid of them. Some mothers specifically complained that my children preferred to stay and interact with them rather than play with the other children. Of course, this made more work for these mothers. Even as babies, my children would not sit in an infant seat unless you were engaged with them the whole time. If I was still in the same room but turned my back for a minute, they would scream for attention. All three of my children made eye contact at birth and were visibly agitated and upset when they couldn't see and interact with a grown-up. I learned later that these are fairly typical behaviors for highly intelligent children.

When Rick was an infant, my husband and I would silently cheer whenever he finally rubbed his eyes and looked sleepy. He never just slowed down; he literally went from totally alert and active to being totally ready to sleep. I've since learned that this fight to stay awake followed by "crashing" into sleep is typical of some highly gifted children, but I didn't know it at the time. I wish I had. It would have made it easier for me to relax about my parenting.

Early School Years

My oldest child, Chuck, was clearly smart and quite advanced intellectually and academically for his age. But Rick, who was only one year behind him in school, was rapidly overtaking him. Rick came home from kindergarten one day saying, "I hate school." Curious and worried, I asked him what was it about school that he hated.

"Frankly, it just wastes so much of my *time*."

He was right. Even though Rick had passed every single pre-test for kindergarten skills, no special provisions were made for him except those I took to the teacher myself. Somehow I just assumed that school personnel would see that my child was exceptional and unusual, and they would know what specific things to do with him. I couldn't have been more wrong.

What was I supposed to do with my two boys? It didn't seem a good idea to skip Rick into the same grade as his brother. I didn't want to hurt the feelings of my eldest, but this second child of ours was a real issue. Finally, the school agreed to test both boys for intellectual level. I knew by then that an IQ of around 130 was the start of the gifted ability range. Chuck scored in the moderately gifted range—in the 130s. Rick scored in the low 140s. Rick's score seemed far too low to explain what I was seeing in his learning and behaviors. Later, I found out that the school psychologist had tested him only until she could see that he was well into the gifted range. Then she stopped the test. She apparently believed that "gifted is gifted"—just one all-encompassing category. She even used the best test at the time for assessing the highest levels of intelligence, but as I learned later, she used it incorrectly. She didn't test him to the highest levels he could successfully complete.

In all, however, kindergarten was actually not too bad for Rick. His teacher recognized his abilities, accepted suggestions and materials I gave her, and remained flexible and supportive of him all year. I gave her activity books and workbooks for older children, and she allowed him to work through those on his own while the rest of the class practiced making their letters. She let him read whatever he brought to school or found in the library, and this gave him something to do while the other children were learning to count by 2s and 5s, or whatever they were doing that he already knew how to do. Besides, kindergarten was only half days and included the types of playtime that Rick enjoyed.

For first grade, though, my husband and I decided that I should home school Rick. I'd been an elementary school teacher for six years before having children of my own, but just so I'd be a little more formal and organized, I took on another highly gifted child. Jennifer's parents were so grateful that I was home schooling her, too, at no charge, that they paid for our youngest son Bill's daycare. In one year of half-day home school, these two highly gifted children finished first- through sixth-grade curriculum. To give them a chance to socialize with others their own age (and to give me a break), I was able to send them to the regular first-grade classroom for lunch and to spend the afternoon with their age-mates.

Radical Adjustments

Our older son, Chuck, sat through nearly a whole year of kindergarten before the teacher realized that he could already read chapter books[1] and did not need to learn the letter poems to remember the letters of the alphabet. Clearly, the school wasn't a good fit. And with Rick, I found that one year of home schooling had exhausted my knowledge of the elementary curriculum. I thought there *had* to be a good school for my children *somewhere*. After discussing alternatives, my husband and I decided to move our children to a larger city where there would be more options.

So the children and I left our small community and moved to Minneapolis, a four-hour drive from where my husband worked. He commuted on weekends to visit us, and we enrolled our two oldest sons in a highly recommended private school that assured us they could meet our children's needs. Bill, our youngest, eventually enrolled in the same school—a selective college preparatory school—and the children attended this same K-12 school for a total of 16 consecutive years.

In their first school year, both boys were invited into the gifted program, and we attended a meeting to learn what the school would do for them. No one mentioned to us that children within the gifted range often differ significantly from one another. Within a few months, I found myself becoming alternately angry and frustrated with this new, more expensive school. The pace was still too slow, and it seemed to have a "watered-down" curriculum. Hadn't they read my notes on what my child could do? It turned out that they had not. The teacher explained that she didn't like to bias herself by reading the children's files. When I complained that Rick could at least be doing higher-level math, she told me that several students in the class were better at math than Rick. Incredulous, I asked how that was possible. She replied that Rick often missed a couple of problems on the "Mad Minute," a daily timed quiz of arithmetic facts—one digit addition and subtraction fact problems that the whole class took every day until everyone could get a perfect score in under a minute. Knowing Rick as I did, I was very surprised he bothered to do the quiz at all.

Taking Matters into Our Own Hands

About halfway through that first year in Minneapolis, I decided to have my two older boys tested by an independent expert—a private psychologist. Chuck, now in third grade, scored solidly gifted and well within the range that the school was prepared to handle. In fact, the school turned out to be a very good place for him. In his years there, he built several solid friendships, encountered good teachers, participated in wonderful activities, and had many good learning and study opportunities.

Our second grader, Rick, on the other hand, scored so high that the school refused to accept his score as accurate. Although the psychologist listed in a four-page test report all of the things that Rick's school should do for him, the school ignored everything the man wrote. The school then decided to test Rick themselves; they gave him the *Stanford Individual Diagnostic Achievement Tests* and discovered that he hit nearly every test ceiling. Although Rick was just 7¾ years old and in second grade, his grade equivalency scores were 7-0 (seventh grade, zero months) for auditory vocabulary, 10-6 for reading comprehension, the test ceiling of 12-9+ for phonetic analysis, and the test ceiling of 8-9+ for all four math sections. It is easy to understand why I didn't want to home school him any more—it would be too hard for me to stay ahead of him!

Educational planning became a problem. Rick could not be "ability grouped" with other bright kids in his class in a way that would close the intellectual and learning gap. Moving him ahead 10 years wasn't feasible, either—at least not without creating many new and possibly greater problems. So the school agreed to let us hire, at our own expense, tutors to teach Rick at his own level during the school day on the school's campus. That year went well as Rick enthusiastically studied and enjoyed Shakespeare, Poe, Roman and Greek history, and general sciences with different tutors. He also studied accelerated math so that, by fourth grade, he could qualify for a fast-paced high school math sequence held at our local university for math-talented seventh graders.

None of this caused embarrassment for Rick's older brother—something that had concerned us. Although we continued to struggle with what was best for Rick, things finally got easier when he was old enough for high school and had other options available to him that are offered for older gifted children. At last, his school experiences were closer to meeting his ability.

Chapter 2
Issues for Parents

*I was so worried, confused, and angry, and I didn't know where
to turn. It was so hard because almost anyone that I talked to
about my child's abilities thought that I was bragging or, if I
tried to paint the difficult side of the issue, that my child was an
aberration. Sometimes people would respond by saying
something like, "Oh, I have a neighbor with a child like that,"
but I could only doubt that this was true.*

~ Mother of a profoundly gifted child

Parents of gifted children usually don't anticipate problems raising them. Many of these parents are intellectually advanced as well, but their own experiences as gifted children—the loneliness and the too slow pace in school—have largely faded. Few gifted adults even recognize or understand the connection that their intellectual level had on their childhood experiences. It takes time before most parents realize that having a highly intelligent child can present problems and that they ultimately need to have their child assessed in order to provide for the child's development. This chapter describes issues that families typically experience as they raise their gifted children, and it includes vignettes from parents of children you will come to know later in this book.

Discovering that the Child Is Different

Parents don't expect to have an unusual child, so the comments of others often take an emotional toll. There is a natural sense of pride when comments about the child are complimentary and positive, yet parents sometimes feel awkward accepting these compliments because they view the child's abilities as natural gifts more than their own doing. They often experience an ongoing conflict between how to encourage their child's ability in an area while at the same time maintaining humility. Parents of other children may see them as pushy and enmeshed, which may provoke resentment from others. But perhaps the most serious issue with parenting gifted children, particularly those who are highly gifted, is the tremendous sense of being alone and misunderstood and having no other parents with the same issues to talk to.

Positive Feedback

Parents of bright children start to hear positive comments very early during the child's preschool years because this is the time when children are free to do what they enjoy and are naturally good at. But these parents are not always sure whether observations of others are accurate or merely polite. Unless there are other children the same age around for comparison, parents don't always know just *how* unusual their child is. When we add in the fact that intelligence has a strong genetic component, other relatives may have so much in common with the young family that they don't see the precocity; this is normal for them.[1] However, when complete strangers in restaurants or stores notice that the child is advanced or charming in one way or another, parents naturally come to think that others, namely school personnel, will also notice these qualities. Trips to the doctor's office often give them their first unbiased feedback.

Debra Sund—Debra's preschool teacher told me that she had to tear herself away from Debra sometimes because they had such wonderful conversations. People who'd hear Debra say things beyond her years would say, "She's really smart! Did you know that?"

Justin Janacek—Our friends, neighbors, and parents of preschool classmates were often incredulous over Justin's abilities and good behavior. We got lots of positive feedback. I never felt any envy or resentment from other parents.

Emily Newton—During her toddler and preschool days, we often got comments about Emily's abilities. While we were proud of her and thought that she was special, I think that we thought people were being nice, and we didn't recognize how truly advanced she was compared to others.

Rebecca Resnick—Rebecca's grandmother pointed out several times when Rebecca was two or three years old that she was sensitive and had compassion for how others felt. A family friend who was also a physical therapist in the school said that I should talk to the schools early about

Rebecca because she was so advanced in her thinking that the schools needed time to get ready for her.

Colin Richards—Casual acquaintances and strangers all reacted with astonishment when they saw how Colin could read, spell, count, etc. at such a young age.

Michael Cortez—Even though I did not disclose anything about Michael's abilities to others except family, relatives, and very close friends, the Montessori school principal, the kindergarten teacher, people in department stores and in the grocery store all noticed his reading and advanced speaking, and they commented admiringly.

Negative Feedback

Most parents are thrilled when their children first sit up, start to walk, say their first words, and so on. When the parents of gifted children try to share this normal excitement and pleasure with others, they soon learn that they should not talk about their children's accomplishments the way other parents do because they sometimes get negative reactions from others—even from their own relatives. It is painful to have people react to your child as though something is wrong, yet some parents of gifted children face this every day. They may be misperceived as bragging, exaggerating, or even fabricating stories about their gifted child's achievements.

William Jones—Sometimes people couldn't follow Will's train of thought. I saw him as an "Einstein type"—and people thought that Einstein was a little odd, too.

Tyler Lundquist—We had never heard a negative comment from Tyler's preschool teacher, but at our first conference in kindergarten, *everything* was negative. The teacher said that he used baby talk, cried over every bump, didn't go to the bathroom on time, held his pencil wrong, and lacked self-control and self-discipline in social situations. We were absolutely crushed.

Keith Sands—My mother-in-law dismissed the idea that Keith was unusually gifted. My friends with similar age children sometimes showed disbelief and resentment.

Seth Cannon—Some adults reacted to Seth with amazement. Others, usually people we knew, were quick to add defensive notes about their own kids' accomplishments.

Bill Arnesen—We got occasional feedback that it made some children feel bad when Bill could read and they couldn't. I think this bothered the parents more than their children, though.

Rick Arnesen—Rick's kindergarten teacher ran an overview pre-test of everything that she would be teaching that year. The test included "challenge activities," which some children might be able to do by spring. She shared the results, without names, during parent conferences the second week of school. Many parents were actually angry when they saw Rick's high results.

It took quite a while for most of our friends and relatives to like Rick. He carried on conversations at a very high level, had a good sense of humor, and remembered everything you told him. But he also argued, was competitive, and was impatient if you didn't catch on to something as quickly as he thought you should.

Michael Cortez—A mother of one of Michael's classmates noticed Michael's abilities and started to ask about him. I felt that I could trust her, so I shared some stories about him with her. The next day, she was aloof and distant. From that point on, I was careful about sharing unique experiences in raising an advanced child.

Conflicting Feedback

Most of the conflicting feedback on gifted children comes from people who notice the child's precocity but do not understand its probable effects on the child's general understanding and behaviors.

Michael Fuller—Michael was quite the topic of conversation in our house. His gym teacher called to report that he'd forgotten his gym bag for the third time that month; his Spanish teacher raved about his extra credit project and his "lateral thinking"—but he still got a D- on the exam; and I called his father to tell him about Michael's creative writing paper juxtaposing a raindrop and a teardrop, with the latter attempting to communicate with the former.

Keith Sands—Keith was a very special child. Strangers found him entertaining, family friends sometimes found him obnoxious, teachers found him challenging, younger children found him great fun and interesting, and older children liked him.

Samantha Forrest—When I mentioned Samantha's boredom at school, my neighbor commented that maybe I should "just let her enjoy kindergarten." When we spoke to my mother-in-law about our plans to keep Samantha engaged in learning, she understood but also commented, "You know, they need time just to be kids, too." Although we agreed, it didn't reflect an understanding of the academic challenges that we were facing.

Bill Arnesen—Bill talked too much in class, but he was constantly asked to share his thoughts with his classmates. Then the teacher pointed out that some of what he said made no sense, and she told him to try to monitor what he said.

How Parents Learn What to Do

Before and after intellectual or medical assessments are done, many parents still don't know where to turn, whom to trust, or what to do in order to support their children's growth and development. Included among the parents' concerns are:

- Who can actually tell us what is best for our child?
- Is there something wrong with our child, or is it the school environment?
- Why do other people show resentment or competitive attitudes?
- How do we talk about this, and who is safe to talk to?
- How do we keep from being lonely and saddened by how time-consuming, frustrating, and difficult it is to find answers for our children?

Who Can We Turn To?

Parents expect schools to both embrace and care for their children. It takes most parents of gifted children a year or two to realize that this isn't likely to happen. If the child appears to adapt well, most parents quit worrying. However, if the child is unhappy with the school experience, parents set off on a journey of trying to figure out what might help. When these parents start to learn about some of the potential problems of gifted children whose environments are inappropriate, they become angry or dismayed that no one warned them of these possibilities.

Frank Price—We had questions. What must the school do for Frank by law? Are there Saturday programs or summer camps in our area for him? Should we be considering a private school? Are there private schools in our area where he would get what he needs? If we advance him now, what will he do later? He's unlikely to be emotionally ready for college until he's at least college-age. Is contact with same-age intellectual peers important? Where do we find that? How much do we push him (in piano, reading, exercise...)? He wants to sit around every minute he's not in school and read maps. Is that healthy? Should we buy him more maps, or should we try to expand his interests?

Arthur Richards—Arthur's response to the stress of school—frequent stomachaches and headaches—was a surprise. I didn't know what to do other than wait for a while before trying to enroll him again—maybe in high school. In the meantime, we home schooled.

Gina Oliver—Although Gina was a fluent reader when she started kindergarten, we had concerns. She had difficulty articulating her words, and people often couldn't understand what she was saying. She was screened for speech services but was not sufficiently behind. Since her birthday was the last day before the cut-off, we were worried about whether she should start kindergarten or wait a year. We ultimately decided to put her in kindergarten even though she was more than a year younger than some of the other students. In January of that year, she was formally identified for an articulation disorder and began speech pullout three times a week.

Author note: Gina qualified for special services for speech, but her school never considered her for acceleration or grouping for instruction at her own level and pace. Her parents didn't know how to find the right balance for her with the choices that they had.

Stephen Williams—When I began home schooling Stephen, he seemed to need time to just do what he wanted for a while. I couldn't get him to stick to a schedule. I could accept that for the time being, but his father couldn't. So life turned into a battleground for us (I wasn't doing my job, I was wasting Stephen's education, Stephen was stubborn, etc.). I alternated between thinking that it was okay that it had been a light academic year because he was still young, and worrying that he'd never learn to work hard and that he'd fall behind other bright kids out there.

Author note: When neither parent knows what the "right" thing to do is, family members can struggle among themselves. As with many other families, this mother left her own professional career to home school their son.

Sophie Fuller—When it was time for kindergarten, Sophie was reading as well as her older brother. Her older sister, realizing Sophie's high abilities, pleaded, "Don't send her! She won't learn a thing!" Even if I could talk the school principal into a full grade skip to first grade, I worried that he would put her with the less adequate first-grade teacher. I knew that the specialist helping us would say soothing things like, "We'll try several different approaches. If one doesn't work out, we'll try something else." But at that point, I needed to hear, "Do XYZ. It will work. It will help. Your child will not feel different. Your child will feel comfortable socially. Your child will be included. There is a good place for her." The source of my frustration was fear, I'm sure. I was afraid that my efforts on behalf of my children wouldn't be good enough—that they could hurt them or keep them from getting where they could or should be.

Brennan Ahlers—I was naïve. I thought that the schools would be thrilled to have such a curious, bright, energetic child as Brennan. But what they saw was a nuisance—a child that they had to "help" since there was no specialist to push him off on. They wanted to take my square peg child and shove him into the round hole of their program. His kindergarten teachers seemed to enjoy him, but I think they pulled in his reins quite often. Even though they were all aware of his capabilities, they still made him do endless tasks he'd already mastered. He seemed able to tolerate this in kindergarten, but later it got worse.

Samantha Forrest—From the time Samantha could verbally communicate, many people told us that she was different from others her age. A psychologist told us that we might want to get involved in a group for parents of the gifted, but we received no advice from others that we should do anything more. Since I didn't know anything about the gifted world, I would love to have been informed by Samantha's preschool teachers that I should read and learn more about the subject of gifted children. When we talked to my husband's sister, a former elementary teacher, about various milestones in Samantha's life, she was very clear about how advanced Samantha was—we just didn't realize it because she was our first child.

Daniel Schmidt—Daniel often felt confused and annoyed by other kids' behaviors, attitudes, interests, etc. He had a group of friends that he hung around with at school, but he didn't really have any close buddies. We knew that there was an emptiness in him, but we couldn't just wish up a compatriot or an equal. We thought that helping him at least understand better why his thoughts and interests were different from most of the kids out there would be beneficial to him.

> *Author note: Children in Daniel's position are treated as though they need to learn friendship skills, as though that will solve all of their problems. Once the parents and youngster are informed about different levels of giftedness and the mismatch with a typical classroom set-up, it helps them understand the child's frustration. They can then find opportunities to increase the child's exposure to others who may become true friends and peers.*

Carol Johnston—Carol was extremely inquisitive, empathetic, and sensitive. She was loving and giving, a peacemaker. In her desire to create harmony, she often sacrificed herself, adjusting to the expectations or wishes of others, often denying her own needs. A special program with other children with similar minds and spirits would have helped her immensely.

Rick Arnesen—It was simply impossible to get anyone else to understand what we were dealing with as far as what Rick was like and how there were no straightforward, simple ways for trying to educate him. It was clear fairly early that he would not be able to just follow the normal plan offered by the schools, but how much adjusting did we need to do? Should I let him accelerate right through high school, take classes with older kids, and go to college early, or should I emphasize the social development instead and not worry so much about the academic? It was nearly impossible to stay even one step ahead of him, so I looked for a team of people and a number of different options to keep him learning and growing. I felt a lot of anger in the first few years that there was no real help available—no road map and very little willingness to see this as anything but our family's problem rather than a gift and a joint obligation of society to help children like this. If he were significantly below average in his intellectual functioning, everything—right down to a personal daily assistant—would have been offered to him for free. It took a while to get over being angry about this.

Jon Crockett—We always had some concerns about allowing Jon to start college young. After he did, though, I came to suspect that kids like this might be better off just learning on their own as long as possible rather than being in formal academics of any kind. Toward the end of college, even Jon questioned our decision and wondered whether he'd have been better off learning informally and having more time to be creative, rather than having to do this project and that homework set, etc. Mind you, he wasn't saying that it was a poor choice, but for the first time, he questioned it in many ways. He thinks that going to college early actually slowed him down.

> *Author note: There is considerable anecdotal information available about radical acceleration and very early college entrance, and most of it emphasizes how well it works. But families also need to know more about how the radically accelerated child feels by the time he is 30 or 40 years old. The family needs experienced professionals to lead them through the process of deciding which normal American rites of passage will (and won't) matter in the long run—things like graduating from high school, attending the prom, driving a car, dating, joining a fraternity, and living in a dorm. These things are important, but they can be managed even with radical acceleration.*

Michael Cortez—When Michael turned eight, I was a bit apprehensive about how he'd be able to juggle school, UMTYMP (the University of Minnesota Talented Youth Math Program), violin, and piano and still have time for play. He said that he could manage, but I think he had a way to go with time management. He insisted that he wanted to proceed with UMTYMP in the fall, and it was his last chance to enter, having almost maxed out the math that was available in his elementary school. He also insisted on still pursuing piano and violin, and although he was good at both, he often didn't practice. We did convince him to cut back one subject in his gifted magnet school in anticipation of the heavy UMTYMP workload.

Pressure from Others

When children are especially capable, others sometimes want to promote them or show them off. In these situations, parents are torn between meeting the needs of the child and succumbing to pressures or opportunities. Many parents go from enjoying their children's abilities to hiding them from others. They worry that their children will become too focused on what they can *do*, rather than their inner character, and they also worry about comparisons with siblings.

Rebecca Resnick—When Rebecca was four, people heard that she could read, and so they would hand her a book and ask her to read out loud. I thought that this was rude and disrespectful, and I discouraged it. I didn't want her to become exploited—like a circus act.

Jacob Jones—As Jacob got older, ages two and up, people were in awe of him. His vocabulary stunned them. People were so amazed with what he was able to do that it put pressure on him and made him feel uncomfortable. The term "freak" may be an overstatement, but we felt a need to protect him from becoming almost like a sideshow.

Jon Crockett—We started to feel pressure from others about what we should expect from our son because of his intelligence, and Jon experienced this directly. People either stated or implied that when you're that smart, you aren't measuring up if you don't accomplish something huge someday. You need to win a Nobel Prize, or get rich, or cure some awful disease, or you've failed. One of Jon's mentors, a wonderful and supportive man who mattered a great deal to us and to Jon, strongly believed that it would be in Jon's best interests if he applied to graduate school as soon as he finished undergraduate school (at age 12). We felt an incredible pressure not to disappoint someone who had been so kind and supportive in the past (and continued so for many years). When we resisted such an early start to graduate school, this man initially saw us as failing our child. It was a very tough time—we felt that there was no perfect solution.

Michael Cortez—We had close friends who marveled at Michael's abilities, but we worried about all of the attention, praise, and pressure (they would ask him to do advanced things). However, Michael enjoyed every bit of it. My mother worried about what would be left for him to learn in kindergarten.

Misdiagnoses of Medical and Behavioral Issues

Many gifted children exhibit behaviors and symptoms that are hard to understand. Their uneven development often puts their intellectual development and understanding ahead of their maturity, experience, and insight. This can lead to anxiety and obsessions over things that others their age would never think about. Where does a parent turn for advice? Parents want someone with experience in these issues, and not many professionals have knowledge of high giftedness and the typical behaviors that often come with it.

Frank Price—When Frank was about 4½, I worried that he was too asocial, except with his father and me, and I was concerned even more when he refused to start potty training. In fact, I was worried that there might be something physically wrong with him because he seemed sincerely to want to be potty-trained, but all of our attempts had failed. So when he was four, I took him to see a psychologist who said— without meeting him—that it sounded like he was perhaps a high-functioning autistic child, so she wanted to test him. She believed that his extreme introversion was caused, in part, by differences in his levels of abilities.

Layne Freeman—Layne's second-grade teacher thought that she might have ADD because she wouldn't do what was asked in the classroom. She sometimes got so overloaded with too much going on around her that she reacted in anger. At home, I'd send her to her room to settle down, and within minutes, she was fine again. Layne also would become so totally engrossed in a subject, especially when reading, that she ignored or shut out everything going on around her—which indicated to me that the problem wasn't ADD; her attention was fine when she got to do something she enjoyed. I just wasn't sure how to really help her. Was there something wrong, or was this just normal for a highly gifted young girl?

Phil Burns—Several specialists diagnosed Phil with ADHD. One psychologist diagnosed obsessive-compulsive disorder because Phil insisted on finishing what he started and had intense interests and passions that were all-consuming for several months. We threw out all of these diagnoses and took him to someone who diagnosed anxiety as a consequence of high intelligence—that is, Phil's ability to cognitively understand the dangers of the world outstripped his ability to deal with those things emotionally, thus causing him great anxiety. This made sense to us, especially in light of his concern about death. At age five, he became intensely fearful of things like burglars, fire, being left alone, and of our possible pending deaths. As a coping mechanism, he developed his own detailed cosmology—a theory of life and death which encompassed way stations on other planets, reasons why babies are born with defects, reincarnation, etc. He'd had no religious training and didn't have a concept of God. At any rate, this last therapist suggested that we resist any attempts to put negative labels on him and just work with the issues that he was facing. It worked.

Maintaining Modesty as Parents

Most parents want to support their children's abilities, confidence, and self-esteem but do not want to appear overly proud or arrogant. It is a delicate balance—one that's not easy to maintain.

Debra Sund—What I found difficult was when my friends saw Debra doing something and started to worry because their own child didn't do that yet. It was hard for me to say, "Don't worry about your child— she's normal. Debra's just early."

Sophie Fuller—At age two, Sophie talked so much and so well that I was embarrassed because none of my friends' two-year-olds were even close to her fluency. I made excuses like, "She hears her older brothers and sisters all day long, and so she tries to keep up with them."

Emily Newton—We spent quite a bit of time with friends whose son was 2½ months younger than Emily, and it became obvious that Emily was hitting developmental stages earlier than he. At a dinner party, the other child's father described some situation between the two kids and got to laughing about Emily practically quoting from an encyclopedia while his son was still drooling and making googly sounds. It was funny, but it showed that our friends knew that she was different.

Loneliness of the Parents

The degree to which parents and children struggle with feelings of isolation or being alone depends somewhat upon the children's level of giftedness and the community in which the family finds itself. Although lots of people think that "gifted is gifted," the range within giftedness is so large that parents need to be careful how much they reveal, even to other parents whose children are gifted. Parents are wise to start by talking about broad common issues like finding friends and see where conversation goes from there.

Gifted and talented organizations and gifted parent support groups are helpful. They give parents a place to communicate with each other and learn from the experiences of others.

Debra Sund—I felt very isolated, like I couldn't talk about the joys and frustrations of having a gifted child. There's a stereotype that gifted children don't have any problems. And if I talked about the amazing things that Debra did, I felt ashamed, like I was boasting.

Michael Fuller—I felt exhausted from years of worry and frustration. I was afraid to answer the phone if it rang at about 3:30 P.M., because that's when school got out, and I was afraid one of Michael's teachers was calling—again.

Keith Sands—The only parents who showed understanding or gave good advice were other parents with gifted children.

Samantha Forrest—Since bragging about how smart my kid is was not something I wanted to do, there were few people for me to talk to. My mother and my husband both got their fill. Year after year (ages one through five), those lonely feelings persisted. I was looking forward to the time when Samantha would enter kindergarten and grade school, where I thought she might find some intellectual peers whose parents I could finally talk to, but I was disappointed when that did not happen.

Phil Burns—Before we had the assessments done for Phil, we had basically ignored the baby books and advice from well-meaning friends and family because that advice just didn't seem to fit. Now we know why. We definitely felt lonely, as there were very few people we knew dealing with the same issues that we were. Later, we discovered some Internet groups and made friends with other families of profoundly gifted kids across the country—and it helped to know that we were not totally alone and that others had the same problems.

Summary of Parent Issues

Most parents of gifted children go through a similar process of discovering that their children are different from others and that the schools won't necessarily recognize or support the needs of their children. Early delight in their precocious, engaging newborns and toddlers turns to confusion and worry as other people point out problems with the children or the children themselves don't conform to everyone else's expectations. These worried parents find themselves having to become activists and advocates for their children through self-education, assessments, and considerable time and effort. Much of this is done on their own and leaves them feeling tremendous frustration, uncertainty, and loneliness. Finally, when they've done everything they can to help their children, most can only cross their fingers and hope that they've made the right choices.

Chapter 3
Intellectual Level and Why it Matters

Bill has superior math skills—head and shoulders above other students in his classroom. He meets an hour a week for math enrichment activities with other first graders working at his level. He doesn't seem to mind an occasional math activity that the other children are doing, but I endeavor to suggest alternatives when they are appropriate. As we were discussing the new decade this month, Bill related it to the millennium.
~ Teacher of an exceptionally gifted first-grade boy

Today we sometimes hear school people say that *all* children are gifted, that people would pretty much be the same were it not for lack of opportunity, and that we should not look at intellectual differences at all. Yet people do differ remarkably in their ability to learn in many different areas. In their book *Genius Denied* (2004), Jan and Bob Davidson note that the field of Special Education developed to better assist children with learning difficulties. In the same way, Gifted Education developed to assist children with high learning ability.

While the field of education is well-known and well-funded, it is perplexing why gifted education is so unrecognized and under-funded. As a society, we should nurture intellectual differences in our schools, in higher education, and in the workplace; otherwise, we waste talent. As our world gets more complicated, it makes sense that we need bright people to solve problems like global warming, worldwide diseases, persistent hunger, and diminishing water resources. This book makes the case that intellectual differences matter—first for the individual, and second for society.

As noted earlier, highly intelligent people are not as common as the majority of people who are average. As both Terman (1925) and Hollingworth (1931) pointed out as long ago as the 1920s and 30s, when people are "outliers,"[1] they are very different from most of the other people around them. Yet they often do not know this about themselves and so may experience feelings of strangeness. They may even conclude

25

that there is something wrong with them. For example, if an unusually intelligent person doesn't know and understand his intellectual level, he may experience great personal turmoil trying to figure out what is going on because he never seems to "fit in." In fact, many highly intelligent people who have not received appropriate support and guidance feel emotionally isolated and very, very lonely (Ruf, 1998; Tolan, 1985; 1989). In her fascinating longitudinal work with exceptionally gifted children, Miraca Gross (2003) makes it clear that gifted children do not thrive either emotionally or socially if their giftedness goes unrecognized. Thus, it would help the overall adjustment of most individuals who are unusually intelligent if they were informed about how they are different and how their intellect affects them and others.

In discussing intellect, it is important to remember that a specific IQ number is only an estimate and a helpful guide to where one fits within a range of intelligence. An IQ number certainly does not—and cannot— explain all of one's inner differences from others. Intelligence testing measures only a small piece of who we are or what we can do. It tells us how we perform on a test of reasoning compared to others who took the same test. It does not tell whether we can weave an intricate rug or create a sustainable farm or compose music—skills which also require intelligence but which are not measured on an IQ test. Nevertheless, that thing we call intellect or reasoning ability or creativity or intelligence is definitely an important part of our personhood—of who we are.

Because children differ so greatly in their abilities, it makes sense that educational programs would allow for the diversity of learning styles and speed. Certainly, this is true in other areas. When physicians prescribe a drug, they must take into account the age, weight, and health history of the patient, because the medicine's dosage must match the individual needs of the patient. If the wrong dosage is prescribed, the treatment could be harmful or ineffective. The same is true for meeting the learning needs of children with different levels of ability.

Some children, even from an early age, exhibit a striking hunger to learn and acquire knowledge and are extremely advanced in skills when compared to others their same age (Gottfried, Gottfried, Bathurst, & Guerin, 1994). Most of humankind's greatest inventors, creators, scientists, and philosophers exhibited the same sorts of very early childhood behaviors, interests, and skills. We know that there is a connection between early childhood behaviors, intellectual level, and the likelihood of later achievement. It makes sense, then, that a society would want to encourage, nurture, guide, and effectively motivate individuals who have the strongest likelihood of developing advances that would benefit the greater society.

The failure to recognize the existence of highly gifted individuals and their needs in our present education system has led to a system that is currently failing these bright minds. The loss to society is, of course, immeasurable.

What Is Intelligence?

So what are we looking at? What is intelligence? Scientists debate over whether or not there is a core element called general intelligence—sometimes referred to as "g"—or if a person's ability to perform is an amalgam of characteristics (Jensen, 1998). The expression of intelligence is influenced by many other factors as well, as indicated in the following summary:

> *Abilities are only one class of underlying psychological traits that are likely to affect quality of performance in real-world tasks. Other traits affecting performance include motivation (or interests) and personality (the style with which one approaches tasks). Motivation affects an individual's willingness to practice or even try out particular tasks, and personality affects the style in which he or she does so. Both motivation and personality can affect the quality of performance. In most important areas of life, the quality of performance represents an amalgam of abilities, motivation, and personality. In fact, there are other important human characteristics, such as identity, leadership, creativity, entrepreneurial character, and values, that probably require particular combinations of these three broad features of the mind (abilities, motivation, and personality), plus developed skills and information acquired through others in society. Others* (Carson & Lowman, 2002) *have referred to such constructs as "aspects of character"* (Roid, 2003).

Background on Exceptional Levels of Giftedness

Profound giftedness has been generally treated as a footnote in the gifted research literature, except for the work of a few persons. Leta Hollingworth's seminal book, *Children above 180 IQ* (1942), is the first in-depth study of school children whose IQs are in the profoundly gifted range. Hollingworth became interested in these children by accident. Unaware of the existence of such highly intelligent children until she was teaching college students how to administer the *Stanford-Binet* intelligence test, she, by chance, discovered a child who scored in the 180s. She thereafter deliberately sought others who might score that high and arranged for a special class at New York's Hunter School where she could observe, teach, and provide appropriate educational and social opportunities for these students. She ultimately focused on 12 of these children to form the basis of her book on profoundly gifted children. An excellent compilation of her work and life, which includes details about characteristics of profoundly gifted children, is the book *A Forgotten Voice: A Biography of Leta Stetter Hollingworth* (Klein, 2002).

Regrettably, Hollingworth contributed to the belief that profound giftedness is more rare than it is. Katherine Kearney, while seeking information for her own doctoral dissertation on the 12 Hollingworth-studied children, now adults, reports the following:

> *Hollingworth goes to great lengths in the 180 IQ book and in other writings to state how "rare" extreme giftedness above 180 IQ is, stating as one reason for this the fact that she only found 12 kids at this level between 1916 and 1939. However, she wasn't always so wedded to the "one in a million" figure she quotes later; an article in the NY Times magazine in the mid-1920s quotes her as saying "one in 250,000." But she overlooks obvious kids right under her nose, quite literally—there are a number of popular press prints about NYC kids above 180 IQ who Leta never mentions in her lit review or anything else. She HAD to know they were around. They were very hard to miss; they were getting national press. Likewise, her colleagues at NYU had a whole clinic and did a number of studies on children above 170 IQ—apparently completely different children than the ones Leta was seeing* (2003).

In the early 1920s, Lewis Terman and his team undertook a vast longitudinal study of California school children, screening thousands of them to uncover the gifted among them. Unfortunately, this was not a screening of all school children, but instead included only those children recommended by their teachers. In other words, preconceived notions of what giftedness looks like in school filtered the school population so that only the students who were pre-selected by the teachers were given the individual IQ test. A subset of children were identified as being pro-foundly gifted, but Terman summed them up as being so different from the majority of gifted students that findings for the majority could not be generalized to them (Terman, 1925; Terman & Oden, 1947).

More recently, in her book *Exceptionally Gifted Children* (1993; 2003), Miraca Gross gives detailed feedback on 10 years in the lives of 15 exceptionally and profoundly gifted Australian children, including their intellectual, social, and emotional development and the educational approaches that worked—and did not work—well for them. Her longi-tudinal research continues.

In 1986, David H. Feldman wrote *Nature's Gambit: Child Prodigies and the Development of Human Potential*. He asserts that omnibus prodi-gies—those profoundly gifted children who have intellectual gifts in virtually every area—are extremely rare—more rare even than the prod-igies who are specialists, like musical or mathematic prodigies. He provides some excellent descriptions of children who are clearly pro-foundly gifted, but no IQ scores are reported. When IQ levels are not reported along with the description of what the child is like, it is difficult for the reader to gain the perspective needed to fully understand which level of ability produces which accomplishments, personality traits, sen-sitivities, communication and learning styles, and problems.

Biographies of profoundly gifted people can shed more light on some of the individuals whose intellectual levels are in the profoundly gifted range. Two favorites are *Genius* by James Gleick (1993), about Richard Feynman, a brilliant scientist, and *The Prodigy* by Amy Wallace (1986), about William James Sidis, a turn-of-last-century omnibus genius who is an example of great promise lost. Notably, the roles of these indi-vidual's parents seemed key to their subsequent accomplishments.

Biographies often depict highly gifted people as poor students in school. Albert Einstein and Thomas Edison, for example, are sometimes portrayed as though they weren't really that smart but only figured out how to work harder as they matured. The "poor student" theme appears in some of the gifted subjects of this book, particularly in primary and middle schools.

A handful of others who have looked at the highest levels of intel-lectual giftedness are Gagné (1985; 1993), Janos and Robinson (1985a; 1985b), Kline and Meckstroth (1985), Kulik and Kulik (1984; 1990), Robinson (1980), Robinson and Noble (1991), Robinson and Robin-son (1982), Roedell, Jackson, and Robinson (1980), Rogers (1986; 1991;

2002), Silverman (1989; 1993), Silverman and Kearney (1989, 1992), VanTassel-Baska (1983), and Webb, Meckstroth, and Tolan (1982). These and other experts who have studied individual differences in exceptionally gifted children have contributed to my understanding about giftedness and levels of intelligence. This work, combined with my own work with individuals, has contributed to the evolution of my concept of levels of giftedness.

Who Are the Gifted and How Do We Find Them?

Not surprisingly, the identification of gifted children—from those labeled moderately gifted to the most profoundly gifted—is fraught with disagreement over criteria, terms, and definitions. Despite discussions of gifts and talents,[2] multiple intelligences,[3] emotional intelligence,[4] a triarchic model of intelligence,[5] and the "giftedness" of *all* children,[6] there is still sufficient agreement in practice to describe two principle methods that are used to identify children as gifted:

- Parent and teacher recommendation based on characteristics and behaviors.

- IQ and achievement test scores usually above the 95th percentile, but sometimes above the 98th percentile.

Even though these are common practices, critics argue that test scores have little real meaning beyond an ability to succeed in school. Some critics believe that a portfolio—examples of things done by the child—is a better indicator of high intelligence or potential than a test score. Others believe that a checklist of behavioral characteristics and achievements is better for identifying children who may not score high on tests.

The characteristics below are ones most frequently found on these checklists, and they are helpful. However, checklists—because they only reflect the presence or absence of a behavior—do not provide the parent with any knowledge of what is early, what is precocious, what is unusual, or highly different, or truly astounding. Some reference point is needed to determine the degree of advanced development. A checklist like the one below would be more helpful if we knew at what ages these behaviors typically occur and how many of these characteristics must be present at a particular age for a child to be considered unusually intelligent (Rivero, 2002, p. 50).

- Precocity, especially early language development
- Uneven development
- Intensity
- A creative nature
- High levels of sensitivity
- Complexity of thought and personality
- Perfectionism and high expectations
- Highly developed or pervasive sense of humor
- Idealism and sense of justice
- Exceptional memory
- Fascination with patterns
- Unusual ability to concentrate on topics of interest
- Strong drive and developed sense of self
- Unquenchable curiosity
- High levels of energy
- Excitability

Part II of this book is a guide toward recognizing which of these behaviors and milestones occur at what ages in different levels of gifted children. This will allow parents to see how their children compare to other very bright children, and it begins to get to the heart of what a gifted child is really *like*.

In 1991, a group of high intelligence specialists, later known as "The Columbus Group," met in Columbus, Ohio, to wrestle with the concept of giftedness as it reflects the *personal* qualities of gifted children. The Columbus Group defined what can be called the *essence* of the gifted individual:

> *Giftedness is asynchronous development in which advanced cognitive abilities and heightened intensity combine to create inner experiences and awareness that are qualitatively different from the norm. This asynchrony increases with higher intellectual capacity. The uniqueness of the gifted renders them particularly vulnerable and requires modification in parenting, teaching and counseling in order for them to develop optimally* (Morelock, 1991, p.1).

This definition may seem more cumbersome than a straightforward test score, but test scores are not as clear-cut and simple as we might like, either. It is the combination of all of these different factors—assessment results, checklist traits and behaviors, and qualitative definitions—that helps us know someone's level of intelligence, their level of giftedness.

31

Giftedness According to Test Scores

Schools almost always use scores from standardized ability and achievement tests as part of their identification process for giftedness. These scores are usually reported using percentiles, and the gifted range typically starts at the 98th percentile. On intelligence tests, the 98th percentile most often starts at about a 130 IQ score. This means that two out of every 100 children could be gifted by this definition. Sometimes, due to the different kinds of scores—and the different kinds of abilities that schools look for—educators will consider students with scores as low as the 90th or 95th percentile as gifted.

However, there are huge differences in capabilities within the highest 1% or 2% of people. The difference in ability between someone at the 99th percentile and someone at the 99.4th percentile may be as large as the difference in ability between someone at the 50th and someone at the 75th percentile. The continuum of ability stretches far wider than most people realize, and percentile scores are not the best way to show that spread.

What is meant by continuum of ability? It means the range of intelligence between individuals in the overall population of people, and more particularly, the range of abilities within a typical classroom. A typical grade school classroom is a heterogeneous (mixed-ability) grouping of children who are all about the same age. An average elementary school has three or four classrooms of children at each grade level. At the end of each school year, many principals ask teachers to list children in rank order according to their demonstrated learning ability so that they can create balanced classrooms for the following year. In other words, the teachers informally identify the students who already know the most and who learn new concepts the fastest, and the principals then create a continuum of students based upon this information. Then the principal "deals from the top" on down so that the three or four most intellectually able students will each be in different classrooms the following year, the second most intellectually able three or four children will be spread out across different classrooms, and so on, until each classroom has a similarly balanced variety of learners for the following school year.

An approach like this gives each teacher one or two of the brightest students, but it also creates the widest possible range of learners for each class and makes it difficult for teachers to address the needs of all students within a single grade level. Children vary greatly in their capacity to learn new material, and teachers can experience difficulty understanding just how different the learners in the low and high ends of the ability range are from average learners. This practice also means that the gifted children are often alone; no one else in their classroom learns as quickly as they, which can make them feel odd, different, and unsure of themselves.

Understanding the Confusion over IQ Scores

Most people know that IQ stands for "intelligence quotient." You may know your IQ score from a test you took at some point in your life. You may have taken a group test with your classmates, or you may have taken an individual test given by a school psychologist. Until about the 1970s, the scales—the possible score range—differed between those two types of tests. This means that although you may know a score from your childhood, you probably don't know what scale the test used or what that score really means.

Schools typically use scores from group tests—tests administered to a group of children at one time. While useful for assessing the learning ability level of a group as a whole, these tests do not always give reliable results for an individual. First, since they are not administered one-on-one, they leave opportunities for children to misunderstand directions, which can result in inaccurate scores. Second, many children simply do not take group tests as seriously as individually administered tests and thus score below their actual capabilities. In an individual assessment, an experienced practitioner is able to coax ideal performances from an examinee by making sure the child fully understands all directions and by encouraging the child to do his or her best.

Unfortunately, neither group nor individual tests make the extent of intelligence very clear because they bunch people who would fit at the very low and high ends of a continuum into a restricted range. As noted earlier, there are huge differences in capabilities within the highest 1% or 2% of people. But on most tests, once a child reaches a score at the 98th or 99th percentile, it is difficult to tell if that child's ability is moderately high or extremely high when compared to other children the same age and grade. In such cases, the experience and expertise of the person administering and evaluating the test is vital for the correct interpretation of the test results.

What do IQ scores mean? What is a high IQ, and what is normal? Since the first IQ tests were designed more than 100 years ago, there have been many types of tests, and they have used different scales. One can't always compare the scores from one test to the scores on another test. Furthermore, most people, if they find out their IQ score at all, are never given information on what their score really means, what scale it was on, or how their measured ability compares to anyone else's.

When the first intelligence tests were designed, an IQ score could be 200 or higher. Modern tests are specifically designed *not* to show the measurement of extraordinarily high ability, apparently based on the assumption that there are too few of these rare "outliers" to warrant the extra expense during test development. A few specialists still use the old tests—specifically the *Stanford-Binet (Form L-M)*—to help them gain additional information about children whose learning abilities exceed what the modern standard scores and use of percentiles can reveal, but those high IQ numbers are no longer available on tests used by the schools.

Many people assume that the scores they got in their early school years used the same scale as the tests that allowed for very high scores. They are incorrect. The group tests that the schools used—when they tested a whole class at the same time—only had a possible high score of 146-150. This is quite different from the older individually-administered *Stanford-Binet* tests that could go past 200 IQ. Some school districts still use the *Slossen Intelligence Test* as a gifted screening instrument, and it is scaled to match the old *Stanford-Binet (Form L-M)* with the very high score range, but the people using it often don't realize that the scores cannot be compared to any other IQ tests in use. Even IQ tests used outside of schools now top out at about 145 to 160 IQ points, again depending on each test's scoring scale.

To get a clearer sense of how scores vary depending upon the test instrument, look at the different score results on the tables in each of the chapters in Part II. There are differences between scores referred to as "ratio IQ" (because of their original formula that compared the ratio of the person's mental age to his or her chronological age) and standardized or "deviation IQ" scores (based on formulas that use statistical deviations from a hypothetical age-group average score). Confusion often results when people try to compare the two, which contributes to the problem of why most people don't think that very many children of unusually high intelligence exist in our schools. Due to the current tests being used, students are getting IQ scores of 130-145 instead of 160 and 170 or above. It takes someone knowledgeable and skilled in different tests and test interpretation to "discover" these highly gifted children. Schools don't typically have such people on their staff, and parents don't often seek outside testing for their children.

The Intelligence Continuum and Education

Intelligence exists on a continuum; people cannot simply be grouped as *slow, average,* or *bright* with clear and distinct lines between each group. Each person is unique. Although each person has individual strengths and weaknesses, all people appear on the continuum somewhere between *very low* to *very high* in their general ability to learn and use information. Children who are below average in intelligence will need more time and more repetitions to learn new material. Conversely, children who are above average in intelligence need less time and fewer repetitions to learn new material. School systems with gifted programs generally have a cut-off score—usually between the 95th and 98th percentile on an ability or achievement test—as part of their criteria for selection of gifted students. Such a score cut-off is artificial. Obviously, people who fall very closely on either side of that cut-off score will be similar in their learning abilities. On the other hand, an IQ difference of just 15 points, or one standard deviation,[7] makes a strong difference in how easily a person can learn and understand new material.

A number of studies, including those by Flanders (1987) and Reis et al. (1993), indicate that an average child (one with an IQ of 100) needs about seven or eight repetitions to learn new material—the primary reason elementary curriculum follows a spiraling course through the grade levels. In a mixed-ability classroom, a child of 115-120 IQ[8] needs about half as many repetitions—or half the time—to absorb new material as a child of average intelligence (Gottfredson, 1998). Achievement test results indicate that a child of an approximate 130-135 IQ requires about one-quarter the time to absorb and use new material as a child of average ability. This increase in learning speed, and the associated ability to decipher progressively more complex material, continues throughout the upper end of the IQ range.

The point to be emphasized here is that a gifted cut-off score used by schools for program eligibility is confusing if it leads people to think that a child is either *gifted* or *not gifted*. There is a continuum of intellectual giftedness, and children at different points along that continuum differ considerably in their learning abilities and their educational needs.

How Common Are Gifted Children?

In addition to the problem of IQ score confusion, other reasons exist for the continued belief among educators and the general public that children with high intellectual levels are rarer than they are. Perhaps it is because unless a person develops into a laudable, recognized high achiever, or the individual somehow has the spotlight turned on her—as in the case of a child prodigy violinist or spelling bee champion—we fail to appreciate that she might be an example of early genius. As long as we group children by age rather than by what they are ready to learn, we simply won't notice which ones learn faster.

Since teachers and administrators are not trained to detect the characteristics of bright children, and since schools are not usually set up to give them opportunities to learn at a level and pace appropriate for them but different from their classmates, it is easy to see that highly gifted children would be under-recognized and practically invisible during their school years. How can a six-year-old math whiz reveal his aptitude in a mixed-ability classroom when all of the other children are learning to count and do simple arithmetic? How can a second-grade future writer blossom when the weekly spelling words are ones she has known how to spell since kindergarten? Our brightest children often must sit back and wait while others learn what these kids already know.

How do I know that there are more children in the highly gifted range than previously thought? I have been fortunate to have had the opportunity to test many gifted children on both kinds of test instruments—both the old ratio IQ tests, with the higher score ranges, and the newer standard score IQ tests, with the lower, compressed score ranges. The results from both have shown significantly more children in the highly gifted range than the hypothetical "normal curve" would suggest. Other specialists have noticed this phenomenon, too, though some of them erroneously concluded that the newer tests were wrong, rather than that they were simply on a different—and more difficult to interpret—scale. Due to the design and structure of newer tests, children with IQs in the 170, 180, and 190 range will obtain IQ numbers that look more like 140s and 150s on the modern tests (Ruf, 2003). The children with the highest scores exist in sufficient numbers that almost any large school district with a substantial proportion of college-educated parents will have at least a few students with IQ scores of 170 and higher on the older tests—and 140 and higher on modern tests—at every grade level.

The children with ratio IQ scores that span from 123 to 170 or above—or newer standard test scores from 120 to 146 and above—can be grouped into five different levels. The chapters in Part II describe the levels of giftedness so that parents and educators can more easily recognize the differences within the gifted spectrum and can better meet the needs of this unique group of highly intelligent children.

The Assessment Process

The following vignettes illustrate what prompted parents to get their children assessed, how the parents felt about the process and the results, and some of their worries and hopes for their children. Most of the children were assessed with the old ratio IQ test, the *Stanford-Binet (Form L-M)*, so the scores that the parents mention are significantly higher than any standard score IQ results that the children would get on current tests.

Emily Newton

Mother: We had Emily tested in second grade because we worried that our happy, enthusiastic little girl was changing, and not for the better. She appeared depressed and unhappy once she started school. We were just looking for some data to present to our school district to try to get some more challenging work for her. We absolutely did not want to make any special requests from the school, though, because we're prominent in our community and didn't want others to think that we were demanding special favors. But our daughter was clearly suffering.

We were a bit surprised by the testing results, which didn't fit our picture of Emily at all. To see the results on paper was quite a shock. We certainly felt a high level of denial—a concern that the testing center was in the business of finding gifted kids, so of course they'd find one in our child. I was also very concerned that Emily would be different and would have trouble finding success and happiness and wouldn't fit in. I wanted children who were bright so that their chances of being successful were good, but not "too bright."

Two years later, I was still concerned that I wouldn't have the inner resources to provide my daughter with the support and guidance that she needed. I saw my role as a parent to ensure that Emily be put in situations where she could safely be challenged and occasionally fail so that she could be learn and grow. I also wanted to make sure that she was in social situations where she could develop friendships, have fun, and be a little girl for as long as possible.

Father: I knew that Emily was gifted, and I admit that I felt very proud that she was bright. I also felt that it was important *not to let on to her how I felt* or to make too big a deal over it. She seemed to understand that she had these talents and wasn't too impressed with herself. I was a little shocked when the testing was complete, but only momentarily. I was more distressed by her mother's reaction, which was one of great concern about Emily's future happiness. I thought that it was great and was very happy to find out what we had always suspected to be true.

Michael Cortez

Mother: We obtained an assessment for Michael when he was 4½ years old to get a clearer idea of his abilities and educational needs—and, we hoped, to rekindle his love for school. We knew that Michael was gifted based on early signs, and we even suspected that he was highly gifted like his father.

We were worried when the evaluation took longer than we expected. We thought that Michael would get tired, but we also knew how much he liked to be asked questions and to talk with adults. We were also constrained by a set budget for the evaluation, and the evaluator didn't have a flat rate fee. During the quick break, I noticed a calm but serious expression on the evaluator's face; he seemed deep in thought. I thought he might be exhausted from dealing with Michael. At the end, we were told that the evaluation went well, that Michael was "gifted indeed," and that the report would be provided to us as soon as possible.

We were beyond our scheduled time, so we were ready to conclude the meeting when the evaluator said that another meeting with us was very important. He revealed to us the exact level of Michael's giftedness. We were stunned and speechless, then immediately afterward felt afraid and lost. What did this all mean? How would things be for Michael from now on? How had he become so gifted? What should we do next? Would we be able to manage, and how? Naturally, we became more afraid and felt incompetent for Michael when the evaluator explained further the rarity of Michael's giftedness. From then on, our lives, attitudes, and priorities changed. We purchased and borrowed anything and everything that we could find on giftedness.

Father: Michael started showing signs that he could be a really smart kid. But the moment of truth was when we got his IQ results that confirmed that he was quite gifted. I still remember being awestruck when he finally came out of the testing room after more than three hours. The feeling changed to a heavy sense of responsibility that we were given this remarkable child to nurture to fully develop his potential. My feeling was, "Okay, we're relatively smart people, but Michael is just several levels higher." Then the feeling came to a firm resolve that we were going to do everything possible to support our son with his future challenges—intellectually, emotionally, and socially. I admit that his mother had always been Michael's strongest and most loyal advocate with regard to his development. Initially, my simplistic mindset was, "Don't rush him—he's so young." My attitude has since changed to, "There may be some holes, but we need to keep challenging him as much as we can. Otherwise, he can lapse into lazy thinking and will end up not tapping his full potential."

The Richards Family

Mother: The realization of the profound giftedness of our children came rather late, since we had always home schooled them. We always knew that they were very bright—beginning with Colin, our oldest—but we were never concerned with quantifying exactly *how* bright they were until we tried to fit them into a school system. We found that we needed some "scientific proof" when we worked with teachers and administrators to get our children's work levels adjusted. It was then that we began learning about the concept of giftedness, and I wasn't sure what I thought about it. I especially wasn't sure what to think about the differences in IQ among my three children and what those implied for their relationships with each other, as well as how we should handle them emotionally and academically. I felt disappointed—and unbelieving at first—about the results of one of the three because I wanted so badly for all of the children to be pretty much the same.

Jon Crockett

Mother: I wasn't ready for the actual IQ number that Jon received when we had him tested. I cried and was shaking and in general didn't handle it very well at all. I'm not sure it changed how I felt about our role as parents, but I did feel that our son's childhood was flashing before our eyes, as his academic testing was all post-high school level and his mental age was already up around that of people who have college degrees—and yet he was physically only seven years old.

Father: I was stunned to find out Jon's IQ. I knew that he was intelligent, but I had no idea that he was so far out there. My wife called me at work, and because I was sitting in a cubicle farm, I was somewhat limited as to what I could say, but I was shocked—and also pleased. I had a hard time focusing on work for the next hour or two. I felt like I should tell someone to somehow make it more real, but then again, I didn't think that I should. I imagined what I would tell someone, how I would broach the subject, how much I would reveal. Finally, the urge overwhelmed me, and I called a good friend of mine, whom I picked because he's the smartest guy I've ever known. I knew that he would understand. I wasn't sure what to tell him or why I was even telling him, but I just had to talk about it, and I told him all of that. It felt good to discuss it and sort of validate the whole thing. After that, I settled down and got back to work.

Stephen Williams

Mother: Stephen was 10 years old when he was tested, and I felt awed, excited, and overwhelmed at times about the tasks ahead of us. I found myself wondering if the results could be wrong, like a false positive. Shortly after the test, Stephen initiated a conversation with his father and me about ancient religions, Paganism, and science versus God that left us shaking our heads and commenting to each other that we hadn't had discussions like that until we were in college.

This whole process made me do a lot of reflecting about my own education. I remember doing a lot of work in school, but it was never hard. However, the first two years of college were difficult, since I'd never had to study before. I also had trouble applying myself to lower-level classes—I wanted to get to the "interesting stuff," and then I had trouble in the upper-level courses because I hadn't learned the basics well enough, but there wasn't enough time to go back and fill in the gaps! I didn't want this to happen to Stephen.

Father: I was quite surprised to find out that Stephen was profoundly gifted. To me, he just seemed like a bright, normal kid—not really out of the ordinary. I just never realized how exceptional he was, probably because I'd had very few interactions with other kids for comparison. In addition to being surprised, I was also very pleased and proud. However, after learning more about giftedness, I had concerns about the social implications for him and the effect that this might have on our family life. There was also a feeling of relief, because it explained some of the differences we had observed, such as his early talking, lack of baby talk, amazing puzzle solving skills, early arithmetic skills, his unusual concern about social injustices, and his comfortable interactions with adults.

Samantha Forrest

Mother: Since Samantha was our first child, we thought that she was normal and that all children were like her. We had her tested for early entrance to kindergarten, and the psychologist mentioned that involvement in a parent support group for gifted children would be helpful. She also said that children with scores at that level are often grade accelerated. What we felt was a roller coaster of surprise, happiness, loneliness, frustration, and satisfaction.

I soon discovered that it is completely up to the parents of profoundly gifted children to make sure that those children receive the intellectual and emotional support that they need to function in society. The job can be overwhelming, because there is no manual on how to educate and emotionally support each individual gifted child. It can also be frustrating, because there are few people one can discuss it with. However, it can be very satisfying to observe a profoundly gifted child's mind at work and to see it go beyond anything imaginable. The joy of having an in-depth conversation with such a child makes it all worth it, because you have succeeded at meeting her special needs and have provided her with the ability to use her giftedness to its potential.

Father: I was fascinated by the probability that if Samantha had been born three weeks earlier (a few days before her due date) she wouldn't have been tested for early entrance to kindergarten, and an awareness of the official term "gifted" or "profoundly gifted" would not have been introduced into the family's vocabulary. I would probably have been satisfied with Samantha's school performance in kindergarten because it was above the expected level, but I would have had no understanding of her disengagement. It has now become clear to me that there are probably many, many gifted children (and adults) who are not recognized, which could explain why so many find the educational experience less than satisfactory.

Debra Sund

Mother: When Debra was young, we knew that she was smart and quick, but we didn't think about her being gifted. For the first few months of school, we got reports that she was just a normal child who didn't finish her work. Even after they had her reading level tested and found it to be at a fifth-grade level, the school wasn't at all concerned that she might be bored in a first-grade reading level. This confused us and made no sense, so we decided to have her IQ tested.

The school suggested that we join a support group for parents of gifted children. It was there that I began to learn about the many aspects of gifted children. But even then, when they talked about profoundly gifted children, I tuned out, because I thought that while Debra was gifted, she certainly wasn't profoundly gifted. When I was later told that her IQ was above 170, I was unprepared. My mouth dropped, and I felt like laughing. It turned out that I wasn't a crazy mother who saw things that weren't there! I had a very intelligent child whose mind was a sponge. I also felt like crying, though, because I could think back to all those talks I'd listened to in the support group about profoundly gifted kids and realized what a huge job it was going to be.

After the assessment, my highest priority was getting my husband and me educated so that we'd agree on what was necessary for our daughter and what wasn't. My husband was much more laid back and believed that Debra would be fine in school. If so, great! But if not, I wanted to be prepared to recognize the symptoms.

Father: Like her mother, I knew that Debra was verbally precocious and loved books, but her reading ability exploded so fast that it caught me by surprise. The reading test in kindergarten didn't scare me, though. My reaction was—and continues to be—"better off gifted than slow." My response to the IQ test has been guarded. I'm not comfortable with quantifying intelligence (the humanist in me, no doubt), and I'm also aware of how such numbers have been misused in various ways. I suspect that it's also because I was quite content and easy-going as a student throughout my undergraduate education, and if indeed the apple doesn't fall far from the tree, then I tend to assume that Debra will be the same way. Clearly, her mother and I differ in our reactions.

The Amundson Family

Mother: We have three boys in our family. We already knew that our oldest, Kyle, was very bright, but even so, we were shocked at how high he tested. We were also saddened by how low—relatively speaking— our second child was, mostly because we worried about how he competed with his older brother and felt bad about himself. The differences had been there even without testing, though—the test results just made it easier to understand and support our children's differences.

Rebecca Resnick

Mother: I had Rebecca tested in fourth grade because I felt that the results could back up my request for differentiated coursework. When I got the results of her IQ testing, I felt quite a mixture of emotions. I was happy, proud, and surprised that it was so high. I also felt validated and scared that if I didn't carefully make choices for Rebecca's education, she wouldn't be emotionally stable. When I myself was in sixth grade, there was an exceptional child in my class, and he was socially pretty weird. I could tell even at 12 years of age that he wasn't going to fit in very well in life. I didn't care whether Rebecca would be popular or not, but I didn't want her to be an outcast or a loner. So I made decisions that tried to balance her emotional needs with academic challenges, and that's why I didn't try to get her placed in classes with older kids.

The Price Family

Mother: We believed from early on that Frank was gifted mathematically. He showed great fascination in mathematical things at a very early age. Of course, parents always think that their kids are talented, but we didn't have anything to confirm our beliefs. When he got to be four and wasn't having success with potty training, we sought advice from a psychologist who thought, from our descriptions, that he might be borderline autistic. So we brought him in for testing, and she saw right away that he wasn't autistic, but that his abilities were at such different levels that he was having trouble with the social aspects of his life. I am very proud of his giftedness. I understood him so much better when I found out what his strengths and relative weaknesses were.

The only reason that we even considered testing our daughter was for early kindergarten admission—she missed the cut-off date by two weeks, and I believed that she was ready, regardless of her IQ, but I had to jump through the school's hoop of having her tested anyway. Frankly, I was shocked to learn that her IQ was so high. She didn't show the same signs of giftedness as her brother.

The Engquist Family

Mother: As far as getting assessments and figuring out why my kids were different from others, it could have been much smoother. My insurance plan would cover ADD testing and treatment, but not testing for giftedness. The problem is that, if there are school problems with giftedness, it often ends up looking like ADD. Our pediatrician, whom I trust, even said about one of my sons, "Well, it looks like he's a candidate for medication." It's as if the ADD diagnosis and med trial is the only thing worth pursuing. No one ever mentioned to me that it might be giftedness. It wasn't until after we pushed for an assessment that I realized we were dealing with a higher level of giftedness than I had formerly thought. Once we knew that and started reading up on kids like this, we were much better able to give him what he needed.

Daniel Schmidt

Mother: By ninth grade, Daniel was very depressed and anxious. No one ever suggested that his adjustment difficulties might be due to his very high intelligence. No one ever explained what his test scores really meant—maybe they didn't know, either. At our wit's end, we finally found a gifted specialist, and it helped. Daniel was very glad that we met and seemed anxious to start pondering all that she told us about high intelligence and how it affects a person. He took one of the books to school, the one on people who create—in a brown paper wrapper, though. We were all shocked at the specialist's explanations about our son's intellectual level, but since then, it's begun to make sense. Now that Daniel's got detailed a description of what his past test results and early milestones really mean, he seems to be in a better frame of mind.

Phil Burns

Mother: We received so much negative feedback from the preschool about Phil's behaviors that we decided to have him assessed for whatever his underlying difficulties might be. He tested as profoundly gifted. We were floored. We had expected a score in the 150-160 range but were told that his IQ was much, much higher—and perhaps even higher than tested because they had continued testing past the point where he was tired instead of terminating the session and continuing at another time. We immediately began researching profoundly gifted children—those with an IQ over 180. We decided to home school and were all much happier and less stressed. My only regret was that I got very little one-on-one time with his siblings, and I worried that they were cheated out of the stimulation and activities that Phil had at their age.

The Jones Family

Mother: When we had Jacob formally tested, I believed that the specialist would say that he was bright but not brilliant. I wasn't prepared for what I did hear—that Jacob was profoundly gifted, a rare individual in this world. I remember driving home wondering how I would parent him, but then I remembered that he was still the same child as before the testing, and therefore, we would sort this out together. We assured Jacob that his character was what we were most proud of; academics came second.

I also quickly learned that as much as I needed to talk to someone about this new information, very few people wanted to hear about it, and even fewer people really understood. I received a great deal of advice from well-meaning acquaintances, which honestly was not much help. In fact, they were quite critical of the decisions we made, like accelerating his academics. We learned along the way to trust ourselves more and stop looking outward for answers from people who knew much less about our child than we did. I have cried, been extremely frustrated, and felt incredibly humbled by this child along the way. His older brother, William, is also gifted, but not to the same degree. This is a problem for William, but it's also a problem for us in helping him cope with feelings of inferiority next to his brother.

Father: I was in shock when I found out the level of Jacob's giftedness. My whole adjustment to it was to give him opportunities and facilitate activities that would further his interest, but not to make him the center of our lives. It is humbling when your 11-year-old knows more about a subject than you do, but it makes me proud of him. The biggest thing is that my focus is not on his profound giftedness as much as is it on his character. I want him to use his intelligence to do good things in his life.

Justin Janacek

Mother: When we first got the results of Justin's IQ test, we were stunned and scared and felt disbelief at his level of giftedness. We had known that he was extremely bright, but not that he was so exceptional. We were scared that we wouldn't be able to provide what he needed emotionally, socially, and intellectually. Also, we felt very self-conscious about sharing this information with others. The people we told reacted with disbelief, envy, or seemed to feel that we were comparing or bragging.

Justin's grandparents held such differences in values and beliefs that there was no emotional support from them. Both sides said, "Well, we already knew he was really smart," and that ended it. My husband's father, who never had anything positive to say about his son, started yelling and putting him down, telling him that he'd been like that as a child and now look at him. He accused my husband of being lazy, and that's why he never got anywhere. My mother thought it would all just work out and that we didn't need to do anything special—it was just great that Justin didn't have a learning disability like my brother or nephew. For my mom, our son's intelligence was a wonderful thing to brag about to others, but she had no interest in hearing about the challenges that we experienced because of it.

Author note: It is interesting that the grandparents didn't see that perhaps not giving their own son what he needed to nurture his abilities and intellect was precisely why he "didn't amount to anything" as an adult.

Father: We've both always thought of ourselves as smart, but not gifted. We both experience feelings of being odd or unique. We know that we are smart and that we make our life decisions based on values rather than on money or societal expectations, but that doesn't seem to be the norm for others in our socioeconomic class (blue-collar/lower middle class). Although we both relate well to others, we still feel that we don't fit in well with either college-educated white-collar folks or with typical blue-collar folks. Thinking of our special sensitivities and intelligence as part of being gifted does explain some of this to us now.

Layne Freeman

Mother: I had no clue that Layne was highly gifted until I got her tested. She was bright and had been reading since about age three, but I'd never felt that her academic growth and development took precedence over her emotional development, so I didn't recognize or look for signs of giftedness, nor did I push formal learning. She began resisting academic work in the second grade, and the teacher referred her for testing. When the school psychologist revealed Layne's IQ score to the principal and her teachers in January, their reaction was interesting. I think it was one of the higher scores they had ever seen, and they seemed to then see Layne with different eyes—no longer as a stubborn, obstinate, ADD child, but a child with intellectual gifts and tremendous potential. We all realized that she had to be moved to the full-day gifted school, and that was accomplished almost immediately. She instantly became much happier and felt more understood and accepted by her new teacher, who had a special and personal interest in the needs of highly gifted kids.

Brennan Ahlers

Mother: We had Brennan tested by a well-known psychologist who had over 25 years of experience working with gifted children, and he estimated Brennan's IQ to be 170. When he told me this, I immediately started to cry. They were not tears of joy. At the time, I knew very little about gifted issues, but I could see that any time someone was so out of sync with "normal," there would be problems. I also felt a sense of relief that we now knew the reasons for Brennan's troubles. His father, on the other hand, said, "Cool!" when I told him. Although he wasn't blind to the problems ahead, I think he was thinking long term on the neat things that his son might be able to accomplish with his life.

After I learned Brennan's score, I spent the next six months reading everything I could get my hands on about the gifted. I talked to as many experts in the field as I could. I became armed because I never wanted to sit across from teachers or administrators and not know more than they did about giftedness. I could have read about a twentieth as much information and still have known more about the issue than the majority of people I came across as I tried to advocate for his needs. I began advocating for the needs of *all* gifted children; I never wanted any other family to have to go through what we did.

My original expectations of schools included *DO NO HARM*. I expected them to educate my child. I expected them to encourage his growth, respect him as a person, respect his abilities, and respect us as parents. Now I have no expectations of any school in our state. After receiving Brennan's test results, we had a meeting with the principal, assistant principal, and school counselor. They said that this was no problem; they had other kids like this, and they could certainly "keep him busy." Yet I saw little understanding or change for my son.

Keith Sands

Mother: When I first learned that Keith, age four at the time, was gifted, I was dismayed and apprehensive. As a psychologist, I was aware of the difficulties ahead in having an "atypical" child. I was surprised by other people's reactions, and I resented having to "defend" the gifted label. People were dismissive, amused, jealous, disapproving, questioning, resentful, or even disbelieving. As new parents living in an urban community, it was important for us to feel like we fit in or were accepted, so we rarely talked about Keith's "gift" unless we felt understood or supported.

When I first met another mother with a gifted son like Keith, I felt utter relief! I could finally talk freely about him. It made me uncomfortable when other people praised our parenting or assumed that we were so lucky for Keith to be so bright. But I had to overcome my discomfort over talking about Keith's giftedness when he started school because I very quickly had to become his advocate.

Summary of Intellectual Assessment

Intelligence tests provide reasonable ways of measuring intellectual ability. However, modern IQ tests generally underestimate the number of children in the upper levels of giftedness. Schools most often identify gifted children as those scoring at or above the 98th percentile on ability tests, but this fails to recognize the great range of abilities that exist within children who score in the upper 2%. Careful assessment beyond the usual IQ tests can be extremely helpful to parents in understanding their highly gifted children.

Part II:

Levels of Giftedness

When I began selecting subjects for this study, I determined that all of the families should have at least one child who tested with a ratio IQ over 170 because I wanted to focus on the higher levels of giftedness. I anticipated that I would be able to line the children up by their test scores and show how early childhood behaviors correlated with score results. It didn't work as I expected. I found that children won't line up in a perfect, predictable pattern, regardless of the assessment instrument used, but tests do give us a good starting point for figuring out a child's ability level.

My primary assessment tool was the *Stanford-Binet (Form L-M)* because I started gathering subjects for the book before I personally switched to a newer test instrument. The *SBLM* was written and its various items compiled over many years. The original 1937 edition was last updated in 1960, and the normative data were most recently updated in 1973. Thus, by anyone's standards, this is an old and outdated test. The downsides to the old test are that: (1) many of its questions are obsolete and unfamiliar to today's children, (2) its scores are unfamiliar and therefore not useful to most educators, and (3) the scores are too high due to the different scale and the very old norms.[1]

In my own work,[2] I no longer administer the *SBLM* because there are now better options available[3]. With the newer tests, it is possible, though difficult, to determine levels of intelligence—including levels of giftedness—and the current, modern test norms, age equivalency information, and standardization actually make the newer tests more broadly useful. We can compare results between different tests and know that we are talking about similar intellectual qualities within the child. Because of this, I have included standard scores from more current tests whenever those results are available.

Each of the next five chapters focuses on one range or level of giftedness, and the Ruf Estimates of Levels of Giftedness follow below. To simplify matters and to avoid loaded qualifiers such as "exceptionally" or "profoundly" gifted, I simply label the categories "Level One," "Level Two," and so on, up to "Level Five." It will be easier for readers to remember that Level Four is higher than Level Three, rather than trying to remember whether "exceptional" is higher than "highly."

In organizing the material for this book, I thought that it would be more meaningful to readers if I began with descriptions well below what some have described as the profoundly gifted range, so I have started with what is sometimes called "moderately" gifted. It also became clear that there is a need for a category that acknowledges various exceptionalities, such as learning disabilities and processing disorders. How to integrate this into the Estimates of Levels of Giftedness will be investigated in a future study, but for the time being, these exceptionalities will be added to the five levels as Level Six. If a child seems to fit Level Two, for example, but has exceptionalities that make the estimate tentative, he would then be described as Level 2/6.

Ruf Estimates of Levels of Giftedness

Level One Gifted:

- Approximately 90th-98th percentiles on standardized tests
- Superior★ to Moderately Gifted range on IQ tests
- Generally top one-third to one-fourth of students in a mixed-ability class

★*Superior is the term utilized by test publishers to designate the intellectual range prior to either Gifted or Advanced.*

Level Two Gifted:

- Approximately 98th-99th percentiles on standardized tests
- Gifted to Highly Gifted or Very Advanced on IQ tests
- As many as one to three in typical mixed-ability classroom

Level Three Gifted:

- Approximately 98th–99th percentiles on standardized tests
- Highly to Exceptionally Gifted or Very Advanced on IQ tests
- One or two per grade level; more in high socioeconomic schools

Level Four Gifted:

- Primarily 99th percentile on standardized tests
- Exceptionally to Profoundly Gifted or Highly Advanced on IQ tests
- One or two across two grade levels; two or three per grade level in high socioeconomic schools

Level Five Gifted:

- Primarily 99th percentiles on standardized tests
- Exceptionally to Profoundly Gifted or Highly Advanced on IQ tests
- Nationally at least 1:250,000, with a higher proportion in metropolitan areas
- An evenly high intellectual profile, great inner drive to learn across domains

Chart 1: Standard IQ Score Ranges for the Levels

Levels of Giftedness	Approximate Score Range	Descriptive Designation
Level One	120-129	Moderately Gifted 120-124/Gifted 125-129
Level Two	130-135	Highly Gifted
Level Three	136-140	Exceptionally Gifted
Level Four	141+	Exceptionally to Profoundly Gifted
Level Five	141+	Exceptionally to Profoundly Gifted

Author note: Because of the limitations of current IQ tests, Levels Four and Five above appear to be identical but are not. The differences between the two levels are in the degree of the individual's behaviors. This chart does not consider ratio IQ scores and is not related to the old ratio IQ results except in the most general way.

Other factors considered when selecting level placement include the following:

- Early childhood intellectual milestones and behaviors
- General personality traits
- Degree of intrinsic motivation to initiate learning
- Sustained intrinsic drive for continued independent learning

Early Indicators of Giftedness

The following bullet points list behaviors that are common and familiar to the parents of gifted children—at all levels—before they start school. The majority of these abilities are beyond kindergarten skills, as well as beyond the achievement of many typical children by the end of first grade. They are all signs of being very advanced.

Children in all five levels of giftedness generally master most—but not necessarily all—of the Early Indicators of Intellectual Giftedness by or before age five. Most of these skills are related to academic abilities, but they are not the only factors considered when determining intellectual level. The Indicators of Uniquely High Ability are not universal to gifted children except at the highest levels. For example, if a child intuitively uses numbers at age five or younger, she would probably show all of the preceding supporting behaviors as well, and she would fit into at least Level Three. The extent of inner drive would still determine the final difference.

Early Indicators of Intellectual Giftedness

- Understands complex verbal instructions
- Shows interest and ability with shape sorters and eight- to 10-piece puzzles
- Speaks in complex, correct sentences using comparatives and connective words
- Can sight read a number of words or familiar signs
- Completes 25+ piece jigsaw puzzles and complex mazes
- Recognizes and/or names a wide variety of colors and shades
- Knows the letters in or out of alphabetical order
- Makes letters by writing or using sticks, utensils, etc.
- Knows the numbers
- Shows keen memory for detail in spatial directions, past events, etc.

- Uses one-to-one correspondence in counting objects
- Spontaneously reads anything with or without previous instruction★

★*Although a sign of giftedness, the onset of this skill seems harder to pin down and relate to a particular giftedness level than most of the other abilities. Also, it may or may not start before age five for any level.*

Indicators of Uniquely High Ability

- Intuitively uses numbers for grouping, adding, subtracting, multiplication, and division—mostly in their head and without instruction
- Shows concern and interest in existential issues and life's purpose

Differences between the Levels

The different levels of giftedness have some variability within them. Some children are incredibly advanced in their mathematical reasoning abilities but less so in their verbal reasoning, for example. When two children are equally able in one ability area—say verbal reasoning—but one also has a quantitative reasoning strength and the other does not—they will not be in the same level of giftedness, even if their overall IQ score is nearly the same.

Some parents might conclude that their children are at a certain high level of giftedness when the children demonstrate obvious abilities, such as talking or reading well before their age-mates, or they achieve a very high IQ score. However, in order to fit a specific level of giftedness, children need to show numerous early indicators of intellectual giftedness (as discussed in each of the chapters in Part II) similar to other children within that level.

People can change their position on the continuum of levels when critical aspects of their environment—particularly their inner environment—change. For example, sometimes something happens that suddenly causes them to have a passion for a topic or a goal, and this changes their level of intrinsic motivation to learn. For instance, an adult who is a generalist in medicine might become strongly motivated to find a cure for the disease that suddenly afflicts a family member. This person could go from being simply good at his medical work and at keeping up in his field to being a crusader always on the forefront of new research. Such an inner drive changes a person's goals and use of intelligence. Some children have strong inner drives to keep reading and acquiring new knowledge, but if those children are placed in school situations where they are not allowed to learn at their own ability level or follow any of their own natural interests, they can lose their inner drive, at least for the time being.

Who Are the Subjects of this Book?

Fifty families participated in the study for this book, some in a limited way and others quite extensively. Most of these families live within the same large metropolitan area. Because they came to me as clients, they are not a random sample; they are a self-selected sample. To fill in some IQ gaps from the subject pool, especially in Chapter 4 in which I describe the ability continuum leading up to the generally accepted gifted range (98th percentile), I used additional information from other families I have worked with over the years.

My study certainly does not include everyone who could have been eligible; many families never seek help, and some families are adamantly opposed to labeling of any kind. They avoid any sort of testing or consideration of level of intelligence; they want their children to be normal and to be mainstreamed with everyone else during their school years. This does not make these children any less gifted or different, however, and the lack of attention or recognition can cause problems, as later chapters reveal.

There are 78 children profiled in this book. The profile of children is as follows:

- Level One (13 children)
- Level Two (21 children)
- Level Three (19 children)
- Level Four (18 children)
- Level Five (7 children)

How the Information Is Presented

As you read through the chapters on the different levels of giftedness, you may want to refer to the appendices at the end of the book. Appendix A: Developmental Guidelines for Identifying Gifted Preschoolers (Hall & Skinner, 1980) was developed to describe normal childhood development compared to what is normal for the average gifted child (who is approximately 30% more advanced than the average child). Parents can use this table to see at what ages gifted children reach milestones compared with more typical children their same age.

Appendix B provides summary grade-level expectations from several major metropolitan area school districts. It shows how, as intellectual ability increases, there is an increasingly poor fit between learner and curriculum.

To offer some perspective, Appendix C provides some examples of historical figures which are taken from a book by an early scholar on giftedness, Catherine Cox. *The Early Mental Traits of Three Hundred Geniuses* (1926) shows some of the childhood behaviors of famous people whose names we recognize for their accomplishments as adults. Cox estimated ratio IQs for each person in her study based on her research. I have attempted to match the abilities and behaviors of these historical figures to the children in each of the levels.

Each chapter about the children at different levels contains a table of each child's available test scores so that readers can see the connection between early abilities and behaviors and later abilities as measured by standardized tests. Each table lists scores from tests, including the *Wechsler Intelligence Scale for Children (WISC-III)*, the *Cognitive Abilities Test (CogAT)*, the *Wechsler Preschool and Primary Intelligence Scale (WPPSI)*, the *Stanford-Binet, 5th Edition (SB5)*, and the *Otis-Lennon* group test given by many schools for many years. Scores from the *Otis-Lennon* test can be misleadingly low. If the children in this book were assessed by the *Stanford-Binet (Form L-M)*, the tables provide the ages at the time of testing, because *SBLM* score results are less reliable indicators of relative intelligence for some age ranges—within the six to seven year age range and again after about age 11 or 12.[4]

Some of the children in Level One and all of the children in Level Two through Level Five received 99th percentile scores on at least some standardized tests that they took, but their scores do not adequately explain how different their intellectual function actually is from that of their age-mates. Children who are sometimes incredibly different from one another earn scores that look very much alike. Parents and others should note that a test score is just a starting place for defining the highest levels of giftedness.

The chapters in Part II present the children in the order of my analysis of their intellectual level based on the reports of their previously demonstrated abilities, rather than in an order that is strictly tied to their test scores. The test scores, which provide important context, can alone be misleading. For example, how old are the norms? The accuracy of percentiles shifts over time, as well.[5] Due to the fact that not all children take the same IQ tests, and the scores between different test instruments are often on different scales, there is the problem of which test, which scale, and which scores to use. To minimize these difficulties and to add meaning, each chapter on the various levels of giftedness groups children whose intellectual, academic, and behavioral characteristics seem similar. Illustrative behavioral anecdotes are included for many of the children, although some parents provided less information than others.

The complexity of the individual intellect defies perfect grouping or ordering. Nonetheless, there are clear consistencies that distinguish each level from the others and which have implications for nurturing a child's intellectual, emotional, and interpersonal growth.

The difficulty of grouping children within levels underscores the pitfalls of cut-off scores. Some children are either far more verbally or mathematically advanced than others, but not both, which makes an uninterrupted continuum unlikely. Although I began this study with some confidence that a child who scores 180 on a ratio IQ test is always more intellectually capable than a child who scores 150, I discovered that this is not always the case and that the child with a 150 score can sometimes outperform the child with a 180 score. An important yet somewhat intangible quality almost always seems to determine where on the continuum children actually belong. An inner drive to learn—a strong intrinsic motivation—appears to make a substantial qualitative difference between children with similar test scores and outcomes and thus affects their placement in the levels. This intensity or inner drive to learn was often the main difference when deciding between a lower or higher level placement.

This book combines children's specific observable behaviors with their tested abilities and then compares and contrasts those behaviors and abilities with what the children encounter in school. Parents reading this book can use this information to estimate the level that their own children would fit into. All of the children's stories reinforce that intellectual level does matter significantly when determining how best to nurture a gifted child.

Chapter 4
Level One Gifted: Approximately 90th to 98th Percentiles

His attitude toward school is one of toleration, although his
teachers have said he is capable of so much more than he
produces with minimal effort. He tends to hurry through
schoolwork, not giving his full attention to it.
~ Mother of a Level One boy

Level One is what most schools and families think of as representing bright to moderately gifted children. Most, like the children in this chapter, have ratio IQs in the mid-120s to mid-140s range and standard scores ranging from about 115 to the upper 120s. Table 1 lists available scores. This level includes bright children who are well ahead of their classmates but who may score below the range typically designated for gifted program inclusion.

Most of the children in this chapter, called "moderately gifted," have ability scores that approach the 97th and 98th percentiles, which are referred to in testing manuals as "superior." These children should be included in any discussion of giftedness levels for two reasons: (1) their advanced abilities must be addressed if they are to maximize their academic potential and their ability to develop into confident and productive adults, and (2) readers need to see how the learning and behavioral distinctions differ between children who are bright and those who are substantially more advanced. This chapter provides a context for comparison.

How many Level One children are there in our schools? It varies according to a school's population type. The average ability level of different schools and school districts can vary significantly. This will always affect how many gifted children are in any school or any classroom. In some schools, children whose abilities are very low are not always placed in regular classrooms, which somewhat raises the average within the school compared to the full population within the school's attendance area.[1] In some very selective or competitive private schools or in districts where most parents are professionals, Level One children may be the average learners and will constitute the majority of the students. A typical suburban elementary school with a 25- to 28-student classroom may have from three to six children who are Level One or higher in intellectual ability in each classroom. Schools that draw from impoverished, culturally deprived, or low educational background families will generally have fewer Level One students,[2] possibly one per 28-student classroom and about four to six per 100 children.[3]

Because of the assumed symmetric shape of the bell curve, Level One children make up a large proportion of the students who are in gifted programs. Thus, there are more children at the 125 IQ level—using standard scores—than at the 135 IQ level, and fewer yet at the levels that are even higher.

Are Level One children truly gifted? Yes, because most school systems define gifted children as those in the upper 3% in ability or achievement. A frame of reference comes from standard score test data collected in the 1950s and 1960s. It was estimated that, in the United States, the mean IQ of high school graduates was about 105, the mean of college graduates was 115, and the mean of people getting medical degrees and Ph.D.s was about 125 (Matarazzo, 1972). This is, of course, different than saying that the average person with a 125 IQ goes to medical school. Psychologist Leta Hollingworth (1926) called a ratio IQ of 120-145 "optimal" intelligence, because such individuals are not so different from most other people that they will feel odd or different, yet they are able to succeed in colleges and universities.[4]

The Children

Children in the various levels are quite different from each other when comparing the onset of developmental behaviors. Even among the gifted, there is plenty of variability in intellectual strengths; however, you will notice a trend as you progress through the levels.

Here, in the parents' own voices, are descriptions of gifted children's developmental behaviors. These children reappear at different ages throughout the chapter.

Birth to Two Years

Clare Gaudette—Clare made good eye contact at about three months, waved bye-bye at six months, and liked us to read to her when she was a little over a year old. Her favorite TV show was *Teletubbies*. She could count by age two, but she couldn't count *things* yet.

Albena Brosch—At 14 or 15 months, Albena said words like "mama" and her sister's name. She enjoyed fairy tales with princesses—at two years old, she would sit while I read stories about them. She had amazing spatial ability; by age two, she turned pieces of 75- to 100-piece jigsaw puzzles to make them fit, although she couldn't do the whole puzzles yet.

Donald Wolsfeld—Donald said "hot" at 10½ months. He always wanted us to read to him and enjoyed it from the time he was born.

Deborah Resnick—Deborah sang *Twinkle Twinkle Little Star* at 18 months, and she had the tune down. The words weren't clear, but she could sing most of the song's first stanza.

Benita Walsh—Benita learned nose, ears, eyes, mouth, etc., by around 18 months.

Kirk Peterson—We think Kirk knew his colors before he was two.

Meridee Crocker—Meridee made good eye contact by the time she was a few weeks old. She waved bye-bye at about five months, and by six or seven months, she could say "ball," "ma," "da," "dog," "doll," "duck," "book," and "no." She loved to be read to. She sat still for TV by nine months and enjoyed *Barney*, *Spot*, *Kipper*, and any show with music and animated characters. Meridee counted to 10 by 18 months. She liked to stack blocks and count them, and when we did puzzles, she counted the pieces. She knew the alphabet sometime between 18 and 20 months.

> *Author note: Sitting still to watch and pay attention to TV is common among the gifted, but it is not common among typical children under one and two years of age.*[5]

Hans Fletcher—Hans laughed at two months. At five months, he played with his Busy Box™ (recommended for ages 18 months and up). He waved bye-bye at 12 months. At 13 months, he put the pieces in his shape sorter accurately. He said "clock," "mom," and "dada" at 18 months and loved puzzles and books.

Kristin Miller—Kristin made good eye contact her very first day. She waved bye-bye when she was about six months old. By one, she could say "mama," "dada," and the names of her brother and sister. Before she turned one, she loved it when we read to her, and she knew the colors by about 18 months.

Ronald Cooper—Between eight and 10 months, Ronald said "dada" for both of us, "bu" for bird, and "og" for dog. We could tell he knew colors before he could actually talk, and he could say about 60 words at 18 months.

Henry Ruggles—Henry made good eye contact at about 4½ weeks. He waved bye-bye at 10 months and said "tickle" ("tee-kuh") and "what's this" ("Dis?") at 12 months. We started to read to him when he was a baby. At about 13 or 14 months old, he could say a number of two-word phrases, although they weren't clear to everyone. His talking moved to four-word phrases by 19 months, and he could rote count by 18 months.

Age Two to Three Years

The most notable aspect of the Level One gifted children between two and three years old is how busy they are and how interested they are in so many things. Notice how often puzzles are mentioned as a favorite activity. Interest in puzzles appears to be highly related to intelligence.

Clare Gaudette—Clare knew colors and some of the alphabet by 2½.

Albena Brosch—Albena sat still for TV at about 2½. Her favorite shows were *Spot* and *Blues Clues*—ordinarily geared toward children ages three and older.

Donald Wolsfeld—Donald recognized colors at two and knew the alphabet before age three.

Deborah Resnick—At age two, Deborah imitated her sister by sitting next to her with a book, looking at the pictures and pretending to read. She also sang and matched pitch to the piano tuner.

Benita Walsh—Benita knew all of her colors before she was three years old. At daycare, she gravitated toward the puzzles and LEGOs®—the motor skills activities. She started to use the computer when she was about 2½, playing an alphabet game in which she found the letters on her own. She started wooden puzzles and went to 60- to 100-piece puzzles by about age three.

Meridee Crocker—By late two, Meridee could control the computer mouse and play sorting and musical games such as *JumpStart Toddler.*[6] She learned to count to 60 before she was three and recognized most colors. She started playing with wooden puzzles at daycare and progressed to 25-piece puzzles at three when she moved to preschool.

Kristin Miller—Kristin sat still and paid attention to musical videos like *Sing Along Songs* and *Grandpa's Magical Toys* when she was about two. She would also draw or paint until we told her it was time to stop. She knew the alphabet when she was 2½ and could count before she was three.

Li Bartrom—Li sat still for TV by 2½ years. Her favorite shows were *Barney* and any educational show with singing or kids. We became aware of her incredible memory at this age.

Henry Ruggles—At the age of two, he did puzzles intended for four- to six-year-olds.

Jonathan Truett—Jonathan's older sister loved playing "school" with him and taught him the alphabet by 2½.

Age Three to Four Years

The majority of Level One gifted children master kindergarten end-of-the-year academic tasks before they turn four. Many of these children can already read street and store signs, which is a developmental milestone that indicates early reading ability and is correlated with general intellectual ability. Also note the increasing use of humor by these children as we move higher on the IQ scale, as they grasp the subtleties of language earlier and earlier. None of the parents actively pushed or taught their children as much as they simply provided activities which the children enjoyed.

Clare Gaudette—Clare knew the whole alphabet shortly after she turned three. At 3½ to four years, she used her fingers or other materials to add numbers from one to 10.

Albena Brosch—Albena read her own name and knew some of the colors and some of the alphabet at three. By age four, she had mastered all of the colors and the alphabet.

Deborah Resnick—Deborah knew the alphabet by the time she was 3½ to four years old, but it was still a while before she could get the sounds or put them together in any way.

Meridee Crocker—When Meridee was late three, she loved simple mazes. She also worked at computer programs with letter and matching games by herself. By four, she could insert the CD and start and end games without parent supervision.

Author note: Young children who are allowed to use the computer do so, and they rapidly become quite proficient. I encourage parents to allow computer use and play, although some children become so absorbed by computer play that their time needs to be limited so that they get physical activity time as well.

Kristin Miller—Kristin read an exit sign one night at a restaurant when she was about three. She could write her name when she was 3½. Puzzles were one of her favorite activities—some with as many as 200 pieces by the time she was four.

Ronald Cooper—At age three, Ronald could joke and banter with adults. He held good conversations and had a great sense of humor.

Li Bartrom—By three, Li memorized what was read to her. The first book she did this with was *Go Dog Go* by Dr. Seuss. She also started to use numbers, counted well, and knew her colors and the alphabet by this time. By 3½, she could read most store and street signs easily. By 3¾ years, she became very interested in the computer.

Henry Ruggles—By age three, Henry recognized many store and street signs. He became independent on the computer shortly after that.

Age Four to Five Years

Children typically start kindergarten at age five, but even the children at the lower end of our IQ continuum are already meeting many, if not all, of the kindergarten expectations a full year before they start kindergarten. For instance, the typical kindergarten class has about one-third of its students "reading ready" at the beginning of the year. It is important for kindergarten and first-grade teachers to provide appropriately advanced instruction and materials for this upper one-third of the class so that they can continue their learning at an interesting and challenging pace.[7]

Clare Gaudette—Clare was almost five when she could phonetically sound out the beginning letter in some words and then guess the words from the pictures.

Donald Wolsfeld—Donald started to use numbers at age four or five.

Kirk Peterson—Kirk read store and street signs at about age four or five. He knew the alphabet by this time. He never showed interest in puzzles.

Meridee Crocker—Meridee began interest in learning what sounds letters make at daycare. Late during her fourth year, we started using *Hooked on Phonics*®[8] at home for lower- and upper-case letter recognition.

Kristin Miller—Kristin recognized her name and some words in print at about four years old. She was more interested in drawing than in writing letters. At her kindergarten screening, she only identified five letters out of the alphabet, even though we thought she had known them all from the time she was 2½.

> *Author note: Many children at Level One can learn academic skills with instruction and guidance from their parents, but this does not always mean that they are independent at these skills. Sometimes children need cuing—hints—from an adult to get them on track before they can recall the alphabet or remember how to do simple arithmetic problems. Even so, children with higher levels of giftedness are academically independent at earlier ages than those at lower levels, regardless of parent support.*

Li Bartrom—Between four and five, Li did simple addition on her own and sounded out words by herself.

Henry Ruggles—Henry started to read *Bob* books[9] with us when he was four, and he knew many words on his own. He showed a preference for nonfiction and loved that section of the library–history, presidents, space, and science. He also loved mazes, and we kept a maze book in the car.

Jonathan Truett—At four, Jonathan read *Hop On Pop* and other Dr. Seuss books that we'd read to him. He started sounding out simple words, so we read the text and stopped at words we thought he could recognize or figure out. He then did this with harder words.

Age Five to Six Years

All of the children described here started kindergarten during this year of their lives. Because of what they were already able to do, school was usually quite easy for them. They got a strong sense that they were smart and that people admired how able they were. Actual schoolwork was not challenging; they had a full school year to learn how to fill their time with lots of play and social interaction.

It is at this point—kindergarten entrance age—when many parents learn how their child compares to others. If they have consulted typical developmental milestones charts, they know that their child is advanced, but they still have no real reference points for discovering whether or not their child is especially unusual.

Differences between boys' and girls' reported interests also start to emerge around age five. Computers and mazes are more often the purview of the boys. The girls tend to focus on reading; however, when boys read a lot, they lean more strongly toward nonfiction. In this sample, fantasy games and imaginative activities are more common among girls than boys.

Albena Brosch—Albena started to recognize street signs, like "zoo" and "stop," when she was five, just before she started kindergarten. I started working with her on sight words with phonics.

Deborah Resnick—Deborah wanted to learn to read and asked me to teach her, which I tried when she was 4½ years old and again when she was five, but she didn't get it until she was 5½. She was very excited about this accomplishment and immediately started reading beginner books.

Benita Walsh—Benita's kindergarten used a phonics system that totally confused her. She started to read beginner books when she was in first grade. She began reading regular chapter books at this age, too, and she enjoyed 1,000-piece puzzles.

Author note: Most gifted children learn to read from contextual clues; phonics can disrupt the process. Basic phonics helps them sound out unfamiliar words until they recognize the word, but this method should not be their primary instruction.

Kirk Peterson—Kirk liked math early. When he was five, he came up with the idea of a paper airplane business. He made paper airplanes, wrote prices on them, 10 cents to $1, and put them in a paper bag in the front yard. He decided to fill the bottom with rocks to keep it from blowing away. He wrote a sign saying, "Paper airplanes for sale. Put money in bag." He kept this up for a couple of weeks. Finally, someone bought a plane for 50 cents (me). We discussed how location is important to a business—we live in a cul-de-sac—and other business lessons. He was very interested. I think he was doing addition, subtraction, and some basic multiplication at age 5½. He started reading beginner books in the middle of kindergarten. He never expressed any strong interest in having us read to him. He enjoyed listening to some books, but not enthusiastically.

Meridee Crocker—Meridee read store and street signs by the time she was about five. She also started to read beginner books. She learned to read primarily using phonics tools and by asking us questions. She also had a good background with letters from her daycare program. It was truly her curiosity that led to her reading, more than us as parents trying to lead her in that direction. She became almost competitive when it came to learning. She loved computer games until she turned 5½. Then she became much more interested in playing make believe or reading with a friend. She spent long periods of time on art or imaginative activities with her friends.

Hans Fletcher—By the time he was five, Hans enjoyed 100-piece puzzles, took a chess class, and loved building with blocks and LEGOs®. He was concerned that he needed to know how to read to enter kindergarten, so he taught himself soon after he turned five

Kristin Miller—Kristin wanted to read before kindergarten. We had *Bob* books, and I showed her how to read the first one by making the sounds of the letters. She took off from there, reading *Arthur* books[10] within a few weeks. When she was five, she was fascinated with the artist Monet.

Ronald Cooper—At age five, Ronald started to recognize words in books. Shortly after that, he surprised us by reading signs at the state fair. During kindergarten, he read beginner books and counted by 2s, 5s, and 10s. He could do all of the basic number facts by this time, too, in both addition and subtraction.

Li Bartrom—Li taught herself to read by hearing others read aloud while she looked at the pictures in the books. She also memorized what was read to her. By 5½ years old, she could read beginner books on her own. She went straight to chapter books before she turned six.

Henry Ruggles—Henry started reading simple chapter books at 5½ years.

Age Six to Seven Years

At this age, children enter first grade. All of our Level One children could already read by this time, even though the first-grade expectation is that they would just now begin to learn the sounds that letters make. As for math, all of these children learned to count years before, and most had advanced far beyond counting. First-grade expectations do not typically make allowances for children with these advanced skills and abilities.

Albena Brosch—Albena started to read beginner books like *Cat in the Hat* and *Sam I Am* by Dr. Seuss at age six.

Donald Wolsfeld—Donald could read beginner books in first grade when he was 6½ years old.

Kirk Peterson—We home schooled Kirk for ages six and seven. I taught him to read, but he didn't enjoy it. He wouldn't forgive himself when he made a mistake. He's always been more of a doer than a reader. He was very good at following picture instructions in order to put things together, like with his LEGOs® and Hot Wheel® kits. He did enjoy it very much, however, when we read books like those by Tolkien and C. S. Lewis aloud to him.

Meridee Crocker—At 6¼ years, Meridee mastered most three- and many four-letter words that could be sounded out. She also worked on sounding out five- and six-letter words. She very much enjoyed daily reading with her teachers and parents, and she still liked puzzles—even the more complex 200-piece ones.

Hans Fletcher—Hans could read chapter books when he was in first grade.

Li Bartrom—By age six, Li began to do addition, subtraction, and simple multiplication in her head. She was completely adept and independent with the keyboard and computer by 6½ years, and she could read chapter books that were for third and fourth graders.

Jonathan Truett—Jonathan read the entire first-grade reading book at the beginning of the year. His teacher often had him stand in front of the class and read to the other students out loud, which he enjoyed a lot. He played a version of the *Math Blaster*®[11] computer game for seven- to 10-year-olds when he was six and mastered it.

Age Seven to Nine Years

Most families of gifted children first contact someone for help when their children are between second and fourth grade. The parents realize that their children are not being challenged, are bored in school, and may not get the chance to learn all they can. Few present day classrooms have any ability grouping—that is, there is no high, middle, and low math or reading group. As a result, rote memorization or drill of arithmetic facts is a common issue with gifted kids, teachers, and parents. Many children find it unnecessary and consequently dislike it.

Albena Brosch—Albena was happy when she learned how to read beginner books, but she seldom picked up a book on her own and did not start to read chapter books until she was 7½ years old. Her favorite pastime was fantasy play. Although she got along well with everyone, she particularly liked anyone who could enter her world of fantasy, especially younger kids, because they tend to really enjoy make-believe.

Donald Wolsfeld—Donald started to read chapter books when he was in second grade, at about 7½. He got really good with the computer and keyboarding at about that time, too.

Deborah Resnick—Deborah started reading chapter books by the time she was about seven years old. She liked the Ramona books[12] and books about animals. She did well enough in school, but her performance was not exemplary. Although she was very good in geometry, she didn't pick up math skills early compared with children her age. She was gifted in language and verbal skills, though, and scored very high in reading in third grade, so she was given several special independent projects in that area. However, she didn't score high enough in math for the school system's gifted program. Deborah did a large poster assignment in third or fourth grade, and her graphic design and placement of elements was so adult that I was compelled to tell the teacher that she did not have help from me.

Kirk Peterson—Kirk started reading chapter books at about age seven. Some of the math in his second-grade public school was too easy for him. He'd known money denominations for years.

Hans Fletcher—Hans loved reading up through first grade, was turned off in second grade, and then hated to read, although he would read grudgingly for information. He had good reading comprehension but preferred to watch videos. Although he was in the high potential program, he liked to go at his own pace, which was much faster than what happened in school. The math instruction was far behind what he could do or enjoy. Math came easily to Hans—at the end of third grade, he was doing pre-algebra, and he had unique methods of adding columns of numbers or multiplying. However, he was prone to computation errors because he rushed and was easily bored with repetition. He liked the *Math Blaster®* CD for the computer and enjoyed playing chess.

Kristin Miller—Kristin really started to read chapter books in first grade. She loved using the computer and enjoyed *Oregon Trail*®[13] and *JumpStart Spanish*.

Ronald Cooper—In second grade, Ronald started reading the *Hardy Boys* books,[14] and his reading ability developed quickly. He loved to read, and he often filled up his free time at school and home with it. Teachers required daily reading, and he took this seriously. In second and third grade, he consistently read more than anyone else. Ronald did not like practicing addition and subtraction in first and second grade and continued to resist until his third-grade teacher made math fun. Multiplication and division seemed to come especially easily in third and fourth grade.

Jonathan Truett—In second grade, Jonathan was able to read fourth-grade-level chapter books like *The Stone Fox* by John Reynolds Gardiner. His achievement tests showed his reading level to be approximately eleventh grade in word decoding skills. His *interest* in reading, however, was more sporadic. He did more reading when there was some sort of incentive, like for a contest. He became interested in tangrams[15] when he was about eight.

Age Nine and Older

Deborah Resnick—Deborah made her own website from scratch when she was 10 and another when she was 12. At 11, she wrote and directed a play while also participating in some school gifted program activities with other identified gifted kids. At 14, she designed a new website with her own artwork. She learned some HTML from her sister and the rest online.

Kristin Miller—Kristin finally qualified for the gifted and talented program and was put in a fourth/fifth-grade mixed age class. Her favorite game was *Sim City*®, a computer city building program. She enjoyed making *PowerPoint*®[16] presentations, and she also liked computer art programs.

Author note: Kristin started her schooling in a major metropolitan area suburb known for its good schools. She was not part of the gifted and talented program because her scores were never quite high enough. Then, for one year, she lived in another state where she was placed in a special class for the gifted. Before moving to the new state, her math achievement scores were near the 50th percentile. After a year of instruction at a higher, faster level, her math achievement score zoomed to the 99th percentile. Back in her original school again, Kristin mentioned that she was getting nothing even close to the same level of instruction.

Unlike reading, math is not learned independently; instruction is needed. Except for the year that she was in a gifted program in another state, the math curriculum and instruction Kristin received in school was considerably below what she was able to handle. The high percentiles that Kristin obtained after appropriate instruction for mathematics provide a clear example of how tutoring can make a significant difference. If all children were taught at their own ability and readiness levels, especially in mathematics, their achievement scores would be quite similar to their ability scores.

Ronald Cooper—By age 10, Ronald went through many series of books in the school library. He especially liked the *Hardy Boys* books (he read more than 40 of them!) and Gary Paulson, and then he moved on to the *Redwall* books.[17] He loved to read so much that we sometimes had to shut off the light and take the book away at night. When he was in fifth grade, he took very little time to pick out a report while typing at the computer, and very soon, he needed no help from us on the computer at all. In a sixth-grade production of *Oliver*, he was fabulous as Fagin, with three solos and 55 lines. He had a great year in sixth grade, even though the only advanced offering was honors social studies. He really liked his teacher and the class.

Summary of Level One Gifted

The preceding group of children displayed a remarkable range of abilities. Virtually all of them started school with skills beyond what they would be taught in their classrooms, and some children were considerably beyond that. The lowest Level One IQ examples, in the low to mid-120s for their ratio and standard score IQs, usually comprise the top one-third of any class that these children would be in throughout elementary school. The children at the top of this range, with mid-140 ratio IQs and upper 120s standard score IQs, stood out as very smart and capable throughout their elementary careers. The ratio IQ scores for these children from the *Stanford-Binet (Form L-M)* are listed in Table 1.

An IQ score of 132 on the *SBLM* was, until recently, considered the cut-off for the gifted range. However, today's standard score tests—for example the *WISC-III-IV, WJ-R, Stanford-Binet 4th* and *5th Editions*, among others—which have a 130 score for the corresponding gifted cut-off, find fewer children who score at that cut-off point. In other words, the children in this chapter, up to about 140 or 145 ratio IQ, would not meet the 130 IQ cut-off point on the standard score tests given today. This is important to note because it means that even children who might not be identified as gifted by their schools today are all still significantly more advanced than the normal school curriculum expectations.

If we look at what Level One children are like and what can they do, we find the following points.

- Most liked someone to read to them before they turned one year old.
- Most knew and said many words before 18 months.
- Most said three- to four-word sentences by 18 to 20 months.
- Most sat still and attended to TV by 18 to 30 months.
- Many recognized colors, letters, and numbers and could rote count before age two.
- Many liked puzzles before age two.
- Many knew how to count and knew most letters and colors by age three.
- Most demonstrated complex speaking and extensive vocabulary by age three.
- Many recognized simple signs and their written name and knew the alphabet by age four.
- Most did simple addition and subtraction by age four.
- Most showed interest in learning to read before age five.
- All read simple signs and most read beginner books by age six.
- Many did 200- to 1,000-piece puzzles by age six.
- Most were independent on the computer and started to keyboard by age six.
- Most fully grasped counting and basic number facts by age six.
- All were reading two to three years beyond grade level by age seven.
- Most enjoyed having advanced-level books and stories read to them by age seven.
- All could read chapter books independently by age seven to 7½.
- Many showing impatience with repetition and slow pace at school by age seven or eight.

Children of Level One ability can easily go on to college, can benefit from accelerated coursework, and are often, although not always, good and cooperative students.

Table 1: Level One Children's Data

Name	SBLM Ratio IQ	Test Age Years-Mos.	Other IQ Tests	Achievement Test Grade Equivalencies/ Percentiles
Clare Gaudette	122	4-9	-	-
Albena Brosch	125	7-8	-	-
Donald Wolsfeld	129	10-3	-	-
Deborah Resnick	128	-	-	-
Benita Walsh	156	8-11	CogAT 123	-
Kirk Peterson	139	8-0	WISC-III: VIQ-117, PIQ-115, FSIQ-117; CogAT: Verbal 79, Quantitative 99, Nonverbal 93, Total 98	Iowa Basics Composite 63: Reading 76, Language 85, Math 54
Meridee Crocker	137	6-2	-	-
Hans Fletcher	138	-	-	Iowa Basics Composite 97: Reading 90, Language 66, Math 99, Social Studies 99, Science 93, Information Sources 86
Kristin Miller	128	-	-	At age 11: Woodcock-McGrew-Werder Basic Skills 94: Reading 98, Writing 68, Math 99, Knowledge 81
Ronald Cooper	145	10-4	-	-
Li Bartrom	165	7-5	WISC-III 139	Explore Test for 8th grade norms taken in 3rd grade: English 52, Usage 66, Rhetorical Skills 48, Reading 66, Science Reasoning 91, Composite 51
Henry Ruggles	141	6-8	-	-
Jonathan Truett	146	9-8	-	-

Chapter 5

Level Two Gifted: Approximately 98th and 99th Percentiles

*She was very excited about bugs and worms and other crawling
things that her brother was fearful of. We finally had to make a
rule at age three that she was not to put living things in her
dress pockets.*

~ Mother of a Level Two girl

Children at Level Two generally score at or above the 98th percentile on standardized tests, a level most schools recognize as gifted. By definition, one person out of 50 is at the 98th percentile and one out of 100 is at the 99th percentile on standardized tests. Despite their similar percentile scores, children in this chapter have a very wide range of ratio IQs (130s to 180s), and standard scores (125 to 146). Available scores for these Level Two children are presented in Table 2.

How many Level Two children are there in our schools? Selective or competitive private schools and schools in districts in which most of the parents are highly educated professionals can expect that fully one-third to one-half of their students may be at this level or higher. A typical suburban elementary school with 100 children per grade level probably has at least four to six of these children in each grade—one to two per class. Schools that draw from impoverished, disadvantaged, or low educational background parents will usually have fewer Level Two students, perhaps one per 100.

The Children

Birth to Two Years

As you read this section, notice how often mothers of Level Two and higher children mention their child's alertness. Usually, this comes in the form of eye contact at a very early age—sometimes as early as the delivery room. Most average children will make little eye contact with anyone until they are many months old. In addition, most children will not sit still for reading—they will often tear at the books. However, Level Two gifted children tend to have long attention spans, and they show great interest and patience in listening to people speak or read to them. Letters, numbers, and puzzles routinely fascinate them, and they enjoy copying what people around them say and do.

Level Two gifted children are especially interactive very early in their lives. As you read, notice all of the indications of understanding and meaningful communication that parents had with these children, even before they could actually speak well. However, once they learned to talk, these children often progressed quickly to very advanced speech, frequently attracting the attention and comments of strangers. Many of the parents in this sample expressed surprise that their Level Two or higher children knew or could do things while still very young that the parents never specifically taught them.

Cory Engum—Cory said his first words—"dada" and "mama"—at nine months of age. He walked at 9½ months and ran everywhere by 10 months. At 12 months, he said "hot," light," and "Rose," his sister's name. By 18 months, he added "mine," "this," "hat," "tractor," "on there," "blanket," and "water." He showed interest in being read to between 12 and 18 months. We read board books[1] and picture books and then progressed to stories as his attention span increased. He sat and looked at some books by himself. We read Richard Scarry's *What Do People Do All Day?* over and over. He liked the illustrations of how things are constructed (plumbing in a house, for example). He also played with a variety of wooden puzzles.

By the time he was a little more than year old, Cory was creating "projects" using whatever materials were available and of interest to him at the time. The first ones were constructions made of paper, tape, yarn, and other objects like tissue boxes. When he was about 1½ to two years old, he liked to watch a video about construction equipment. He also began playing with DUPLOs®[2] and computer games, particularly the *JumpStart* series educational games. He drove our electric toy car around the yard very proficiently. He could navigate obstacles, stop, change gears, and drive in reverse. Other children as old as five had more difficulty doing this than he did.

Gary Lundquist—Gary was smiling at us at seven weeks. By the time he reached six months, he wanted us to read to him. He repeated sounds we made to him at 10 months, and by 12 months, he could say "uh-oh" and "bye-bye." At 19 months, Gary asked specifically, "Color, paper," when he wanted to draw. He also knew his own version of many songs, including *Twinkle Twinkle What You Are*, parts of the alphabet song, and *Happy to You*. Gary could count to 14 by the time he was two, spoke in sentences, and started to have some favorite television shows.

Glenn Richards—At 11 months, Glenn said "bear." By 12 months, he could say many animal sounds, "brother," "dada," "ka" for car, and "kafa" for careful. By the time he turned one, he loved to look at books and be read to all day long. He recognized some letters and all of the colors by 15 months, started working puzzles, and was a good imitator. He loved dogs, cars, trucks, and planes, and he was dexterous, opening shampoo bottles and throwing a ball well. At 18 months, his favorite playthings and activities were balls, balloons, cars and trucks, drawing, magnetic letters, and filling and emptying containers.

Boyd Uphoff—Boyd made eye contact in the delivery room. He liked us to read to him when he was six or seven months old. By 10 months, he could say "airplane," "mom," "more," and "bus." He recognized and said store and street signs at 11 months. Before he was one, you could tell him to "go to the kitchen, get a towel, put it in the blue bowl, and then go to mommy" and he would crawl off and do so. He said some numbers by 16 months, and he seemed to sight-read a few words at about 17 months, like "peas," "car," and "boo." At about 20 months, he repeated memorized words of his favorite books and soon recognized words in other contexts. He recognized colors by 19 months. By 20 months, he could fetch one object of one type and two objects of a different type, and by 22 months, he could count to 10 and hand us three and five things when asked.

Bradley Ruhl—Brad made eye contact between one and two months old. He said some words by about 11 months, but they were hard to make out. He said whole sentences by 15 months, which weren't very clear for awhile, and then, rather suddenly, he was understandable.

Noa Collins—Noa made good eye contact almost from birth. I could understand her by seven months. For example, she responded to "Where's your brother Nicholas?" by looking at him. By nine months, she brought me books to read to her. She did simple puzzles at one year. She didn't talk at all until she was 20 months old. Among her first words were "bih" for bird, "tee-tue" for thank you, and "pee" for please. Although she started late, she was talking in eight- to 10-word sentences within two weeks. Noa sat still for TV at about 18 months, recognized colors by 20 months, and did 35-piece puzzles by age two.

Betsy Dunkirk—Betsy made good eye contact when she was just a few weeks old. She said "dad," "ma," and "ball" before she was one. She also loved to be read to. She recognized colors by 18 to 20 months, and by the time she was two, she talked well, knew the alphabet, and was definitely using numbers. She liked to watch animal shows, cartoons, and musicals on TV at this age. Although she liked puzzles well enough, she was never very interested in them.

Chrissy Quan—We started reading to Chrissy as an infant, and she loved it. She started to play with 12-piece puzzles when she was one. She said all of our names, plus "all done," "more," "balloon," "no," and "bye-bye" when she was 14 months old. She sat still for TV and enjoyed *Barney*, *Thomas*, and animated videos. When she was 18 months old and playing with plastic alphabet letters, she surprised us by saying each of them correctly. She could even tell which was a "W" and which was an "M" if we held them upside down. She must have picked this up from an educational video.

Tamara Lundquist—By 11 months, we could tell by the context and inflections that Tamara was saying "dada" and "thank you." She also seemed to make the connection between books and the words in them, and she started turning the pages at the right time.

Arthur Richards—By 10½ months, Arthur waved bye-bye. He said some words by 11 months, like "thh" for fan, "mamam" for mom, "nana" for banana, and "dzhiss" for this. "This" became such a practical word for him—he pointed to all kinds of objects asking, "This?"—that he didn't develop the need for other words until he was about 18 to 24 months old. By the time he was 1½ years old, he looked at books on his own, colored pictures, used the computer, played some card games, and played with toys like DUPLOs®, Mr. Potato Head™, and blocks.

Tony Matthews—Tony made good eye contact at six weeks and waved bye-bye at eight months. He said "mama," "dada," and "baba" (grandma) at seven months. Many people understood his large repertoire of words by 11 months. He loved when we read to him and was very interested in books. He knew several store and street signs by 14 months. It was clear that he recognized many colors and started to use numbers when he was one year old. Around this time, he became interested in puzzles and could quickly put together ones for children above his age level. He sang the alphabet song at 13 months and recognized all of the letters by 17 months. He counted by 15 months and recognized printed words and numbers by the time he was about two.

Nicholas Collins—Nicholas was immediately unusual. At six weeks, he spent half an hour intensely exploring a small rattle, passing it from hand to hand to mouth to belly to foot and back. When he started eating cereal at six months, he understood, "Do you want more?" He began playing with simple puzzles and shape sorters at nine months. He pointed to a dozen or more named items in a picture by 10 months, and he also said his first words, including "kah" for clock, "bah" for ball or circle, and "buh" for book. By 15 months, he placed all 18 pieces in the shape sorter cube, counted to three, and identified the color red. He knew all of the colors by 18 months. He built elaborate DUPLO® structures and BRIO®[3] train tracks, and he constructed towers, roads, and bridges out of blocks, books, or any available material. By 21 months, he assembled 35-piece puzzles and built tall structures out of preschool blocks. Nick recognized the letter "D" at 15 months and knew all of the letters by about two years. He recognized many words in books and newspapers, and he read store and street signs, as well as the names on friends' mailboxes.

Frank Price—The earliest signs that Frank was talented were his large vocabulary by the age of two and his intensity of play and concentration. It was clear when he was slightly over one year old that he really understood things. At 13 months, he could say "door," "juice," and "truck." At 15 months, he said "silly," "gentle," "chair," "tractor," "bubble," "pepper," "diaper," "more," and "night-night." By 17 months, he said 41 words; at 18 months, he started two-word sentences, and his vocabulary was 114 words; at 19 months, he started three-word sentences. We all understood him as soon as he could talk—he was always particularly clear. At two, he would say things like, "Actually, I meant…."

Earl Langer—Earl made good eye contact at six to eight weeks. He said "cheese" and "kitty" when he was 11 months old. When he was an infant, he sat in our laps while we read the paper and looked at the words. By one year, daily reading was a big part of our lives. Earl really enjoyed books and had a long attention span from an early age. He read stop signs at 16 months. Other signs quickly followed, and he also started to spot specific words in the newspaper. He began counting by 14 months, like counting down the numbers on the microwave. He knew some colors by 16 months. Puzzles were a favorite activity by age two.

Zachary Hackner—Zach made good eye contact by one month and expressed interest in our reading to him before he was two years old. He liked to watch TV, especially musicals like *Mary Poppins*, *Willy Wonka*, music videos, and *Barney*. He knew his colors by 20 months.

Debra Sund—From the first week Debra was born, everyone commented on how alert she was. At 3½ months, I held her in front of the bathroom mirror and said, "Where's Debra?" and she'd search for us in the mirror. At eight months, when we said either "mommy" or "daddy," she would look at the right person. When she was nine months old, she searched for the ball when we got to a page in her book with a ball on it. At 9½ months, her father asked, "Where's daddy's foot?" and Debra grabbed his foot. He asked, "Where's Debra's foot?" and she grabbed her own foot. She said "dup" for yes at 15 months, and then life got infinitely easier when I asked her what she wanted and she'd respond. She could even follow simple directions. She said some words at 17 months and recognized the letter "E" on a sign. She could identify the letters "O" and "T" a month after that.

Greg Cooper—Greg always had "wise eyes," even as a baby, and made good eye contact about a month after birth. Between eight and 10 months, he said his first words, including "mama," "dada," and "up." It was clear that he knew some different colors, too, picking items out by the color we named. By six months, he sat still endlessly when we read to him. He loved to do puzzles, and he started to count between 18 and 24 months. Greg had an incredible ability to communicate without words. He was quite a mime, using gestures and intonations to tell us what he wanted. When he did start talking more than a few words at a time, he spoke in sentences and progressed quickly to well-organized verbalization.

Harry Vassar—Harry made good eye contact at about one month. He waved bye-bye at nine months and started to enjoy having us read to him. At 10 months, he loved to watch his sister play on the computer. He had a good attention span for TV before he was one. Shortly after he turned one, he recited numbers up to 13. He knew the color blue at 15 months and played with 24-piece puzzles two pieces at a time. He knew all of the colors at 20 months, recognized Florida on a weather report, and did puzzles labeled for three- to five-year-olds. He loved the U.S. map puzzle and could do about one-third of it. At 21 months, he mastered the computer mouse, and we'd have to drag him away from the computer kicking and screaming. He was obsessed with *Barney* videos by 20 months, taking them out, showing them to people, stacking them, lining them up, naming them, and identifying the people on the cases. He read books to himself in his crib at this time also, like *Go Dog Go* and *Ten Apples on Top* by Dr. Seuss, which are supposed to be for children four to eight years old.

Spencer Hayes—Spencer smiled at birth. He showed interest in having us read to him when he was four to five months old, and at six months, he sat while his brother flipped through the books telling him the stories. He knew all of the colors by two years.

Age Two to Three Years

Many parents of Level Two children know from looking at developmental milestones charts that their children are advanced. Few suspect, however, that what their three-year-old child can do is so far ahead of expectations for five- and six-year-old children who are in kindergarten.

Cory Engum—Cory knew the alphabet and started to read store and street signs at about 2½ years. He also had several large floor puzzles that he liked to put together. He didn't talk much until after his second birthday, but then he talked in sentences. At 28 months, he said, "Where is the little one?" and "Mom, I want to sit by you." By 30 months, he said, "Grandpa, this is for you." At or just before age three, I kept him busy by putting the newspaper in front of him and asking him to circle the letters he knew.

Glenn Richards—After he turned two, Glenn learned the alphabet and numbers, looked at books on his own, and used a fork. Sometime between ages two to three, he learned how to use the VCR to turn on a *Barney* video, and he spoke in one-word sentences.

Boyd Uphoff—Boyd knew the alphabet by age two. At about 30 months, he could do 1+1, 1+2, etc. on his fingers.

Noa Collins—When Noa was two, she knew the alphabet and read store and street signs. By 2½ years, she seemed to know letter sounds, recognized words in books, and counted to five. Two weeks before she turned three, she read her first words and a sentence in the phonics book. She wanted to write words, so I started her in a first-grade book in which we did lots of circling the picture with the specified beginning sound, and she traced words I'd written.

Chrissy Quan—When Chrissy was two years old, she drew people with a head, eyes, eyeballs, nose, mouth, teeth, ears, chin, legs, and feet. A few months later, she started crying one day because "I just can't draw hair!" She sat and drew for hours.

Author note: Developmental charts list the above drawing skills as typical for six-year-olds.

Arthur Richards—Arthur started taking an interest in talking—in both English and Spanish—around age two and said 15 to 20 words. He progressed rapidly to phrases like, "No I not!" He also recognized and said the names of several letters. At 2½ years, he knew all of the letters, recognized many numbers, and could play card games like *Go Fish*. He could also ride a two-wheel bike with training wheels. We really noticed that he was bright when he was able to play games like chess with his older brothers at 2¾ years old.

Nicholas Collins—Nicholas consistently enjoyed puzzles recommended for children one to three years older than he was. When he was two and three, he spent about an hour every day doing puzzles.

Frank Price—We noticed special talents when Frank was two, like when he took 80 miniature cars and made a detailed snowflake pattern out of them with lots of symmetry.

Zachary Hackner—Zach started to use numbers when he was two. He could count, do 24-piece puzzles, knew the alphabet, and recognized or read store and other signs by age three.

Debra Sund—By the time she was three, Debra was able to count up to four things in her head and tell how many there were. She also amazed us with some of the things she noticed and remembered. On a trip when she was 2½, we stopped in a little town and pulled up to a plain brick building. Debra kept saying, "Why are we going to the post office?" We said, "We're not," puzzled. As we pulled away, I noticed on the very top of the building the postal emblem of the eagle. It was a vague symbol—I had to look twice to see that it was an emblem for the post office.

Bernie Walker—By two, Bernie enjoyed *Barney*, sing-along shows, and musical programs on TV. By 2½, he recognized store signs, counted to 20, played with puzzles a lot, and knew the alphabet and colors.

Greg Cooper—At 2½, Greg surprised us with, "PU! Dat smells putrid!" His favorite joke at that time was, "Is you wefrigrator wunnig? Den go catch dat!" Curled up with his father at a nap, he said, "You like boat, me like boat at dock." When eating a carrot, he explained, "Me like beaver eating a tree." When he was 2-2/3 years old, he said, "Dat banana filthy!" Another favorite memory of ours is when, after eating a cupcake, Greg said, "Danks! Dat was a tasty meal."

Harry Vassar—At 2¼ years, Harry impressed people by what he knew. He recognized the letters, spelled his name, and liked to watch sports on TV. By 2½, the daycare teacher commented on his vocabulary, remarking that he knew the alphabet and could type his name on the computer. At age 2¾, he moved up to the preschool room at daycare and said that he liked being around the "bigger boys." He knew the names of the Maryland basketball players by then, too. By the time he turned three, he could count objects.

Jo Anne Price—Jo Anne was really good at learning things through songs. At two, she loved a number of reading and math educational computer games. She always had a good vocabulary and a good command of the English language. She knew the months of the year and the days of the week pretty dependably by age two. When she was about 2½, she pretended that she was going to work, and she stuck her head in my bedroom door and said, "See you later, alligator." I answered "After a while, crocodile." Jo Anne threw the door open and screamed, "I is not a crocodile!" and slammed the door. A moment later, she opened the door again and said, "Oh, you's just jokin.'"

Author note: Jo Anne knew the days of the week by age two, but according to the normative scoring on the Stanford-Binet (Form L-M), the average child knows the days of the week in order by about 7½ years old.

Age Three to Four Years

There is a tremendous diversity of activities and interests among preschool-age Level Two children. They catch on to complex games and activities very quickly. The parents of such children try to find anything that will keep the child busy.

Most of these children love to try writing and will work on it independently for long periods of time. Most can also read many words before they turn four. They appear to have memorized stories that are read to them, but their memories merely cue them to expect and read the words as they come up.

Cory Engum—At three, Cory liked to watch "do-it-yourself" home videos about plumbing, framing a house, and wiring a home. We had one videotape about do-it-yourself home plumbing projects that he watched over and over until the tape wore out. He liked to play with sections of plastic PVC pipe and connectors—we gave him ropes, pulleys, clamps, and piles of plumbing supplies to play with. We noticed when building our house that Cory could read a blueprint. He drew a wiring diagram, a floor plan, and a map. He was very aware of where we were in the car, knew how to get to where we were going, and questioned me if I took a different route. At age 3½, he switched from DUPLOs® to LEGOs®, which are much smaller and more advanced building block sets.

Cory liked TV shows like *Blue's Clues, Theodore the Tugboat, Arthur,* and *Mr. Rogers.* When he was about 3½, we started to read chapter books to him like Laura Ingalls Wilder's *Little House on the Prairie,* which we read several times. He was fairly effective at keyboarding when using the computer by this time. We played a game practicing math facts, and I'd asked him things like, "You have two apples and add three more." He figured it in his head without counting on his fingers. He could do addition and subtraction up to 14 or 15 in his head. One day, he sat down at the counter and created "The 13 Game." He took a piece of paper and drew boxes on it, and then he wrote the numbers 1 through 13 in the boxes. You were supposed to role a die and move a marker. I hadn't realized that he knew how to write numbers up to 13; it wasn't something we had practiced.

One of Cory's early interests, beginning about two or three years old, was tractors and farming. He became quite an expert, both in the sense of identifying different kinds of tractors and noticing small details about them, but he also knew the history of many types of tractors such as which tractor companies bought out and merged with others, how John Deere started out by making plows, etc. Before he was four, he would take these facts and make his own analysis and value judgments, such as "Massey Ferguson makes the best tractors because...."

Glenn Richards—By his third birthday, Glenn could count to seven and spoke in full sentences like, "Ooh, look, this is cool, Daddy!" and "Why does that dinosaur crack out of the egg?" He recognized and wrote a number of simple words. He loved daily reading and several rather complicated computer games—programs designed for much older kids. He watched TV shows like the science show *Nova* and the adult game shows *Jeopardy* and *Wheel of Fortune*. He also liked Disney movies.

Bradley Ruhl—Brad started to read simple books between ages three and four.

Noa Collins—When Noa was 3¼ years old, she started writing letters of the alphabet. She could read a dozen pages in some very simple beginner books. We started a preschool number facts book at this time, and she counted to 20 after a month of practice. She read clocks to the half-hour, extended three-unit patterns, and distinguished 1s and 10s in two-digit numbers. When she was 3½, we started a first-grade-level math facts book. She did simple addition and subtraction, before and after numbers, and identified the greatest and least of three two-digit numbers. At age 3¾ years, she read bits of second- to third-grade books or more advanced material, and she read entire first-grade books with minimal help. She increasingly recognized words she'd seen frequently. She measured objects in inches or centimeters and counted out money to "buy" items from food ads.

> *Author note: Most children who are advanced in their academic skills are not coached or specifically taught by their parents during their preschool years. This parent is unusual in that she actively taught and drilled her child since Noa was quite young. After she taught Noa at home for several years, she had the girl tested for IQ, but she initially felt that her daughter's tested IQ must be wrong—too low—because Noa was capable of achieving to a level twice as high as children her age are expected to learn. Does giving the child extra exposure to academic skills increase the actual IQ? Although this might increase the measured IQ score, it is unlikely to increase a child's intellectual potential or basic intelligence.*

Early academic coaching enhances the achievement portions of IQ tests. In order to estimate intellectual potential, however, it is important to notice what very young children of higher giftedness levels are doing *without* specific instruction. There is more to high intelligence than academic achievement. It is also about the child's pondering, interests, self-motivated drive to learn, and feelings that go along with complex reasoning ability. There was certainly nothing wrong with Noa's mother giving her specific instruction, though, because Noa truly enjoyed it.

Chrissy Quan—By age three, Chrissy put together 50-piece puzzles easily. She started doing mazes at about this time, too. She used long, full sentences and did not hesitate to use big words. She also wrote us little notes, sounding out the words to spell them. When she was 3½, I used the *Bob* books to show her how to read. She figured out the connection between adding the sounds of the letter to make words in a day or two.

Arthur Richards—Arthur played card games like *Canasta* at three years and *Hearts* by four years. When he was three, he counted up to 15, talked in full sentences, and liked shape-sorting toys and blocks. By 3½, he wrote numbers and many letters and could print his name.

Nicholas Collins—By three, Nicholas was interested in letters and their sounds. I sounded out the titles of all of the books I read to him, and he gradually started to associate letters with words. By his fourth birthday, he reasoned how many feet were under the table when we were seated for dinner—and how many more there were if someone were visiting. He figured out how many apricots each could have if there were 12 of them and three children who wanted them.

Frank Price—When he was three, Frank told us about "numbers with middles and numbers without middles," along with a bunch of properties that these numbers held—facts about odd and even numbers, etc. He continued this kind of discovery of mathematics throughout his childhood.

Earl Langer—After he turned three, Earl was very interested in instructional videos that came with products, like the one that came with our bread maker. He started to read beginner books just before he turned four, and soon, he understood some numerical relationships between things—as when three pieces out of the pizza meant that it was half gone, and six people at the table meant 12 feet underneath it.

Zachary Hackner—Zach started adding and did one-to-one counting at three. He could add and subtract in his head at four. We heard him say at 3½ years old that something had vanished, and when we asked him what that meant, he said that it had disappeared.

Debra Sund—At 3½, Debra asked for 10 crackers. I poured out a bunch and asked her how many she had. She replied, "Seven." I asked, "How many more do you need?" With very little hesitation, Debra responded, "Three." At this point, she could count up to 20 on her fingers and toes. Right before she turned four, she made up a new game of giving me numbers to add up starting with lower numbers and gradually getting higher, like this:

> Debra: "What does 800 and 800 make?"
> Me: "1,600."
> Debra: "What does 1,600 and 1,600 and 1,600 make?"
> Me: "4,800."
> Debra: "What does 4,800 and 4,800 make?"
> Me: "Um…."
> Debra: "9,600!"

We had never done that set of numbers before. When her father asked, "How did you know that?" Debra replied, "Because I'm three!" She was a couple of weeks away from her fourth birthday.

Her verbal concepts were even more dramatic. At three, she'd have us say words and then take turns coming up with words that rhymed. One day, when Debra thought she was eating a ham sandwich, I said, "No, it's turkey." Debra responded, "Oh, ham and turkey are similar." We had no idea that Debra knew the word "similar." Right before she turned four, there were snacks on the table along with a big bowl of grapes. Debra said, "Can I have some chips?" I looked around but didn't see any chips, so I asked why she thought there were chips. She pointed to the bowl that had the word "chips" written on it. She was too short to see that it actually contained grapes.

Bernie Walker—At three, Bernie counted by 2s just by looking at the things he wanted to count—no fingers. We showed him how to add numbers on a tape measure, and from that point on, he did all math in his head.

Greg Cooper—When Greg was 3-1/3 years old, he said, "Look, come quick, there's an eagle in the backyard." When we asked where, he replied, "Perched on that limb. April Fool!" By age four, he didn't need our help with the computer anymore.

Spencer Hayes—Spencer started to use the computer at age three. He was self-sufficient entering CDs through DOS, and although his keyboarding skills were not perfect, they were adequate. He read or recognized words on stores, signs, in books, and on papers by 3½ years. He played with the *Reader Rabbit*®[4] software for about two weeks and then began reading books out loud. He read aloud to his preschool class by the time he was four. He could count endlessly and even add by then.

Jo Anne Price—When Jo Anne was three, she could count to 30 with no problem.

Age Four to Five Years

One year before most children start kindergarten, virtually all of the children in Level Two have mastered letters, colors, and numbers, and most have also started to read, use numbers for solving problems, and have rather advanced computer skills. In addition, their interests are usually beyond what is typical for their age. Preferring activities with older children and adults becomes more and more common with the higher intellectual levels.

Cory Engum—By four years old, Cory recognized words he saw on signs, and when asked to bring his favorite book in to preschool, he brought *Farmer Boy* by Laura Ingalls Wilder, which is written at about a fifth-grade reading level. When visiting his sister's elementary school, he put together a three-dimensional pyramid wooden block puzzle. He liked to do mazes anytime he could; it was the first thing he'd choose in an activity book. He continued to enjoy making things, so his father built him his own workbench in the garage. He asked questions all the time. For example, after driving by an ethanol plant, he asked, "What is that place? How do they make the corn into ethanol? What do we use ethanol for? How does the factory run? I mean, what makes it run? Electricity? How long do they have to cook the corn to make ethanol?"

Gary Lundquist—Gary listened to all of the *Chronicles of Narnia*[5] books as a preschooler. He also loved puzzles. Instead of starting with the outside edge pieces, he did them in chunks by color. He thoroughly enjoyed computer and video games, and he stopped needing any help with the computer—not even with the Internet.

Glenn Richards—By age 4½, Glenn played lots of chess and was nearly as good or better as anyone else in the family. He studied chess strategies in chess club, wrote down chess moves and chess notation, and competed in his first chess tournament. At 4¾, he took second place in the

State Kindergarten Chess Championship. He worked fairly complex mazes by this age. He also began sounding out words, got the idea of reading, and understood the concept of rhyming words. He was so interested in science that he found science in everything and loved to watch *Bill Nye the Science Guy* and nature shows on PBS. In math, he excelled; for example, he could add 7+7, 84+4=88, and 40+7=47, and he knew that if 60 minutes equals one hour, then 120 minutes equals two hours. He also began learning that multiplication is simply addition.

Noa Collins—Noa progressed greatly in academic, physical, and social skills—and in symbolic thinking. She started silent reading shortly before her fifth birthday, and she could read some of the hymns in church. She did math problems such as 1,234 divided by 6 with each day's math work and really seemed to understand it. Math facts came very slowly, but with lots of daily practice, she got to know more and more of them without specific drills.

Betsy Dunkirk—At age four, Betsy thought it was fun to decipher people's nametags.

Chrissy Quan—Chrissy no longer needed help with the computer by four or five years old.

Tamara Lundquist—Tamara did 50-piece puzzles by herself when she was four.

Arthur Richards—At four, Arthur was able to play *Hearts* and *Monopoly*® with his older brothers; both games involve adding, subtracting, and complex strategy. He also played computer games using educational software like *Number Munchers*® and *Number Maze*®, which are for children ages eight and up.

Nicholas Collins—When he was just over four, Nicholas read me his first simple book—just eight pages long. He read it in about 20 minutes with almost no help. I encouraged him to read to me every day. He'd read a short book or just a sentence, paragraph, or page of a more difficult book. I explained phonics rules to him, as he seemed to need them.

Author note: When Nicholas was four, his mother started him on home school materials, and he made progress quite quickly. In general, though, I prefer that parents respond to demonstrated interest on the part of the child; otherwise, there is the risk that the child will feel pressured. Gifted children enjoy learning, but that is not always the same as enjoying instruction.

Frank Price —When he was four, Frank could beat me at the matching game *Memory*®.

Debra Sund—At four, Debra read the label on the graham cracker box. Before she turned five, she read long words like "elevator." She didn't seem to learn to read by sounding out the letters. Instead, when she saw a word she didn't know, she would ask what it was. After she heard and saw the word once, she knew it on sight. At 4½, while walking home from the park, Debra asked about wind and what we needed in order to live. Her father explained there was something in the air that we needed to breath. Debra replied, "You mean oxygen?" Where she heard that is anyone's guess.

Bernie Walker—Bernie began to enjoy doing mazes at about four. He recognized words in books by 4½ and could play a large number of solitaire card games.

Greg Cooper—At four years old, when his mother left for work, Greg said, "She waved to me as she started off on her journey." He was about 4½ when he started sounding out signs and words.

Harry Vassar—Between three and 4½ years of age, Harry taught himself to read using the *Reader Rabbit*® computer software, and then he started to read beginner books. He always enjoyed being around adults. At age four, we were at a party where he preferred playing bocce ball with the adults to playing with the kids. He played advanced sports games on the computer by then, also, such as *EA Sports*™ games. He also played checkers and several card games.

Spencer Hayes—Spencer read beginner books, especially fiction, before he turned five.

Jo Anne Price—Jo Anne loved books—though she showed no real interest in reading herself until she was about 4½; then she started to sound out three-letter words. She recognized the names of family and friends without sounding them out, learning phonetically at first. She loved the *JumpStart* computer games and all popular educational software for young children. She had a fabulous attention span for whatever she was interested in. She could play for a long time by herself, but she also had a good sense of humor and enjoyed talking to others.

Age Five to Six Years

By the time they reach kindergarten, most Level Two children have begun to read. Spontaneously starting to read is an increasingly familiar phenomenon as we move higher up the giftedness continuum. Gifted children pick up contextual clues of vocabulary and meaning—especially when they are interested in a topic—and simply start to read. There is little evidence of "sounding out" among most gifted early readers, and many resort to silent reading soon after they begin to read because it is faster.

Cory Engum—Cory enjoyed *Learning Channel* shows about how things work or how they were built, like engineering marvels, bridges, the Eiffel Tower, and Mount Rushmore. He liked *Bill Nye the Science Guy* and *Junkyard Wars*. By age five, he was proficient on the computer and played a variety of computer games for children, including *JumpStart First Grade, Arthur's First Grade Visio*™ (for drawing pictures and diagrams), and *My First Amazing World Explorer*. He started to read beginner books by the time he was 5¾ years old. In his kindergarten class, they learned 50+ sight words and word families. Cory learned them easily, but he wasn't really that interested in reading, although he did read simple books when in the mood. We read the first two *Harry Potter*[6] books to him, editing some of the darker parts.

By age 5½, Cory's constructions became more and more complex. He sat in on a couple of classes at the gifted co-op, and they let him make some creations—he was in heaven. After one class, he came home and wanted to make a boat. He took two empty pop bottles, attached and wired a battery-operated motor with a propeller, and added an on–off switch—completely on his own. He put it in the tub and it ran, but did not go straight, from which he learned that it needed a rudder. He then made a rudder and attached it to his boat.

Gary Lundquist—Gary started to read beginner books when he was five. By kindergarten, he did a number of adult-level computer games. At 5¼ years old, Gary brought home a *Berenstain Bears*[7] book and said, "I'm going to read this to you," and he did. We didn't know he could read. Before he was out of kindergarten, he read the *Power Boys*[8] books, which are comparable to the *Hardy Boys* books that I read in fourth grade. It took him two months.

Glenn Richards—At age five, Glenn could add with poker chips, knew what half of 60 equaled, could multiply 3x6, and counted money.

Bradley Ruhl—Brad started reading chapter books when he was in preschool, at about age 5½.

Betsy Dunkirk—Betsy started beginner books when she was five and pretty much knew how to read by kindergarten. Her older sister taught her a lot of phonics.

Tamara Lundquist—Tamara started to read beginner books and became good at using the computer keyboard when she was in kindergarten.

Arthur Richards—When Art was about to turn five, the *Pokemon*™ phenomenon hit. He wanted to play so badly, but he had to be able to read. So within a few months, he was reading with no trouble—big words, too, like "opponent" and "paralyzed." The game also involves multiplying 10s by single digits, as well as adding and subtracting double-digit numbers, which he could do. Arthur wrote a thank-you note by hand: "Dear Grampa thanks for the car and labyrenth thar fun. Arthur."

Tony Matthews—Starting at age five, Tony read adult materials on topics of his interest. For example, he decided that he loved flowers, even though no one in our family held this interest. He quickly learned, in great detail, the names of dozens of different flowers, whether they were perennials or annuals, came from seeds or bulbs, etc.

Nicholas Collins—At five years and two months old, Nicholas was finally quiet during prayers at church because he was reading silently. By the time he started kindergarten at age 5-1/3, he was reading second- and third-grade books for fun. He particularly liked nature books, *Magic School Bus*[9] chapter books, and adventure comic books. When he was 5½ and in kindergarten, I worked with him some on an arithmetic series at home. He could tell time to the minute, read thermometers and graphs, add and subtract three-digit numbers, and knew the times tables for one through five times one through 10. He could do simple division in his head and two-digit by one-digit multiplication and long division. We spent a few hours each afternoon going over spelling, English, and phonics at home. We finished up third-grade-level language arts; I didn't do much teaching except getting him started writing stories and reports.

Author note: This mother considered achievement as the truest form of intelligence and enjoyed tutoring her children in math facts, phonics, spelling—the details of schoolwork. While her daughter enjoyed this and was quite cooperative, her son was more resistant. My professional opinion is that this is too much work time for a young child, especially when the child is not interested. I think a child's welfare is better served by letting him find his own interests through reading, videos, and unstructured play.

Earl Langer—There was a noticeable increase in Earl's computation interest when he turned five. He asked when he would have his first communion; when he learned that it was at age seven, without hesitating, he said that he could wait two years. He asked several times a day what one number added to another number is, what year things happened, and when that time was in relation to the current year.

Zachary Hackner—When Zach turned five, he got to stay up for naptime with the big kids and was determined from that day to read. He started with the *Bob* books, and it took him about one month. At a restaurant at 5½ years old, he saw a dessert for $1.39 and said if his sister and I each got one, that would be $2.78, and if we each got two, that would be $5.56. His kindergarten teacher said that he could borrow, carry, and multiply, plus he knew some dividing and fractions. She said no one else in the class came even close to understanding these things.

Bernie Walker—Bernie picked up reading all of a sudden at five years old, recognizing words and sounding them out. He could read the easy readers in kindergarten.

Age Six to Seven Years

Gary Lundquist—Gary read the abridged version for children of *Great Illustrated Classics*—a collection of books for children substantially older than he was at that time. When he was in first grade, Gary and I attended an NBA basketball game with several other dads and first-grade boys. The boys sat together at one end of a row of seats with the dads at the other. At one point, Gary leaned forward and yelled down to me, "Dad, I'm famished." The dad sitting next to me was amazed to hear a first grader use a big word as a matter of course.

Bradley Ruhl—At 6½, Brad read three *Harry Potter* books, which are middle school and young adult-level books, in three weeks while keeping up with other reading at the same time.

Betsy Dunkirk—Betsy started reading chapter books between ages six and seven.

Chrissy Quan—Chrissy started reading chapter books when she was six and in kindergarten. She also did lots of puzzles at this age—up to 200 pieces.

Tamara Lundquist—Tamara started reading chapter books in first grade. She read *Arthur* chapter books, the *American Girl*[10] books, and Gertrude Chandler Warner's *Boxcar Children* books, all for children ages nine to 12. We also started reading the *Chronicles of Narnia* to her that year.

Nicholas Collins—Once he turned six, Nicholas became interested in books about children with problems, such as Louis Braille and Helen Keller.

Frank Price—When Frank was six, his interests changed to geography. He came home from school each evening and spent three hours without interruption tracing maps from atlases and making lists of countries. He had an unusually good visual memory. One night I asked him to name all of the countries he could without looking at anything. He named something like 170 from memory. I asked him how he did it, and he explained that he pictured a page in one of his atlases and just read off the countries from that picture. He could also look at a flag and tell you which country it belonged to and which countries border any given country.

One day I came home to find a piece of paper on the table with "1+2+3+4+5+...+35" written out. Frank said he wanted to add up the numbers from 1 to 100. I asked him how big that would be, and he told me "Bigger than 100!" He cracked up laughing at this—he loved silly humor—but then added, "Oh, 1+99=100, so it would be bigger than 200. Oh, and 2+98=100, so it would be bigger than 300. Oh, you can keep doing that down to 50+50." I'm a math professor, so I knew how to guide his progress, but the mathematical insights he had were all his own. I asked him to put together what he knew, and he said that the sum would be 5,050. He just did it in his head.

We never taught Frank about fractions, and his exposure in first grade was simply to color in one-fourth of a circle. When we had pizza one night, however, and he had one-fourth, then another one-fourth, and his dad carried over the last piece and said it was about one-third. Frank immediately asked, "Who ate the other one-sixth?" Along with fractions, he did his own investigations into percents. When reading Dr. Seuss's *Hooray for Diffendoofer Day!* in which the principal announces that the students have scored 10,000,000%, Frank laughed and said, "Ten

92

million out of a hundred?" as though it was the funniest thing he had
ever heard.

*Author note: Some children are actually more brilliant in math concepts than
their overall IQ score suggests. Frank's ability to figure out so many things for
himself is a sign of very high giftedness in mathematical reasoning. In fact, his
IQ subtest results indicated as much. Teachers are more likely to notice high
verbal and reading skills, though, than Frank's kind of math ability. As a
result, most mathematically brilliant children receive absolutely no advanced
or appropriate instruction until they are in fifth or sixth grade or later, depending on the school. In the meantime, they endure endless arithmetic details and
drills. Many incredibly able math children come to believe that they hate
math, when what they really hate is needless repetition.*

Zachary Hackner—Zachary was 6½ when he started reading chapter
books. By age seven, he loved to learn about Egypt, chemistry, and
magic. We read the *Harry Potter* books to him four times. He also read
trading cards and instructions for board games and computer games.

Harry Vassar—Harry read chapter books by age six, and at 6½, he loved
Calvin and Hobbes books.[11]

Spencer Hayes—When Spencer was five, he read chapter books that
were at about fourth-grade level. He craved nonfiction by the time he
was six, and he read *Zoobooks*—a series of science fun/reference books—
from cover to cover. The second time Spencer logged on to the
Internet, he demanded to "surf" by himself.

Age Seven to Nine Years

The achievement difference between the skills of average children
and the Level Two gifted children has widened to a startling degree by
third and fourth grades as the slopes of ability and difficulty level diverge.
A number of the children have received standardized achievement tests
by this point, and their grade equivalency scores reveal just how imper-
fect the fit is between what they are ready and able to learn compared to
curricular expectations for their age and grade level. Most remarkable
are the extremely high achievement scores in the subjects that Level
Two children can teach themselves due to high reading ability, interest,
and ever-accumulating knowledge. In contrast, their achievement scores
are substantially lower in subjects that they must be taught in school,
such as math or writing skills. In other words, Level Two gifted children's

time in school appears to be far less helpful than one would expect (McCoach, 2003). However, when Level Two children are moved into accelerated classes, they are no longer ahead of or different from their classmates. As a result, they feel "normal," and their time is filled with real learning and academic progress.

Gary Lundquist—While Gary was in second grade, he independently read 40 of the original 56 *Hardy Boys* books, as well as books by Roald Dahl and Bill Peet. Third grade was his year for reading the *Goosebumps* books by R. L. Stine, which are actually intended for children ages nine to 12. He had a wonderful third-grade teacher and spent a lot of time laughing at things only the two of them found funny.

> *Author note: Humor is a trait often associated with the gifted, but what is funny to some gifted children may not always be appreciated or understood by their same-age classmates.*

Betsy Dunkirk—Betsy was always ahead of what was being taught in school, but that changed in third grade when, fortunately, she got into an advanced math class. She read about one simple chapter book a day, usually about animals or places in the world, whenever she had time.

Chrissy Quan—Chrissy read chapter books like those in the *Harry Potter* series when she was eight years old, but she still loved little kid books, too.

Tamara Lundquist—At seven years of age, Tamara read the first *Harry Potter* book—although it took quite a while. At age eight, we read about Betsy (from the *Betsy-Tacy* series, by Sharla Scannell Whalen) as a high school senior. Tamara used computer programs for 10- and 11-year-olds. She participated in Fermi math—a school system consortium extracurricular activity in which children must solve a very challenging math problem with a partner or team—and she loved it.

Arthur Richards—At 7½ years old, Arthur completed our local library's Summer Reading Game in 18 days, reading a hundred 20-minute books, generally from the *Goosebumps* series (fourth- to fifth-grade level). Both before the contest and after he finished winning all of the prizes, he continued to read the *Goosebumps* books just because he liked them.

> *Author note: Gifted boys whose first choice is fiction tend to read humor, fantasy, and adventure.*

Tony Matthews—Tony had no interest in routine computations and disliked math worksheets. He did, however, like to figure out more complicated math problems such as how many seconds there are in a year, etc. Once he became familiar with the Internet and the possibility of pursuing his areas of interest, he became fascinated (obsessed?) with the computer. By age eight, he loved to do *PowerPoint*® presentations telling funny stories about his friends. He independently learned how to download pictures using his digital camera and how to incorporate graphics and his voice to narrate stories, thus creating short "movies."

Nicholas Collins—At 7-1/3 years old, Nicholas was most interested in science books about electricity, magnetism, power plants, ships, aircraft carriers, and airplanes.

Frank Price—Right before he turned eight, Frank wanted to learn all about animals and classify them. Looking through a children's encyclopedia of animals, he laughed and said, "Mom, I made it all the way to 'U' before I found an echinoderm!" If you needed to know a small Pacific island was that had a name beginning with "T," Frank was the one to help you out. He was not interested in writing.

Author note: Writing is another common problem area for gifted children, their parents, and the schools. Teachers will point to a child's lack of advanced writing ability (usually normal for the age but not for the intellectual level) as evidence that the child is not really gifted.

Harry Vassar—At just over seven, Harry loved to read the *Animorphs* books by Katherine Applegate (for nine- to 12-year-olds).

Spencer Hayes—Spencer skipped halfway through second grade to third grade. Subjects like the Titanic fascinated him, and he was especially interested in adventure and natural disaster books when he was 7½. For a project on Africa, he chose to read *A Short History of African Art* (a 416-page book by Werner Gillon) but had to change to a shorter book due to the scope and timeframe of the project. He then chose African inventors. He rarely had difficulty with word pronunciation and always asked for meaning or usage (for instance, "The structures were built with pisé...." Spencer would stop and look up "pisé"). He also liked to read diagrams for any type of truck, submarine, fighter jet, etc.

Age Nine and Older

Gary Lundquist—When Gary was 11 in sixth grade, he read all of the *Harry Potter* books on his own and started to read Michael Crichton and the other adult authors. He made it to the regional semi-finals for the Spelling Bee in sixth and seventh grades.

Summary of Level Two Gifted

The preceding group of children is composed of very smart, capable young people. Their measured IQs on school ability tests and individual standard score tests qualify them for a gifted program—if there is one—and alert their teachers to their high ability. Nonetheless, Level Two children are quite different from the higher levels. The following developmental features characterize Level Two children.

- Several children were alert and made eye contact at birth—most by one month.
- All children paid attention while someone to read to them by five to nine months.
- Almost all of the children understood adult directives and questions at six to 12 months.
- The majority independently looked at and turned pages of books by 11 to 15 months.
- Most of the children knew and said many words by seven to 17 months.
- About half of the children said two-word phrases by 15 months.
- A number of children played with shape sorters by 15 months.
- Many recognized some colors by 10 to 15 months.
- Most knew many letters at 15 to 18 months.
- Many knew and sang songs by 19 months.
- Most knew the majority of the colors by 15 to 20 months.
- Many liked eight- to 10-piece puzzles by 12 to 15 months.
- Most knew and called out names on signs and stores between 11 and 16 months.
- Most did some recognizable drawing and coloring by 19 months.
- Several read numerous sight words at 16 to 24 months.
- Almost all were speaking in three-word and longer sentences by age two.
- Most had favorite TV shows or videos by 24 months.
- Most could rote count past five—many counted higher—before they were two.

- Many recognized and picked out specific numbers by 12 to 22 months.
- Several enjoyed 35-piece puzzles by 21 to 24 months.
- About a quarter of them knew the entire alphabet by 17 to 24 months.
- Many used language to make jokes by age 2½.
- Many enjoyed rhyming by age three.
- Most did one-to-one counting by age three.
- Most knew letters and colors by age three.
- Most had extensive vocabularies and did complex speaking by age three.
- Many could print letters, numbers, words, and their names between three and four years.
- Several had high interest in facts, how things work, and science by 3½ to 4½ years.
- Most knew many sight words by age four.
- Several read easy readers by age four.
- Most were independent on the computer by age 4½.
- More than half played games designed for children ages eight and up before they were five years old.
- Most fully grasped counting and basic number facts by age five.
- Many showed an intuitive grasp of number concepts by age five.
- Most enjoyed having advanced level books and stories read to them by age five.
- Most read easy reader books before age five, nearly all by 5½.
- Most read for pleasure and information by six.
- Many, primarily boys, showed interest and knowledge of maps by age six.
- Most read youth-level chapter books by six to seven years.
- All read two to five years beyond grade level by age seven.
- All read chapter books independently by age seven to 7½.
- Many showed impatience with repetition and slow pace at school by age six to seven.

Children of Level Two ability can do accelerated coursework almost from the time they enter school. They eventually take advanced courses and hold many leadership positions in high school, are capable of getting into competitive colleges and universities, and often go on to some form of graduate school. Although many Level Two children are excellent students, a number of them may resist general school requirements.

Because instruction is typically aimed at average–level students, many Level Two children achieve less than they are capable of.

Table 2: Level Two Children's Data

Name	SBLM Ratio IQ	Test Age Years-Mos.	Other IQ Tests	Achievement Test Grade Equivalencies/ Percentiles
Cory Engum	145	5-10	WISC-III: VIQ-142, PIQ-131, FSIQ-140	-
Gary Lundquist	n/a	-	SB4 138; SB5 131 (VIQ-135, NVIQ-128); Otis-Lennon 125-144	Woodcock-McGrew-Werder Reading in 8th grade: all 96-99th percentiles; Basic Skills, Reading, Writing, and Factual Knowledge: all >16-9, Mathematics 16-3; SAT-V 560 and SAT-M 630 at age 13-9 in 8th grade
Glenn Richards	150	10-8	SB5 125 (VIQ-120, NVIQ-128)	Metropolitan Achievement Test-7 in 7th grade: Social Studies 76, Science 82, Language 80, Math Procedures 98, Math Concepts 98, Reading Comprehension 76, Vocabulary 97
Boyd Uphoff	142	4-5	-	-
Bradley Ruhl	144	-	WISC-III 134	WIAT-II in 4th grade: Word Reading >12-9, Comprehension 9-5, Numerical Operations 8-3, Math Reasoning 8-4, Spelling 12-4, Written Expression 8-5, Listening Comprehension 11-4, Oral Expression >12-9; School Achievement: Math 99, Reading 97
Noa Collins	145	3-9	SBLM 145; SB5 139 (VIQ-146, NVIQ-128)	Woodcock-McGrew-Werder: Reading 99, Writing 99, Math 84, Knowledge 72
Betsy Dunkirk	155	8-4	-	Reading 99, Math 99
Chrissy Quan	132	8-2	-	NWEA Tests 99th except 93rd Reading

Name	SBLM Ratio IQ	Test Age Years-Mos.	Other IQ Tests	Achievement Test Grade Equivalencies/ Percentiles
Tamara Lundquist	152	8-8	SB5 132 (VIQ-136, NVIQ-126); SB5 w/o WM 134* (VIQ-139, NVIQ-127)	NEAA Levels Test in 2nd grade: Math 99, Reading 98
Arthur Richards	173	6-5	-	Metropolitan Achievement Test-7 in 3rd grade: Social Studies 92, Science 74, Language 99, Math Procedures 99, Math Concepts 91, Reading Comprehension 91, Vocabulary 95
Tony Matthews	152	8-0	WISC-III 131	-
Nicholas Collins	181	6-5	WISC-III 131; SB5 126 (VIQ-129, NVIQ-121); SB5 w/o WM 128* (VIQ-131, NVIQ-123)	Woodcock-McGrew-Werder Achievement Test in 1st grade: Reading 7-2, Writing 7-0, Math 3-7, Factual Knowledge 2-2
Frank Price	159	7-1	WPPSI 142	
Earl Langer	143	6-0	-	-
Zachary Hackner	170	7-1	-	-
Debra Sund	172	6-11	-	-
Bernie Walker	165	8-3	WISC-III 139	-
Greg Cooper	180	6-1	SB5 131 (VIQ-134, NVIQ-126); SB5 w/o WM 137* (VIQ-141, NVIQ-130)	-
Harry Vassar	160	7-3	-	Reading 99, Math 99
Spencer Hayes	172	6-2	Otis-Lennon 121	Woodcock-Johnson Achievement at end of 1st grade: Writing 6-6, Math Calculation 4-8, Applied Math 10-2, Science Info 9-5, Social Studies 4-5, Humanities 3-4
Jo Anne Price	177	4-4	-	-

*w/o WM is one method of calculating an experimental gifted composite score for the *Stanford-Binet 5th Edition* in which the working memory subtest is omitted.

Chapter 6
Level Three Gifted: Approximately 98th and 99th Percentiles

At two years old, our daughter made friends with a woman at
church by telling her, "I like your shoes!" They got into a
five-minute conversation about shoes. She would do that sort of
thing often. She assumed parity with adults the way some
household pets seem to think they are human.
~ Mother of a Level Three girl

Level Three gifted children are often described as "highly" or "exceptionally" gifted. As in earlier chapters, the following cases are presented in ascending order of precocious behavior. Ratio IQ and standard scores are provided in Table 3. Although none of the IQ scores, either ratio or deviation,[1] is precisely accurate in identifying which children rank above or below others in their early childhood behaviors and abilities, readers will notice how the ratio IQ points toward behaviors and characteristics beyond school performance and how these abilities become more pronounced in a fairly linear fashion. In our particular sample, the ratio IQ scores range from 159-188, which contrast with the deviation IQ scores that range only from 128-152 on individually administered tests.

How many Level Three children are there in our schools? Selective private schools and schools in districts where most of the parents are highly educated professionals can expect that about 5% of their students will be at Level Three or higher. In other words, most classrooms will have one such pupil. A typical suburban elementary school with 100 children per grade level has one or two of these children in each grade, which means that not all classrooms will have a Level Three student. Schools that draw from impoverished, disadvantaged, or low educational background parents will generally have only one or two in each school across all grade levels at any one time.

The Children

Birth to Two Years

Books about babies tell us that babies cannot see very well in their early months, but parents of Level Three and higher gifted children almost all report an intensity of eye contact either from birth or soon thereafter. Now I ask parents about early eye contact on my intake questionnaire because it does appear to separate the highly intelligent babies from those of average intellect. Parents also report that medical personnel in the hospital comment on their child's alertness.

Another distinguishing characteristic of Level Three gifted children is that they clearly know and understand many things before they actually talk. Most of these children talk in full sentences before they are two years old, and the quick transition of not speaking at all to speaking in full sentences is a hallmark of exceptional intelligence.

Chuck Arnesen—Chuck focused and made eye contact as soon as he was born. The doctor and nurses all commented on how alert he was, how unusual. By eight weeks, he and I deliberately repeated each other's sounds. He said "hi" when he was six months old and started vocalizing real word syllables at nine months. His early words, before he turned one, were the names for our family members and our cats, then "moon," "pretty," and the words for many colors, numbers, and shapes. He had a very advanced vocabulary as soon as he started talking. At about 15 months, he could correctly say most of the colors when we pointed to them, and he started doing simple wooden puzzles. He absolutely loved *Sesame Street* and said many letters correctly. By the time he was 20 months old, he knew all of the letters, talked a lot, and did some counting. By two, he clearly recognized numerous store signs and logos. He also knew many nursery rhymes and songs and would say or sing them.

Chuck showed an early interest in music, and at just 12 months old, he could play records on our record player. I restricted him to his own children's records and kept a supply of new needles handy, but he was actively playing and changing records before he could walk. We had a set of records that came with books so that he could play the record and follow along in the book, and he could do this by age two with no trouble.

William Jones—I read to Will from birth, and we enjoyed that time together. He read many of the words himself at just over one year old.

Reading was a huge part of our life. He read store and street signs by about two. He also counted, which he probably learned from books. He knew his colors by then, too.

Peter Koos—Peter made good eye contact from the time he was born. At 10 months, he said "bottle," 11 months "ball," 12 months "baby," "thank you," "truck," and "busy," 13 months "outside," and 26 words total by 15 months. At 11 months, his favorite toy was the shape sorter. He always listened to books, and by 12 months, he loved being read to. By 19 months, he counted to 10. He enjoyed puzzles and games, and at 22 months, he was proficient at floor puzzles with many pieces.

Derek Fondow—We read to Derek from birth. By 12 months, he said "mama," "dada," "sis," "hi," "bye," "baby," "bounce" (for Tigger), "grouchy, grouchy, grouchy" (for Oscar the Grouch), "peas, mommy hall" (when he wanted me near at bedtime), and "sis sad" (if his sister was sad and he wanted me to check on her). He enjoyed puzzles before age two.

Stephen Williams—Stephen knew the colors by the time he could say them. He learned the alphabet the same way. He always loved puzzles— at 15½ months, he put together a six- to 10-piece puzzle.

Michael Fuller—Michael's first word was "boo" at nine months for "balloon," which he knew from the book *Goodnight Moon* (by Margaret Wise Brown), then "dada" and "mama." At 10 months, he said "ba-ba" for bottle; at 12 months, "num-num" (food), "bae-bae" (bear), "dja" (yes), and "baw-baw" (ball). At 14 months, he said "bay-bay" (basement), and he started to add "ya?" to sentences to mean "May I have…?" or "Can I…?" "Bay-bay, ya?" meant "Can I go to the basement?" At 15 months, he knew many animal noises, and by 16 months, he knew so many words that I couldn't keep track anymore.

When he was 14 months old, Michael's daycare teacher reported that she saw him finish coloring, put the crayons back in the box, carry the box across the room to the cabinet, open it, and put the crayons back on the shelf from which he had seen her take them. At about 20 months, he memorized the *Sesame Street* book *Don't Cry, Big Bird* word for word—his favorite story since he was 12 months old. He corrected us if we substituted "the" for "a" or some such blunder. He sat in my lap and read the words to this fairly long book to me. His pronunciation was not keen, but I still smile to think of his reading *"No Ky, Bee Bir"* to me.

Sophie Fuller—Sophie said her first words starting at about nine months. She had the best vocabulary of any of our children at the earliest age. We all understood her by the time she was one, and she spoke in full sentences by two. She wanted us to read to her and liked having books with her in her crib by the time she could walk. I noted "Good sense of humor—six months" in her baby book. She made funny faces to amuse us and seemed to have a sense of humor that involved self-awareness rather than just pure mimicry. She also knew many colors, including the more unusual ones.

Layne Freeman—Layne made good eye contact almost immediately after birth. She started to wave bye-bye at four or five months, and she said "dada," "ball," and "mama" soon after. I don't know when she actually began to read things like signs, but she recognized them by about age two. Shortly before that, in response to my offering her a cookie, she bargained with me to give her two.

Franklin Hayes—Franklin made good eye contact from birth; he even smiled at us several different times the day he was born. He loved to sit and be read to by four months. He sat still for TV at about nine months. Although he started talking late, he talked in full sentences at 18 months. By then he also knew most colors, and by age two, he knew the alphabet.

Tiana Bardy—Tiana said "dada," " mama," " duck," " up," and "ball" by 11 months, and she was up to about 24 words by 14 months. She knew her colors and started to use numbers by 18 months. She spoke in six- to eight-word sentences by 19 months.

Andrea Dolan—By the time Andrea was four months old, she sat for longer than I cared to sit while I read to her. She said "dada" by seven months, and between 9½ and 10½ months, she said "hi," "dad," "up," and "gentle." We did homemade phonics in the car by the time she was one. Learning the alphabet was easy, although she didn't know it in order until she was over two years old. She knew how to say "A is for apple" and could recognize printed alphabet letters by 20 months. She also sat for hours doing puzzles.

Brennan Ahlers—Brennan made eye contact as soon as he was born. He loved it when we read to him almost immediately, too. He said the usual first words—"mom," "dad," " bye"—when he was nine months old, and he started to read store and street signs when he was about two.

He was also proficient with puzzles. Brennan had an odd obsession with cars, and before he was two years old, he'd go through the newspaper page by page to find the classified ads. He'd then color in all of the cars in the ads. He also always begged for the *Auto Trader* magazine sold at the gas stations. As a big treat, we'd buy them, and he'd sit at the table for hours coloring each and every car ad. He started recognizing the different models of cars and would name them in the parking lot as we walked into a store.

Janet Lewis —Janet's verbal abilities were remarkable at a very early age; she spoke several single words by eight months and began reciting rhymes, the alphabet, and number songs well before others her age.

Angelica Plomin—Before she was six months old, Angelica was able to sit and enjoy listening to short books being read over and over. While reading *Goodnight Moon* one night, I read "goodnight light" and she looked directly at the light in her room. She could look at the correct item if I named just about any object in the book that was in her room, the rest of the house, or outside. Shortly thereafter, she began pointing and had a huge receptive vocabulary. She said her first words between seven and eight months.

Angelica sat through an entire one-hour episode of *Sesame Street* by age one and spoke at least 20 words clearly by then. At 15 months, she could identify numbers between one and nine, combine words, rote count to 10, and name colors—including unusual ones like lavender and gray—and shapes, including hexagons and ovals. She knew all of the letters of the alphabet, upper and lower case. By 16 or 17 months, she could tell the sounds each letter made and recognized numbers through at least 10. By 20 months, she was counting objects to five with correct correspondence, easily put together eight- to 10-piece puzzles, and recognized stop signs, school signs, fast food signs, and logos. At 23 months, she began sounding out short words, and she corrected me if I took a different route to a regular destination: "Wait, turn there, Mom." She did 30-piece puzzles before her second birthday.

Justin Janacek—We always described Justin as intense. When he was just a couple of months old, he craved eye contact, and not just "look at me" attention, either. He needed to feel that someone was really engaged with him. He said "mama," "dada," and "up" at about 11 months. He could say several simple words by 14 months, many words by 18 months, and he spoke in full sentences before he turned two. He knew several songs—the alphabet song, *Twinkle Twinkle Little Star*, and *Jesus Loves Me*—and *Mother Goose* rhymes before his second birthday. He had a great vocabulary and was easily understood by everyone. One day at the library when he was 1½ years old, he chose *The Wizard* by Bill Martin, a book for kids ages three through eight. It made him laugh; books, evening story time, and the library were a big deal after that. He knew the colors and the alphabet—and that letters have sounds—by the time he was two. He also realized that numbers had value, and he learned to count quite high.

Age Two to Three Years

Note that incredible memory is prominent in the higher gifted levels, even at a very young age. This information helps when trying to estimate a child's true ability level.

Chuck Arnesen—When Chuck was 2½ years old, he could sing *You Are My Sunshine* with no help. He could count items up to 50 before he was three years old and knew when a number was larger or smaller than others.

Peter Koos—Peter got a wooden train set for his second birthday and immediately recognized it as being like Grandpa's—model trains he had not seen for nine months and even then had only seen a couple of times in his life. By 2½, he loved to watch *Barney*, *This Old House*, *Home Time*, and the *Masters' Golf Tournament*. At 28 months, he recognized and spelled his name. By three, he read all of his friends' names, knew the alphabet, and could spell many words.

Derek Fondow—By 26 months, Derek counted "1, 2, 3" before running, jumping, etc. When he was 28 months old, he asked if I would read to him. If I was unable to, he would say, "Sis, read!" asking his older sister to read to him instead. About a month later, he discovered the airplane section in the children's encyclopedia and looked at it for hours at a time. He began working on sandpaper letters and sound cards during his first year of Montessori starting at age 31 months.

Michael Fuller—Michael knew all of his colors by age three. He knew the shapes fairly early, and his baby book includes artwork from age 25 months in which he identified a drawing as a "wircle" because he was scribbling "wownd and wownd." He sang the alphabet song early on and began to incorporate letters into his artwork by his fourth birthday.

Candice Richardson—When Candice was 28 months old, we were staying in a hotel, and she went to the bathroom by herself. She announced that she had done so, then immediately piped up, "And don't say 'Good job!'"

Author note: Level Three gifted children are sensitive very early to any hint of condescension. Most strongly object to being treated like little kids.

Sophie Fuller—I think the main reason that Sophie became interested in numbers is because, at age three, she was concerned with getting the same number of things as her older siblings. She knew the alphabet by two, but by three, she changed around the letters that rhyme just to be goofy, laughing uproariously. At age two, people would ask, "*How* old is she?"

Layne Freeman—Layne showed an interest in the written and spoken word since birth. Her attention span when being read to was very long. She also had an amazing memory, and from very early, maybe age two, she was able to repeat a story after it had been read to her just once. She could also recite a song after she heard it once almost verbatim. When she was tested for early entrance to kindergarten at age 4½, I was told that she was having trouble decoding words at the fifth grade level! I nearly fell over—I had no idea that she could read at all. I later found out that she'd been reading to others for many months.

Franklin Hayes—Franklin liked to watch *Bill Nye the Science Guy* and *Magic School Bus* when he was about two, and he could count to 10. He recognized words in stores and on signs before he was three. He had an incredible memory. He remembered what kind of car we had rented on our vacation—including the color, both exterior and interior.

Tiana Bardy—Tiana always liked to be read to and recognized words on signs and stores by about 2½ years. She pointed out words in books and in the newspaper by two years eight months. She liked to count items in the house and, by age two, could count to six, but then she skipped right over to 20 and 100. She learned names of letters by 3½. She always had an amazing memory. At age two, she recalled events from when she was one.

Andrea Dolan—Andrea read the word "ice" on the ice machine when she was 2½ years old. She was interested in mazes by this time but really liked connect-the-dots.

Janet Lewis—Janet could be quite creative in getting her point across. When barely two and sitting in a grocery cart pestering me for a treat, I reminded her that I didn't allow candy for a snack and I wouldn't respond to her whining. She turned to her rabbit puppet and told him, "Mommy said I can't have any candy!" She gave the rabbit a voice, muttering, "I don't like your mommy very much, Janet," to which she responded, "I don't either, Rabbit!"

Once when we were scouting for a nearby restaurant, Janet saw a sign for a family-owned pizza parlor off the highway—not a chain with a familiar logo—and yelled out "pizza!" She was barely three. Her vocabulary was unusual as well. Once, when I admonished her in a crowded store to stay by my side, she ran off anyway, announcing to amused fellow customers that she needed to see something and she didn't "want a consequence, either!"

Author note: This is an example of a child who might seem to be impertinent and need correction. But due to the relatively high-level thinking that is going on—coupled with lack of experience and hindsight—Janet wanted the freedom to make decisions for herself. "Because I said so" does not work for many parents of the very gifted. These children need explanations, patience, and respect from their parents; then their cooperation can be won.

Angelica Plomin—Angelica used advanced vocabulary, like "irritating" and "difficult," when she was 27 months old. She didn't completely master pronouns until about 28 months. She began recognizing time on a digital clock by 2½ years. She wrote her name at 33 months and began to understand the concept of days of the week and other time periods. She knew the order of the days—and "tomorrow" and "yesterday"—and what our schedule was on any given day. She wrote some words by 35 months. She began playing on the computer independently at this age and enjoyed *JumpStart* games and *Reader Rabbit®* software.

Justin Janacek—Justin started to read gradually. At around 2½ to three years old, he asked what the words were on signs, sweatshirts, books— anything printed. He also asked what sound letters make.

Age Three to Four Years

By ages three to four, most Level Three gifted children are doing things that Levels One and Two children did when they were between four and five years old. For instance, Level Three children progress from simple readers with only a few words on each page to easy readers in a matter of weeks. Their reading usually moves to first- or second-grade level within a few months, and they accomplish this simply through access to reading material, not instruction. This is probably one of the most significant differences between the academic abilities of gifted children and average children during the first years of school.

Chuck Arnesen—When he was 37 months old, Chuck said to his 16-month-old brother, who was eating a breakfast of bananas, "This is a bwanna, Rick. Can you say bwanna?" While boarding an airplane when he was 40 months old, Chuck heard the instrumental music piped in and exclaimed excitedly, "Barry Maninow! Barry Maninow!" The flight attendants were astonished. By age three to 3½, Chuck read all store signs and many traffic signs. He also loved animated movies and cartoons.

Gina Oliver—Gina was willing to risk punishment if it was for something she wanted. One night, at age three, she spent half an hour coming up with whatever reasons she could to delay bedtime. (This had become a nightly ritual for her.) Once we finally got her into bed and went downstairs, she yelled from her bed that she wanted us to get her some water. We told her no, but she continued to yell. Then she said she would get it herself. We again told her no, go to sleep. She was quiet for the next 15 minutes. Then she came down to our room, tears streaming down her face, and said, "I don't care what you said, I'm going to get it myself," and proceeded to the kitchen. It was such a funny sight—her first real act of defiance—that when she left the doorway, we started to laugh.

Peter Koos—Peter started playing computer math and reading games at age three. He got into video games later when we let him. At three years 10 months, he read "fire," "exit," and "banana" on signs.

Derek Fondow—Derek put sounds together to read simple words by 3½. He also was engrossed with the alphabet through magnetic letters, letter bingo, and *Bob* books during this time. Just before he turned four, Derek was reading beginner reader books and progressed quickly to nonfiction—encyclopedias, anything about airplanes, space, and whales. He later became interested in fiction at age four with the *Magic Tree House*[2] books.

Stephen Williams—At 3½, Stephen did a 70+ piece USA map puzzle himself and helped others on 500- to 1,000-piece puzzles.

Michael Fuller—Michael started to read store signs at about age three. I used to go *crazy* when he was quite small because I got so little rest with him. He was always the last one to fall asleep and the first one up. He gave up naps early. He wouldn't go to bed. A scrapbook notation that I wrote when he had just turned four reads: "Exasperating situation with interjection of humor: 9 P.M.—1½ hours after being tucked in bed—Michael exclaimed, 'Well, I just can't handle going to sleep.'"

Author note: It is probably the intensity of Level Three and higher gifted children that makes it difficult for them to "turn off their brains" at night. Many such children need parental suggestions for slowing their thoughts down so that they can relax and go to sleep.

Candice Richardson—On Christmas Eve, when she was 44 months old, Candice asked me to write a note to Santa on a chalkboard. I waited an eternity for her to fall asleep, which was not long enough, because as soon as I'd written Santa's reply, she came out and inspected the slate. She asked if I had seen Santa, because she knew that the current message on the slate was not the same as what I had written earlier. We then had to talk about whether or not Santa was real. I was not prepared to have this discussion with a three-year-old at midnight on Christmas Eve, and I was torn between continuing the fantasy and telling the truth—which she seemed so badly to want. I assured her that Santa was magic and that I had fallen asleep on the couch and hadn't seen him.

Author note: The Santa Claus dilemma is a common issue for the parents of Level Three and higher gifted children. Parents are unsure of how to respond for a couple of reasons: (1) they want the child to enjoy the wonder of it all, and (2) they don't want the child to tell other children that Santa isn't real.

I do not recall the age at which Candice began using numbers, except that she was doing so quite well by age four, when she had her preschool screening. One incident stands out. She was riding in the car with her father when he missed an exit at a cloverleaf. He exited at the next loop and explained that he was going to have to go around two more times to go the direction he had intended to go. She said, "Oh, that means you will have to go around three times."

Author note: Many adults have trouble with the problem of a cloverleaf. Candice's ability to visualize the number of turns in a highway cloverleaf was

> *part math and part spatial reasoning, but it was all very advanced reasoning for a young child.*

Franklin Hayes—Without my being aware of it, Franklin began reading at age three. One day I suddenly realized that he could read some words on an advertisement for a local bank. Once I knew that he could read, I let him use the computer. He liked the *Reader Rabbit®* program, but that was short-lived. He was no longer challenged once he figured it out. He asked scientific questions like, while driving around a sharp curve, "Is this centrifugal force?" He counted into the 100s by age four.

Tiana Bardy—Tiana started reading beginner books when she was three—she taught herself from being read to. I taught her the phonic alphabet rather than letter names, but she took off from there. Tiana was not as interested in math as she was in reading, but at 3½, she could count and used small numbers in practical life—for example, "Two kids and two mommies means we need four plates." She loved mazes and puzzles and did 50-piece puzzles by age 3½ to four.

Brennan Ahlers—Brennan started to put together 30+ piece puzzles and read beginner books when he was about three. He just did it; we didn't teach him. He wrote many words when he was 3-1/3 years old. Interestingly, even when he was very young, he always referred to his father as "Mark" instead of "Dad." This bothered me, and I asked Mark to talk with Brennan about it.

> Mark: "Brennan, Mom would like it if you called me 'Dad' instead of 'Mark.'"
>
> Brennan: "Why? Because you're my dad and I'm your son?"
>
> Mark: "Yes."
>
> Brennan: "Then are you going to call me 'Son'?"
>
> Mark: "Would you like me to call you 'Son'?"
>
> Brennan: "No, I'd like you to call me 'Brennan,' and I'm going to call you 'Mark.'"

End of story. My husband and I looked at each other and figured we couldn't argue with a three-year-old's logic. To this day, 90% of the time, Brennan calls his dad by his first name.

Author note: The early use of logic is a common theme among Level Three gifted children. It is confounding when the child's logic runs counter to societal expectations.

Brennan's grandfather was a huge car buff and thought Brennan's keen interest in cars was great. He gave Brennan a subscription to *Motor Trend* and *Auto Week* when he was three. They started going to auto shows together each year, and the salespeople were always amazed because Brennan could name the make and model of nearly all of the cars on the showroom floor. One time, Brennan said that a particular car was a Dodge, but his grandpa said that no, it was a Chevy. He then noticed that the car had Dodge hubcaps, and that was what Brennan was reading. Brennan later spent hours poring over the car brochures from the show.

Author note: Brennan was incredibly self-motivated from an early age to learn about cars—they fascinated him. Parents and teachers often ask how to get their school-age children motivated. I like to point out what the children were like before starting school and being required to comply with someone else's ideas about how they should spend all of their time. Very bright children are naturally motivated to learn; for such children, the environment must be set up less to motivate learning and more to allow it.

Angelica Plomin—Angelica went to a non-academic preschool at age 3½. She could tell time to the half hour on an analog clock, and she knew it in five-minute increments before she turned four. Also at four, she could count by 5s and 10s and do simple addition. Within a few weeks of wanting to learn to read, she could sight read in an easy reader, and she sounded out complex words shortly after that. By three years 11 months, she was reading at a first- to second-grade level, going quickly through books like *Little Bear* (by Else Minarik) and *Henry and Mudge* (by Cynthia Rylant).

Justin Janacek—Justin really started to use numbers when he was about three, although he counted long before that. He loved mazes by this age. I had a hard time finding enough maze books for him that were appropriate for his level. He started to show interest in the computer but not in video games yet. He would pick an interest and focus on it until it was totally mastered. For example, at three, he became interested in sign language. We checked out every available book on sign language, and he taught himself the alphabet and various signs and then used them for several months.

Age Four to Five Years

At four, these children are just one year from kindergarten. What Level Three gifted children are already doing at home and in preschool is dramatically beyond the typical curriculum for kindergarten and first grade.

As you read, notice the speed with which many of these gifted children move from beginner books to chapter books. In most children, this is related to level of giftedness. A Level Three gifted child, compared to a Level One child, rarely goes through any stage of phonetically sounding out words. Intense interest in complex mazes is also a strong clue that the child is probably at least at a Level Three.

Chuck Arnesen—Chuck had an advanced vocabulary and started to read whole sentences by the time he was 4½ to five years old. By the time he was five, he could read any beginner book and showed great interest in humor books such as the *Garfield Comic Anthologies*.

Gina Oliver—When she was four, Gina woke us one morning by coming into our room and asking where she could find an 11/4 measuring cup. We explained that she probably needed 1 and ¼. She said, "Okay" and turned to leave, but as we became conscious, we asked her why. She told us that she was baking a cake; she had been reading the recipe on the box. She began reading slightly earlier than her brother. I think that this was mainly due to her exposure to computer reading programs and our heightened awareness that it was within the realm of possibility that she could read before kindergarten. Her progression with reading was slower than her brother's but still much advanced compared to other kids.

Peter Koos—Peter read beginner books by 4½ and could add and subtract before kindergarten.

Derek Fondow—Before Derek was four, he used the computer by himself to write notes, add and draw pictures, send and receive e-mail, and surf the Internet. By 4½ years, he was reading biographies more often read by children age eight and older. He began more advanced math work in his Montessori classroom with number beads and number rods, worked on telling time to the hour and half hour, and could do four-digit addition.

Stephen Williams—Numbers seemed to come naturally to Stephen— we never had to drill or quiz him—and he understood the concepts of adding, subtracting, and multiplying before kindergarten. He enjoyed mazes by age four, and by age seven, it was hard to find mazes difficult enough for him.

Sophie Fuller—Sophie started to use the computer a lot when she was about four. She was self-motivated to move from coloring-type games to math and reading, and she liked to write letters to her friends on the computer.

Franklin Hayes—Franklin started to read beginner books on his own when he was four. He also knew all of his addition and subtraction facts through the 12s.

Andrea Dolan—Just before Andrea turned four, my mother-in-law helped her sound out some words, and that was all it took for her to learn to read. She began reading beginning books and has been reading everything since. She read the large Dr. Seuss books, a Children's Bible, and many more.

Brennan Ahlers—Brennan started to read chapter books when he was about four. He did simple division and multiplication in his head at 4½. When he started preschool, I didn't know enough to ask for any adjustments to be made for him. His teacher tried to keep him challenged, but he complained that it was boring. He was already reading and writing while many students couldn't write their names. He was puzzled at having to memorize his address and phone number, because it seemed so basic. He thought every kid knew that.

Author note: Level Three gifted children usually know their home addresses by the time they are five. It is very unusual for them not to have personally insisted upon knowing such things.

Angelica Plomin—Just over four, Angelica began working her way through the *Boxcar Children* books. Four months later, she knew addition facts up to 24 and could add three-digit numbers without carrying. By 4½, she could add with carrying. She could also subtract fairly reliably but didn't like it as much. She soon learned to multiply and had a good grasp of basic fractions. Her word recognition skills were at about fourth-grade level, but she preferred books at a second- or third-grade level with lots of pictures, which made selecting reading material difficult.

Justin Janacek—Justin started to read beginner books at 4¾. As we read each evening, he recognized more and more words until one day, he read Joanna Cole's *Bug in a Rug*—a book that was new to him—by himself. He had known for some time that numbers stand for something, and when he was five, his father began doing worksheets with him and taught him to carry 1s. Justin thought that this was fun—we never pushed. However, subtraction was harder for him than addition.

Age Five to Six Years

By age five or six, all of these children can read simple books, and many can read chapter books. All of them count well and figure simple problems in their heads. In addition, all have large vocabularies and good speaking and discussion skills. It is not uncommon to assess children like this at about age five or six and discover that their reading skills and comprehension are already in the upper elementary school range—without any direct instruction.

However, many Level Three children are weak in one or two areas. The weaker areas or deficiencies worry parents because they suspect that their child may not really be gifted after all. Parents are confused as to whether their child is simply being stubborn, not applying herself, or has substantially less potential in some areas. It is reassuring to them to discover that uneven interests or abilities are entirely normal for most gifted children and nothing to worry about.

Chuck Arnesen—By the time he turned five, Chuck read beginner books to himself silently, including a number of children's books that were first- and second-grade reading level. At church, he liked to read to the younger children in the nursery when I volunteered. He read with great expression and took the time to answer their questions. He was like a mini teacher, very patient and solicitous. When asked early in his kindergarten year what his hardest subject was, he answered, "Scissors." It was true. He had no trouble with the academic subjects.

Gina Oliver—Gina read fluently when she started kindergarten. With an August birthday, we were concerned about whether to send her to kindergarten or wait a year. We decided to start her right away even though she was more than a year younger than some students.

Peter Koos—Peter could read easy chapter books in kindergarten. It seemed that he taught himself to read by paying attention to labels at daycare. By six, he read books like E. B. White's *Charlotte's Web* independently for recreation. When five, he asked about the differences between even and odd numbers. He liked to be quizzed on multiple digit addition and subtraction for fun at the dinner table.

Derek Fondow—On his first day of kindergarten, Derek walked with his sister and me to the fourth-grade classroom; he promptly found a biography of Wilbur and Orville Wright's adult years and asked the teacher if he could borrow it. He had already read the *Childhood of Famous Americans* books. He read E. B. White's children's books, laughing loudly through each. By age five, he worked on division with remainders. At 5½, he wanted to figure out how many months old he was. He used addition, multiplication, and estimating with subsequent correcting to compute the number of months in five years (5x10 + 5x2) to come to the correct answer. Before age six, Derek acted as banker in board games such as *Life*.

Candice Richardson—At age five, Candice read *Ramona the Pest*, by Beverly Cleary (a book for nine- to 12-year-olds!), and wondered, as did five-year-old Ramona, if the Tooth Fairy was real. She announced that she was sure that her dad was the Tooth Fairy, and then she also asked about Santa and the Easter Bunny. At that point, I confessed.

Sophie Fuller—Sophie started reading beginner books by the time she was about five, knew her numbers to 100, could count by 10s, and learned Chinese numbers from 1 to 10. During car trips, she enjoyed doing computer-generated mazes. At 5½, she was a night owl and went through six or eight books a night. Oftentimes, she stayed up until 10:00, sometimes 10:30, and the next morning, her bedroom was littered with books on the floor. She read anything in the bookcase but was partial to fairy tales. Her teacher said that she was the best reader in her class. She was reading the *Harry Potter* books before kindergarten and had read them all by the end of her kindergarten year. At the fall conferences that year, her teacher asked me, "Are you sure this is the right school for her?"

Layne Freeman—Layne was reading chapter books by age five, and her first chapter book was *Cam Jansen*.[3] She read three of the *Narnia* books before discovering *Harry Potter* just after she turned six, and she read and re-read all four volumes until they fell apart. She didn't need help with the computer within minutes of first using it at not quite 5½ years old.

Tiana Bardy—Right after Tiana turned six, she scored in the 98th percentile on the second-grade *Iowa Basics Test*, two years ahead of grade level.

Andrea Dolan—At almost six, Andrea read all of the *American Girl* series on one girl character in 24 hours, and she quickly finished the entire series. With no pressure from us, she easily learned her 11-times-tables series, as well as easy addition and place values. She loved music, gymnastics, dance, and swimming. I was glad that I hadn't sent her to kindergarten yet but simply allowed her to participate in plenty of activities.

Justin Janacek—Justin started to read chapter books at 5½ years old. He quickly jumped several levels in his reading. He read silently or out loud with lots of expression. He either sounded out words or used context. He liked a sophisticated story or plot, so I had to choose picture books carefully at this stage. He also liked poetry books and atlases, and he usually chose to bring home from the school library nonfiction books about planets, plants, shells, and books about the nature of science and matter.

Justin didn't know how to type yet, but he used the computer independently. During preschool after his fifth birthday, his father taught him to add and subtract double-digit equations, even carrying 1s. However, that skill declined with lack of practice, and his desire to do it didn't continue. He was more advanced than others his age, but math didn't come as easily as verbal skills. In fact, so much came easily to him that he eventually balked at any challenges. He had difficulties with money and time. When we worked on money, he seemed to have the skills (count by 1s, 5s, and 10s) but just didn't make the connections. He had a good concept of time and the passage of time, but he couldn't master the clock. These skills seemed relatively simple when compared to some of the advanced material he could read.

Age Six to Seven Years

Chuck Arnesen—By the end of kindergarten, when Chuck was 6½ years old, he was reading at the fifth- or sixth-grade level. He loved *Ramona* books and all manner of easy reader chapter books, including mythological and historical stories. He always preferred fiction to nonfiction.

Gina Oliver—When tested for fluency in first grade, Gina was reading 168 words per minute on the fourth-grade assessment. The next closest child in her class was reading 19 words per minute on the first-grade assessment. She enjoyed stories, historical fiction, and mysteries. When she already knew material in school, she tended to pass the time by sneaking a book. When reading orally in class, her mind raced ahead of her, and she paraphrased instead of reading word for word.

Author note: The ability to paraphrase can cause problems for gifted children. They may be academically judged as being incorrect, going too fast, or having attentional problems. They can also have difficulty with short-term memory tasks because they look for the "big picture" rather than parrot back exactly what they have heard. I encourage parents and teachers to help the child determine when exact replication is needed so that the child can learn to focus on it. I also encourage the adults to let go of a requirement for precision when precision is not needed.

Derek Fondow—Derek read the first *Harry Potter* book and half of the second one before first grade. He also read *The Little Prince*, by Antoine de Saint-Exupéry for nine- to 12-year-olds, more than once. He liked to play *Scrabble*™ and do the computations to determine which words earned the most points. He enjoyed being the banker when we shopped together—especially counting back the correct change. He liked exploring fractions and how to reduce them. Once when his immunologist was explaining test results, she asked him if he knew what the immune system is. He labeled a sheet "Immune System" and drew his version of how a body fights a germ. She said that he understood it better than most med students and asked if she could copy the picture to use in her medical school immunology class.

Stephen Williams—Stephen was slow to start reading on his own, but he went from simple sentences in kindergarten to easy chapter books in first grade; his reading really took off in second grade. He wanted math problems to "go to sleep with," such as two-digit by two-digit multiplication or simple variable equations like $2x+4y=36$ that could keep him thinking for hours.

Michael Fuller—I didn't let Michael watch *Power Rangers* or *Sesame Street* because I thought it would diminish his attention span. He started reading in first grade in school. He was given beginner books and took off like a rocket. By end of first grade, at age six, he had read J. R. R. Tolkien's *The Hobbit* (for children ages 12 and up!) twice and was totally bored with the easy reader books. He just loved to read. I ordered an anniversary edition of *The Hobbit* for myself, but Michael claimed it for his own.

Author note: Michael started reading quite late for a Level Three child. My research suggests that there are two possible reasons why this happens: (1) the child's parents do not expose him to TV shows that teach reading, and so the child gets the basic message that he's not supposed to read yet,[4] or (2) the child has a vision tracking or coordination problem and needs to see a specialist. In Michael's case, it appears to be a lack of exposure to reading.

Layne Freeman—From age six or so, Layne enjoyed doing the maze for adults in a local freebie newsletter, which we picked up whenever we ate out. I didn't provide much in the way of additional mazes, but she loved them. She started at the end and worked backwards, or she picked a point in the middle, and she seemed startlingly adept at figuring them out. We didn't own a *PlayStation®* or a *Nintendo®*, and we didn't get a home computer until she was five, so her first experience with electronic games and programs was in late kindergarten. She started out with simple games and progressed to about grade 4/5 in the *Reader Rabbit®* software and the *JumpStart* series. She loved advanced math and logic computer games. Once when playing one of these games, she announced, "This is *not* right, Mom!" One of the multiple-choice questions was: "What emerges from a cocoon?" with three possible answers. One of the answers—and the only one that was remotely close—was "Butterfly," and she was quite indignant that the response was incorrect, because "*Moths* emerge from cocoons; butterflies emerge from chrysalises!"

Author note: Layne is a good example of how a Level Three child can quickly fill in her own learning gaps and catch up once exposed to learning opportunities. Although she did not have access to a computer until she was in kindergarten, she quickly became as adept as equally intelligent children who had access much earlier. The general population doesn't understand this. Parents of gifted children are often disheartened when others imply that any child would be so gifted and talented if given the same opportunities. But it is not parents who make their children gifted; the parents react to what their children are already like.

Justin Janacek—Justin wasn't ready until age five for me to read a chapter book to him without pictures, but after that, he enjoyed easy reader chapter books on his own, as well as more mature stories read by me, such as *Harry Potter*.

Age Seven to Nine Years

Achievement test results for young Level Three gifted children are almost always well ahead of their school grade level due to these children's extensive reading and excellent memories. The subjects that tend to be the lowest are the ones that need direct instruction, such as writing and math computation. This explains why you will often see a much higher math concepts score for the same child who has a low math computation score; their intelligence level makes it possible for them to devise ways to solve problems before they are taught specific methods.

Sophie Fuller—Sophie stayed up late reading—she loved to read. She got into Lemony Snicket books—*The Ersatz Elevator* and *The Reptile Room* (for readers ages nine to 12)—and loved Roald Dahl books. We had a 10-volume set of *Collier's Junior Classics* that she often read—the best dollar I ever spent!

Layne Freeman—Layne was a voracious reader by age seven, and she often preferred reading to any other activity. She could easily read four to five hours a day. She also read to calm herself when overexcited or upset. She usually had a book with her if she had a choice, and it was difficult to get her attention when she was engrossed in a story. For pleasure, she read books like the *Magic Tree House* series, the *Magic School Bus* books, the *American Girl* books, and all sorts of chapter books. Sometimes she went back to old favorites that were a bit easier, like the *Berenstain Bears* books. She liked fiction because she found nonfiction boring, although she showed some interest in geography, as with the question: "Is there land under the North Pole, and if there is, why isn't it a continent like Antarctica?" She asked questions that made me wonder where she got her information. She also liked poetry and magazines, usually kid-oriented ones like *Crayola Kids* and *Time for Kids*.

Franklin Hayes—Second grade was a rough year for Franklin, as he already knew almost all of the curriculum. He was able to do long division well by then, but he had no opportunity to practice it in school, so he lost the methods.

Author note: Franklin's parents had him assessed on the SBLM and the Woodcock Johnson Tests of Achievement. His grade equivalency scores when he was in the second month of second grade were between sixth- and ninth-grade level in subjects related to reading, and in the fifth- to seventh-grade level in subjects related to math. Because his IQ score was in the

Level Three to Four gifted range, his parents wanted him tutored until he caught up with his real level of potential. After six months of twice-weekly tutoring, his grade equivalencies were all between upper sixth- and upper eleventh-grade levels. His elementary school then allowed him to skip third grade and go to fourth grade.

Tiana Bardy—At age seven, Tiana did single-digit multiplication and division in her head, as well as multi-digit fractions, decimals, area, volume, and perimeter on paper. She was also very good at word problems. She read everything and anything but preferred fiction about girls, horses, and elephants. She also enjoyed nonfiction on diverse topics. She read several books a day, sometimes to the detriment of getting other work done. She also liked to write stories and draw mazes for other children to do.

Brennan Ahlers—Brennan was home schooled three days a week when he was technically in second grade. He took the *Iowa Test of Basic Skills* in May that school year. His grade equivalencies were from mid-fourth-grade level in listening and math computation to the end of eighth grade in science. The remaining 13 subtest scores were all at fifth- and sixth-grade levels.

Age Nine and Older

Level Three children typically enjoy a wide array of reading. Every now and then, however, they prefer light reading that is "below their level." This is nothing to be alarmed at. In fact, many parents observed that their Level Three children who once read a lot independently sometimes seem too tired from school to come home and read. It is not hard, then, to understand why they may periodically choose books that are easy for them to read.

Chuck Arnesen—Chuck's creative writing started to gain him considerable attention. He wrote a complex mystery, and it became the under-pinning to a screenplay he wrote a dozen years later and turned into a feature length independent film. The germ of the idea, we later discovered, actually first came from a *Garfield* cartoon book. Chuck attended a private college prep school after second grade, which was ideal for his ability level and talents. That first year, his achievement test scores were all in the 92nd to 98th percentile except math, which was lower. Chuck qualified for and stayed in the accelerated math sequence at his school, but in his own mind, he struggled.

> *Author note: Math requires more effort for most people than talking and reading, so many bright, verbally adept students underestimate their quantitative reasoning abilities.*

Michael Fuller—At age 10, Michael enjoyed *The Eagle and the Raven* (by James Michener), the *Redwall* series, Clive Cussler books, Tom Clancy books, and classics in either junior or original versions. He loved doing anything on the computer and made his own website, purchased from e-Bay, programmed, and designed and played games. However, he still played with LEGOs® and enjoyed spending time with his friends.

Candice Richardson—Candice's favorite reading material at 11½ was fantasy. She loved the *Redwall* series, Lloyd Alexander books, and anything with fairies or princesses in it, interspersed with *Sweet Valley Twins*[5] books.

Franklin Hayes—By age 10, Franklin was captivated by television documentaries. He still read on his own but devoted less time to it outside of school. Although his reading skills were very high, he sometimes struggled to give the correct answers on tests, as he often read "beyond the question."

> *Author note: Many Level Three children do not know what the teacher is really asking for. Directions that seem too simple or make no sense to them stymie their ability to understand the thrust of what the teacher wants them to do.*

Brennan Ahlers—Brennan did very well playing the violin. He amazed his father and his teacher when he off-handedly told them that he could recite all of the fingerings on every song he had ever learned. Challenged by his teacher on this, he recited a minuet by the fingerings. His teacher was dumbfounded. Little things like that crept up whenever we started to think he was normal.

Janet Lewis—Janet went to academic summer camps each year after seventh grade through the Duke Talent Identification Program and the Midwest Talent Search. These were very positive experiences for her. In high school, she took all enriched and AP[6] courses and fit in an extra course before the official start of the school day. She received credit for three AP courses as a sophomore and took three more AP exams the next spring. Her social life at age 15 primarily revolved around fellow members of the varsity speech and debate teams, although she also enjoyed friends and activities related to the cross country running and ski programs. She spent four weeks at Stanford University's summer debate camp.

Summary of Level Three Gifted

- Most Level Three gifted children are dramatically different from their age peers. Their abilities with numbers, colors, the alphabet, speaking and reading, and sense of humor are recognizably advanced. All 18 Level Three gifted children, for example, knew how to read, count, and do simple math before they started kindergarten. During their kindergarten year, almost all of the children had moved from simple books to chapter books. In kindergarten and first grade, many of the children were assessed as having third- to fifth-grade reading levels. The following developmental features characterize Level Three children.
- Most were alert at birth or soon thereafter.
- Almost all paid attention within months of birth while someone to read to them.
- Most had books as a favorite interest before age one.
- Almost all understood what someone was saying to them by six months.
- Most independently looked at and turned pages of books before 10 months.
- Most knew and said some words by 5½ to 10 months.
- Most made their families understand what they wanted before 12 months.
- Many said two-word phrases by 12 months.
- A number of children played with shape sorters by 11 months.
- Many recognized some colors, shapes, numbers, and letters before 12 months.
- Most had favorite TV shows or videos between nine and 18 months.
- Most had large vocabularies, receptive and expressive, by 16 months.
- Most knew many colors by 15 to 18 months.
- Many liked 35+ piece puzzles by 15 to 24 months.
- Most knew and sang songs before they were two years old.
- Most read names on signs and stores between 20 months and 3¾ years.

- Many read numerous sight words between 15 and 20 months.
- Many memorized the books that were read to them before they were two years old.
- Many showed interest in letter sounds and sounding out short words by age 2½.
- Most were speaking in complex sentences of more than four words by 15 to 24 months.
- Many could rote count to 10, several higher, by 15 to 24 months.
- Almost all knew the entire alphabet by 17 to 24 months.
- Many used language to make jokes by age 2½, and several showed humor earlier.
- Most could print letters, numbers, words, and their names between 2¾ and 3½ years.
- Most knew many sight words by age three to 3½.
- Half could read very simple books—perhaps memorized—by age three to 3½.
- Many had high interest in facts, how things work, and science by three to four.
- Most grasped skip and backwards counting and basic addition and subtraction by three to four years.
- Many questioned the reality of Santa Claus or the Tooth Fairy by three to four years.
- Most were independent on a computer by age three to 4½ years.
- Many were keyboarding by three to 4½ years.
- Most could read easy readers by age four to five years.
- Most read children's level chapter books by 4¼ to 5½ years.
- Many understood some multiplication, division, and some fractions by age 5½.
- Most read for pleasure and information by six.
- All were reading two to five years beyond grade level by age six.
- Almost all played many adult games by the time they were age six to 6½.
- All read youth and young adult chapter books independently by age seven to 7½.

Level Three gifted children are delightfully energetic and inquisitive during their preschool years. However, because their skills are so far beyond their age peers, problems may occur when they enter school. Teachers are often incredulous about what these children can do, and they are seldom prepared to provide opportunities for them at their level of readiness.

Families of Level Three children rapidly discover that the usual educa–
tional and parenting methods and expectations simply do not apply and
that they must consider alternative and nontraditional approaches.

Table 3: Level Three Children's Data

Name	SBLM Ratio IQ	Test Age Years-Mos.	Other IQ Tests	Achievement Test Grade Equivalencies/ Percentiles
Chuck Arnesen	-	-	WISC-R at age 6, 128; WISC-III at age 14, 136; Otis-Lennon 115, 119, 124, 135	ERB Achievement Test: 65th-99th; SAT-V 570; SAT-M 710
William Jones	-	-	WISC-III 145	Explore for 8th graders taken in 6th grade: 92nd percentile
Gina Oliver	160	7-10	-	-
Peter Koos	164	8-4	-	-
Derek Fondow	175	7-0	-	-
Stephen Williams	188	10-7	WISC-III 144	Woodcock-McGrew-Werder Achievement Test in 5th grade: Reading 12-5, Writing 6-0, Math 14-5, Knowledge 10-9
Michael Fuller	185	11-2	WISC-III 133	WJ-R in 5th grade: Reading 136, Math 122, Passage Comprehension 129, Calculation 116, Applied Problems 118
Candice Richardson	185	-	-	Woodcock-McGrew-Werder Achievement Test: Reading 161, Writing 159, Math 161, Knowledge 132
Sophie Fuller	177	5-5	-	-
Layne Freeman	177	7-10	CogAT 145; SB4 152	W-J Achievement Test: Reading 99.8, Math 99.7

Name	SBLM Ratio IQ	Test Age Years-Mos.	Other IQ Tests	Achievement Test Grade Equivalencies/ Percentiles
Franklin Hayes	188	7-8	-	WJ-R in 2nd grade: Letter-Word Recognition 9-7, Reading Comprehension 6-9, Calculation 5-0, Applied Problems 6-8, Writing 5-9; in 3rd grade: Dictation 6-8, Proofing 9-1, Writing 7-0, Math Calculation 6-8, Applied Problems 11-6, General Info in Science 11-6
Tiana Bardy	177	7-6	SB5 136 (VIQ-136, NVIQ-134); SB5 142 w/o WM*	-
Andrea Dolan	178	4-4	-	-

*w/o **WM** is one method of calculating an experimental gifted composite score for the *Stanford-Binet 5th Edition* in which the working memory subtest is omitted.

Chapter 7
Level Four Gifted: 99th Percentile

Rebecca was not easy going. She was spirited. Her emotions were so big that they would overwhelm her and she would lose control. As a preschooler, they manifested as inappropriate outbursts, and these typically were unexpected by the adults who interacted with her. On the other hand, she was so enjoyable for adults to be with because they could have meaningful conversations with her.
~ Mother of a Level Four girl

Level Four children exhibit the IQ range previously referred to as exceptionally to profoundly gifted. The children in this chapter have *Stanford-Binet (Form L-M)* ratio IQs that range from 176 to 220. The children in this chapter—and the next—are spectacularly intelligent. Table 4 provides the Level Four children's ratio IQs and standard scores from various tests.

How many Level Four children are there in our schools? I believe that there are more of these amazing students than many people might otherwise realize,[1] particularly since some of the students will never be formally identified as gifted because their challenging behaviors in a regular classroom may work against their identification. Furthermore, the prevalence of these children in any one school or district is greatly influenced by parental efforts to find a good "fit" for their children. This means that while some Level Four children may start school in a neighborhood public school, the family may move or send the child to a place where they think educational opportunities are more appropriate. Many parents of Level Four and higher children turn to home schooling, so fewer Level Four and Level Five children remain in regular schools.

Selective or competitive private schools and public schools in districts where most of the parents are highly educated professionals can expect that about 2% of their students, two to three per grade level, will be at Level Four or higher. Selective private high schools—college prep schools—can have from two to seven Level Four students within a class of 100, because such schools, with their track records of graduates gaining admission to highly competitive colleges, may attract more high ability students than do other schools. Large public high schools in professional communities will generally have six to 12 students at this intellectual level in a class size of about 400.

Most public elementary schools with 100 children per grade level will have one or two of these children across every two grade levels, which means that the school might not have a student this intelligent every year. By the time the students from such a district are all drawn together for high school—approximately 1,200 students total—there will be about six to 12 Level Four students in the school. Schools that draw from impoverished, disadvantaged, or low educational background parents and very rural, isolated schools do not often sustain students who are at Level Four; the parents of such children usually seek other schooling options.

The Children

The children in this chapter are substantially ahead of others their age—even typical *gifted* children. When extremely bright children head off to kindergarten, their parents often do not yet understand how very unusual they are, expecting that educators in the school will know what to do for them. The general public assumes—naively and incorrectly—that all children will be given the opportunity to learn at whatever pace is right for them.

Every child in this chapter started kindergarten and first grade with other children who were within a year of his or her own age. Every child in this chapter had parents who asked the schools to recognize the abilities that their child possessed and to guide him or her appropriately. Every parent and child encountered one problem after another.

There can be no doubt that the children in this chapter are quite amazing in their intellectual energy and precocity. These children pick up information from everywhere, whether it is specifically introduced to them or not. Their attention to detail, ability to make sense of details to form conclusions, and capacity to induce theories of their own sets them apart from more typical children. It is important to note that most of the children in this book are from a single large metropolitan area of about two million residents. The majority of these children did not have any other children in their classes that were as highly gifted as they, and when they took high school advanced courses, they were still usually—but not always—the most highly gifted students there. I asked the older Level

Four children if they knew anyone else like them who seemed as smart as they. All of them had encountered others as smart, but usually only at inter-school contests such as Quiz Bowl, Math League, Talent Search, or similar events.

Birth to Two Years

Notice in this section the ways in which parents describe when their children first demonstrated an interest in being read to, as well as the children's reactions to books. Reading to young children helps them to begin building a knowledge and experience base, so that a Level Four gifted child is able to make seemingly spontaneous, theoretical observations at a very early age.

Level Four children also often make dramatic leaps from just starting to do something to being remarkably good at it, as with simply saying words to speaking in full, meaningful sentences, typically by age two, or with beginning to count and then suddenly being able to count well into the hundreds.

Also at the Level Four gifted range, there are several examples of amazing memories in the children—even for things that happened before they were two years old.

Patricia Walker—When Patty was three to four months old, it was clear that she enjoyed being read to. At six months, she wanted more story—simple books with big pictures weren't enough. At eight months, she sat on the floor by herself and flipped through book after book. She said words at 9½ months, including "pooh," "daddy," and "mommy." By 13 months, she knew 40 to 50 words and spoke so clearly that it shocked people. She also could count to 10. At 14 months, she was putting two words together, and by 16 months, she started using three to four word sentences, such as, "Me want cookie," "Elmo tape in," and "I love you, Daddy." She could also count past 20 by then. She got an alphabet puzzle for her first birthday, and at 15 months, she could recite all of the letters. By 17 months, she knew all of the letters if we showed them to her randomly, and she could tell you what each was for: "'P' is for 'papa,'" "'E' is for 'egg.'" Sometimes she said "'P' is for 'pizza'" instead of "papa." Between 12 and 18 months, she understood and correctly used abstract words in sentences, like "Unusual," "I'm thinking," and "I'm using my imagination." She memorized board books such as *Goodnight Moon* and *The Three Bears* (by Byron Barton) and could recite them without looking at the book.

At 14 to 16 months, Patty knew all of the colors, including the more difficult ones like magenta. She also knew many complicated shapes, including oval, star, and diamond. Simple puzzles, in which shapes fit into a board, were easy for her by 18 months. She sang her first song—*Old MacDonald Had a Farm*—at 15 months. At 16 to 18 months, she played regularly by herself with her dollhouse or with Play Dough® or markers for up to two hours without interruption. She also loved playing the "rhyme game," in which we gave her a word and she said words that rhymed with it. At 20 months, she memorized and recited longer books, like *Ten in the Bed* (by Penny Dale), without the book in front of her. She corrected me if I made a mistake when reading to her. Sometime between 18 and 24 months, we discovered that she knew her street and city, even though we had never talked to her about it.

Nathan Webster—Nathan started to say words at about 11 to 15 months. He knew colors between 18 and 24 months. He was always interested in being read to.

Emily Newton—When Emily was not yet two, she was sitting in her high chair eating dinner when a friend walked in for a visit carrying a book. Emily looked at the cover, and said, "Oh, *Miss Smilla's Sense of Snow*. My mother is reading that book," and went back to her dinner. My friend, a preschool teacher, was amazed and still tells that story.

Rose Engum—Rose loved to be read to from the time she was four months old, said "mama" when she was eight months old, and started walking at 11½ months. By 14 months, she could say many words, including "dad," "ball," "gone," "car," "bottle," "tree" and "hat." By 16 months, she said simple sentences like "Mommy gone work" and "Daddy gone car." She showed real interest in watching TV by the time she was a year old. She loved *Barney* and *Sesame Street* in particular. At 14 months, she counted to 14—just did it out of the blue; we had never practiced with her. At 18 months, she greeted people saying, "Hi, how are you?" and by 20 months, she could speak in complete sentences, such as, "What happened to the other one?" and "Look what happened to Dolly's face." At 19 months, she knew the colors. She also knew and sang the entire alphabet song. At 22 months, she said, "Grandma's microwave goes round and round in circles," and "My mommy cuts my sandwich into triangles."

Rebecca Resnick—Rebecca always had a long attention span. From very early, probably 1½ years and younger, she would sit in my lap without losing interest while I read to her. At one year old, she got magnetic alphabet letters, and she pointed and made noises until I picked out a letter and said the letter name out loud. I didn't know what else to do with it, and she seemed satisfied when we went through all of the letters. She knew the first half of the alphabet, "A" through "J," by 18 months. At 13 months, we took her on a train trip. The porter showed her how to "high five," and she got it immediately. Every time he came by, he said, "High five, Rebecca," and she'd hold up her hand to slap palms. When she was two, Rebecca's grandmother asked her what TV show she watched, and Rebecca said, "*Mr. Rogers*, and after that show comes the *Nightly Business Report*." She was also counting by then. At 22 months old, she visited her out-of-town grandparents, who had a remote control for their TV. She called it the "mote." We didn't have one at our house. Six months later, when we visited again, the first thing she asked for when we got in the door was the "mote."

Tyler Lundquist—Tyler made good eye contact by six weeks. He was always interested in having us read to him. He loved the TV show *Mr. Rogers* as soon as we first turned it on for him. He said our dog's name when he was one, and he said "Grandpa" at 13 months. By age two, he spoke mostly in full sentences.

Keith Sands—When Keith was born, he was very alert, and as my husband proudly carried his new son around, Keith's eyes remained focused on his father. When Keith was four weeks old, a maternal health nurse, during a routine check-up, used a toy to see if Keith could "track" it. She commented that he was very alert and exceptionally good at following objects with his eyes. From birth, we read to him every night, and he was always calm and focused on the books. He stared at the TV for long periods even before he could sit properly. I first put him in a highchair at about four or five months, and he pointed to his bottle on the bench. He knew his colors by the time he could talk and said the usual first words between 12 and 14 months. He started to really pay attention to TV at about 13 months. He especially liked commercials with music. He recognized store and street signs between 16 and 18 months.

Adam Schaefer—Adam's eyes flew open every time he heard a sound the first night he was born. At five weeks, he made good eye contact and smiled at both me and his father. At six weeks, he could follow us with eyes and head 180 degrees around the room from four feet away. By 8½ months, he said "mama," "dada," "baby," and "go"; at 10 months, he said "this"; at 11 months, he said "ta-ta" for trash truck, "bop" for bear, and "baby go!" By eight months, he fussed for all of the books he saw at the bookstore, and he loved it when we read to him. At 13 months, he begged all day for a "boo" (book). We read to him two or three times each day, 20 to 30 minutes at a time.

Author note: The interaction and attention that Level Four gifted children require can be draining for their parents and other caregivers. It is typical for such children to want someone to read to them often and for long periods. Although many parents admitted to being wracked with guilt over it, they learned to take advantage of the child's favorite television shows and videos because it gave them a break. Life got a lot easier for most of these parents once their children learned to read on their own.

At 15 months, Adam knew the letters "O," "E," and "D" and would call out the gate names at the airport as we strolled by. By 17½ months, he said "airpay" if he saw an airplane and "two" if he saw two of them. Before he was 18 months old, he recognized and said numbers in books and magazines. At about 18 months, he enjoyed watching TV and liked *Thomas the Tank Engine*, Disney's *Dumbo*, and anything with fire trucks. He also took a real interest in puzzles. His first puzzle was an eight-shape one with knobs, but he was more interested in learning the names of the shapes than in progressing to other puzzles. One day at this age, when he saw the doctor's eye exam light, he said, "Like a moon." He knew the colors by 19 months. At 21 months, he could count to five. By 24 months, he knew the entire alphabet. Before he was two, he listened to and understood Neil Ardley's science book for four-year-olds called *How Things Work*.

Samantha Forrest—When she was about one, Samantha started to speak. We began spending time with other children her age and older, and her vocabulary increased rapidly. Once she knew a handful of words, she started putting them together in sentences. She could pronounce any word we said. She also asked for definitions of words she didn't know. She was always friendly to other children and was best friends with Eric, a boy who was one year older. At 18 months, Samantha asked, "Why does Eric pronounce his words incorrectly?"

Kayla Bardy—Kayla paid attention to being read to from birth. At nine months, she said "mama," "dada," "ball," and "cup." She said 15 words by 11 months and about 50 words by 13 months. She also used many two-word phrases. She recognized and said most colors by 18 months, and she started to use numbers and could count by the time she was 20 months.

Daniel Schmidt—Daniel said his first word, "bubble," quite clearly shortly after his first birthday. As a toddler, he wanted book after book. His favorite TV show was *Sesame Street*. At 19 months, his favorite shows were *Wheel of Fortune* and painting and sewing shows. Before he turned two, the computer screen mesmerized him. He dove into computers and never came up for air.

Seth Cannon—By three weeks old, Seth deliberately "cooed" at me. By four weeks, he purposely grabbed the antennas of a toy caterpillar and paid attention to entire books. By 4½ to five weeks, he tried to imitate his father when he stuck out his tongue. His constant babbling was quite directed, as when he "talked" to the toys tied to the side of his crib. By seven weeks, I noted Seth's long attention span; he easily looked at all the pictures in a book like *Brown Bear, Brown Bear* by Eric Carle. At nine weeks, our real estate agent was convinced that Seth said "Hi!" to her. At three months, we left Seth in his bouncy seat in the living room with a football game on TV. In a few moments, we heard him laughing and squealing, and we ran in to see Seth delightedly watching the game. He watched *Sesame Street* for 15 to 20 minutes at a time. At the zoo at four months old, he watched the fish, dolphins, and sharks with great intensity.

From a very early age, Seth made very intense, direct eye contact with people. At eight months, he picked up a toy phone and seemed to say "hello." More words started coming definitively and quickly. He said "duck," "dog," and "cracker." He started speaking understandably, plainly articulating two- and three-syllable words, including "crocodile," at 9½ months. Before he was 1½ years old, he recognized and named primary and secondary colors, plus black, white, and pink. By two, he read store and street signs, knew the alphabet, and asked questions like, "How do they get the crane off the top of that building (when the construction is done)?" and "How does the ceiling stay up?"

Phil Burns—Phil was unusual from the moment he was born. He was totally aware of his surroundings, staring wide-eyed at the delivery room and its occupants. He showed interest in being read to by about four months. He recognized colors at about nine months, the alphabet at around 15 months, and full words before he was two years old. By 14 months, he excelled at doing jigsaw puzzles and shape sorters. He could count to 20 by 1½ years and 100 by age two. He spoke in three-word sentences by two years old.

Bill Arnesen—Bill made eye contact while still in the hospital after birth. He smiled responsively by eight weeks and followed movements with his eyes. He started handling and observing objects by six months and purposefully babbling by the time he was seven to eight months. He enjoyed having us read to him from before he was a year old and showed an interest in signs and calendars, too. His favorite show was *Sesame Street*, and he ran into the TV room for favorite commercials when he was one. He was good at puzzles from about 14 months—he needed no help putting together 15-piece puzzles for three- to six year-olds that he saw for the first time, and he quickly did a 35-piece puzzle on his second birthday. Before he was 17 months old, he climbed on counters, kitchen stools, etc. Also at 17 months, Bill followed along in books that had records to them. He only said about 10 words clearly by 18 months; however, he knew store signs and other signs like "exit" and "open" as soon as he could talk. He started doing one-to-one object counting sometime between 18 to 24 months, and he had no difficulty with games that required numbers and number concepts, like *Chutes and Ladders*®, *Candyland*®, and *Go Fish*.

Age Two to Three Years

At the toddler stage, most of these parents are aware that their children are advanced. For one thing, they have to find toys designed for older children in order to keep their child's interest. Attention span is relevant because the typical school day is set up around the attention span of the average child, not the exceptionally gifted child. In teacher training classes, teachers are taught that attention span increases with age and that lessons should be no longer than about 20 minutes for kindergarteners and slowly increase to about 30 minutes for first and second graders. Level Four gifted children often have trouble in school transitioning from one activity to another when the teacher says it's time.

Early dexterity, fine-motor skill, and good eye-hand coordination are also common among Level Four children. Many of them are able to handle toys, equipment, and objects that are somewhat fragile without any problems. I specifically asked parents if their children tried to put objects in their mouths when they were under three years old. Very few did, and almost all of the children understood why they should not do so.

Patricia Walker—By the time she turned two, Patty could entertain herself for hours with her dollhouse or at other activities. She had an incredible imagination and wanted to role-play with other children or play school or princesses, and she could play the same story for hours. Other children her age didn't understand what she wanted them to do.

We gave Patty a book with lots of story but few pictures for her second birthday, and it was the only book she wanted to read. She wrote the letter "T" by herself and started making letters out of her eating utensils (T, X, V, E, etc.). At about 2¼ years, Patty used abstract, qualitative adverbs and adjectives regularly, like "This giraffe has a long neck." While washing her face after dinner, I asked her if having a clean face was better. She responded, "Yes, it's *much* better!" She also started to do regular jigsaw puzzles. Sometime before she turned three, she recognized words in books and newspapers.

At just two, Patty knew 100+ songs. She remembered and sang songs that had been sung to her only once or twice, and she knew the entire *University of Minnesota Rouser, Jingle Bells,* and *Rudolph the Red-Nosed Reindeer.* At 2½, she recognized that several songs had the same tune but different words, like the alphabet song, *Twinkle Twinkle Little Star,* and *Baa Baa Black Sheep.*

After a walk with her father when she was two, Patty told me "Ellen's Mommy gave me a treat." I asked if they'd seen Ellen on their walk, but her dad had no idea what she was talking about. Then Patty said, "Ellen was dressed up as a pumpkin." She was talking about Halloween, 5½ months earlier. We had been to about 40 houses that night, too.

Nathan Webster—Nathan was always been able to count as high as he knew the words for the numbers, although he showed some confusion with "teen" numbers when he was 2½. He never officially learned addition and subtraction—just knew them, as though they were common sense. He started to use the computer at 2½. He was clearly cognizant of letters, concepts of words, and word meanings by 33 months.

> *Author note: At Level Four, we see examples of children who intuit math the same way less-gifted children intuit reading. It takes an extremely high intellectual level to teach oneself reading, but it takes an even higher level to teach oneself math.*

Rose Engum—By the time she was two, Rose easily read many street and store signs and started playing with puzzles. At about 2½, she started to use the computer. She quickly became quite adept at typing on the keyboard.

Rebecca Resnick—Rebecca could count by age two, and at 2¼, she counted to 200 over and over again when we drove in the car.

At two, Rebecca was listening to tapes with books and turning pages to go along with the story. At 2½, she recited everything from her beginner poetry books. I'm not sure if she was actually reading, though, because she didn't read books that I hadn't read to her. She was able to correctly pronounce any word that she learned. I always had water in the sipper cup for her no matter where we went, especially in summer, and I'd say, "Here, drink some water so you don't get dehydrated." Later when we were out in public, a woman who thought she was cute said, "You sure must like your juice." Rebecca answered, "It's water; I have to drink it so I don't get dehydrated." She didn't know what "dehydrated" meant, but she used it correctly.

Sometime before age 3½, Rebecca noticed that Santa used the same wrapping paper as Mom and Dad.

Tyler Lundquist—Just before he turned three, Tyler noticed that two rented movies were in boxes of different shades of green. He recognized most of the letters by this age, and after seeing his preschool teacher's name in print, he told her that both of their names ended with an "R." Noticing that two different names end in the same letter is something that can be expected of seven-year-olds, not children who aren't even three yet!

Keith Sands—Keith counted his toys after placing them in order at about two years old. He loved jigsaw puzzles and put them together with his father. He did a 50-piece puzzle by himself by the time he was about three. He started using computers and was adept at the keyboard almost immediately, and he did the *Reader Rabbit*® series on his own.

Adam Schaefer—Before he turned three, Adam understood how air pressure and air brakes work.

Kyle Amundson—Kyle started to read store and street signs in his second year. He knew the alphabet by 2½. When we saw a stop sign, he'd say, "S-T-O-P, stop!"

Samantha Forrest—When we were trying to teach Samantha to talk, we began with the typical questions, like, "Can you say 'dog'?" but we quickly progressed to questions like, "Can you say 'environment'?" Our friends and family commented that her clarity was advanced for her age. A friend of ours who was a doctor liked to ask Samantha, "Do you know what my job is?" Samantha would answer, "Doctor." When she was 2½ and we knew we were going to a party at the doctor's house, I spent some time teaching Samantha to say "anesthesiologist," and I told her that this was a different way of saying our friend's job. At the party, when our doctor friend asked, "Do you know what my job is?" Samantha answered clearly, "Anesthesiologist," and it just about floored our friends!

Kayla Bardy—Kayla loved being read to but was always fanatically independent—the original "me-do-it-myself" kid. She read signs by 2½ years and recognized many words in the paper by the time she was three. I taught her a few letter sounds and blends between ages 2½ and 3½ because she was desperate to read like her sister.

Seth Cannon—When Seth was 27 months old, the name "Andy" came up in adult conversation. Seth said, "Andrea," who had been his father's summer student, and I asked, "Do you remember Andrea coming for dinner three weeks ago?" He said, "Yes, she came with Tiffany and Doug and Mary Ellen." Then he added, "We ate lasagna."

Seth and his father played tic-tac-toe when Seth was 27 months old. At 28 months, Seth was put down for his nap, but he wasn't quite ready to fall asleep, so he called for me, "Mommy. Mommy. Mommy." I was busy, so didn't respond right away. He then switched his approach to, "Ellen Givens Cannon. Ellen Givens Cannon" (my full name).

By two or so, Seth was interested in talking on the phone, and he was capable of holding a decent conversation. He not only answered questions in great detail, but he also initiated new topics and made original inquiries regarding the caller's activities. He called his father at work without any assistance. Friends with a similarly aged child were amazed that Seth could do this.

At 2½, Seth played with his horse and told me it wasn't real; it was a toy. "It can't neigh; I have to neigh for it!" He asked me if babies could talk. I explained that they communicate by crying and making other sounds, and then we talked briefly about other ways of communicating. That night when his father came home, I asked Seth, "How do dogs communicate?" and he said, "They bark." I asked, "How do babies communicate?" and he said, "They cry." I said, "How do we communicate?" and he said, "We talk."

At this point, we decided that Seth could probably handle the movie *E.T.* The movie opens with E.T. running through woods, trying to get back to his ship and being chased by men. Unable to reach his ship, his family leaves without him. It's a pretty intense scene, and I worried that Seth might be upset. I asked him if he was okay. He said "Yes, of course." So I asked, "What do you think is going to happen?" He said, "I think the spaceship is going to come back to get him." I didn't even know he knew the word "spaceship," not to mention the fact that he'd already figured out the whole plot of the movie. I asked, "How do you know the spaceship is going to come back to get him?" and he said, "*Because*, I know a lot about spaceships!"

When Seth was about 2½, we took him to see a high school production of *Oklahoma*. He was completely absorbed in the play and was extremely disappointed when it was over after three hours. He observed set changes, noticed when a character was wearing a hat in one scene but not the next, and demanded to look in the orchestra pit during intermission to see where the music came from.

Phil Burns—Phil spoke in nine-word sentences by 26 months. At 2½, he used the computer for video games and educational programs. He also discovered that letters have sounds that, when put together, make words, and he began reading simple words. He then began reading simple sentences, but he didn't read whole books until later. He always asked questions like "How do you spell X?" and "Where does Y come from?" and he enjoyed little science experiments like putting Christmas tree needles in water to see if they'd sprout. He constantly surprised us with his vocabulary—he picked up sophisticated words and phrases from books we'd forgotten we had read to him. He thrived on challenge; his idea of "fun" was to take three or more 15-piece puzzles, dump them out on the floor, and do them all at once, mixing up the pieces first.

Bill Arnesen—A week after turning two, Bill could say about 50 recognizable words, and he spoke in long, detailed sentences by the time he was 2½. By 26½ months, his vocabulary had grown tremendously. He used comparative words like "big," "little," "hot," "cold," "enough," "too much," "good," "bad," "fits," "doesn't fit." He typed all letters and digits when named. He also recognized all letters and numbers anywhere he saw them and loved calling them out when they appeared on *Sesame Street*. He sang to his records and loved *Davy Crockett* and the *Sesame Street* record. He also played tapes on our stereo; his favorites were Michael Jackson's *Thriller* and the *Beatles 20 Greatest Hits*. In addition, he loved to make up songs and dance. He was very interested in naming colors, consistently identifying many of the more complicated ones, and he started some counting. At 2¾, he was the youngest in his first Montessori class; everyone else was three to five years old. But he began getting on his own underpants, pants, socks, and shoes by himself, and his teachers said that he fit in well, was well liked, and that he was their "little intellectual." They were surprised at his advanced ability to do complex puzzles. Also at this time, he mastered the four- to eight-year-old labyrinth board.

Age Three to Four Years

By the time Level Four gifted children are between three and four years old, most are intellectually ready for typical kindergarten material that is designed to challenge children between the ages of five and six. Schools often use the expression "developmentally appropriate." This suggests that children are not expected to do more than they are ready to do developmentally. Most school curricula are based on rather rigid age and grade-level expectations. As you read through the descriptions of what Level Four gifted children can do before they are three, four, and five years old, remember that the typical school curriculum through third grade is based on the assumption that children can do none of these things until they are older.

Patricia Walker—By three years old, Patty knew opposite sets and could complete even obscure ones. She could do simple computations, such as, "If you had two apples and I gave you one more, how many would you have?" She also read simple words like "dog," "cat," "mom," and "dad." By the time she turned four, she was reading beginner books. She taught herself phonics, sounding out words by breaking down the sounds, not just by recognition of the word. She tried to recite the alphabet backwards and got as far as the letter "T." Mazes became fun for her around this time, but she wasn't very good at them until she was nearly four. We didn't have a computer until she was about 3½, but she quickly figured out the mouse, how to play games, and how to turn off the computer without help. Until she was about four, she preferred playing with adults or older children.

During this time, Patty used phrases and sentences like, "Well, that's progress," "I discovered that I didn't like it," "I'd prefer to read this one," "This interests me," "Perhaps the blue one" (while choosing a crayon), "Carole and I could both enjoy this" (while looking at a toy catalog), and "I didn't realize my lunch was already on the table" (when I had called her three times for lunch). One time I said, "Patty, what a beautiful day," and she replied, "It's gorgeous!"

Nathan Webster—Nathan enjoyed listening to chapter books by age three or four. In preschool, he was advanced compared to any of the other children his age. He was always interested in puzzles and mazes—he could make his way through some pretty complicated multi-page mazes. He played video games with friends by the time he was four.

Rose Engum—When Rose was three, I put cookies on the table after dinner and asked her how many each person would get. She figured it out without having to sort them. Between three and four, she enjoyed mazes in activity books and a computer game with a maze-type activity—luggage moving through an airport baggage system.

Rebecca Resnick—At 3¼, Rebecca read the *State Farm* slogan: "Like a good neighbor, State Farm is there." At the same age, at a restaurant, she asked for a menu, read it, and ordered the strawberry cheesecake. At about 3½, she did simple addition and subtraction with objects like spoons or blocks. Her attention span was quite long; others remarked about how she attended to one thing when most kids just hopped from activity to activity. As a preschooler, she sat and read instead of moving around like the other kids. By four, she was reading many books.

Tyler Lundquist—At almost four, Tyler became very interested in mazes. There was a maze in his preschool room that asked to help a bird find its nest. Tyler suggested other mazes to his teacher, such as Sesame Street's Oscar finding his garbage can.

Author note: Notice the increasing references to enjoying mazes. This interest developed about a year earlier in the Level Four gifted children as compared to those described in the earlier levels. Strong interest in mazes seems to occur most often in Level Four and particularly in Level Five children.

Keith Sands—Keith's great aunt came from the Czech Republic to live with us for six months. She spent a lot of time teaching him Czech. He in turn read to her in English. Around 3½, he wanted to read simple books to us. From then on, he absolutely devoured books. He read the street directory in the car and the labels on items in the supermarket. He loved completing activity books that included mazes and puzzles.

Adam Schaefer—Adam first showed an interest in mazes when he was three. That year also, he explained to a photographer that the photo umbrella was like the moon because it reflected light but didn't make its own. When he saw a neighbor child's expensive self-propelled ride-on dump truck, he said, "I can make that." He told me how to cut the cardboard, and then he decorated a little washtub with construction paper. We attached it to his riding fire truck, thus converting it to a dump truck, and he was so happy. He did large 25-piece dinosaur floor puzzles at preschool with assistance at age four.

Kyle Amundson—Math came early and easily to Kyle. His great-grand-father gave him double-digit math problems to do over the phone when he was a preschooler. He also loved sitting at the table with his father and learning about negative numbers and other math concepts.

Samantha Forrest—Samantha could add and subtract in her head and do simple multiplication at age three. One of her favorite people was the preschool assistant teacher, who spent lots of time answering her questions. One day they spent half an hour on how a pencil sharpener works. The teacher was amazed that a three-year-old would ask about something like that and then stay interested enough to take it apart for further investigation.

Author note: Samantha's intense interest and attention to how a pencil sharpener works was unusual for a three-year-old. Typical school expectations list such technology explorations as normal for second- and third-grade students.

Kayla Bardy—For a while at 3½, Kayla seemed stuck on some letter sounds, but she was so eager to read. Then one day, it just clicked, and she took off reading beginner books. She liked numbers, counting, and math problems, and she could do simple addition. She adored puzzles and put together ones with 50 pieces by then.

Daniel Schmidt—When Daniel was in preschool, his favorite TV shows were *Reading Rainbow, Square 1 TV*, a PBS math show, and *PBS Nightly Business Report.*

Seth Cannon—As a three- and four-year-old, one of Seth's favorite TV shows had a group of 10- to 12-year-old children doing experiments, playing games, telling jokes, and preparing recipes. His other favorites were *Mr. Rogers*—especially the videos of how things are made—a PBS reading program, and *Whose Line Is it Anyway?*, a comedy show for adults.

Author note: A hallmark of Level Four giftedness is interest in videos and television programs designed for older children or adults. When these children start school, they find it difficult to sustain interest in the activities and curriculum that is designed for most of the children their age. Unevenness of development—a difference between intellectual and emotional development—is quite normal in the highly intelligent, too, so age-appropriate behaviors and interests are not uncommon for these children as well.

At Seth's third birthday party, he decided to count the people sitting at the table. There were seven. He started to count 1, 2, 3, 4, and then he was number 5. He wanted to be number three since it was his third birthday. He started over, but started with the same person. Again, he wasn't number three. I began to explain that he needed to start with a different person, two people away from himself, but he cut me off. He started counting with the same person as before, but this time, he counted 1, 2, 4, 5, 3, 6, 7!

Seth could do some simple addition and subtraction. By 3½ years, he had taught himself to count to 100 and beyond. He also counted by 10s but tended to lose track of where he was in his counting. He liked to make jokes that were plays on words. He recognized written words by then, too. He was only marginally interested in puzzles, but we went through periods when he couldn't do enough mazes.

Phil Burns—By three years old, Phil could count indefinitely and had a thorough grasp of numbers. Before he turned four, he understood and could use negative numbers and could do multi-digit mental addition and subtraction. We bought Phil an adult puzzle-solving game as a reward for giving up his pacifier around his fourth birthday. It was an interesting contrast—a difficult adult game exchanged for a pacifier. He was already quite adept with keyboarding skills by this time.

Bill Arnesen—Bill had a very long attention span and was meticulous about whatever he was doing. He started to write letters and numbers when he was about three years old and worked very long and hard on the task each time. He didn't need to look at examples to do this, and no one told him to do it; it was totally initiated by him. At 3¾ years old, he could write quite a few letters, numbers, and words. He read easy reader books by the time he was four.

Age Four to Five Years

Up to a year before they start kindergarten, Level Four children already do many of the activities that are in the second- and third-grade curriculum in most school systems. Said another way, between the ages of four and five, Level Four children can perform many academic and intellectual functions of children who are already eight years old. Watch for conceptual understanding and self-generation of problems and their solutions as opposed to simply learning how to perform academic tasks. Also notice the speed with which Level Four children move from the introduction of an idea to near mastery.

Patricia Walker—Just before her fourth birthday, Patty read her first beginner book by herself, though very slowly. She read simple books by sounding out each word. She was frustrated, though, because she wanted to go faster, and the books she *could* read didn't have as much story as she liked. She could do slightly difficult computations, often using her fingers to figure them out. She solved problems like, "If we had 10 teddy bears but five went away, how many would still be at our picnic?" She could count to 50 by 10s. She also remembered what people gave her for presents 10 to 12 months later.

Nathan Webster—At four, Nathan expressed interest in powers of two, and he doubled numbers in his head up to 2,048. He was adept at using the keyboard before he was five.

Author note: Using the keyboard means that the child also knows how to spell some words.

Rose Engum—Rose pointed out words in books and the newspaper by the time she was four. She also read and reread the *Magic School Bus* books. One day, imitating one of the characters, she got a notebook, a calculator, and a pencil. She punched numbers into the calculator and then copied them into her notebook. She continued this for days, filling up pages of this notebook, calling it her "research." She started to read beginner books between 4½ and five. She simply taught herself to read. We gave her beginning readers, and she learned from them. She sight read and read from context. She didn't like or want any help with phonetic rules, and she got annoyed if we told her a word that she hadn't asked about. Once she got started, she quickly progressed to more and more difficult books, and by kindergarten, she was reading chapter books. When we went to the library, Rose checked out stacks of books and read them all. She brought books with her everywhere we went.

By the time she was four, Rose no longer needed any help using the computer. She wasn't much interested in numerical concepts, but she showed strong numerical skills. She was very interested in inductive and logic skills and especially enjoyed extracting "rules" about how things in our world interact, as when she said, "The reason there are schools is because kids need to be somewhere safe while moms and dads are doing important work and making money to take care of the family, and the *kids* are learning how to do important work, too, but their bodies have to get bigger before they can drive cars to go to work."

Rebecca Resnick—When she was four, Rebecca's babysitter played school with her and gave her addition and subtraction worksheets. Rebecca filled them out correctly. Her teacher said that she always had more complex and interesting ideas for play than the other kids. When she got frustrated that "they didn't get it," she went to the bookrack and read. She was really into jokes and told one joke after another to my mother on the phone. She also loved colored beads and made perfect geometric patterns with them.

Tyler Lundquist—When Tyler was about four, he and I entered a building where the entry area was being redone. Tyler saw the big yellow caution signs and asked me what they meant. I told him it was to be careful—workers had ripped up the carpet and didn't want anyone to trip. Weeks later, Tyler saw caution signs somewhere else. He looked around, confused, and asked, "Where is the carpet ripped up?"

> *Author note: Tyler's observation about the caution sign is a good example of how young Level Four children can remember details and transfer learned information to new situations.*

Keith Sands—Keith read regular chapter books by the time he was 4½ years old. He played with a calculator and completed advanced math-like games on the computer, but he wasn't really motivated to do mathematics until he started school.

Adam Schaefer—Beginning when he was about 3½ years old, we taught Adam the sounds that letters make. He occasionally used the *Blue's Clues ABC's*™ computer program, and then suddenly, during his last year of preschool, he could sight read. He never went through a period of sounding out words. When he was 4½, he could read the directions in activity books and kept himself busy reading for long car rides. He read atlases and beginner books by himself before he turned five.

Kyle Amundson—Kyle loved puzzles at around age four and would rather stay inside to do his 30-piece puzzles than go outside to play with other kids. He got interested in mazes, and it was hard to find enough complex mazes that were not too expensive.

Samantha Forrest—Samantha started to use the computer at age four and easily mastered the preschool programs, so she moved on to more advanced programs. She enjoyed music, especially classical, and liked to describe what might be happening during a piece, such as, "the storm is coming, the girl is walking through the field, she's chasing butterflies now…." Her father gave her a few beginning piano lessons, and she also had many children's instruments that she played at home. Her memory for music was very good.

Kayla Bardy—By 4½, Kayla could do very simple subtraction and 100-piece puzzles. She liked mazes but had trouble staying in the lines at first. She started to read chapter books when she was 4¾.

Daniel Schmidt—Daniel knew how to read at 4½ years old. I have no idea how. He looked at the sticker on the window of his grandfather's car and asked, "Why does it say 'Warning Radio Alarm'?" That's when I knew he could read. The numbers on the speed limit signs always excited him. He could count to at least 100. He also was completely adept with computer, keyboard, and mouse, and he never needed our help with any of it.

Seth Cannon—At an early age, probably four, Seth could count by 2s, 3s, 5s, and 10s. He counted by 3s to 100 really fast. When we worked on math, he learned the concepts pretty easily, but he wasn't a fan of workbook and worksheet learning. He read quite well but still got frustrated because he wanted to read absolutely fluently and couldn't. It's interesting that he did better with more difficult words.

Phil Burns—At four, Phil played computer games designed for six- to 10-year-olds. He was very good at 100-piece puzzles. He did simple, single-digit multiplication in his head.

Bill Arnesen—By the time Bill was four, he played lots of complex, advanced video games designed for kids 12 and older. He was constantly befuddling adult audiences with his extensive talking about video game story lines. He mentioned every character, detail, and action. He didn't seem to realize that these games were totally unfamiliar to most of us.

When he was 4¾ years old, Bill's older brothers and I were watching *Wheel of Fortune*, and the clue was "Place." The letters to that point were: _ _ T E L L _ _ _ _ We were all working on it, but Bill blurted out the answer, "Hotel Lobby," before any of us came up with it. He read well and with good expression before he was five.

Age Five to Six Years

Children in the United States usually start kindergarten after they turn five years old. Despite their incredibly high abilities, most Level Four children are not offered any instruction beyond what their average classmates receive unless their parents actively intervene.

Patricia Walker—Patty loved kindergarten. She didn't seem that interested in reading, but whenever she did read to us, we were amazed at how much she had improved in just days—seemingly with no practice or effort. She read at about the 2½-grade level, according to her teacher. However, she preferred that we read to her—maybe because she was frustrated with her own slow speed. She resisted reading early readers; the stories were too simplistic and boring to her. She preferred the *Junie B. Jones*[2] series, the *Jigsaw Jones*[3] mysteries, and the *American Girl* books.

Nathan Webster—Nathan didn't really want to read beginner books but instead wanted them read to him. He then simply started reading chapter books himself when he was between five and six years old. He went from reading *Bob* books to chapter books within one month. He also liked fact books, such as those about animals. He rarely read aloud. At age five, he was doing all of the math concepts in *Operation Neptune*™[4] for fun, including percentages, multiplication, and division in story problem form. He stopped needing parental help with the computer before he was six years old.

Rose Engum—Rose read and enjoyed chapter books by the time she was 5½. She always had excellent comprehension and retention and read very quickly. In kindergarten, she brought home an *American Girl* series book and read it before supper. I quizzed her on it, because I was surprised at how quickly she read it, but she had indeed read and comprehended the entire book. Once, while in the car, she asked what time we would be home. I told her 6:00. A few minutes later, she correctly said, "That's 18 minutes."

Rebecca Resnick—At five, Rebecca read one of my parenting books that pictured a mother and a child in a cartoon. She said, "That mom wasn't talking to the child correctly. She should have said…," and then proceeded to tell me what the book said was the proper response to a kid jumping into a puddle with no boots on. So she was not only able to read, but she could apply reasoning and point out a parallel example.

Rebecca got books for her birthday that were way beyond what a normal child her age would be interested in reading, and she'd finish reading them all in one day. We could see her eyes moving very fast across the page when she was absorbed in a book. Her first-grade teacher tested her reading speed at more than 210 words per minute with excellent comprehension. She was like a sponge. It was a real challenge to find reading materials that were at her reading level but that also fit her emotional level. Many of the books that she could read contained inappropriate subject matter for her age.

> *Author note: Finding appropriate reading material for young, advanced readers is a common problem for parents. Some of My Best Friends Are Books by Judith Halsted (2002) is an excellent resource. And parents can ask librarians for help.*

Tyler Lundquist—Tyler started to read beginner books when he was in kindergarten. Before he started kindergarten, he asked, "How much is six fives?" We asked him if he knew, and he *immediately* said 30. We asked how he figured it out, and he said that six 10s is 60 and five is half of 10, so it must be 30.

Keith Sands—By the time he was five years old, Keith was already so adept on the computer and at reading that we began allowing him to use the Internet unassisted. Once he started kindergarten at age 5½, he read to other children in his classroom. Around that time, he became obsessed with dinosaurs and read everything he could about them. Before he turned six, he began to learn how to read in Czech, his mother's native language.

Kayla Bardy—At five, Kayla liked to read three to five easy reader books a day, but she still enjoyed being read to at night. When I was tired, she'd read to me instead. She read *Charlotte's Web* to herself over a span of five days, but she mostly preferred shorter books. She liked numbers, counting, and math problems. At 5¼, she added and subtracted numbers up to about 15, multiplied some simple one-digit problems, and divided by two or three. She understood basic fractions and counted to 1,000 with occasional lapses (for example, she'd say that the number after 320 was 330).

Seth Cannon—Just after he turned five, Seth asked me: "How did the world begin?" Before I had a chance to reply, he continued, "Because as far as I can tell, there is no beginning and no end." I said, "Well, the Bible says God created the world and everything in it...."

He cut me off, "I know, I know...but the people who wrote the Bible don't know very much about science."

"That's right," I replied." So some scientists think there was a big explosion, called the Big Bang, and the earth formed as a result of the explosion."

"Mom, *how* could the earth start from an explosion?"

"Well, I don't know that much about it myself. Maybe we should get a book...."

"Hey, maybe God created the explosion."

"Maybe." The irony of this conversation is that it all happened in a bathroom down the hall from my office. I accompanied Seth because, well, he was five and still preferred to get help.

Author note: At five, Seth provides a wonderful example of how existential questions can occur to very young Level Four children. Notice the distinction between issues of religion and issues of existence. Seth's theorizing is representative of children at intellectual levels Four and Five. These conversations take place a year or more earlier than for children whose intellectual levels are Two or Three. They also take place about a half year to a year later than they will for children in Level Five. Children whose IQ scores are in the average range of about 100 sometimes show interest in topics such as these by the time they are about 12 years old.

At age 5½, Seth asked, "Mom, is there such a thing as a fourth dimension?" (I didn't know he had any concept of the first three dimensions.)

"I think so. I'm not sure what it is. Let's ask your dad. You already know about the first three?"

"Sort of." His father and he had reviewed the first three dimensions (points, lines, volumes) and discussed the possibility that time is the fourth dimension. The conversation then moved to the possibility of other dimensions, physics, and string theory.

Once, we were at a public restroom in an older restaurant, using the handicapped stall because it was easier for us both to be inside, when Seth noted, "I don't think this stall is really wide enough to be a handicapped stall. Angie probably wouldn't fit in here." Angie is one of my university students whom Seth met who is in a big electric chair. This led to a very interesting series of conversations about the Disability Act and the codes that enforce it, as well as a fairly graphic discussion of the car accident that caused Angie's paralysis. I told Angie about Seth's observation that the bathroom stall was too narrow; she was amazed and said that most adults don't recognize that reality.

Seth was able to sound things out before he was four, but by five, he still wasn't reading very fluently, so he wouldn't tackle books with more than one or two lines on each page. However, he read pretty much any length word, and he particularly liked to read signs, as in "Please leave door open when you leave." In kindergarten, though, Seth's reading took off in leaps and bounds. During this time, Seth drew a picture and explained that it was actually a symbol for something else. He seemed to have quite a sense of the concept of symbols. When Seth was 5½, we bought eight donuts. I asked him how many he, his father, and I each could have. Almost immediately, he answered, "2 and 2/3."

Phil Burns—Shortly before he turned six, Phil built a museum in our family room with detailed, labeled exhibits and a sign announcing the museum's hours and entrance fee. He offered free entrance but charged 25 cents to let someone *out* of the room. The museum included a rock collection, homemade perfume made of pine needles, a butterfly exhibit with freshly caught butterflies and information about them, and myriad constructions and contraptions built out of blocks, LEGOs®, etc. The museum also included a paper exhibit with a suit of clothing, flowers, and a 20-foot-long miniature golf course with hills, obstacles, holes, and dead-ends—all made entirely from 8.5 x 11 inch paper folded, crumpled, and taped together.

Still five, Phil read books labeled "Grades 2 to 4," including Judy Donelly's adventure book series *True Life Treasure Hunts*. He moved on to learning about rocks—he knew the names and properties of 50 or so rocks in his collection—and insects, weather, atoms, and the periodic table of elements. He was particularly fond of gears, mechanics, electricity, and magnetism. One time at a science museum, he refused to leave the electricity room until he had figured out every do-it-yourself circuit, and then he wanted to go home and build more himself. He got a science construction set (ages 7+) for Christmas and, with his father, loved to combine various gear capsules and batteries to make working fans, cars that moved forward and backward, and robots.

Phil was fascinated by the computer and by educational computer games (we did not allow arcade-type games). He particularly enjoyed problem-solving games, such as *The Incredible Machine* (an adult-level game in which you solve puzzles by finding Rube Goldberg-type contraptions using gears, belts, ramps, etc.). He enjoyed strategy board games such as *Monopoly*® (the adult version—and he needed no help counting out money, making change, or devising a winning strategy). He also liked paper and pencil puzzles, mazes, and 100- to 300-piece jigsaw puzzles. When he especially liked a game or puzzle, he'd design one of his own for us to solve.

Phil's vocabulary was huge, and he enjoyed playing with words. He was fond of creating stories using as many words as possible that rhyme with a given word. Sometimes he would answer a question with a word puzzle, such as, "The answer has five words and the first word has three letters and begins with a 'T.'" He loved playing *Twenty Questions* and word games such as *Boggle*® or a cooperative version of *Scrabble*™. He had a *Macmillan Children's Dictionary* and looked up definitions and spelling on his own. He wanted to understand the reasons why words are spelled the way they are, and he made a "word book" for his sibling's elucidation.

Foreign languages fascinated Phil, and he constantly asked us the French or German word for something. His favorite placemat depicted the contents of a house and the French and English words for each item. Similarly, he loved secret codes and cipher, sign language, and pig Latin, and he wrote us many messages which we then had to decode while he waited eagerly nearby. Other interests included maps of all kinds and U.S. geography. Phil identified most of the U.S. states by shape alone and could quickly put them together in a puzzle. We wrote letters to tourism offices of a few of his "favorite" states, and he happily pored over the materials they sent us.

Phil also loved numbers and math. He counted to the 100s by age three and was comfortable with the 1,000s by age five. His favorite number was the googolplex. He added and subtracted numbers up to 20 on his fingers, up to 99 with no carrying using pencil and paper, and understood the concepts of multiplication and division. He worked at second-grade level in the computer game *Number Maze®*. We made number concepts a natural part of our lives, introducing measurement, exponents, or division whenever they were relevant to what else we were doing. We discouraged him from rote memorization.

Bill Arnesen—Bill read simple books by the time he was four, and he preferred fiction and humor, especially Jim Davis's *Garfield* and Bill Watterson's *Calvin and Hobbs*. At five to six years old, he sat, read, and chuckled for hours. His reading level was about third to fourth grade by 5¾ years old. At five, he said, "You're trying to steal my warmness," when I touched him with cold hands. He had no difficulty with games that required numbers and number concepts. His math achievement was at an upper second-grade level by kindergarten, and that was with Montessori continuous progress in workbooks—not direct instruction. When Bill turned five, he visited a prospective school for a half day. As we left, he asked, "Do you think they were impressed?"

Age Six to Seven Years

Level Four children's interests and abilities become increasingly sophisticated and complex as they mature. Much of what they do and read at their ability level is done on their own time, usually at home.

Nathan Webster—Nathan read *Harry Potter Book IV* (600 pages) in a few days with excellent understanding and retention when he was six years old.

Rebecca Resnick—Shortly after Rebecca turned six, she pointed to an animatronics magician and said, "Look, that's a prestidigitator!" Another time, in a restaurant, she saw a fish tank that was made from a series of tubes. She exclaimed, "That's an architectural feat, not f-e-e-t."

Tyler Lundquist—When Tyler was almost six, we had the following conversation.

Tyler: Two times two is four.

Dad: That's right. Do you know what three times three is?

Tyler (almost immediately): It's nine.

Dad: How about four times four?

Tyler (again almost immediately): Sixteen.

Dad: Five times five?

Tyler: Twenty-five. (I wasn't too surprised he could go this far, although his first-grade class was just starting to add single-digit numbers.)

Dad: Six times six?

Tyler (not quite as fast): Thirty-six. (This impressed me, but I thought the next one would probably be too hard.)

Dad: Seven times seven?

Tyler (after some thought): Forty-nine.

Dad: How did you get 49?

Tyler: Well, six 6s is 36, so seven 6s is 42 (adding six), and then seven 7s is 49 (adding seven).

This clearly signaled to me that Tyler operated at a different level, at least where math was concerned. Getting from six 6s to seven 6s isn't a big step, but going from seven 6s to seven 7s is a different level of processing. I expect if he tried his explanation on one of his elementary teachers, they wouldn't have understood how it applied to the problem at hand.

Keith Sands—Around first grade, Keith was fascinated with the dictionary and thesaurus. By age six, he was changing computer programs and downloading files independently.

Adam Schaefer—During kindergarten, Adam started reading chapter books like *Nate the Great*[5] and the *Magic School Bus* series, both for children four to eight years old.

Kyle Amundson—Kyle was reading at sixth-grade fluency by about age seven.

Samantha Forrest—Samantha read very fast at about third- to fourth-grade level and improved daily. When the material was interesting to her, we couldn't get her to put the book down. She did very well in all of her subjects except math and penmanship. Her penmanship was age appropriate, although it improved greatly with her vision therapy.[6] Although she was uninterested in math since the school instruction moved at such a slow pace, she enjoyed figuring out interesting things like square roots.

Phil Burns—At 6½ years old, Phil's math knowledge was about third-grade level, with some gaps, and his abstract reasoning abilities in math were at an adult level.

Age Seven to Nine Years

Most Level Four children read copiously any chance they get, and their store of information and exposure to other people's viewpoints and experiences continues to mount. As they get older, background information that they have gained, largely on their own, greatly enhances their own writing, speaking, general knowledge, and recall of information.

Emily Newton—In second and third grade, Emily always had several books tucked away in her school desk, and she pulled them out whenever she could. We encouraged her to engage in other activities, go outside, or play with her brother, but she always preferred to read. She liked topics aimed at her age but read the books extremely fast because they were too easy for her. She enjoyed some books intended for junior and senior high school students, like books that summarized Shakespeare plays or Greek myths, but the story had to grab her. When almost eight, she read one to two books a day all summer. I would almost describe her as addicted—she picked up anything.

Rose Engum—By the time Rose was seven and still in first grade, her reading included a lot of nonfiction. Sometimes a subject was of particular interest, and she read everything she could find on it. Once, she became quite an expert on wolves. Another passion that year was ancient Egypt. She read book after book on pyramids, pharaohs, etc. Some other areas of interest were Norway, horses, and lots of American history. She also started to use the Internet, and although we didn't let her use it totally unsupervised, she was proficient at searching for and finding information.

Rebecca Resnick—In second grade, Rebecca was published in the *Minneapolis Star Tribune's* "Mindworks" column. Children were asked to select the top three priorities for government spending if they could advise the President. She was chosen again when the question was "What are you afraid of?" She actually wrote what she considered to be a humorous answer: "I'm really not afraid of anything besides monsters, haunted houses, horror movies, my head being chopped off, getting left home alone, and Mom dying." I talked to her about it because I was concerned if she was truly worried about me dying. She said that I didn't have to worry about her fears because she wrote it as a joke, not as the truth. Several months later, an issue of *Life* magazine re-published Rebecca's "What I'm Afraid Of" answer.

Author note: Level Four children can have many adult ideas and abilities, and their fears can become quite complex. Like all young children, their intellectual maturity does not make them less vulnerable to fears; they still need supervision, emotional support, and guidance.

Tyler Lundquist—When he was a second grader, Tyler read chapter books, including all of the Roald Dahl books. He read the *Goosebumps* series as a third grader. It wasn't until third grade that the school tested him to see if he should be in the gifted program.

Adam Schaefer—In first grade, Adam read *Silverwing* by Kenneth Oppel, a long fantasy chapter book about bats for children ages nine to 12. He also liked to read about how the human body works. However, he still enjoyed being read to. He started borrowing in three-digit subtraction problems and said that word problems were harder, but he actually seemed to do them more easily. He knew some multiplication and division of single-digit and two-digit numbers, and he discovered by himself that 3x4 is the same as 4x3. He had worked a lot with shapes in preschool and seemed to have an easy time with geometry. He started 500-piece puzzles of favorite places. He badly wanted an old car from the junkyard with a working battery because he was pretty sure that he could build an airplane with it. The woman who administered the WISC-III test remarked that he had better comprehension and retention about a passage after he had thought about it a while rather than directly after hearing it.

Author note: The Wechsler tests such as the WISC-III award points for speed. Some Level Four children enjoy the challenge of speeded activities and tests;

others do not. Responding well to time pressure is more related to personality and temperament than it is to high intelligence.

Daniel Schmidt—Daniel always loved to read a lot, but he was bored with grade-level material. His favorite book on his second-grade bio sheet was *Tom Watson's Strategic Golf.* He loved *Highlights, Kids' Discover,* and *3-2-1 Contact* magazines. He was really taken by the conceptual side of mathematics and always found plain computation uninteresting. In the elementary grades, he had trouble with math facts and often wouldn't finish worksheets, all the while scoring in the 99th percentile on standardized tests.

Author note: Balking at rote memorization is a real problem for schools, parents, and teachers to resolve. My recommendation has always been to forget the drills, move the gifted child higher in math, and let him learn from experience that knowing the math facts will be useful. When Level Four children find something interesting and useful, they memorize what they need to know very quickly.

When Dan was in second grade, he received a *QBasic®* programming book, which he read and then started to program. He later taught himself *Visual Basic®* and *C®*, and he programmed lots of utilities for his graphing calculator. He liked some computer games, too.

Victor Schultz—When Victor was in third grade (age eight), one of his classmates innocently asked the teacher how the age of a fossil is known. Victor eagerly raised his hand and gave a small lecture on carbon dating of fossils.

Age Nine and Older

Rose Engum—At nine, Rose read almost every free moment, fiction and nonfiction. She learned, retained, and applied what she learned. Occasionally, we quizzed her on something, such as an article from the *Wall Street Journal*, and she always showed great comprehension and recall. She was like a walking encyclopedia in the way she conversed on topics, recalling facts and information that she'd read somewhere along the way. In fourth grade, she took the S.T.A.R. computer adaptive reading test and scored a 13+ grade equivalent, comparable to reading beyond a typical high school graduate.

> *Author note: Rose advanced with her own intellectual ability through reading and doing things on her own and with her family, not with direct instruction or classes. Her family finally decided to home school Rose for fifth grade so that she would receive instruction at her own ability level. One has to wonder how much more someone like Rose could have learned if she had been instructed at her own level all along.*

Rose qualified for the Scholarship Awards Ceremony for the Midwest Talent Search for Young Students (MTSY) sponsored by Northwestern University. She took the *Explore Test* as a fifth grader and placed in the 99.6th percentile among fifth graders. Only eight MTSY fifth graders, out of 2,085 who took the exam, earned a higher score. She also scored in the 99th percentile with respect to the general population of eighth graders who took the exam. She qualified for the Talented Youth Math Program at the university (UMTYMP)[7] a year earlier than most participants and started weekly classes of algebra and geometry during sixth grade.

Rebecca Resnick—Rebecca always got 100% on her spelling pre-tests, so she got to choose her own words to study each week. When she was 11½, the words she selected were "abstractionist," "banquette," "desideratum," and "entrepreneur." She went to Math Masters competitions, and her group won first place both years. She placed eighth overall in individual competition in sixth grade from around the entire metropolitan area. Despite all this, by ninth grade, she was still in enriched math only one year ahead of her classmates.

Tyler Lundquist—In sixth grade, Tyler started the university's Talented Youth Math Program (UMTYMP), in which the first year is a High School Algebra I and II sequence. Of the 947 applicants who were all in the top 5% of their classes from around the area, Tyler was one of only 127 admitted. Seventeen students scored higher than he did, and 16 more were tied with him. His *Stanford Achievement* scores in sixth grade were 99th percentile for both national and local norms.

Tyler read the *Redwall* series in fifth and sixth grades. At 13, his leisure reading included Tom Clancy, Michael Crichton, and books suggested by teachers, such as Harper Lee's *To Kill a Mockingbird* and Joseph Heller's *Catch 22*. He really enjoyed the *Chicken Soup for the Teenage Soul* books. In ninth and tenth grades, he received the top score at his school in the national AIME test (American Invitational Mathematics

Examination), and he was second in eleventh grade. He was a varsity member of the math team for three years. In his junior year at age 17, he was nominated for National Honor Society, and he applied for and was accepted into Mentor Connection for his senior year. He was sixth in the state in his category in Speech. After spending less than an hour on a practice exam as his total preparation effort for the SAT, he scored 1570 out of a possible 1600.

In his senior year, Tyler was on the state team for the national American Regional Math League competition in Iowa City. He was second in the state in his category discussion. In college, he got into a program called Great Conversation, studying the classics with faculty and other students for part of each of his first four semesters—a perfect fit for him.

Author note: Although Tyler was in gifted programs in his school system, his parents and teachers constantly doubted that he really was gifted because he was not always a cooperative student. He was so far ahead of his classmates that he would refuse to comply with certain expectations at school. Nonetheless, when he chose to perform, he still had many impressive achievements which could only be attainable by a highly intelligent child.

Kyle Amundson—During middle school, Kyle focused on "fluff" books like *Pokemon*, *Garfield*, and *Star Wars* (easy version), but he also read *Scientific American*, *Newsweek*, and *Money* magazine. In general, he still read voraciously.

Daniel Schmidt—When he was in fifth grade, Daniel read *A Brief History of Time* by Stephen Hawking, *Chaos: Making a New Science* by James Gleick, and *Gödel, Escher, and Bach: An Eternal Braid* by Douglas Hofstadter. At 14, he enjoyed reading *Scientific American*, *MIT Technology Review*, *Time*, and *Newsweek*.

Phil Burns—When he was 10 years old, Phil started Beginning Algebra through EPGY online.[8] He attended a two-week summer school class where he designed and built his own website.

Bill Arnesen—As an eighth grader, Bill played the lead in his middle school's production of *Joseph and the Technicolor Dreamcoat* and did a great job. When he was 12, he was recommended by his school's drama teacher to perform as Sam in an inaugural presentation of Dr. Suess' *Green Eggs and Ham* with the Minnesota Orchestra and several professional singers at Orchestra Hall.

Author note: High intelligence can be expressed in activities other than the traditional academic subjects like math and science. Great artists, poets, and filmmakers are often as highly intelligent as physicists or mathematicians. Being highly intelligent makes it easier to memorize lines. Many Level Four gifted children find great enjoyment in performing in the arts and in competitions such as debate, math, science, and trivia contests. Highly intelligent children often find others like themselves through such pastimes.

Summary of Level Four Gifted

All of the Level Four gifted children in this chapter likely knew their colors, shapes, letters, and more well before Level Two and Level Three children did, but it is difficult to determine how much sooner because most children cannot physically speak much before they are one year old. Level Four children clearly outpace lower levels of giftedness in their powers of reasoning, the complexity of their speech and interests, and in their grasp of math concepts. The learning trajectories for these children, particularly in reading, raised them from an average third-grade level as kindergartners to an average upper high school level by fourth and fifth grades.

The following developmental features characterize Level Four children.

- Most were alert at birth or soon thereafter.
- Almost all paid attention within months of birth while someone to read to them.
- Books were a favorite interest before three or four months.
- Almost all understood parental directives by six months.
- The majority independently looked at and turned pages of books before eight months.
- Most knew and said some words by 5½ to nine months.
- Many said two-word phrases by 12 to 15 months.
- Many had large vocabularies, receptive and expressive, by 14 months.
- Most had favorite TV shows or videos between nine and 18 months.
- A number played with shape sorters by 11 to 15 months.
- Many recognized and picked out specific numbers and letters by 12 to 15 months.
- Many could rote count to 10, and some could count higher, by 13 to 20 months.

- Most knew many colors by 15 to 18 months.
- Many liked 35+ piece puzzles by 15 to 36 months.
- Many read numerous sight words between 15 and 20 months.
- Almost all knew the entire alphabet by 15 to 22 months.
- Most were speaking in complex sentences of more than four words by 15 to 24 months.
- Many knew and named shapes before age two.
- Most knew and sang songs before age two.
- Many memorized the books that were read to them before they were two years old.
- Most read names on signs and stores between 20 months and 3¾ years.
- Many showed interest in letter sounds and sounding out short words by age 2½.
- Many used language to make jokes by age 2½, and some showed humor earlier.
- Most printed letters, numbers, words, and their names between 2¾ and 3½.
- Most knew many sight words by age three to 3½.
- Half read simple books by age three to 3½.
- Most read easy readers by age 3½ to 4½ years.
- Many had high interest in factual information, how things work, and science by age three to four.
- Most grasp skip counting, counting backwards, addition, subtraction, and concepts of "more and less" by age three to four.
- Many questioned the reality of Santa Claus or the Tooth Fairy by age three to five years.
- Most were independent on a computer by age three to 4½ years, and most were keyboarding by five.
- Most read children's-level chapter books by 4¼ to 5½ years.
- Many understood some multiplication, division, and fractions by five.
- Most read for pleasure and information by five.
- Almost all played adult-level card and board games by the time they were five to 5½.
- Almost all read two to five years beyond grade level by age six.
- Almost all read youth and adult chapter books independently by age six to 6½.

Most Level Four children are capable of finishing all academic coursework through eighth grade before they reach third or fourth grade, but few have the opportunity to live up to their capabilities. When we hear about the amazing children who go to college at ages 10, 11, or 12, we think they are one in a million. Any of the children described in this chapter could have done the same thing. They all could have finished the elementary curriculum in two years or less, and they could have moved on to interesting and enriching coursework after that.

However, most parents want to maintain as normal a childhood for their children as possible and so reject radical solutions. Though it requires instructional and structural flexibility, there are ways to address the needs of these children without removing them entirely from their normal rites of passage. Parents may need to advocate for modifications such as acceleration or partial home schooling. Leaving these children completely at grade level is one of the least effective solutions—not helpful for the children and ultimately cumbersome for educators. Doing nothing at all, which is what most often happens, is an unconscionable waste of natural ability.

Table 4: Level Four Children's Data

Name	SBLM Ratio IQ	Test Age Years-Mos.	Other IQ Tests	Achievement Test Grade Equivalencies/ Percentiles
Patricia Walker	180	4-0	-	Wechsler Individual Achievement Test (WIAT) at age 6 yrs. 9 mos.: Reading Comprehension 5-2, Math Reasoning 3-9, Calculation 1-9, Oral Expression 11-9 grade equivalencies
Nathan Webster	185	7-3	-	-
Blake Hauge	181	8-7	WISC-III 143	WJ-R: Reading 99th, Math 97th, Developmental Skills 97th
Jerrod Engquist	220	-	-	-
Emily Newton	183	7-3	WISC-III 145	WJ-R: Reading 143, Math 130

Name	SBLM Ratio IQ	Test Age Years-Mos.	Other IQ Tests	Achievement Test Grade Equivalencies/ Percentiles
Rose Engum	180	9-5	-	4th grade WJ-Achievement Composite grade 10-9, and 7 of 14 subtests at 12th grade level; S.T.A.R. Computer Adaptive Reading Test in 4th grade: 13+ grade equivalency; Explore Test in 5th grade: 99th percentile in 8th grade norm group; Iowa Basics in 3rd grade: Reading 7-6, Math 8-6; 4th grade WJ-III Achievement Writing Samples and Story Recall >18-0 GE; at age 12: SAT V-670, SAT M-540, ACT English 27, Math 23, Reading 33, Science 23, Composite 27
Rebecca Resnick	178	10-6	-	ACT 35; SAT I end of 11th grade: Verbal 710, Math 410, Writing 760; SAT II beginning of 12th grade: Writing 760, Math IC 680, Math IIC 640
Tyler Lundquist	N/A	-	SB5 146; Otis-Lennon 132-140	11th grade: SAT Math 800, Verbal 770; ACT 34; American Invitational Mathematics Exam 138 (8th in the state); American Regional Math League Team: 7th of 90 nationally
Keith Sands	180	8-11	CogAT: Comp. 149, Verbal 150, Quantitative 131, Nonverbal 144	Iowa Basics: Reading 97th, Language 99th, Math 94th, Composite 99th national percentiles
Adam Schaefer	193	7-5	WISC-III 142	Wechsler Individual Achievement Test (WIAT): Reading 153, Math 134; WJ-R: Reading 135, Writing 138, Math 137

Name	SBLM Ratio IQ	Test Age Years-Mos.	Other IQ Tests	Achievement Test Grade Equivalencies/ Percentiles
Kyle Amundson	195	10-9	CogAT 148	Explore Test in 5th grade: 99th percentile for 8th grade norms; at age 11½: SAT Verbal 650, Math 540
Samantha Forrest	199	5-7	WPPSI-R 154; SB5 Abbreviated Battery 148; Otis-Lennon 140: Verbal 146, Nonverbal 123	Stanford Achievement Test in 3rd grade: Reading Comprehension 86th, Total Math 95th, Math Problem Solving 94th, Math Procedures 89th, Language 99th national percentiles
Kayla Bardy	205	6-2	-	-

Chapter 8

Level Five Gifted: Above the 99th Percentile

For some time now—and she's only six—Carol has been driven to investigate big philosophical questions of meaning. She devours books on the origins of the universe, the beginning of life, evolution, human history and progress, and religion. She is trying to answer the universal "Who am I?" "Why am I here?" and "Who is God?" questions not typically addressed until late adolescence or adulthood.

~ Mother of a Level Five girl

Level Five includes those children with an IQ range that has been previously referred to in the gifted literature as profoundly gifted. Level Five children fit the description, coined by David Feldman (1986), of omnibus genius—unusual occurrence of profound ability across all ability areas. These children exhibit an even intellectual profile along with behaviors that enhance their potential to learn at the highest levels. The term "profoundly gifted" has lost some of its impact because it has been overused to describe a broader range of intellect than the truly exceptional children in this chapter.

Level Five children have *Stanford-Binet (Form L-M)* IQs that range from 195 to 230—extremely rare results. When tested on modern standardized individual IQ tests, these children receive scores in the mid to upper 140s because today's tests now compress the highest scores to force them into a standard bell curve. While this score compression makes percentile comparisons across different tests reliable, it understates how very different children at Level Five are, because their scores often appear quite similar to Level Four children. The accompanying Table 5 provides both ratio IQ and standard scores.

Several children in the previous chapter had *SBLM* scores that were as high as the children in this chapter. However, they were designated Level Four either because they didn't manifest abilities across all of the

163

domains or because they seemed to lack the strong inner drive for their own continued learning, both of which are criteria for inclusion in Level Five. If the environment is non-supportive, children may not exhibit such an inner drive until the environment improves, for example when a child is finally allowed to take advanced courses with intellectual peers, or when the assignments finally seem relevant and important, or when the instructors value their insights. Thus, placement within a specific level can change over time for some people, up or down, depending on the individual's current environment—both internal and external.

How many Level Five children are there in our schools? I estimate that at least four in a million—possibly as many as 10 in a million—Level Five children are born every year. Anyone who is a high intelligence specialist has no doubt discovered and worked with at least one or two children very much like those whose abilities appear here. An important point should be apparent: the children in Level Five are *not* a one-in-a-million occurrence. If that were so, the sample size presented in this book would be substantially smaller.

If there are those in the world who are more intelligent than these individuals, we do not know who or where they are. What we see here is likely the upper end of human intellectual capability. For persons at this level of intelligence, the added factors of personality, opportunity, interests, motivation, and other environmental enhancements make the difference between those who are simply highly intelligent and those who become the true geniuses—those who will become eminent.[1]

Of course, not all Level Five children ever come to the attention of those who could help them live up to their potential.[2] Some languish within the regular school system and never know how truly unique they are as they endeavor to lead normal lives and fit in with people their own age. Their thinking processes as adults continue to be exceptional, but there is no assurance that their adult-level *achievement* will be exceptional; the reasons are complex and are explored later in this book.

Although in earlier chapters I have estimated the number of children that one could expect in suburban, urban, and rural schools for Levels One through Four, a similar estimate is not possible for Level Five. The incidence of Level Five individuals in any particular geographic area is less common than with previous levels. For example, in order to find a small representative sample of these children, I had to include both a broader age span and a broader geographical range.

There are seven children in this sample; five have siblings who are intellectually gifted in Levels Two through Four. Although the siblings share the same set of parents and their environment is quite similar,[3] this does not predict or guarantee that another Level Five child would ever appear in the family. The ages and levels of education of the parents vary considerably, but all the parents are gifted at Level Two or higher.

This population is quite rare and spread out by age, location, and time. Not one of these Level Five children has ever had someone else in their classroom as intellectually able as they. When the older youngsters were asked if they knew anyone who seemed as smart as they are, they uniformly said that they didn't think so. However, all have taken comfort in the knowledge that there are others like them somewhere.

The Children

Parents of Level Five children soon recognize that their child is different from others and seems to be unusually gifted. In many cases, however, these parents do not yet understand just *how* atypical their children are, and they expect that educators in the grade schools will know what to do for them. There is no federal mandate in the United States that requires schools to identify or provide services for gifted children, and states vary considerably regarding mandates and funding for gifted services. It is often left to individual school districts to decide what they will provide.[4]

All but one child in this chapter had significant parent-arranged alterations of their educational paths, and as you will see, getting flexible educational arrangements for the children was far from easy. Gifted education specialists continue to work to bring current information to the schools showing that acceleration and curriculum modification are beneficial for these children. The recently published *Templeton Report* (Colangelo, Assouline, & Gross, 2004), which supports academic acceleration, is available free to schools that request it. This author, for one, hopes that this report and other recently published books on the topic of equity for gifted youngsters will result in a willingness from schools to be more flexible with these bright students.

Birth to Two Years

Level Five children often demonstrate advanced speaking and verbal comprehension levels before they are 18 months old. In addition, competency with shapes, puzzles, and sorting before age 12 months, and numbers and mazes before age 18 months, are hallmarks of profound innate math ability. Many of the Level Four children have either language or math as an obvious strength, but not necessarily both. The combination of many incredible aptitudes is what differentiates the Level Five children.

Level Five children seem to learn things in a jumble. As soon as they become able to talk, they already know letters, numbers, shapes, and lots of vocabulary, and they express themselves in sentences. They quickly figure out how to read and work with computers, too. It may be shocking to learn that Level Five children show almost all of the expected kindergarten readiness intellectual abilities *before they are two years old*.

Jacob Jones—Jacob's father knew when he first saw Jacob that something was different about him—about how he observed things with an unusual intensity. Jacob stared at things intently from birth. He had an insatiable love of books. He loved to be read to, and before he was two, he was reading board books to me. I never thought anything about it—we just went on to more difficult books.

Ross Oliver—When Ross was just weeks old, he seemed interested in everything around him. His eyes were always wide, and he seemed to take everything in. By four months, when we referred to an object, he turned to look at it. When he reached nine months, he started saying very simple sentences, while his cousin, who was six weeks older than he, hadn't really begun talking at all. By 10 months, Ross was speaking in full sentences with accurate grammar.

At 12 months, Ross showed great frustration in putting together a puzzle if a piece was missing. At 14 months, he asked "Why?" about everything, and he also asked intelligent follow-up questions. By 16 months, he talked in paragraphs and came up with language constructs of his own. Once, when I was nursing his baby sister, he asked me if my nursing bra was a "booby hat." Our punishment for him usually involved counting—we told him that we would count to three before doling out the punishment that we threatened, but Ross pointed out that there are numbers greater than three.

Carol Johnston—Carol recognized colors when she was about nine months old. She was so far ahead of the developmental milestones charts that they were irrelevant, so we suspected extreme precocity from the very beginning. She was a quiet, alert baby, taking everything in, missing nothing. It felt like her first word was "Why?" She seemed to understand everything we said or did, regardless of the difficulty level. She began talking at a very early age—she had a vocabulary of at least 150 words by 12 months and almost double that at 15 months. I don't recall exactly when she started speaking in sentences, but it was almost immediately.

Carol knew the alphabet well and could recognize letters on signs by 15 months. She read full words on signs and picked them out of books before she was two years old. I distinctly recall a dinnertime conversation just before she was two in which she told a joke that she made up about an elephant pretending to be a strawberry by hiding in the bushes. She squealed with laughter at the incongruous vision of an elephant pretending to be a small berry.

Jon Crockett—Jon seemed to understand my saying "I love you" at 10 weeks of age, as he would respond with a very large smile and bright eyes. He said "I love you," "hello," and "dada" at five months. He seemed born with understanding, and this is why we never had to put away the fine crystal and other breakables, even when he was a baby—he just seemed to understand what was okay to touch and what was not.

Jon loved books from the day he was born, and he was always happy to sit on anyone's lap and listen to them read. He was also born loving music, and he always had access to our piano, as his father literally bounced his little bottom on the keyboard just hours after his birth. His attention span was unusual from early on. At five months of age, a family friend pointed out to me how atypical it was that our son could focus on just one toy for long time. At 10 months, Jon enjoyed playing with his shape sorter, and his grandfather saw him putting the shapes into it on his own faster than another grandchild could who was six months older. About the time he was 12 months old, Jon began using the computer, and he loved it.

Jon counted to nine by 17 months, and soon after, he counted to 12 with no errors. At 18 months, he plopped himself on the floor with a new set of state magnets, studied it for two hours straight, and was thereafter able to name 30 states using the black side of the magnet in any orientation or by drawing the state shape. It wasn't long after that before he knew all 50 states.

At 1½, Jon could match items with the first letter of their names— for instance, he put a fabric picture of a ball in the "B" letter pocket of an alphabet wall hanging, and the violin in the "V" pocket—all by himself.

He started reading words at about that time, including "closed," "game," "clean," "stop," "walk," "edit," and "reading"—all words he saw in one place or another. He liked saying the same thing in several different ways, such as "finished, all gone, empty," when finishing a bottle. He loved experimenting with plurals. He liked singing the alphabet song with me by singing every other letter. He said, "Bonjour" if someone said "Good day," and vice versa. He appropriately used "Bless you" when anyone sneezed, "Thank you" and "Excuse us" if we were trying to get by people in an aisle, and "How are you?" on the phone.

At 20 months, when I said 87, Jon said 88. He started seeing numbers everywhere, even imagining two hoops hanging together at a circus as being an 8. He started to count lots of things on his own, like stairs and flags on his toy castle. He said things like "Need octagon" while trying to go to sleep, because he was trying to work out a dominoes puzzle in his head. He also counted backwards from 24 while talking himself to sleep. He began noting what "isn't," such as "Yellow, no blue" in a picture and "Y, no X" when reading a shopping directory which listed all of the letters except X and Z. He began learning our phone number and address, too.

At 20 months, Jon broke his cereal into pieces on his chair and commented, "Messy, messy. Shame, shame." At breakfast, he told me, "Pull up a stool. Sit down." At 22 months, he had a spoken vocabulary of more than 1,500 words—above that of the average four-year-old. Once, he asked, "What's after 8:54? 8:55!" Later, he said, "It's quarter to six" when he looked at his analog clock at 5:45. When asked how many shoes he had if one pair was here and another upstairs, he said four. Still before two, he started announcing the page numbers he saw songs on; page nine was *Old MacDonald Had a Farm*. He read, "June 18, 1993" off a T-shirt. He also read car registration stickers and knew which month each of the 12-month numbers corresponded to. He liked playing the card game *War* and knew which cards won. He did a dot-to-dot backwards from 19 to 1. When a babysitter read, "There was a blizzard outside and it was snowing," Jon commented, "That's redundant." At 23 months, he took his first subway ride and said, "Isn't this a nice ride?" When a Cookie Monster figure in a car raced off a track, he said, "Is Cookie Monster hurt? Feel sorry for Cookie Monster."

Rick Arnesen—Within a few weeks of birth, Rick watched everything and was very alert. He'd stare up at me as though he was this "being" trapped in a baby body. It was clear that he understood a lot of what we were saying and doing by the time he was five or six months old. He walked at 13 months—not early. He had excellent dexterity and eye-hand coordination, though, and could pick up tiny pieces of food, like a piece of cereal, from the time he was six months old.

Rick was very interested in shape sorters before he was one year old. He had a couple of stacking-type toys that he played with over and over again, sorting the colors and shapes. He started playing with simple puzzles before he was one. He had a wooden toy bench with different colored pegs that he pushed or hammered into their places. He paged through books all of the time, and he loved music, playing with the record player and plunking away at the piano without pounding aimlessly. He enjoyed watching TV, especially *Sesame Street* and sports games, loved having us read to him, and demanded lots of interaction and attention from the time he was born.

Rick didn't start actually talking until he was between 17 and 19 months old, but he talked in phrases and sentences right away. He understood what we asked him to do long before he talked. If you said, "Hand me the blue box," he would. If you said, "Give me three raisins," he would. At a Christmas party with all of the relatives when he was 17 months old, he was the only child under two who seemed interested in what was in the packages rather than just playing with the wrapping paper or running around. He sat down and successfully completed every puzzle in the room that had been given to any of the other children through age six. He could stack a tower of cubes as well as any grown-up. He also showed a natural propensity with numbers—before he actively talked, he could put magnetic numbers in order, and by the time he was 18 months old, he could count out loud to at least 20.

Colin Richards—Between six and nine months, Colin knew the colors and names of many objects, showed a fascination for things with numbers—calculators, phones, and thermostat controls—and liked to watch the TV show *Jeopardy*. He liked to get up very early in the morning, so we tried an alarm clock radio. We carefully explained that we would not come and get him in the morning until "Mr. Radio said beep, beep, beep." After a couple of days, he got the idea; he would wait in his crib and play quietly until the alarm went off, and we were able to get some more sleep! When I read him a Dr. Seuss book at 10 months, *Marvin K. Mooney, Will You Please Go Now*, he laughed and laughed at the repeating sounds of the words. He spent lots of time looking at books on his own, and he always loved letters; between 10 and 12 months, he learned all of the letters of the alphabet with magnets, and he learned all of the colors with toy keys. He also recognized "stop" and "exit" by then. He understood the concept of numbers before 12 months and enjoyed playing with shape sorters, too.

Colin liked to color feverishly at 13 months, and by 15 months, he enjoyed using letter and number games on the computer. He got the concept of reading after typing letters and repeating sounds on the computer—simple words like "mama" and "poo poo." When I took him to the park at about 1½, instead of playing on the playground, he picked up sticks and noted how they looked like letters. He preferred to read books in his stroller at the zoo instead of watching the animals. By age two, he could read just about anything, and he could spell words like "Albuquerque" and "Washington." He counted quite high by 1½ and to over 100 by age two. As he sat in the grocery cart, he counted higher and higher and amazed everyone within earshot.

Michael Cortez—Michael was alert upon delivery. He showed an intense interest in patterns, colors, movement, and music by three months old. He was fascinated with numbers by six months, and he learned to recognize numerals and counted to 10 by one year old. At eight months, he worked with 10- to 15-piece board puzzles. At 15 months, he could count to 20 and could associate an actual group of items with the numbers. At 16 months, he could count backwards. Also at 16 months, Michael recited the names of all of the planets; at 17 months, he wanted to count all things including the planets, so he counted the planets' moons. Astronomy was his favorite topic then. He loved house numbers, telephone numbers, ages, birthdays—just about everything with numbers. By 18 months, he could count up to 100 in multiples of 10.

Regarding learning to talk, when he was only two months old, Michael said the last syllable of "hungry" several times when we kept asking him if he was hungry. His first word was "water" at eight months. "Daddy" was clear at 10 months and "mom" at about 13 months. He spoke in full sentences and was easily understood by others by the time he was 15 months old. Michael also knew the alphabet and recognized words in books or in the paper at 15 months. He could read his own beginner books by then—books that had been read to him by us. He could read new words independently at 17 months, but we only knew that he could read for sure when we showed him a simple list of words, which he was able to read back to us when he was 21 months old. His favorite book at this age was *Pigs from 1-10* by Arthur Geisert. He identified 11 colors at 15 months, and he used the words "light" and "dark" to distinguish shades of a certain color when he was 1½. Also by 1½, he could write the alphabet. His love for books along with his fascination for the alphabet, letter sounds, and numbers enabled him to read early. He always preferred toys that somehow incorporated the alphabet and/or numbers (tactile and auditory), and so we got him that kind of thing—in books, toys, tapes, and even software.

Michael started to use the computer mouse and keyboard when he was 1½. To keep him occupied in his baby high chair longer, we put the keyboard on the chair's tray to see if he could interact with the program *Elmo Preschool*™. After a month, it was difficult to snatch him away from the computer. He loved preschool and kindergarten computer programs, especially those with the alphabet and numbers. He managed to bend the CD tray at two years old when he attempted to change the CD himself. He continued to use the computer on a regular basis, adding more difficult software as needed. He started to use a word processing program and spell at 20 months.

Age Two to Three Years

Jacob Jones—Before he was 2½ years old, Jacob talked in full sentences. One of the first things he asked was, "What time is it?" He repeated this over and over with many different inflections.

Carol Johnston—Carol started to read words at two years five months, and she read actual beginner books by three years old. She started to use the computer before she was two, earlier than her sibling. She did simple addition in her head by 2½.

Jon Crockett—From two years on, Jon read quietly in his crib each morning, and we read each night before bed. He used his free time to play on the computer, do puzzles, play with all sorts of toys (a BRIO® train set was a favorite), have fun with other kids, and read. At age two, he could correctly figure 7+13 and 8+11. He could also fill in missing numbers in series problems such as 100, 200, (blank), 400, 500. He started putting together multiplication—7x7=49, for example, and anything multiplied by 0, 1, or 10. He seemed to put together multiplying by five from knowing how an analog clock works. He talked out loud and would spout out things like, "Negative 200 plus negative 200 equals negative 400." He understood the context of the hyphen ("-"), as in when it meant "subtract," when it meant "negative," and when it meant "to,"—for instance, when he saw a 4-3 baseball score, he said, "That means 'to'; it doesn't mean 'negative'!" He could follow problems like 5+5+5+5 and answer 20 very quickly. When he heard 18+8=26, he responded, "28+8=36, 38+8=46, 48+8=56..." and so on. The next day, he suddenly shouted out, "88+8 is the same as 48+48!"

Soon after his second birthday, Jon held up two lacrosse sticks perpendicular to each other and asked, "Is this a plus sign?" He pointed to "100%" on a grated cheese container and said, "It says one hundred percent." He understood the concept of rhyming at 25 months of age. He often asked what letter words start with, and he spelled out words on signs and asked what the words were.

At 26 months, Jon played *America the Beautiful* on a keyboard correctly after hearing the song from a TV in the next room. At 27 months, he heard an Elton John song at the mall and said, "This is Elton John." We have no Elton John albums at home. He had an uncanny memory for notes, songs, singers, and rhythm.

At 27 months, Jon repeated our six-digit health insurance member number after he heard me say it over the telephone. He could dial our home phone number and his father's work number. His singing and talking himself to sleep was even filled with numbers: "Oh no, this is terrible! $50!" and "The best mix of the 60s, 70s, 80s, and 90s," and then the radio station's number and call letters. He would also draw numbers at this age, and while doing so, he announced, "Eleven in square" and "Twelve in triangle," and whatever else he drew. He woke up one morning correctly saying, "Today is December 10th." I asked him how many days there were until Christmas, and he said, "Fifteen!"

Once, Jon put his fork down on his plate so that the prongs were at the bottom and the handle was at the top and said, "Six o'clock! It's a clock!" In a hidden words puzzle, he found the words "fossil" going down, "jaws" going across, and "eggs" going up. He could type sentences on the computer one word at a time. I suggested that he try typing the states, and he said, "The first is Alabama," which it is, alphabetically, but nobody had ever taught him that. He seemed to be alphabetizing the colors as he said, "What comes after black? Blue! What comes after blue? Brown!" Before he was 2½, he was typing words into his pocket data bank like "Amadeus" and "JCPenney."

At about 2½, when Jon saw page 127 in a book, he joked, "Who lives on this page? Joe Rivera!" Joe was a man he'd met briefly five months before whose house number was 127. On a walk, he would see someone walking a dog and say, "That person shops at aisle 10." I asked what he was talking about, and he explained that aisle 10 in the grocery store is where the pet food is (we have no pets and buy no pet food). He was interested in percentages and loved estimating what percent full his glass was. He liked using a calculator to figure out 15% tips in restaurants. He read full pages with expression in books that were new to him, like Crockett Johnson's *Harold and the Purple Crayon*. Soon after turning 2½, he not only read, but he spelled more than 100 words from memory. He knew the concept of conservation of matter the first time it was tested at 31 months when I put equal amounts of water in two glasses, then poured one into a bowl, and asked "Which has more water, the glass or the bowl, or are they equal?"

Rick Arnesen—Rick got a plastic bat and baseball for his second birthday and enjoyed trying to hit the ball when it was gently tossed to him. He hit it about half the time. When just 28 months old, he begged me to show him how to use a knife to cut apples into chunks, and I decided that he was coordinated enough to do it. He was very musical, and he recognized and sang songs by the time he was 2½ years old. He also enjoyed plunking on the piano and xylophone, and he started to play tunes he'd heard by the time he was three.[5]

Colin Richards—Colin liked puzzles. He sat focused for a very long time at age two—hours if we let him—using a computer program with letters and numbers. He even left his own birthday party to use it. He often read on his own in his room, in his highchair, in the car, on field trips, even on the toilet. He loved to color and turned out endless piles of scribble-drawings. He also liked to play with clay, paint, and mud, and to draw—mostly pictures of letters and numbers. Calculators and the computer fascinated him.

Michael Cortez—Michael could write his name and simple words at age two. Although he was not fond of drawing, we noticed that he could draw faces with details like a circle within a pupil within round eyes, nostrils, eyebrows, ears with circles inside them, and round or oval mouths.

Author note: Such drawing detail is not expected before age four for the average gifted child and six years for average children.

Our family had just moved from the East Coast to an apartment in the Midwest. I couldn't remember our assigned parking space, and I drove around looking for it. Suddenly, Michael uttered the numbers—which I did not take seriously at first. But he was right, and we found our parking space. At not quite 2½, while at the pharmacy, Michael surprised me when he read the word "prescription," clearly. Addition and subtraction came easily at that time, too. He worked 25-piece puzzles by age two, 50-piece puzzles by age 2½, and a 100-piece puzzle by 3½. He has been interested in geography since he was 2½. His favorite puzzle was of the United States, and he was able to identify each state puzzle piece just from its back shape. He started to show interest in mazes, too, and continued to love mazes, word puzzles, and number puzzles. At about the same time, he became interested in the concepts of death and aging. His interest in pure facts, like almanacs, data lists, and so on began when he was about three years old.

Age Three to Four Years

Ross Oliver—Ross started using the computer at about age three. He enjoyed using preschool programs but could be afraid of the animations or frustrated if time limits were imposed. He was very much into patterns and counting. We didn't really teach him any math skills, but he was very intuitive with math. When given a problem, he could apply multiplication ideas before age four.

Carol Johnston—Carol read chapter books and could add three-digit numbers by the time she was 3½. She also consistently solved problems using simple division and multiplication. She was good at keyboarding and computer use before she turned four.

Jon Crockett —At just three, Jon did a new 60-piece jigsaw puzzle of Europe in 10 minutes while watching TV. He noticed patterns in numbers used in the play-by-number notes of the song *Twelve Months* and said that it looked like *London Bridge*, but he was not looking at the *London Bridge* page as he made this observation. I told him in March that he could call someone in a couple of weeks, and he said, "Oh, on April 3," exactly 14 days from the date at hand, and there was no calendar in the room. Playing Black Jack, he uttered, "I turned up an ace to my six. I think I'll double down because I have a soft 17. I was going to bet $404, but with a soft 17, I'm going to double my bet to $808!"

Also at age three, when I asked Jon what word could be made from H-blank-R, I was expecting "her"; he said, "helicopter." Jon often critiqued what he read, suggesting better words. He found a typo in a dictionary. He read the words "publication," "electronics," and "hallelujah" from a friend's book. Asked to circle the things that started with a given letter, he circled a horse for "R," stating, "It's a race horse!" That same day, he was to draw two things that start with the letter "Y," and he drew a yo-yo and wrote quite clearly "2001," adding, "That's a year." Asked to draw a picture of words that start with "P," "Z," and "F," he drew a sheet of paper and an arrow and clearly wrote the word "paper" next to it, a zipper and made an arrow to a nicely written "zipper," and an orange with an arrow and "Fruit (an orange)" printed neatly. When asked to circle the pictures to answer the question, "Can it go?" he circled a drawing of three sets of circular tables with people eating around them, saying that this was a restaurant and, "Well, it could be on a boat, so I'll say, 'Yes'!"

Author note: Children who think like this will not always answer questions on multiple choice tests the way the test designers have in mind. At only three years old, Jon illustrates how highly intelligent children answer questions more creatively than most teachers or parents expect. In some instances, it helps to instruct such children to give the most direct answer, although at home, this is seldom necessary—parents are used to the child's divergent thinking.

Jon and I read a poem in one of his books with the words, "Sit down on the road and eat with me, little mouse," and Jon said, "But they'll get run over by a car!" He played *Bazaar: The Trading Game*, a game to teach algebra concepts, very well, figuring out how many points he earned and keeping score. He showed regular interest in *Simple Science Experiments* books, Isaac Asimov's *Great Space Mysteries*, and the Chelsea House *People and Customs of the World*. He enjoyed using the library computer to look up books by topic and author and then finding the books he said he had "researched." He read a 113-page book called *Zoo Clues* by Sheldon Gerstenfeld; I later asked him if he wanted to know what the average height of a zebra is, and he said, "Sixty inches," remembering it from that book. When I read a book with a reference to a refrigerator, he said that he was thirsty. I told him that he was only saying that due to the book reference, but he said, "No, I'm not thirsty because of the refrigerator; I'm thirsty from life!"

One day, Jon played *Three Blind Mice* on the piano upon request, having never played it before. He also played *Mary Had a Little Lamb* and *America*. He played an original composition of his on his grandparents' harpsichord and hopped off the chair saying, "That was Sonata in F!"

Before turning 3½, he taught himself, among others, *Joy to the World* and *Ode to Joy* from memory. He identified a hammer dulcimer at a musical performance and a sitar at a music teacher's house. In the car, he told me, "Valiha is a type of zither" and later showed me how to look it up on the computer; he was pronouncing it correctly, too—"va-lee." A Suzuki teacher and two other piano teachers who normally won't take children under age five interviewed him; all three said they would take him on immediately, as he was quite precocious.

Rick Arnesen—When Mt. St. Helens erupted, Rick was fascinated by all of the stories about it, even though he was only 2½ when it happened. When he was 3½, he and his father were lying on the bed poring through an atlas, and he observed, "Look, Dad. You're California and I'm Nevada," as he noted the positions of their bodies. He got very involved in planets and stars, too, at about this time.

We got a plastic bowling set, and Rick bowled often and was quite serious about how he well he did. He knew all of the scoring rules for spares, strikes, and end of the game figuring, and he kept track of his progress when he was just 3½ years old. He loved illustrated fact books that listed sizes, heights, weights, speeds, and other numerical details about thousands of topics. He was a trivia buff, and his interests leaned strongly toward anything that could be quantified. He loved ranking things by size, numbers, weight, and so on. He used to drill me while we were driving in the car, and I could not get him off the subject until I, too, had memorized and correctly answered questions such as, "What are the 10 biggest countries in the world by size? Okay, now by population? What are the five tallest mountains and where are they? Who was the tallest man who ever lived?"

Author note: When children are so intent upon sharing their interests, many parents take the time to listen or go along with them. If parents belittle or ignore or, worse yet, regularly suppress such a child, the child will not likely blossom into a well-adjusted, confident person. Nonetheless, parents need to help these children know when to wait or show patience, because the adults cannot be constant playmates, either.

When Rick was about 3½ years old, he started going to local college basketball games with his father. The scoring, playing, rules, and general competition captivated him. He gave rapt attention to the game. He added, subtracted, predicted, and remembered the statistics for the games from the entire season and talked openly and animatedly in front of others in the stands, to their astonishment. He also wanted to know how everything worked. He didn't take things apart mechanically—he didn't want to know how the insides worked—he wanted to know how electricity worked. When I told him how the electrons move through the wires, he wanted to know why and how that happened. I bought all sorts of books that went into great detail with photos, diagrams, and written descriptions so that I could answer his questions. He started reading them himself about a year later, at age 4½, and merely expected me to pay attention when he told me about things. Before he was four or five, I thought that he was a born physicist.

We didn't think of Rick as necessarily reading by the time he was 3½, but we assumed that he began to recognize—or memorize, perhaps—the topics and data in a book on comparing different things as his father read them to him or pointed them out to him. Looking back, we realize now that he must have been doing at least some reading.

Colin Richards—Around age three, Colin discovered shows with numbers and letters like *Wheel of Fortune, 3-2-1 Contact,* and *Sesame Street,* though he only liked to watch the parts that had the letters or numbers in them. He loved *Jeopardy.* He was especially fascinated by logos and theme music to various shows. He begged to watch the PBS introductory theme that came on before a certain show—he didn't want to watch the show, just the introduction. He liked to read books by himself and spell words with magnet letters. He used the computer a lot to type or draw pictures. By age four, he was doing addition, subtraction, and simple multiplication.

Michael Cortez—Michael did word and number puzzles by age three. He began crosswords and showed a deep interest in trivia and almanacs from about three to 3½ years old. He attended kindergarten at age 3½ in a Montessori preschool that worked for him for about five months. We had chosen the Montessori school for its reputation that it was good for gifted kids; they have children of different ages work together. But Michael was ahead of even the oldest child there, and they couldn't keep him busy enough. He took too much of their time.

At 3½, Michael was completely independent and confident using the computer parts and peripherals (printer, scanner, CD and disk drives, power switch). He knew how to boot and reboot the computer, install and start a program, add new paper to the printer, and change the printer ink. Other things such as the TV and VCR were inaccessible to his reach, but he freely controlled them though the remotes. He knew multiplication and division up to 12 by age 3¾. He also won second place in the highest category in his first spelling contest. By four, he knew multiplication by two to three digits, simple fractions, and the addition, subtraction, and multiplication of decimals, and he finished grades three and four EPGY math. He also liked using the camera when he was four years old.

Michael received his first formal instruction on a musical instrument—violin—at age three. He learned to read musical notes at 3½ and taught himself to play piano at age four. He also learned to compose and write lyrics for his compositions.

> *Author note: It is generally not difficult to get Level Five children enrolled in special advanced opportunities, such as music or art. Museums, preschools, art and music instruction, and community classes are usually very flexible and will accept the parents' decision that the child is ready for the activity or instruction.*

Age Four to Five Years

The progression from just starting to read to reading at an adult level is very common in Level Five children—most of them can read just about anything they choose by the time they are five years old. When children start school already reading, parents hope that something can be done to enable their child to continue to progress. Educators often tell parents that the other children will "catch up" by the time they are all in fourth grade, but this is simply not true—nor is it possible unless the other children are also as highly intelligent.

All of these Level Five children also enjoyed computer programs designed for kids ages 12 and older by the time they were five years old. By this age, they all had keyboarding and spelling skills that facilitated full use of the computer and the Internet.

Jacob Jones—By the age of 4½, we'd go to the library and Jacob would head to the section with computer manuals. Nobody imagined that he was really reading them, but he was. We allowed him access to any level book, which led to some interesting questions when this five-year-old was reading about human reproduction in a large book with pictures during church.

Ross Oliver—When Ross, at age four, heard us mentioning that adults just can't program a VCR, he was determined to learn how to do it and very quickly succeeded. He was given a computer CD on reading for Christmas when he was 4½. Although he hadn't demonstrated reading prior to that, within three months, he went from being a nonreader to being able to read from college textbooks, and although total comprehension wasn't there, the phonemic awareness was amazing. When he first started reading, he enjoyed stories the most, and within a month, he was reading chapter books. He hasn't stopped reading since. We had to take books away from him at night because he wouldn't stop to sleep. He was interested in both fiction and nonfiction.

Jon Crockett—Just after his fourth birthday, Jon figured out that a gallon is equal to eight pints —after he learned that four quarts are equal to one gallon and two pints are equal to one quart. He loved codes of all kinds and intently studied Braille and the Mayan number system, plus binary, octal, and hexadecimal numbers bases and Roman numerals. We played an oral game in the car in which the letters in words we passed on the road would be assigned a value, added together, and then converted into Roman numerals. He read about factorials at age three, and just after he turned four, he asked what 10 factorial is when he wanted to know how many ways his electronic dictionary game could scramble the letters in a 10-letter word if all of the letters were different.

Jon learned exponents on his own from studying his father's scientific calculator and how to convert metric measurements of weight, length, volume, and temperature to and from American measures. He asked an adult friend, "Did you know 4 to the 31st power is the same as 2 to the 62nd power?" At age four, he could pretty much read anything. Asked to name five things he'd like if he could have anything at all, he answered, "A mandolin, a checkbook, a mortgage chart, deposit slips, and an account balance." Soon after that, he pulled *Personal Investing* off a bookshelf and, after reading some of this 612-page book, said, "I don't think you should invest in zero coupon bonds." When I asked to see the book, he pulled *Contrary Investing* off the shelf and said I could have that instead, as he hadn't finished with *Personal Investing*. Later he noticed me reading about land as an investment and handed me *The Complete Guide to Home Buying* and said, "Here. This relates to what you're reading."

At about 4½, Jon wrote a creative story called "The First Car that Flew," and after printing it by hand, he typed it on the computer and added graphics and a cover page. During the summer he was five, he read 260 books. His favorites were chapter books like *The Borrowers* by Mary Norton, *Charlie and the Chocolate Factory* by Roald Dahl, *Through the*

Looking Glass by Lewis Carroll, and the *Goosebumps* series—all books at the mid to upper elementary reading level. He also enjoyed Shakespeare synopses. He continued to have terrific recall for where within the books he had read things, even to the page number.

At age four, Jon announced that he was playing *Ode to Joy* in G sharp and A sharp, and he also played the tune correctly starting with C and F sharp on his first try—he had taught himself to transpose music. He recalled *Trumpet Voluntary* being the last piece played on the antique organ at the Arts Festival five months prior. While packing for a vacation that year, he suggested we pack medicine, and when I said we could buy medicine in the state we'd be in, he said, "True, but that would be wasting money that we could better spend at restaurants or at an amusement park or something."

Rick Arnesen—When he was four, Rick and I played a memory game together, and he could beat me almost every time. He must have already known how to read more words than I realized when he insisted that I show him how to read at 4½ years old. Since about 1½, he liked to follow along in books that had records to them, and he corrected us when we read the wrong word, which we did sometimes for fun. He knew what all sorts of signs said and meant long before I thought of him as truly reading. We went through an early reader book for about 20 minutes, and that was the end his reading lessons. Within two weeks, he was reading quietly to himself after the rest of us complained about him being noisy when he read out loud. Within three months, he was reading at about second-grade level and zoomed to chapter books almost immediately. He reached the fifth- or sixth-grade level by the time he was five. He read a series of books about natural disasters throughout history (volcanoes, plagues, earthquakes, floods) and became an existentialist, truly taxing his father and me with his questions, conversation, curiosity, worries, and dreams.

Colin Richards—At age four, Colin wrote and illustrated long, multi-page stories on the computer. In preschool, he scored at the second- and third-grade levels in math and reading achievement.

Michael Cortez—At age four, Michael attended a gifted magnet school. He was the youngest child in the building and spent most of his time in fifth grade the first year; he then split between first, fifth, and home school the next year. He read chapter books, sorted words, and used a dictionary. He read fifth- to sixth-grade-level books by age five and started doing 200-piece puzzles. He completed grade five math in his magnet school and in an EPGY course.

Michael loved the computer, sometimes too much. He started using the Internet unassisted at four years old, e-mailing and using favorite websites independently. He wanted software for his birthday and for Christmas. He mostly worked on software for grades five and beyond, and his selection was always broad, covering all areas of learning and creativity.

Age Five to Six Years

Jacob Jones—In kindergarten, Jacob was reading short chapter books in one day. We couldn't believe it, so we questioned him and saw that he did indeed know what he read. We went through books very quickly. At about that same time, he moved on to reading computer manuals, and this was his idea of bedtime reading. In fact, he was never without a book; he read anything and everything he could. He also liked to write, but not by hand—he preferred to type.

> *Author note: Once these children get over the thrill of learning to write, most lose their taste for actual handwriting, which, of course, eventually causes problems for them in school.*

Ross Oliver—Our punishment of counting down from three quit working when Ross, at age five, told us that there are negative numbers, too. During kindergarten, we were asked by the teacher to make sure that Ross had his snow pants with him every day. We replied that he *did* have them every day, but the playground supervisor said that he often didn't wear them. When she had asked him about it, he'd said, "I'm making a pattern." She told us, "Ross just doesn't seem to understand." When we talked to Ross about it, we asked what he meant when he said he was making a pattern. He explained that if you have snow pants on, you have to play on the playground; without snow pants, you play on the sidewalk or sit and talk with the adult supervisors. He told us that he'd made a pattern in which every Monday, Wednesday, and every other Friday he wore his snow pants, and every Tuesday, Thursday, and every *other* Friday he didn't, so he could have variety in his play.

> *Author note: Most early childhood teachers are nurturing and truly enjoy working with children. However, they are sometimes slow to understand the quirky ideas of Level Five children. Ross's teacher had no idea how to*

interpret what he meant by "making a pattern." She thought he didn't understand her question, when it was she who didn't understand his response.

Jon Crockett—Soon after his fifth birthday, Jon did equations while walking along the beach—things like, "If $y^2=49$ and $x+2y=19$, what is x?" He solved Math Olympiad problems, such as, "Sue has five times as many apples as Jay, Narian has three times as many as Jay, and Sue has 16 more than Narian, so how many does Jay have?" The test allowed five minutes to solve the problem, but Jon responded in just one minute with, "That's easy. It's just $5J-3J=16$, so all I have to do is divide 16 by 2 and I get 8 for J."

Author note: It is difficult to accurately compare Jon's math ability to the other children in Level Five because his mother was considerably more comfortable with math than some of the other mothers and provided him with more opportunities to develop his abilities.

At five, Jon was not interested in his third-grade math so much as studying a scientific calculator and asking about trigonometric and logarithmic functions. In just moments, he could change an exponential equation into logarithmic form and solve basic logarithms in his head, such as log base 3 of $1/9=-2$. When asked how many times the earth turns in one year, he said, "There are 365 days in a year; therefore, the answer must be 365." In his writing, he started to use not just commas and exclamation points, but also parentheses, hyphens, footnotes, colons, and semicolons. He liked labeling his compositions as autobiographical or fiction. He once did some "hangman" words while waiting for a show to begin, and some of the words he included were "extravagant," "spectacular," and "auditorium." While flipping through *The Little Webster* (a tiny dictionary with more than 7,000 words), he pointed out that it was missing the words "auditorium," "extravaganza," and even a little word like "queer."

Rick Arnesen—During the month that Rick turned five, we went with friends to the Field Museum in Chicago. There was a large overhead panel display of the development of a baby from conception to birth, complete with photographs and written explanations. Although other children, both younger and older, and adults were quickly ready to move on, Rick needed to stay until he had finished reading every last interpretive panel to himself.

In the 1980s, an early computer game called *Zork* was developed by and for MIT students. It was an interactive adventure game with no graphics, only words. When Rick was 4¾ years old, a relative showed the game to her two children and to Rick and his brother. Rick was the youngest of the four, yet he was the only one who could play the game because it required typing, spelling, and reading, as well as very advanced problem-solving ability. By this time, he read anything at any level that interested him. He loved geography, science, history, World War II and the Civil War, how things are made, and how things work, and he started the first of many years of reading the *Guinness Book of World Records* from cover to cover, remembering what he had read. By the time he was six, Rick could figure a restaurant tip faster than I could, so I put that part of my brain on idle for the next dozen years and let him figure the tips.

Michael Cortez—Michael started computer programming at five years old, learned web page design and production in a one-week class, and started a *Visual Basic®* programming course in which he was able to produce some simple programs. By the time he was 5½, he was always asking us to purchase puzzle books, brainteasers, and Mensa[6] books. He read and worked on these books constantly, and they and almanacs were his choice for leisure and bedtime reading. His progress in his musical instruction was rapid. He was well advanced in note reading and music theory at age 5½.

Age Six to Seven Years

By six to seven years of age, all of the Level Five children were tested for intellectual level, and many were tested for achievement. A clinician who understands standard scores would recognize a *WISC-III* score of 154 as being exceptionally or profoundly gifted, but most people still believe, as mentioned earlier, that a score closer to 200 should be possible on any test if the child were truly "that smart." These people have been conditioned by the old *SBLM*, which had that scoring range. In fact, today's tests with standard scores do not allow a child to attain a score of much over 160, and it still depends upon the scale of the test.

Children who are six or seven years old are usually in first or second grade. Most of the Level Five children started school after they turned five, and all of their parents tried to make school adjustments—sometimes drastic ones—for their children.

Carol Johnston—At age six, Carol read a science dictionary cover to cover and was in love with encyclopedias. She devoured a book about math concepts called *G is for Googol* by David Schwartz in a single sitting and then proceeded to lecture us on its contents. She rarely asked for help—she was very much self-taught and preferred to learn on her own. She most surprised us with her mathematical abilities. She was able to solve very difficult conceptual problems. She used an intuitive approach and had an innate understanding of surprisingly sophisticated concepts. She particularly liked lateral thinking puzzles and logic problems. She almost instantaneously came up with the solution to a logic puzzle while we adults were still using our tried-and-true methods to derive an answer. She thrived on computer games—the more difficult, the better. She quickly completed the children's games we owned and progressed to adult puzzles and problem-solving games.

Jon Crockett—Jon never went through any of the typical grades in school. He did K-4 using a home school program with an advisory teacher, which is a certified teacher who graded his work, thus enabling him to have a transcript. He typically read books of 100-250 pages, such as the *Chronicles of Narnia* series. At six, he started a fourth-grade curriculum, though he had already gone through a fifth-grade reading and study workbook, and the work wasn't challenging for him. Also at six, he entered a national Merrill Lynch Savings Month essay contest for grades four through seven and won second prize, a U.S. Savings Bond.

At age six, Jon took a *Sylvan Learning Skills Test* and scored ninth-grade level on six out of the nine subsets. That same year, he correctly solved a problem that 77% of American high school students missed on a national test: "If 36 soldiers fit on a bus and 1,128 soldiers need to go somewhere, how many buses are needed?" He had never even divided by a two-digit number before, yet he somehow knew how to set up the problem, do the long division, and round up to 32. He enjoyed setting speed records in his class for the written number drills of math facts. Once when he was swinging the pantry door back and forth, I told him that it wasn't a toy and asked what he was thinking when he did that. He said that he was thinking 180 degrees, 45 degrees, and 90 degrees.

Rick Arnesen—When he was tested at 6½ to enter a new school, Rick read well orally to the twelfth-grade level and had good reading comprehension at the eighth-grade level. He definitely preferred nonfiction and read whenever possible. He became a primary information resource for the rest of the family on a huge variety of subjects, especially anything related to dates, names, geographical locations, and solving math problems.

Michael Cortez—Michael was accelerated in his gifted magnet school, so instead of first-grade, he took seventh-grade math and history; sixth-grade science, reading, and writing; and a few third-grade courses in music and art.

Age Seven to Nine Years

Carol Johnston—At about age eight, Carol was completely home schooled. She completed pre-algebra and some science courses, study-ing physical science and earth science via textbooks and CDs. Her study of biology included an extensive unit on plants, but she missed a more interactive laboratory approach. She studied world history, govern-ment, law, and philosophy, and she participated in summer programs for gifted students. She greatly enjoyed writing poetry. She read exten-sively for her own pleasure, especially fiction. Carol also studied Latin independently, but she couldn't go further without a Latin teacher. She was a gifted and creative artist, enjoyed drama and played the lead in a drama class production, and sang in a children's choir.

Jon Crockett—When Jon was between seven and nine years old, we did something called "unschooling," in which he just studied with what-ever books and materials he wanted to, although I made sure that he covered all of the subjects that the school district required, including music, art, and physical education. He used programmed-learning spelling and poetry books up through the tenth-grade level, as well as books like *Trigonometry the Easy Way* and *Calculus By and For Children.* He read books on astronomy and biology, attended many lectures at area museums, and went to lots of free lectures by scientists at the university, including a couple on physics. He also joined a book discussion group for adults.

Jon's uncle, who has a master's degree in electrical engineering, showed him a truth table soon after Jon turned seven. Jon solved the problem himself. He also figured out how to graph a snowman using equations that would form three tangential circles. Still not eight, he solved 44^2-43^2 in his head by squaring each number and holding the numbers in his head to do the subtraction. He found how many 9x8x4 solids could be placed in a 72x60x36 solid in his head. Rather than mul-tiply 9, 8, and 4, he said, "This is easy. Just divide 72 by 9 to get 8, divide

60 by 8 to get 7.5, and divide 36 by 4 to get 9; then multiply 8x7.5x9 to get 540." His math tutor, who had him doing Algebra I work, asked him to try and come up with a six-digit number that had no two of the same digits and was evenly divisible by 45, and Jon was able to do this on his first attempt. He bought himself a calculus book and read more than 100 pages in it in the first two or three days after it came in the mail. We hired the tutor because Jon wanted to learn calculus, but the tutor insisted on going in a normal, orderly progression of algebra through calculus. She wanted her students to take calculus for college credit and mentioned that Jon would be ready for college classes in short order. At age seven, Jon took a *Sylvan Learning Skills Test* and scored 11.9 grade-equivalent (the highest possible score) on all nine subtests. He hadn't finished seventh-grade coursework yet.

> *Author note: It is entirely common for Level Five—and many Level Four—children to score exceptionally high on achievement tests before they have covered the tested material in school. They do this by absorbing information without consciously attempting to do so in what psychologists call incidental learning.*

Jon won a $100 scholarship to ACE Computer Camp for an essay he wrote. He also won two new computers—the grand prize for the fifth grader division—in an essay contest on how to make the world a better place—all when he was the age of most second graders.

> *Author note: Before he turned nine, Jon won many awards, sat on numerous panels with erudite adults to discuss scientific and humanitarian topics, spoke at conventions as an invited speaker, and also took various musical, dance, and sports lessons. He is unusual among these Level Five children in this regard. It is hard to imagine how he and his family managed to balance their lives, even though Jon is an only child.*

Michael Cortez—By age seven, we home schooled Michael but hoped to get him into available classes at some point. That year, Michael took and received high grades in the following subjects: sixth-grade life science, English, and writing; seventh-grade American history; and eighth- and ninth-grade math. He also passed the Entrance Exam for the Talented Youth Math Program (UMTYMP)—the accelerated math sequence at the university—as one of the youngest ever to do so. He was a member of his school's sixth-grade Continental Math League, which placed first in the state. He personally placed second in his own sixth-grade school standings for the Continental Math League (remember that this is a gifted magnet school and he was still seven), and he was the youngest representative on Capitol Hill in a school computer exhibition. He still enjoyed and made time for music and sports. He was in *Suzuki Book 4* for violin, and he auditioned and passed the state level of the National Association of Piano Teachers. He showed significant improvement in swimming, tennis, and bicycling. At eight, Michael read everything from the latest *Harry Potter* books to Clive Cussler novels to puzzle books to boys' magazines and the Sunday comics.

Age Nine and Older

Jacob Jones—Jacob's special talents included advanced reading and computer skills. He was very creative and built elaborate LEGO® structures, then concocting long, detailed stories about them. His reading interests included computer manuals and chapter books such as *Animorphs* and the *Wishbone* series—all upper middle school reading level. He read at least eight hours two to three times per week and almost always had a book in his hands.

Ross Oliver—When given an opportunity to pursue his own reading or other activities, Ross focused on learning as much as possible about *Nintendo*®, even though we didn't have the game hardware. He was accelerated with a grade skip from third to fifth. Even though he was almost two years younger than many of his classmates, he placed first in our county in the Knights of Columbus Knowledge Bowl for math. He went on to place first for the entire northern half of Wisconsin. (He was in the regular fifth-grade math class at the middle school.) After the Knowledge Bowl, we had him retake the EPGY math placement test, and he tested into algebra even though he had only completed the fifth-grade math program.

Jon Crockett—Jon started full-time on-campus college classes soon after he turned nine years old. As a college freshman, he was still the same happy child. He did very well in his biology class, received the only A+ in a 30-student discussion class, and did amazingly well in a lecture class with more than 300 students—without studying. Some of his college friends came to our holiday open house party, and Jon was invited to the holiday party of one of his college friends. He continued to play with the friends he'd had since kindergarten, while also keeping himself occupied with all sorts of things at home.

Author note: This example illustrates that highly intelligent individuals need to progress intellectually, but they can still have a variety of friends for different activities. Jon may have preferred other nine-year-olds for certain kid-like activities but older friends for discussions of history or philosophy.

Jon was selected as a student speaker at a large conference for the International Food Policy Institute in Bonn, Germany, when he was just 10 years old. He wrote and delivered a two-page paper that made observations and suggestions about what the developed world could do to help the under-developed peoples of the world. He finished his fourth semester in college when he was not quite 11. His finals went well, and he got the highest score—86%—on the Calculus II exam; the next highest grade was a 72%, and most students scored in the 20s or 30s.

Rick Arnesen—Tutored in math as a third grader, Rick caught up to his ability level in fourth grade, completing Algebra I and II and qualifying for UMTYMP—the accelerated math sequence offered by the university—just after he turned nine. On the year-end test normed for ninth graders in the U.S., he scored in the 95th percentile. He also took eighth-grade science as a fourth grader in his own school. The teacher admitted that he was one of the two brightest, most knowledgeable students in her class, but she objected to his being there because she thought that he was too young. As her primary example of his inadequacies, she pointed out that he did not keep a good lab notebook. However, he enjoyed the class and did just fine.

Author note: A nine-year-old's handwriting and record keeping will not be as good as that of older children. This, however, does not seem sufficient reason to deny an advanced child the opportunity to learn at his own level. Mechanical skills will eventually catch up with intellectual abilities out of necessity. This is yet another example of asynchronous development—the child's physical abilities are not commensurate with his intellectual performance.

Even after all of the adjustments that we tried with Rick's education—home schooling, private tutors, and subject acceleration—it was clear that Rick learned more when he simply read on his own than with any of the arrangements we made. At eight, after seeing the filming of a TV show during a family trip to Los Angeles, he expressed interest in acting. So back home, we signed him up with some local talent agents to see if he could be cast in commercials. We weren't worried about his missing school. He landed several commercials and radio spots when he was nine and then got a major role in a movie the week he turned 10. After that, he was tutored on the set. Strange as it sounds, we let him go into acting because school was not working well for him, and kids in show business get tutors as part of their job. Both the movie work and the tutoring were good for him because there was only a three-hour daily school requirement, and he liked that. An 18-year-old played his older brother in the first movie and got a big kick out of dragging Rick around and telling actors, crew, the producer, and the director to ask Rick a question from the *Guinness Book of World Records*. Rick almost always knew the answer.

Rick finished the first movie in November and resumed his UMTYMP classes in geometry, then left after two months to make a second movie. At the end of the semester, having missed five of the 12 math lessons but studying with his tutor, he took the *Cooperative Mathematics Test* and received a 99.3 percentile score—which qualified him for high school credit in geometry. He completed the trigonometry sequence while still 10 and got a B+ in all four math courses.

Back in school and technically in sixth grade after making two movies—and mainly in class again with students his own age—Rick took science with seventh graders and math through the university program. He was allowed to take advanced high school courses right at his school, including functions and statistics. At age 11, he won first place on the Minnesota Mathematics League State Championship test.

Although Rick had made two motion pictures when he was 10, neither was released until he was nearly 12. He did a great deal of publicity work for each, which meant being interviewed on talk shows and press junkets. He thoroughly enjoyed the attention and interaction with the adults. Because he was obviously highly intelligent, interviewers often asked him if he liked school; he always answered that he hated school and that part of the reason he was making movies was to get out of school. It was true.

When Rick was 12, he was away from home most of his seventh-grade year making movies. The directors and actors treated him well and accepted him as an equal. He got to be himself. His tutoring was sometimes inadequate, though, because he was too advanced for any one tutor. For example, his tutor was excellent in language arts, but it was difficult to keep Rick progressing in math and science at that tutor's level. Rick took university correspondence courses, and the tutor helped by guiding him and setting deadlines. He earned an A in college biology and an A- in a college literature course, but he didn't finish the other courses because he went back to his regular school.

Rick acted until he was 13 and had missed half of his eighth-grade year. We tried to keep most of his experiences at grade level while giving him accelerated instruction on the side. But he was homesick when he worked away from home for long periods of time. Sitting with the family at dinner one night, he had no stories to tell that any of his siblings could relate to. Shortly after that, he asked me if he could stop making movies. We made the decision together as a family that we would say no to any offers for at least one year in order to give Rick the chance to figure out what he really wanted to do. We got a great deal of supportive feedback on this decision—usually along the lines of, "It's good that you're letting him just be a regular kid." It was hard, though, because he had never been a regular kid, and all of the choices we made were to try to find what worked for him.

Back in his old school for the second half of eighth grade, Rick won first place in the Mathematics League State Championship test for a second time. In ninth grade, he was put in a French class with kids who had previously taken French. He had no background at all and was not willing to direct as much of his attention to it as would have been necessary to catch up. He claimed that when he really wanted to learn French, he'd go to Paris. He said that he was glad he went to high school—he enjoyed the students, teachers, and the activities. He was in all of the school plays, he was in math league and quiz bowl (captain senior year), and he ran lights for the middle school drama production every year. He wrote commentary for the school newspaper and was the emcee for the Homecoming Coronation. He took the highest level courses that the school offered for his last three years of high school. He got the school's highest score on the *Math Olympiad Test* his junior and senior year. Although he was eligible for a National Merit Scholarship, he didn't do the final step because he planned to attend a college that didn't offer Merit Scholarships.

Colin Richards—Colin progressed rapidly in his music lessons and began composing his own songs around age 10 or 11. I gave him his music lessons until he was age 11; then he switched to a formal teacher. He won the National Spelling Bee that year, after winning for the state the year before. He handled all of the interviews very well and was very proud of himself. He studied regularly and hard.

Author note: Notice that Colin "studied regularly and hard" despite the fact he was a Level Five gifted youngster. All of these children worked hard at their learning, and they worked hardest at learning that was of their own choosing.

Summary of Level Five Gifted

The Level Five gifted children described here were incredibly advanced in every intellectual domain—a primary distinguishing factor in contrast with the children in previous levels. They knew numbers, letters, colors, and shapes before they started talking, and they were all proficient at naming these things virtually immediately upon talking—generally by 15 months, but often earlier—and then they then began speaking in full, complex sentences. The learning trajectories for these children diverged from an average third-grade level as preschoolers to an average upper high school level by age 7½ years old. With all that they know and can do, grouping these children for learning with same-age children makes no sense whatsoever.

To understand Level Five children, it is helpful to think back to the earlier levels. Remember that the achievement of children in Level One is generally two to three years above grade level by the time they are in sixth grade. Level Two children are generally two to three years above grade level by first or second grade, and five to six years above grade level by sixth grade. Level Five children are five to six years above grade level before they enter school, and they are quite capable of finishing all academic coursework through high school before they turn 12. The children in this chapter could have finished the entire elementary curriculum in less than a year, given the opportunity.

Most Level Five children are so obviously different from age-mates in intellectual ability that either their parents or the school arrange for dramatic changes. It is clear from my study and from others, including Gilman (2003) and Smutny (2001), who work with highly intelligent children, that in order for such exceptional children to receive a chance to learn at their own pace, they need to have parents brave and strong enough to challenge an education system that strongly discourages them at every step of the way.[7] In most school districts, there is no legal recourse for the parents of gifted children, not even Level Five children whose needs are so obvious. Often, one parent will need to postpone a career in order to advocate for the child. The cost of special education accommodations such as tutoring falls entirely to the family, and this expense can be considerable. Only one child in this chapter, Ross Oliver, had no substantive changes made to his academic path; he lived in a very small community with few resources, his parents were 15 years younger than the average age of other parents in this book, and both parents worked full time.

Because there are only seven Level Five children in this particular study, we cannot generalize that it is necessary to show all of the milestones listed below by the same age in order to belong to Level Five. None of the levels has strict boundaries or cut-offs.

- All were alert at birth or soon thereafter.
- All paid attention within weeks of birth while someone to read to them.
- Books were a favorite interest of most before three or four months.
- All appeared to understand parental directives between birth and four months.
- The majority independently looked at and turned pages of books before six months.
- All had favorite TV shows or videos before six to eight months.
- Most knew and said some words by 5½ to nine months.
- All had large receptive vocabularies by eight to nine months.
- Half spoke well before age one.
- Many recognized and picked out specific numbers and letters by 10 to 14 months.
- Most played with shape sorters before 11 months.
- Most were good at simple puzzles before 12 months and 35+ piece puzzles by 15 months.
- All knew colors, numbers, the alphabet, and shapes by about 15 months.
- Many read numerous sight words by 15 months.
- Many spoke in complex sentences, more than six to eight words, by 15 months.
- Most could print letters, numbers, words, and their names between 16 and 24 months.
- Many could rote count to 10 or higher by 13 to 20 months.
- All showed musical aptitude before 18 months.
- All memorized books read to them before 20 months.
- Most read board books by 18 to 24 months.
- All read words on signs and simple books and labels before two years.

- All spoke at near-adult level complexity by age two.
- Many used language to make jokes by age two, and most showed humor earlier.
- All showed high interest in factual information, how things work, and science by two years.
- Most grasp skip counting, backwards counting, addition, subtraction, and concepts of "more and less" by two years.
- All were independent on a computer by age two years, and all were keyboarding before three.[8]
- All questioned the reality of Santa Claus and the Tooth Fairy by three or four years.
- All read children's chapter books by age 3½ to 4½ years.
- All showed interest in pure facts, almanacs, dictionaries, etc. by age 3½.
- All played adult-level games for ages 12 and up by the time they were 3½ to four.
- All understood abstract math concepts and basic math functions before age four.
- All read any level fiction and nonfiction by age 4¼ to five.
- All read six or more years beyond grade level by age six.

It is important to note that, just as intelligence scores do not completely identify all of the unusual characteristics of children, high intelligence does not manifest itself in school task achievement alone. The children in this chapter are stunningly intelligent, and that intelligence reveals itself in surprising ways. Whatever educational rules and expectations we have, we must include flexibility if we are to nurture the exceptional abilities of children like these. There are definitely more of these extremely bright children at all five levels than most people think, and we need to embrace all of them. We must leave no child behind, and that must include bright, gifted children.

Table 5: Level Five Children's Data

Name	SBLM Ratio IQ	Test Age Years-Mos.	Other IQ Tests	Achievement Test Grade Equivalencies/ Percentiles/Standard Scores
Jacob Jones	208	9-5	WISC-III 153	WIAT at age 8: Basic Reading 10.5, Math Reasoning 7.7, Spelling 9.2, Reading Comprehension >12.9, Numerical Operations 9.1, Listening Comprehension >12.9, Oral Expression >12.9, Written Expression 7.9, Reading Composite >12.9, Language Composite >12.9, Writing Composite 9.8, Total Composite >12.9 grade equivalencies; WIAT at age 9: Composites for Reading 12-9+, Math 7-2, Language 12-9+, Writing 9-8, Total 12-9+
Ross Oliver	183+	9-3	WPPSI-R 146; WISC-III 151	WJ-R: Reading 154, Math 162, Science 169, Social Studies 160
Carol Johnston	221	6-5	-	WIAT at age 6½: Composite Reading 11¼, Math 10½, Reading Comprehension 13½ age equivalencies; Peabody Achievement at age 8: all >12.9 grade equivalencies except Spelling 8th grade; Peabody Individual Achievement Test at age 8-11: grade equivalencies at >12.9 for Total Reading, Math, and Composite, and 9-0 for Spelling, percentiles all above 99.9; out-of-level 9th grade for PIAT also at age 8-11: Total Reading 86th, Math 79th, Spelling 39th, Composite 82nd percentiles
Jon Crockett	N/A	-	-	At age 6, 4th-6th grade level Sylvan Learning Skills Test: 9th grade equivalencies on 6 of 9 subtests; at age 7, 7th-9th grade Sylvan Learning Skills Test: maxed all 9 subtests at 11.9th grade equivalencies

Name	SBLM Ratio IQ	Test Age Years-Mos.	Other IQ Tests	Achievement Test Grade Equivalencies/ Percentiles/Standard Scores
Rick Arnesen	195+	7-8	Otis-Lennon 150+; SB5 144, 148 w/o WM*	At age 6½: Oral Reading 12th, Reading Comprehension 8th grade equivalencies; Stanford Diagnostic Achievement: Auditory Vocabulary 7-0, Reading Comprehension 10-6, Phonetic Analysis 12-9+, all Math sections 8-9+; Cooperative Mathematics Test in 4th grade: 95th percentile on 9th grade algebra, 99.3rd percentile in 10th grade geometry; at age 17-18: AP U.S. History 5, AP Calculus AB 5, AP Calculus BC 5, Physics B 3; SAT 1580; ACT 33; LSAT at age 22: 178/180
Colin Richards	N/A	-	WPPSI 155	MAT-7 test percentiles in 10th grade: Social Studies 99, Science 99, Language 99, Math 99, Comprehension 99, Vocabulary 99; at age 14: ACT English 35, Math 33, Reading 28, Science 30, Total 32; at age 15: AP U.S. History 3, AP Music Theory 5
Michael Cortez	223	4-8	SB5 146	WJ-R at age 4: Broad Reading 6-4, Letter-Word Recognition 7.9+, Reading Comprehension 4-5, Calculation 5-4, Applied Problems 6-1, Broad Math 5-9, Writing 3-9, Broad Language 4-4 grade equivalencies; Metropolitan Achievement Tests for 4th grade norms when 4 yrs. 10 mos. old: all scores average to above average except Reading Comprehension at 38th percentile

w/o WM is one method of calculating an experimental gifted composite score for the Stanford-Binet 5th Edition in which the working memory subtest is omitted.

Part III:

Gifted Children, School Issues, and Educational Options

Many gifted children exhibit behaviors, interests, and abilities that are quite positive but still cause difficulties for their families or teachers. For example, their early sense of humor can be delightful, but it can also be embarrassing in the wrong social circumstances. The chapters in Part III focus on areas of concern for parents, particularly with regard to how schools are structured and how parents and schools can develop appropriate educational plans for gifted students. This information could make schools friendlier and more effective for children at all intellectual levels.

Chapter 9
What These Kids Are Like

One mother at our babysitting co-op used to put babies in an infant seat so that they could watch the older kids play, and this made most kids happy. Not my kids, though, because if you weren't looking directly at them and talking to them, they were miserable.
~ Mother of gifted children

What is a highly intelligent child like as a baby or a toddler? What is normal, and what should a parent worry about? Are there common personality, temperament, and behavioral characteristics as these children develop? Behaviors that are normal for gifted children are often misunderstood and can lead to difficulties, lifelong problems, or even misdiagnoses as emotional disorders (Webb, Amend, Webb, Goerss, & Olenchak, 2005).

The anecdotes in this chapter, provided by the parents of the children from Part II of this book, describe common behavioral issues that parents face with their young gifted children. Some of these issues are more common than others. Unless someone knows ahead of time what is normal for gifted children, many of these behaviors can be misinterpreted and can become problem areas, particularly regarding cooperation, emotions, and general sociability.

Degrees of Compliance and Cooperation

While some gifted children are naturally cooperative and easygoing, other equally bright children begin their lives as feisty and challenging. These children are often spirited and strong-willed, and many parents are not sure how to react to their behaviors. Parents may worry that discipline will stifle their child's spirit, while others fear that their child will become unmanageable and unpleasant for others to be around unless they continually reprimand them.

When children do not quickly or easily comply, adults may misunderstand the reasons for their behavior, respond inappropriately, and actually worsen the problems. For example, many gifted children have difficulty moving from one activity to another and appear to be stubborn or defiant, when the actual issue relates to their long and intense attention span, their ability to concentrate, and their drive to learn more. If adults mistake the child's intent, the child could be reprimanded inappropriately.

Gifted children are more likely than other children to question *why* they must do something. Once they feel comfortable and secure and understand the reasons for things, most are happy to cooperate.

High Demand for Attention in Infancy

People who have not been around highly intelligent children who constantly demand attention, answers, and interaction often assume that these children are spoiled or poorly behaved. Many parents in this sample described children who had a high need for eye contact and direct, continual interaction almost from birth. This seemed most evident in children in the highest gifted ranges—Levels Three through Five. It is very common for children at all giftedness levels to seek interaction with other people, particularly those who will talk directly to them. Although some might suggest that babies will become spoiled or overly demanding if parents give in to them, the opposite appears to be true. When the need for interaction is consistently met for an infant or young child, that child is more confident and trusting and demands less attention later.

As a result of their gifted young children's need for constant interaction, however, many parents in this book commented on how difficult it was to get anything done while their children were infants and before they could walk on their own. This was also a result of unpredictable napping, since about 20% of gifted children seem to need less sleep than average children, although some need more sleep (Webb, 2000). Many parents said that their very young gifted children simply weren't content to stay in their crib. These children are not always what our culture would describe as "good babies."

Chuck Arnesen—As an infant, Chuck was only fussy when he couldn't interact with someone. At Thanksgiving, when he was one month old, I put him in his automatic swing so we could eat dinner. He screamed and howled the whole time until I picked him up and held him—then he was fine. I never did get to eat my own dinner.

Justin Janacek—Justin didn't really like toys of any kind until he was about 12 months old. Instead, he wanted someone to look at him and talk to him. This made him hard to care for, though, because one can't always be looking at or talking to the baby.

Rebecca Resnick—When Rebecca was an infant, there was a period of a month or so when I couldn't leave the room or she would start crying. I couldn't even go downstairs to do laundry or go into the bathroom to take a shower. Later, I enrolled her in a preschool two mornings a week just so I could get a break, and she never had any problem with going. It seemed she just wanted something to do.

Feisty, Independent, and Strong-Willed

Although some gifted children don't start out as cooperative, many parents described how they won cooperative behavior. They stressed the importance of listening carefully to their child in order to figure out what the child really needed or wanted. Many of these children actively objected to activities that were too structured or group-oriented, and several just wanted time to decide before they jumped into activities. When the parents were consistent, established limits, and showed respect for their child's needs, most of these strong-willed children became more adaptable and cooperative as they matured.

Even when parents were successful in getting their children to cooperate, however, many of them—especially parents of Level Four and Level Five children—found that others still had difficulty with the children as toddlers and preschoolers. A number of grandparents also complained about the willfulness of the children. Adults involved with these children need to learn how to work with them—not fight against them—to become more cooperative.

Ronald Cooper—Ronald was contemplative and would assess a situation and refuse or decline to participate if it seemed too wild, risky, or boring. For example, he refused to play "Ring Around the Rosie" and chose to observe rather than be dragged around by the other three-year-olds.

Glenn Richards—Beginning at seven months, Glenn just laughed when I scolded him. He liked to do what he knew he shouldn't in order to get attention, like play with electrical cords or climb on the table. He threw his first temper tantrum at five months when he got mad that I wouldn't let him play with the plants; he cried and wouldn't be distracted by anything else for almost an hour. He could be very dramatic, as when he choked and gagged about taking medicine.

Nicholas Collins—Before Nicholas was three, I took his diaper off, and he fought and refused to let me put a new one on him. I told him, "Either you let me put a diaper on you or you'll have to wear underwear." He told me that he wanted underwear and was pretty much dry all day after that.

Author note: This is the typical age of successful potty training—often a battle of the wills for mothers and children. Notice the discussion involved here, though.

A significant number of the children were not toilet-trained until older than age three, and a many still had nighttime wetting well into elementary age. Several parents reported control issues with bowel training in their young gifted children. Being gifted does not mean that these children are early at everything.

Jo Anne Price—Jo Anne toilet-trained herself at age 2¼ and showed signs of fierce independence after that. She liked picking out her own clothes. If we made a choice for her in clothes, food, friends, or toys, she screamed with displeasure and frustration.

Gina Oliver—Gina was very independent. She often got frustrated if someone offered to do something for her, even if it was just a common courtesy. When serving the family at dinner, she missed the fact that we dished up everyone's plates—even adults—and she'd yell, "I can do it myself! I'm not a baby!"

Candice Richardson—Candice's love of reading caused some power struggles when we tried to play games as a family. On the one hand, she would rather read than play a game—and thus, she'd be angry and disagreeable during the game—but other times, she'd say that she felt left out if we all played a game without her, even if it was her choice to read instead.

Rebecca Resnick—In preschool, if the other children weren't interesting enough, Rebecca would go off and read a book. She got frustrated when the other kids didn't understand what she wanted to do or respond at her level. When she was older, she hated marching band and band camp because the regimented group thing did not appeal to her. She did well in high school math, but she decided that she liked art and graphics better, so she didn't take math her senior year.

Samantha Forrest—Samantha was always interested in music and hummed and sang all of the time, but she didn't enjoy kid's choir at church—it was too structured. She loved to dance at age four but didn't want to take tap or ballet for the same reason.

Seth Cannon—At 2½, Seth had very definite ideas about how things should be. He only wanted to eat off of breakable dishes and wanted nothing to do with plastic ones. He sat in a booster chair at the big table and rarely agreed to sit in the high chair.

Phil Burns—Phil held strong opinions and argued as an equal with his teachers, much to their surprise. He was strong-willed and not easily intimidated.

Bill Arnesen—Bill frequently threw little fits, but we generally ignored them. Many of these were over food—he wanted ice cream and cookies at every chance. For about three years, all he wanted for lunch was macaroni and cheese from a box. A week before he turned five, our family went on a short cruise. We suffered through scenes at the dinner table on the cruise in which Bill fussed, turned down choices, and was a general pain. I finally pulled him aside and tried to set him straight on how to behave, realizing that it probably wouldn't help much. A few weeks later, I asked him what he liked best about the cruise. He said, "Oh, I just *loved* the restaurant!"

Rick Arnesen—Rick was generally mellow unless he was frustrated or angry. He disliked being treated like a helpless little kid, which is how he thought some adults behaved toward him. When he was about 1½, I picked him up from a babysitting co-op where the mother kept picking him up and handing him to me, not letting him walk. He was so angry and humiliated by the time we got out of the house that he was just furious. I started to put him in his car seat, but he was still outraged. I asked him if he wanted to go back to the porch and walk by himself, and he indicated that he did. I took him back, set him down, and he held my hand so we could both walk to the car.

> *Author note: The intensity of feeling exhibited by Rick is common for gifted children in Levels Three and higher. A sense of fairness, justice, and respect emerges very early in these children—something adults simply do not expect from a child. When parents figure out what is bothering the child, the child feels validated and calms down.*

When he was 2½, Rick went to a childcare class at the local high school. He didn't like having a masking tape nametag on his back, and so he ripped it off right away each day. While the group sat dutifully in a circle and learned to clap and sing songs, Rick roamed around the room looking at books, putting puzzles together, and watching. He wasn't disruptive; he just wasn't interested in doing what they were doing. Fortunately the young class leaders didn't try to force him.

Michael Cortez—At 3½ and in kindergarten, Michael refused some activities. His teacher noticed that he often surveyed the classroom, the materials, and the ongoing activities to look for a challenging activity. Montessori school allowed him the flexibility and freedom to choose his activity, and he was happy with that part of it. He disliked "circle time," though, when the children had to sit specifically with their legs crossed and listen.

Easy-Going and Flexible

While the children described above were at times stubborn or difficult, the next set of anecdotes shows that some very bright youngsters are easy to deal with.

Debra Sund—Debra was always very easy-going. At age eight, she still let me pick out her clothes and didn't really care if what she wore matched. If she ever actually got angry about something, I knew that she felt strongly about it and that I needed to listen.

Brennan Ahlers—Brennan was pretty unflappable. He was a happy and contented child—not real emotional. He seemed to just go with the flow. Although quiet, he took in everything around him. Even as a toddler, he avoided some frustrations because he could verbally express what he wanted. As he got older, if he needed down time, he would just go sit with a stack of books.

Samantha Forrest—At about six months old, Samantha bonded to a soft stuffed bunny. Then, when she was three years old, her sister accidentally threw it away. I thought that this would be devastating for her, but after a few tears, she just talked about how much she missed her bunny. She never threw a tantrum.

Ross Oliver—Ross was always rather easy going. At age two, his grandfather was cutting meat on the tray of his highchair, and Ross whimpered ever so slightly. This was unusual enough that we noticed, but since it wasn't loud or long lasting, we went on with our meal. Later, we realized that his hand had been pinched under the tray, and when Grandpa was applying pressure to cut the meat, he was actually pinching Ross's hand harder.

Carol Johnston—In a group, Carol was quiet. However, one-on-one, she was quite verbal and loved to share her thoughts. She wasn't shy but rather deliberate in what she said and did.

Concentration and Attention Span

Within their own areas of interest, children from Levels Two through Five exhibit incredible attention spans. Parents noted that their children didn't seem to hear them when engrossed in their own thoughts or activities, and they had to either touch the children or gain eye contact in order to pull them out of their intense concentration. These children often are offended when an adult tries to distract them from what they want to do—if adults are able to distract them at all. Parents also related how they sometimes had to talk with the child about the need to move on to a new activity.

Frank Price—Frank did a lot of things in his mind. In fact, many people thought that he was spacing out, and even I was frustrated sometimes that he wasn't listening to me, but he was usually really working on things in his head. At age four, while visiting his grandmother, I asked him if he would please help us reach a bowl on a high shelf by standing on the counter. He was sitting on the floor, spacing out at the time, and he seemed to ignore me. I asked him again. He still ignored me, so I went over to him, stood him up, and asked him again. It was clear that he hadn't heard me the first or second times, and he said, "Oh, sure, but can you remember the number 89 for me?"

Blake Hauge—Blake seemed "lost in thought" as early as age two, and at one point, we thought he might have hearing problems.

Keith Sands—If Keith was focused on his own ideas, he could not be distracted; nothing could move him. But if he wasn't interested, he would do something silly or act out and be unable to focus. This was very frustrating for us as parents.

Seth Cannon—My friend had a child Seth's age. We'd go to the zoo together, but we'd take separate vehicles because Seth and I would usually stay several more hours after they left. We always went to the dolphin show ourselves because her child couldn't sit that long.

Ross Oliver—Involved in his own play, Ross could be so focused that he wouldn't even notice if someone was talking to him. At times, it was as though he heard you but had some other pressing thing on his mind: "Okay, fine, I need to tie my shoes, but what I really want to know is how fast somebody can travel."

Schedules and Transitions

Because of their long attention spans, gifted children can get so involved in their own thoughts that they react strongly to interruptions. Although some parents and teachers might describe them as stubborn or strong-willed, these children respond surprisingly well to schedules, especially if they can be part of the planning. In fact, many of these children have an intense need for schedules and greatly desire to manage their own time and activities—even those children with ordinarily pleasant or easy-going temperaments. Some of their more common behavior issues in school stem from a lack of control over the time that these children get to spend on certain activities; instructional strategies and child-rearing concepts must be significantly adjusted in order to get optimal behavior and give the best support to these highly intelligent young children. Parents and teachers need foresight, diplomacy, and good planning skills in order to cope with them.

Gina Oliver—In preschool and kindergarten, Gina had a very difficult time transitioning from one activity to another. Unless she was finished with what she was working on, she wouldn't move. She had her own schedule and didn't deal well with doing anything piecemeal.

Rebecca Resnick—Rebecca had a very long attention span and had trouble moving from one activity to another. I learned to give five- and 10-minute warnings that it would soon be time to eat, go to bed, go to preschool, and so on.

Keith Sands—Keith was much calmer when he had a routine and a structure. He liked to plan his school holidays with different activities written down next to a time schedule—including lunch and play time.

Bill Arnesen—Bill always wanted to know when things were going to happen so that he could plan ahead. From the time he was three, we kept a calendar in his room, and he wrote events on it and then planned his days around the calendar. Everything needed to be planned or he felt at a loss or unhappy. When it was time to go on a trip, he packed his own suitcase, unhooked and arranged any electronic equipment that was going along, and was ready ahead of anyone else.

Ross Oliver—At times, transitions couldn't happen fast enough for Ross because he was bored, but if they meant taking him away from what he was interested in, they could be very difficult.

Michael Cortez—Michael liked questioning and negotiating schedules as much as planning them by himself. As his activities and interests grew at ages four and five, he saw the benefit of schedules to enable him to do and enjoy everything, and he was more cooperative. He liked using his own appointment book and giving his own time estimates for trips and activities.

Perfectionism

Perfectionism is fairly common among gifted children and probably stems from two main sources. First, these intellectually advanced children get a lot of positive feedback on how quick, correct, and perfect they are—at least in their early years. When anything gets more difficult, they worry that they will lose that positive feedback and that they cannot live up to their own—now entrenched—high expectations. In this way, parents and teachers unknowingly encourage perfectionism. Second, high intelligence makes it possible to envision very lofty goals and performances, and no matter how intellectually able the individual, performance is bound to fall short now and then. Gifted children need help interpreting the difficulties and failures that they encounter so that their self-concept remains strong. They need to understand that being perfect is not always the goal—that mistakes are normal, everyone makes them, and they help us learn.

Although some gifted children do not show any tendencies toward perfectionism, children with talented siblings frequently exhibit this problem, probably because of the perception that others are doing better than they, which can lead to fear or shame.[1]

It is quite common for Level Three and higher gifted children to hold back on participating in an activity until they have watched it first, and many very talented, bright children simply refuse to try things rather than reveal that they can't do them well. It is almost always better to respect this hesitancy and give these children more time. Part of the indecision may be worry over whether or not they can do an activity well, particularly if they are doing it in front of others. Even though practice would improve their performance, their fear of making fools of themselves or failing publicly can undermine their confidence or willingness to try. Some of the hesitation may be their need to feel control. Either way, they respond best when the choice is theirs. Patience and encouragement are needed, and parents might suggest that the child work on the skill in private until he or she feels more confident.

Ronald Cooper—Ronald seemed critical of himself, and by the time he was 11½ years old, he was getting angry with himself if he couldn't get something right away or had to work at it awhile.

Justin Janacek—After several years of loving his "art" (writing by hand), Justin became more aware of the fact that letters are supposed to be neat and legible, and he simply didn't want to put the time into mastering printing. If it didn't look great or perfect, why bother?

Rose Engum—Rose didn't really engage in sports. She was an average player at best, and she seemed to feel that if she couldn't be the best, she didn't want to participate.

Seth Cannon—Once Seth decided to do something, he practiced until he had it down. At 2½, he decided that he wanted to be able to wink, and he practiced all day until he could do it. The best example of his perfectionism was with piano lessons. He started taking lessons and was doing really well, but he decided that the next piece in the lesson book was too hard. He refused to practice that song, which made the difficulty of the piece somewhat of a self-fulfilling prophecy. Once he was persuaded to practice the song and play it, he was fine.

Bill Arnesen—Bill took several classes at the science museum. The first one was "Witches' Brew" and seemed perfect for him. It was a series of chemistry-type science experiments, but he just watched the first session and refused to participate. We didn't make a big fuss over it, and by the second session, he joined in and enjoyed himself very much.

Jon Crockett—Jon was very talented musically, but he didn't have much patience for lessons. Things usually came easy for him, but reading music didn't. He was happier just improvising, and he soon became very good at it. We wanted him to take formal lessons and learn to read and play classical music, but several attempts at formal training only pushed him farther away. We were glad when, some time after the lessons stopped, he eventually returned to the piano.

Author note: The music lesson story is common among the families of gifted children. Most parents are comforted to discover that their child—no matter how talented—is like most other gifted children in this respect. I encourage them to relax, the way Jon's parents did, because a large percentage of gifted children take lessons or teach themselves to play when they are older.

Issues with Authority

When gifted children interpret a situation accurately and make a rational decision, they look for authority figures to back them up. When they do not get that reinforcement, they can lose confidence and respect for those who have, in their view, unreasonable power over them. This can apply to inappropriate school assignments, as well as to social situations. The examples below are from children at Level Three or higher.

Michael Fuller—Michael hated arithmetic in school and frequently received zeroes on his math sheets because he refused to show his work. He understood that it meant a lower grade—about which he cared nothing—but he had drawn his "line in the sand" and refused to budge on showing his work. He said that the rule about showing one's work was stupid. Once he realized that he could use math to his advantage and that it was in his best interest to pay attention, his attitude toward that subject quickly changed for the better. After years of saying he hated math, he looked forward to attending math/technology camp at the local university. His thoughts later ran along the lines of, "Why didn't you tell me this would help me with my C++ computer programming? NOW we're getting somewhere!"

Author note: It is quite common for children who are Level Three or higher to refuse to show their work, memorize math facts, or even turn in "stupid" assignments that do not seem fair or right. This problem resolved itself when Michael started to see the advantages of the math work.

Layne Freeman—Layne tended to challenge authority. Always opinionated, she was at times downright rude. She was suspended twice from school during third grade and had numerous in-school suspensions. People generally responded well to her, in spite of the fact that she had difficulty conforming to adult expectations. She once questioned a teacher in the cafeteria about something fairly benign and was sent to the office for "back talking." Layne also had trouble with anything she perceived as unjust, and she was compelled to have the last word with adults. She was the epitome of the "Walking Argument," although she learned to temper herself somewhat as she got older. Being in the full-time gifted program helped her a lot because her questioning there was no longer automatically assumed to be challenging authority.

Janet Lewis—Janet was the best reader in her first-grade class and read all of the time. Seatwork was different, though. No matter what the assignment, she dragged her feet, despite being kept in at recess for failure to complete work.

Author note: Many Level Three through Five gifted children correctly assess some assignments, seatwork, and homework as being a waste of their time. As a result, these children may develop issues with authority that include resistance and hostility.

Rose Engum—Rose corrected adults if they misstated something, which was sometimes a little disconcerting to those who didn't know her well.

Author note: Many Level Three to Five children do not hesitate to correct adults. Parents and teachers need to work with such children non-defensively to teach them how to let some adult mistakes slide rather than risk embarrassing someone publicly. Or parents can suggest that the child talk about it politely and privately later.

Phil Burns—During a testing session, Phil had trouble waiting for the test directions to be fully explained before starting the test. When the examiner asked if she could hold his pencil until the directions could be completed, Phil held the pencil to the examiner's face and said that he would poke her eye out. For a few moments, he appeared angry. When asked again to hand over the pencil, he did. He then listened to the directions and completed the task.

Author note: When Level Four and Five children become very frustrated, tempers and behaviors can flare. Three different boys from Levels Four and Five had a very similar experience to the one above, although only Phil's is reported here. In each case, adults set clear limits by telling the children that their behavior was unacceptable.

Rick Arnesen—In a Sunday school class for three-year-olds, Rick didn't like either the stories or the coloring activities. He questioned a number of the lessons and argued openly, even dismissively. He was ultimately kicked out of Sunday School.

Demonstrations of Emotions and Feelings

Affectionate Behavior

Degree of affectionate behavior does not appear to be related to level of intelligence but rather to general temperament. All levels of gifted children display a wide range of preferences regarding when and how much cuddling or hugging they want. Although most of the children in this sample were relatively affectionate, many were so physically independent and active that reading time was the only time for cuddling.

Ronald Cooper—As a toddler, Ronald had a very loving nature and was readily affectionate. He was especially sweet at bedtime and needed parent time each night.

Jo Anne Price—Jo Anne was always affectionate, but not to the point that it would get in the way of her independence.

Debra Sund—Debra loved her teachers, and even though she was not especially demonstrative, she liked to give them hugs.

Justin Janacek—Justin hated breast-feeding because he had to be held so close to do it. At the same time, he was affectionate and hugged, kissed, and woke us up by snuggling in bed in the morning, but he was never a lap sitter or a cuddler for any length of time.

Keith Sands—Keith was very affectionate and cuddly, even by age 10, when he was still attached to a particular soft toy.

Samantha Forrest—Samantha didn't like to be hugged or kissed. She put up with the grandparents when they wanted to hug her but asked that no one kiss her. However, she loved to sit in our laps at church and eventually became a hand holder.

Intensities and Sensitivities[2]

One of the earliest issues that parents of gifted children face is the varying degrees of intensity present in their children. This intensity affects not only what the child is like at home, but also how he or she appears to others. For example, an extremely talkative child who loves to interact with adults may not be welcome in a setting with people who think that children should be seen and not heard; in that kind of situation, parents are expected to curb their child's behavior and are at risk for social censure, along with their too-talkative child.

Empathy is something that many adults notice early about gifted children of all levels, and this sensitivity seems to increase with intellectual level. Parents are often unsure whether to shield their children from experiences that will worry or sadden them or to use the occasions as opportunities for conversation and growth.

Some intellectually advanced children are also unusually sensitive to sights, sounds, temperatures, and feelings (Winner, 1996). Their reactions to their environment are quite different from those of most typical children—some parents even take them to a healthcare specialist to find out whether or not something might be wrong. Interestingly, the incidence of allergies is also common among the gifted (Geschwind & Galaburda, 1987).

Some people see these intense, sensitive gifted children as odd or as having something inherently wrong with them; others attribute the child's differentness to poor parenting. As parents experience their child's emerging personality, they must often decide when the child's behavior is a problem and when it is better to respond positively to the child's reactions.

Frank Price—Frank didn't like organized sports—too rough and too loud—but he always enjoyed playground equipment. There was one odd exception. At about age four, he was doing gymnastics, but one night he woke up screaming because he was scared of the rings. The next day, he was having anxiety attacks—his breathing would become rapid, and he'd start whimpering. I asked him what was wrong, and he just said, "Swings and rings." He couldn't go near a playground for quite a while without "freaking out." He told me he wanted to move to the moon because "it doesn't have...you know." We stayed away from playgrounds for about four months, and then he was fine with them again.

Debra Sund—At around 2½, Debra loved the book *There's a Nightmare in my Closet*, but a few months later, she became really scared of it. She wanted us to get rid of the book completely and wouldn't go to sleep until we had taken it out of her room. Once the book was gone, she relaxed and went to sleep. The book stayed in my closet for more than a year.

Author note: Sensitivity to a scary story is common. Many gifted children have tremendous powers of imagination, but they do not have the experience or hindsight to comprehend what is truly threatening and what is not. By not forcing the child to be braver than she felt, these parents showed respect for her worries, and her fears eventually passed.

Chuck Arnesen—When a Charlie Brown show called "No Dogs Allowed" aired on TV, Chuck, who was about three, was beside himself with sadness for Snoopy, who wasn't allowed in any stores or restaurants. He cried convulsively when he went to bed that night, and we needed to talk for a long time about Snoopy, why restaurants have rules like that, and whether or not Snoopy understood the reasons for those rules.

Chuck showed great interest in understanding what made people tick. His first-grade teacher said that he always complimented her when she had a new haircut. He cheered people on during games and was unusually generous and noncompetitive during them. As he got older, he quit playing games with anyone who was too competitive or too far beyond his own skills.

William Jones—My sister always told me that I needed to "toughen William up." She thought that he was too sensitive. I told her that his sensitivity is what made him who he was—unique.

Patricia Walker—At age two, Patty got a dancing dinosaur for Christmas. She was afraid of it, so we got rid of it the next day and never mentioned it again. Ten months later, she made a comment about the dancing dinosaur. We could hardly remember what she was talking about.

Samantha Forrest—Samantha started watching TV at age two and picked the non-scary shows on PBS—she frightened easily—like animal shows on the *Discovery Channel*. She was very frightened at movies that were the least bit scary but wasn't bothered by nature shows that demonstrated the food chain. At age three, she was so frightened of loud noises that we had to sit inside the car with the windows closed to watch the Independence Day fireworks.

Jacob Jones—We were told that Jacob might have ADHD[3] and that we should have him tested. We knew that he didn't have this disorder; he could concentrate for hours on LEGOs®, books, and computers. He was always "more" in every area, and not many people appreciated that.

Jacob liked to be outside as long as it was 70 degrees with no humidity and no bugs. He enjoyed bike riding as long as he didn't sweat, get thirsty, or have to go up hills.

Idealism, Compassion, and Sense of Fairness

The high reasoning ability of gifted children leads them to an early concern for fairness, justice, and doing what is right. They are strongly offended by any perceived injustice, whether toward themselves or toward others, and they have the advantage of an excellent sense of reasoning, fair play, and the confidence that they can explain a situation to their benefit that allows them to stand up for what they believe in. They also tend to notice and care about others in pain. This is sometimes called emotional giftedness (Piechowski, 1991; Roeper, 1982). If gifted children are belittled for being idealistic, they can lose their sense of power to make a difference.

Kindness toward others is an especially common theme in Level Three and higher children when they are quite young. Many of them stop this generosity, especially toward siblings, during their school years. However, there appears to be an innate altruism in Levels Four and Five gifted individuals.[4] In fact, a number of researchers have noticed an early idealism and moral character in gifted children. These children are able to think about the long-term greater good rather than their own immediate satisfaction, and it is easier to teach these concepts to children who are intellectually advanced than to average children.[5]

Keith Sands—When Keith was about 6½, he wrote a note to his teacher: "Dear Mrs. Jones, I have a comment about giving Willy a buckaroo ticket because he took your tray to the cafeteria. I took your tray to the cafeteria *seven times*! It's just not fair! How come *he* gets a buckaroo ticket and I don't? Love, Keith."

Chuck Arnesen—Chuck was always small in his classes, and he used to get teased about his size. Once, in sixth grade, when another boy wouldn't let him have the only remaining seat on the school bus, Chuck sat down anyway and took just a small portion of the seat. When the boy tried to shove him off the seat, Chuck punched him in the nose, causing a nosebleed. The other boy told Chuck that he'd be in big trouble, but Chuck said that he looked forward to telling his part of the story because he would not be the one in trouble. He was right.

William Jones—Will seemed to feel more, care more, and absorb more than others his age. When he was four, we had an Easter egg hunt, and he found the egg with the $5 bill in it. His grandpa said that he should share the money with his brother, so without hesitation, Will ripped the bill in half.

Gina Oliver—Gina liked to play with others, but she could be very stubborn if she felt that their actions or expectations infringed upon her sense of freedom, independence, or fairness. The emotions that were strongest for her were sadness, anger, and frustration. She became very sad when she felt that her peers treated her unfairly. Although she seemed self-possessed, if her peers were critical of her, she took it to heart. If her older brother was ever in trouble or feeling bad, Gina would try to cheer him up by giving him things or trying to fix whatever was making him sad.

Layne Freeman—Layne tended to frustrate easily and got upset when things were unfair. She was very vocal about it, noncompliant, and stubborn.

Brennan Ahlers—Brennan had a keen sense of justice once he hit preschool. He was very compassionate and cost me a small fortune in charitable contributions. He either wanted to join or contribute to any cause-related fundraiser or walkathon. When he was very young, he thought that homeless people should come live with us. He wanted to give his unused toys to children's homes and became very emotional whenever he saw anything about the less fortunate.

Samantha Forrest—Samantha was sad when people were not nice to each other, and she was very concerned about peace and harmony on earth. She couldn't understand why some people do bad things intentionally.

Jon Crockett—At age five, Jon raised the most money in the state for the Multiple Sclerosis Read-a-thon; he read 154 books in four weeks, had 42 sponsors, and raised $1,361.09. Jon not only called everyone whose phone number he could get, but he went door-to-door to neighbors and typed letters and e-mails to get sponsors. When he was getting donations for $1 per book read, I called people back to suggest that they lower the amount they pledged, as he was likely to read more than 100 books in 28 days. He got upset with me and asked, "Why are you doing this? This isn't for me. It's for people with Multiple Sclerosis. Why are you taking money away from them?"

Asynchrony of Development

Asynchrony of development describes the misalignment of intellectual concerns and abilities with maturity—thus, a gifted child is academically or mentally older than he or she is physically, emotionally, or experientially (Silverman, 2002). This means that the child's reasoning, vocabulary, and goal-setting capacity, as well as the ability to read, absorb, and remember information, is often way ahead of the child's experience or judgment. The more intelligent and advanced the child, the more likely he or she is to experience problems or fears based on the gap between intellectual development and actual experiences. These children may also have difficulty interpreting what is really going on in some situations, which can lead to embarrassment.

Brennan Ahlers—Brennan was very concerned about Y2K. At seven years old, he lost precious hours of sleep over what would happen on December 31st, 1999. He envisioned God setting the earth on fire and bringing us all up to heaven. He was consumed by the fact he'd be there for eternity and also worried sick that he'd be bored.

Ross Oliver—It was difficult dealing with Ross at times because he conversed using the language structure and vocabulary of an adult, but he still had the moral development of a preschooler. Expectations were often set much higher for his behavior because one could believe that he understood adult requirements, but he definitely had the emotions of a young child.

Rick Arnesen—The summer Rick was nearly four and his brother was not quite six, they traveled by air as unaccompanied minors to visit their grandparents. Chuck expressed great worry that someone would find out that they weren't old enough to go alone—the age limit was five. Rick impatiently explained to his older brother, "Chuck, we simply won't tell them." Later that week, Rick didn't want to leave an amusement park when it was time to go. He hurled himself down on the ground, kicking and screaming and carrying on. His grandfather was red-faced with embarrassment and angrily hauled him away.

Author note: These examples reveal the asynchrony of the young Level Five gifted child. This three-year-old could show wisdom and maturity well beyond his years in one situation and typical age-appropriate behavior in another.

Rick worried about the things he saw on the news and in books. Between ages four and five, he was truly apprehensive about the possibility of flash floods. We didn't live in an area where flash floods occurred, so I repeatedly explained this to him, hoping to set his mind at ease. He had nightmares about the Johnstown Flood for a long time. He read and reread all of the details and memorized all of the statistics, circumstances, and mistakes that led to the disaster.

Jon Crockett—At age three, Jon didn't want to take an over-the-counter allergy medicine "because that can have bad side effects," but he agreed to take it on the condition that he be shown the list of ingredients. At age five, he voted in a mock election for kids, and he voted for Dole. His reasoning was that, "I want everyone's wishes to come true, and since Clinton has been President, Dole should have a turn." Moments later, he added, "I'm also all for someone who wants to lower taxes."

Sense of Humor

Advanced sense of humor is another frequent characteristic of gifted children, though it is not universal. Many Level Three and higher children end up playing the class clown, which can lead to difficulties, but teachers often enjoy the subtle and mature humor exhibited by some gifted children. When children the same age do not understand a child's humor but an adult does, it makes sense that a gifted child would be drawn to the more appreciative adult audience.

Gary Lundquist—Most teachers loved Gary's enthusiasm and sense of humor, though some considered him disruptive. I felt a huge sense of relief when adults appreciated his humor, because if they didn't, they probably didn't like him. He had a wonderful third-grade teacher, and the two of them spent a lot of time laughing at things they found funny. She told us about the time when she encouraged the kids in the class to tell jokes, just to practice speaking in front of others. One asked, "Why did the man's car go off the road?" and without missing a beat, Gary responded, "Because his wife drove him over the edge." The teacher practically fell out of her chair from laughing so hard. None of the children thought it was funny at all.

Samantha Forrest—Samantha didn't laugh until she was about a year old. She smiled, but nothing tickled her funny bone until later than most babies.

Colin Richards—Colin had a sense of humor, but there were many, many times when he was so literal that he was offended if anyone laughed.

Seth Cannon—At Seth's fourth birthday party, he convinced one of his young friends that the red frosting on his fork was actually blood. This child became upset, and she came over to tell me that Seth was eating blood. I told her he was just teasing—that it was red frosting from his cake. She returned, very confidently, to tell him it was frosting. He responded in an affected vampire voice (which I don't know where he learned) that no, it was yummy blood. She needed more reassurance that he was just teasing.

Seth also talked to himself with some regularity. One day when he was talking to himself in the car, I thought he was talking to me, so I asked him what he said. He responded, "I was just talking to myself, Mom." I asked him why, and he answered, "Because it confuses people."

General Sociability—How They Spend their Time

Social Interaction with Others

There are children throughout the giftedness levels who do quite well in social situations, especially when parents expose them to a range of ages and experiences. As the children start school, however, they are usually placed with classmates who are not intellectually attuned to them, and intellectual differences often means differences in interests. As a result, many bright children seek out older children and adults for companionship.

Many gifted children find it hard to find others with whom to form close friendships. Unless they get support in developing both friendship skills and finding venues where others who are like them congregate, they may feel that something is wrong with them.

Cory Engum—As a toddler, Cory was intent on keeping up with his older sister and other older children. Once, when I picked him up from a play date with a preschool friend, Cory was talking with the mother and helping her with gardening while his friend was off doing something else. The mother remarked that Cory was good company and that they'd had quite a nice chat.

Glenn Richards—Glenn never had any trouble playing or getting along with other kids and was generally very popular because he had a good sense of humor and was fun to play with. Adults usually found him polite and cooperative. When he was older, between ages seven and 10, there were a couple of boys—energetic, strong-willed boys like him—who he had trouble getting along with. They had to work out the pecking order among them.

Chuck Arnesen—In preschool and kindergarten, Chuck loved school and made many friends. When at home, however, he preferred playing with his younger brother rather than with neighborhood kids. Both boys had problems with other children damaging their possessions.

Author note: Although it doesn't mean that they aren't messy, it is common that highly intelligent children like to take care of their things.

Derek Fondow—Derek had a close bond with his older sister and, at 2½, happily joined her in a mixed-age classroom filled with three- to six-year-olds. He liked to work on his own or play with the other children, and he asked the older ones if he could "observe" them working. By first grade, he socialized with everyone and pointed out qualities that he liked in his friends—sense of humor, similar interests, etc. Walking through the hallways of his K-12 school, he always spoke to everyone, and he looked forward to his weekly meeting with a twelfth-grade mentor very much.

Debra Sund—Although Debra sometimes made friends quickly, she was comfortable playing by herself and letting other children join her. When she did make friends, they were strong friendships with children whose imaginations and intelligence were similar to hers.

Jo Anne Price—Jo Anne attached easily to others. She loved her aunts and her cousins—especially the girls—her daycare provider, and four or five other girls at daycare.

Sophie Fuller—Sophie shined at interpersonal interaction with others. She charmed adults from the age of two on, and she had a gift of engaging them with her mannerisms and desire to relate with them. Surprisingly, at school, she was sometimes at a loss to relate to a gaggle of girls. In first grade, for example, she invented games but didn't share the rules before beginning to play them.

Franklin Hayes—Franklin got along fine with most children but never felt like he fit in. He really wanted a best friend. He did make a good friend at one point, but he still couldn't find someone who thought like he did or was interested in the things that he enjoyed.

Justin Janacek—Justin didn't particularly like being around younger children and tended to ignore them. Although he was sociable, out-going, and made friends easily, I watched him struggle to tone down his communication and imaginative play when interacting with kids his own age.

Author note: It is common for gifted children (and adults) to adjust their conversation and activities to the levels of those around them. Many do it so often and so naturally that they don't even know they are doing it. When they find themselves in a group where they are normal—with other very bright people—it is exhilarating. It is only then that they realize what they have been missing.

Rose Engum—Adults always seemed to find Rose charming. She was cheerful, talkative, had an extensive vocabulary, and was interested in everything. As a toddler and preschooler, she had almost daily play dates with other children. With peers, she usually preferred to engage with one or two others and would withdraw if the group got too large or rambunctious.

Rebecca Resnick—Rebecca never had separation anxiety. She had a great time at daycare and never wanted to leave. She played with the other kids and generally got along fine with everyone. When she was three and four years old, she would stand very close to people and talk loud while looking off to the side instead of looking at the person she was speaking to. I was concerned that she wasn't learning to socialize normally. She outgrew it, but it lasted a few years.

Author note: A number of these children had some odd mannerisms but out-grew them. Parents must guide children toward what is socially acceptable with explanations like, "Look at people's eyes when you talk to them. It makes them feel that you are really paying attention to them."

Kayla Bardy—Everyone liked Kayla. She was funny and behaved well. She was reserved at first with unfamiliar adults but went from hiding behind me at age 2½ to good interaction after some warm-up time. After age three, she became very social and always had best friends.

Daniel Schmidt—Other kids taunted Daniel often, especially from second grade on. He was different and sensitive, so he was a satisfying target. He found a few good friends in elementary school—other bright boys. In middle school, he had a nice group of friends with similar interests. Adults generally found him charming, friendly, witty, and sunny.

Bill Arnesen—Bill was very social at 3½, but he often preferred older children for friends. He was not willing to play with the younger children of our friends, and his lack of willingness to get to know others caused our family difficulties in getting involved in some larger social groups. He always had so many friends that he didn't feel the need to develop the skills of actually acquiring friends until much later.

Carol Johnston—Carol waited for other students to initiate interaction, but she was always willing to join a group when invited. She seems to have been largely passed over in school. She ate lunch alone in the school cafeteria, and school staff didn't know how to support her. Her school experience was largely to quietly acquiesce to the classroom standard, avoid embarrassing attention, and endure social isolation and academic neglect.

Author note: There are plenty of Level Four and Five children who behave like Carol. They appear aloof from time to time, and their extreme intelligence complicates others' initial understanding or acceptance of them. Such children benefit from adult guidance about how others might see them and what they can do to make others comfortable. It might help if the parent or teacher demonstrates various approaches to joining a group's activities.

Rick Arnesen—Once, when Rick was talking with an adult, they were both talking over each other, so I asked Rick not to interrupt. Both of them snapped their heads around toward me and blurted out, "We're listening!" As a young adult, Rick still talked over people unless you very specifically asked him not to and he agreed. It never bothered him if you interrupted him.

> *Author note: Many Level Three and higher children are able to carry on meaningful conversations in which both people talk and both people listen. These children need to be directly taught that most people cannot do this. It is a relief for many gifted people to discover this is a normal tendency in extremely smart people and not a sign that they are rude or insensitive. They still need to learn what works for others, though.*

Bossiness

Accusations of bossiness are common among young gifted children. It is not so much that these children need to have their own way, but more that they need to do something more interesting than simple activity without rules. Normal young children play together in "parallel play." Levels Two and higher gifted children, however, have high energy levels and tend to pour their energies into complex games and activities more often than their intellectually average age-mates. They can see ways to make the play activity more interesting by adding rules or embellishments, and they endeavor to guide their less verbal age-mates in this direction. These children simply do not yet have the more subtle social skills to use along with their high organizational skills. Thus, they are often described as "bossy," " too competitive," or "a bad sport," when they try to get others to use their strategy and rules. Consequently, many of these children gravitate toward older children whose mental ages are closer to their own. It is also very common for highly gifted children to cross the gender line for friendships.

Layne Freeman—Layne tended to be bossy and was basically clueless regarding social skills. She got frustrated when she wasn't in charge.

Andrea Dolan—Andrea was aggressive and bossy when she was young. Her outside free time usually ended up in poor, negative, or overzealous behavior. She wanted to direct others, and she was good at organizing learning activities.

Keith Sands—Keith was always very social, but being bossy made it harder for him to be with same-age peers. He would become frustrated with them, and others found him too intense or too verbal. He overwhelmed children who were quiet. With children who were boisterous, he got wound up and silly. He gravitated toward older children, particularly girls.

Phil Burns—Phil's main social weakness was that he liked to direct play, and he often ordered other kids around to fit his grand scheme. He didn't understand when they resisted.

Sportsmanship and Competitive Nature

Being competitive is natural, but losing and winning graciously have to be learned. Many parents are initially embarrassed that their children are competitive or show poor sportsmanship. They are relieved to learn that this is normal in a young child and that most Level Two and higher children are very competitive. These children are intense, though, and their competitive nature can overwhelm friendships, siblings, and parents. It takes careful consideration to guide them into appropriate reactions to winning or losing, and most get their tempers, intensities, and interactive social skills under control by the time they are about 10 to 12 years old. The higher-level children are also sticklers for procedure and rules, which can get them into trouble when the adults just want the children to have fun. Most gifted children approach contests with more fervor than the organizers intended.

It is not necessary to try to get these children to be less competitive. Competition is enjoyable and can help individuals hone their skills. Highly intelligent children and adults seem to know that strategy and effectively taking advantage of the rules is a big part of what makes competition challenging and fun.

Michael Fuller—The library summer reading program was always popular with our family, and one would think that the tallying of books read would be an easy matter. Not at our house. Michael constantly challenged the rules of the summer reading program: "Does 'Read 25 books' mean 25 I've never read before? What about *The Lion, the Witch, and the Wardrobe?* Can I read it again if I haven't read it since my birthday? Why doesn't *The Hobbit* count as more than one book if it takes 10 times as long to read? Do they want me to read just little kid books? What if I have the same book as the library? Can't I just read that if it's the same book and I haven't read it before?"

Jacob Jones—Jacob was quite competitive in certain situations, like when playing board games. He'd quit if he wasn't winning and got angry if it looked as if he might lose.

Ross Oliver—Ross was always intense when it came to playing games. He lost interest quickly playing just with his sister or with friends; he wanted to play with adults. He also wanted to win when playing a game and sometimes could not let go if he didn't win—he wanted to play again and again. He often tried to cheat to win or came up with rules that sounded official but were not accurate. He became a better sport as he matured and started to accept that losing at a game didn't necessarily mean that someone was better than he.

Rick Arnesen—When Rick was in fourth grade, his gym teacher said that he often became frustrated with his teammates. He needed to take the game less seriously and have more fun playing.

Interests and Approach to Play

In general, the play of intellectually advanced children is complex and detailed, and their interests are usually at least several years ahead of what their age-mates are interested in doing. Although a number of experts on gifted children have noted imaginary playmates as more common among these children than average children, only three children in this sample had parents who mentioned them, although many of the children did exhibit a rich fantasy play.

Kirk Peterson—Kirk was very good with detailed graphic instructions, like K'NEX™ and LEGO® MINDSTORMS Robotics Invention System™. He was always creating things—a pretend computer, a fort, decorations from scrap paper, and more.

Ronald Cooper—Ronald regrouped or relaxed with books, the computer, playing outside, playing with LEGOs® or PLAYMOBIL®, and sometimes by watching TV.

Jo Anne Price—Jo Anne always played with her big brother's toys, which were for older kids. She also loved anything to do with babies, dolls, families, kitchens, make-up, or princesses. She liked wearing dresses and said that she wanted to "look like a mom and wear nail polish and jewelry." (I don't wear dresses or nail polish or jewelry; I don't know where that came from.) She was very social and loved playing with other children, especially other girls, and was very influenced by the kids at her daycare. She had many questions about music stars, getting her ears or tongue pierced (!), getting married, having children, and dying.

William Jones—Will had an unbelievable imagination and was always coming up with new inventions. He built many things with LEGOs®. He spent approximately three hours a week reading on his own, specifically science fiction and military books, with a special emphasis on autobiographies and books about constructing and inventing things. He also collected Star Wars™ cards. His special activities included piano lessons, golf, baseball, going to the science museum, and attending Summer School for the Gifted.

Gina Oliver—Gina sang, listened to music, and literally danced everywhere. She took great joy in music, even as an infant. She was always very active with her stuffed animals, and although she never really wanted to play with Barbie™, she did like the *American Girl*™ dolls. She created stories that were complex.

Candice Richardson—In many ways, our biggest challenge was to get Candice to stop reading and try to get information about the world in other ways. Once, I asked her to choose at least one nonfiction book during each library visit. She very quickly discovered that all of the folk and fairy tales are in the nonfiction section. Aargh! She never expressed regret at discovering early that Santa, the Tooth Fairy, and the Easter Bunny are not real, but she truly wanted to believe in magic. She was convinced that she was magic and tried to do magic spells on the playground. Her teacher asked her to stop because she might scare some of the other children.

Sophie Fuller—At age five, Sophie was usually asleep by 10:15 P.M.—with books everywhere. I got a great old set of readers for her, and Sophie just churned through them. All of the bookcases in our house were full.

Justin Janacek—Justin enjoyed art museums, theater, dancing, art activities, being with other people, camping, biking, and swimming.

Rose Engum—At Brownie meetings during first and second grade, Rose actively participated at the beginning of each of the structured activities. When I came to pick her up at the end of the meeting, though, I often found her sitting in the book corner reading while the other girls were still playing. She liked preschool, but she withdrew sometimes when her class went to the gym for large motor activities, not wanting to participate. Her teacher said that she showed a mixture of solitary and social play throughout the day.

Seth Cannon—Seth loved running—running was allowed in our house, necessarily! He ran laps between the kitchen, dining room, family room, toy room, and living room, and he always wanted us to time him. He ran and ran, trying to shave time off his record. He even mentioned running in the Olympics.

Author note: A great many of these children, particularly boys, have very high energy levels and are quite physically active. As with the girls, most develop their skills in individual rather than group activities. All levels of gifted children love an audience and need feedback and praise.

Phil Burns—Electronics and robotics interested Phil once he passed age 11. He accumulated a large collection of electronic components—bulbs, switches, wires, resistors, capacitors, transistors, etc.—and constructed sophisticated devices, including alarms, sensors, and toys for his brother—for instance, a pinball game and a quiz game. He progressed to robotics using the LEGO® MINDSTORMS Robotics Invention System™ to build, program, and test various robots.

Birds fascinated Phil, and he learned to identify them by sight and sound, their feeding and nesting habits, egg size and color, and flight patterns. He maintained a bird feeder and birdbath, built bluebird and other birdhouses, and closely monitored a parent bird and nestlings in one house. He used up many rolls of film trying to get good photographs of them. He also undertook the study of plants, taught himself the names and characteristics of various houseplants, and used his allowance money to purchase them. He experimented with food, water, and sunlight, and he collected seeds from the wild. He planned to conduct genetics experiments with peas.

Ross Oliver—Ross was reading chapter books by the time he entered preschool daycare, but the school always had other activities scheduled, and he wasn't given time to read. Additionally, they had no books that were at his level. After we spoke to the daycare staff, they let him use materials that belonged to the daycare provider's third-grade daughter. Later, Ross focused on learning about *Nintendo®*, even though we didn't have a system, because it gave him the ability to be the "smart kid" within the realm of the other kids' experiences.

Carol Johnston—Carol's passion was whales. She read almost every book on whales in her school library, created artwork about whales, and researched whale behaviors, habitats, and declining populations. Not yet seven, she was thrilled to meet and communicate with a Beluga whale at the local aquarium. She loved to read, and we sometimes had to drag her away to join the "real world." She often fooled us by waiting until we were asleep and then reading in her room until 3:00 A.M. She read almost anything, including books we bought for reference.

At age seven, Carol also discovered the world of the microscope, and she made slides and identified objects and structures. She enjoyed creating "movies" of microscopic organisms using time-lapse photography. She had an inborn need to create, build, or invent things. She came up with ideas for combining household objects in unique and unusual ways to create elaborate artwork, sculptures, new objects, puzzles, and games. She invented a dust cloth consisting of a balloon covered by a cloth. The static electricity from the balloon attracted dust particles to the cloth, which could then be removed for washing. Filling the balloon with helium allowed one to clean the ceiling and other high places. She made things out of materials that she found around the house; she turned a piece of cardboard into an elaborate gift for her teacher. She also made herself a three-note drum using old cut-up balloons for the drum skin. When I insisted we didn't have anything from which to make a drum, she announced tartly, "I always use balloons for my rubber."

Performance and Leadership

A rather large number of the Level Three and higher gifted children in this book were involved in performance activities. They acted, sang, danced, played instruments, and competed in spelling, geography, and quiz bowl-type competitions. Interestingly, many of these children were introverts, perfectionists, or otherwise unsure of themselves, yet somehow they were drawn to these very public activities. In most cases, parents did not specifically encourage the children—in fact, many parents were actually surprised when their child was selected for an acting part because no mention of it was made at home first.

Whereas many people find their greatest enjoyment, social interaction, and acceptance through sports, others find it through non-sports performance. When they are involved in sports, gifted children usually choose individual sports like swimming, golf, tennis, and skiing rather than active team sports.

Derek Fondow—Derek surprised us at age seven when he climbed up on a chair in front of an adult audience of business and law professionals and asked Sally Ride, the speaker, if there is friction on the moon.

Brennan Ahlers—When Brennan was 7¼, he was selected to give a speech at the only sounding of the *R.M.S. Titanic*'s whistles since its maiden voyage in 1912. He lined up on the outdoor stage with dignitaries including our mayor, a U.S. Representative, a variety of CEOs, and every *Titanic* expert in the world. When he was introduced, he stepped up to the podium, faced the crowd of 60,000, and read the poem he had written about the importance of following one's dreams, just like the people on the *Titanic*. There were rows of photographers, television stations from across the world, and a live broadcast on the Internet. When he came off the stage, his eyes were shining, his hands were frozen, and he shivered with cold.

Janet Lewis—Janet always loved performing, and in third grade, she quickly memorized a very large number of lines to play a lead role for the regional theater in our area. She seemed to lose interest in performing, however, after one of the adults in the troupe ridiculed her dream of appearing on Broadway.

Samantha Forrest—Samantha loved to do free-form dance at home with her sister. Once she hit age four, though, she didn't really enjoy dancing in public. Most likely, she was more self-conscious and aware that no one else was dancing.

Bill Arnesen—Bill was a natural at singing and movement, and he started violin and piano lessons when he was four and five years old. He played violin for a TV commercial when he was 5½. He got a national art award for an art piece he did as a first grader and was very pleased.

Androgyny of Interests and Behaviors

Research suggests that as intelligence increases, so does androgyny (Hollingworth, 1942; Kerr & Cohn, 2001). This means that gifted children and adults have many preferences that are not typically associated with their gender group. Many highly intelligent people are glad to discover that androgyny is common among the gifted.

Kirk Peterson—In some groups of boys, Kirk pulled away and played by himself. Even though his interests were quite masculine, he got along best with girls.

Gina Oliver—Many of Gina's closest playmates were boys.

Derek Fondow—Derek asked why kids think that you should only play with boys if you are a boy.

Justin Janacek—Justin was very social and adapted well to most other children, but not to younger kids or aggressive boys. He preferred girls who were a little older than he as playmates, maybe because girls are inclined to be more verbal and less aggressive. Girls also tend to like pretend play more than boys, and he loved that. He was a pretty nontraditional boy. We worried that his preferences could be a challenge for him as he got older, when kids begin to identify "boy" things and "girl" things more often.

Summary of Gifted Behaviors and Traits

What are these gifted children like? And how can the adults in their lives guide them toward well-adjusted lives? Not surprisingly, the most significant characteristic that binds these children together is that they are very intellectual in their interests from an early age. Like all children, they see everything through their own eyes. Unlike normal children, however, cognitively advanced children care about and respond to the logic of different viewpoints while still very young. Discussion and reasoning work well to move these children toward increased levels of cooperation. It is important that they feel included in the basic direction and details of whatever they are asked to do. When adults in their environment do not make sense, gifted children tend to stick to their own interpretations.

Normal qualities for highly gifted children include high intensities and sensitivities, extensive concentration and attention spans, high idealism, competitive nature, sense of humor, and androgyny of interests. Qualities that can, with guidance, change or improve over time are high need for attention, difficulty cooperating with others, rigidity with their own schedules, perfectionism, bossiness, poor sportsmanship, and asynchrony of development.

Chapter 10
The Crash Course on Giftedness and the Schools

*In kindergarten, the students were supposed to count to
at least 100. The teacher stopped Jon at 300 because
she was afraid he would continue all morning.*
~ Father of a Level Five boy

It is easy to see why typical schools cause problems for gifted children
and why gifted children pose problems for their schools. Most schools
are not prepared to accommodate children who are this intelligent.

Once you know a child's level of giftedness, what's next? Most
important is to decide what matters most to both the parents and the
child. What do you value and need, and how much effort are you willing
or able to expend to satisfy those needs?

In my consulting for highly intelligent people—whether children
or adults—the key session is the one that follows the intelligence assessments. I call it my Crash Course on Giftedness because it gives clients
needed information about their own circumstance and options. Parents
who seek professional guidance should request such a detailed explanation and review of the assessment results. Each client's intelligence level,
gender, personality, goals, and other factors should be considered. The
crash course—designed to make important points quickly—includes
theories, interpretations, and summaries, which are supported by cita-
tions, relevant handouts, and additional reading recommendations tailored
to the individual. This chapter is a brief adaptation of the highly individualized Crash Course on Giftedness.

Why Is There a Problem?

Regardless of what level of giftedness their children are at or where
they live, families frequently tell stories of frustration regarding experiences with their children's schools. These families initially expect that the

school will recognize their child's abilities and address them appropriately. They are soon disappointed, frustrated, and sometimes even furious.

Why don't schools customarily provide an array of advanced coursework or challenging programs for exceptionally able students? The main reason seems to be that the fundamental concept of individual differences in above average intellectual ability is an uncomfortable concept for many school professionals. Though willing to recognize differences in ability at the low end of the spectrum, educators seem less willing, and perhaps less able, to notice differences at the high end. Perhaps it's easier to detect the slow learners; they stand out because of their difficulties and frustrations. Children at the high end have frustrations, too, but for different reasons. For them, the work is too easy, but teachers are not inclined to interpret the signs of frustration that accompany what looks like success. Teachers have no idea how high a bright child can go because schools typically don't ask students to do ever-higher, more difficult work. Schools are satisfied to have students work at grade level. Knowing this, many smart kids learn to just fit in, blending with others so as not to get teased or called names like "nerd."

Perhaps most important, teachers are not trained to look for students who are brighter than normal, so they don't expect them to be operating at levels far above the majority of the students in their class. If they have never learned about characteristics of gifted children, teachers, counselors, and administrators are simply not aware that these children exist, so they don't notice them, even when they have one right under their nose.

Schools are measured on how well students meet grade-level standards. Since the passage of the *No Child Left Behind Act* in 2001,[1] there has been an emphasis on raising the achievement of children with learning difficulties. This Act, along with similar accountability legislation, has brought about the practice that children in the lower one-third of the class set the pace of learning. But optimally, we should measure school success by what schools do, or don't do, to facilitate individual learning, building upon children's individual abilities—not just by whether all students meet minimum grade-level standards. We need to close the learning gaps that exist within each student—not focus on the composite gaps between groups.

Groups don't have abilities; individuals do. We should gear our educational system and its functions toward enabling every student to learn to his or her highest ability level. To do so demands recognizing the individual differences that children bring with them to school. If acknowledgment of those differences is denied, then we will continue to fail to meet individual needs, and our children will continue to fail to reach their potential.

Schools Are Problematic for Gifted Students

If more school professionals recognized the full range of abilities that face them every day, with some children in need of challenge at a higher level, the learning situation for highly intelligent children would be much improved. Awareness that these children exist is the first major goal. Once there is awareness, well-meaning school personnel will be able to begin making changes to accommodate bright students. The actual changes necessary to meet the educational, social, and emotional needs of gifted children—without taking anything away from the other students—can be done easily for Level One and often Level Two students. Accommodations for Level Three children may require additional effort or expense, and Levels Four and Five children necessitate more radical change.

There are more reasons why gifted children today have a difficult time getting their needs addressed in our schools. These include the general physical structure and layout of school systems and how they impede individual learning; grouping children by age; attitudes toward grade skipping, tracking, and ability grouping; and finally, changes in educational philosophy and advocacy, resulting in a shift in values, priorities, and funding.

The Configuration of School Systems

The physical configuration and organization of our school systems—i.e., separate buildings for elementary school, junior high, and high school—creates a significant artificial barrier to meeting individual needs. The old one-room schoolhouse allowed students to progress through the available curriculum at their own pace regardless of age; students got materials and instruction when they were ready and graduated when they had finished. There was no kindergarten; younger children stayed at home. School was for grades one through eight. Many students went on to four years of high school, but just finishing eighth grade was considered a worthy goal, especially in rural areas, until the mid-1900s. Skipping grades was quite common for the brightest children, and such advancement was possible because curriculum for all grades was available in the same building.

After World War II, public school systems built consolidated school districts where schools would feed into one large central high school. Most school systems attempted to have smaller schools for the younger children—usually kindergarten through sixth grade—throughout the district in neighborhoods. This physical separation of age groups by grades continues into the 21st century. Each school district usually has a handful of elementary schools, one or two middle schools, and one centrally located high school. In large, urban districts, there may be several high schools in a district, with several middle schools and elementary schools feeding into each high school. Middle schools then supplanted junior high schools with the intention of providing less academic rigor and a more social, family atmosphere for adolescents,[2] who were thought to need more emphasis on socialization at this pre-adolescent age. The problem with the current three-building configuration of elementary, middle, and high schools is that it results in a school "ceiling effect" for those students who out-pace or learn ahead of their age-mates. When they're ready to move into the next building and higher challenges, they can't; they have to wait until they reach the appropriate age.

Age Grouping and the Demise of Ability Grouping

For each grade from kindergarten through eighth or ninth grade, instruction is delivered to children who are most often grouped solely by age. Such grouping makes about as much pedagogical sense as grouping children by height or some other random factor. But regardless of its origins, age grouping is by now a strong tradition, and most people unthinkingly accept that age is a logical way to organize schools, with little or no regard for when and what children are ready to learn, how physically mature or immature they are, what their interests are, and so on. Unfortunately, grouping by age is so much a part of schooling that altering an individual child's normal educational path is difficult and can create new problems as it attempts to fix others.

Despite grouping by age, individual classrooms in elementary schools are set up to reflect the widest possible array of abilities, ethnicities, behavior issues, and genders. The children grouped in a first-grade classroom, for example, are supposed to "look" about the same as the group of children in the other first-grade rooms in the school. That is, each class will have the same number of girls and boys, the same number of slow learners and rapid learners, the same number of minority children, the same number of behavior problems, and so on as all of the other classrooms at that grade level. This "balanced grouping" practice leads to the widest possible range of learning abilities within each classroom. It also makes it very difficult for teachers who want to teach to each student's learning ability.

Then, too, as a result of gifted children's rapid learning—even when instruction is not geared for their level—the gap between gifted and average-ability children grows as children get older because the more rapid learners keep building on their faster growing foundation. By second grade, it is not unusual to find achievement results within each classroom that range from first- to twelfth-grade equivalencies (Lohman, 1999). This also sets up a very difficult task for classroom teachers who try to individualize.

Although numerous professionals, such as Heacox (2002), Reis et al. (1993), Starko (1986), Tomlinson et al. (2002), VanTassel-Baska (1992), and Winebrenner (2000), have all contributed excellent curricula to the gifted field for differentiated instruction[3] at the classroom level, such adjustments only work best for Level One and sometimes Level Two gifted children. Because Levels Three and above need far more advanced learning experiences, these gifted children end up having to work alone and independently for much of each day—an arrangement that does not take care of their need for social and intellectual peers.

Some students in the 70-90 IQ range who are given differentiated instruction also qualify for additional daily pullout[4] instruction in special education classes. Although it might make sense to similarly offer the brighter students instruction at their own levels during that time, it is seldom provided.[5]

In order to deal with the wide array of learners in a classroom, teachers generally teach to the top of the lowest one-third of their mixed-ability class. By doing this, they don't immediately lose those at the bottom, and yet they still manage to hold some attention from the average group in the middle. Children in the upper one-third, however, spend considerable time waiting for the average and below-average students to catch on. Slower children require more repetition of material to learn, which then dictates the pace of the class. When teachers refine their instruction to a lower, more repetitive level in order to increase the chances of a higher overall passing rate and higher composite scores for the class as a whole, the brightest students must sit through additional repeated instruction while gaining nothing from it. These children can frequently pass tests without having *any* instruction in the material, and they score high despite the lack of attention. Teachers think they don't have to worry about these children. The teachers' attention is entirely consumed by those whose failure would be noticed and by which they are judged. Who can blame them?

Looking at a typical composite classroom test result, one might conclude that more than half of the class learned the lessons well and that their overall ability level was quite similar. Levels One through Five children in the class likely mastered the material quickly—or already knew it—but still could not perform better than perfect on tests because the tests were designed to be easy for any student who paid attention in class.

A mixed-ability classroom can stymie learning for gifted students. Children at the top of the middle one-third, depending upon the school population, are often Level One gifted children. The children in the lower end of Level One are the most at risk for underachievement because they are less capable of filling in their own learning gaps without specific help. Reasons vary, but in general, Level One children require more time to do the worksheets and general assignments than the higher levels of gifted children. When compared to Levels Two through Five children, they have less leftover time for doing their own reading, are not as capable of remembering what they read, hear, or see with just one repetition, and are usually comfortable enough with their classmates that they don't want to miss what is going on by doing supplemental work that no one else is doing.

Levels Two through Five children can fill in their own learning gaps if they skip grades, work at a higher level for some subjects, or daydream away several years. They have superior memories, higher perceptions for what is going on around them, and are usually excellent readers who can teach themselves if allowed to do so. Ability grouping for appropriate instruction would definitely lessen the problem of these children learning to underachieve.

The very brightest students who don't turn in all of their assignments but who still ace the tests are often graded down for having poor attitudes, despite achievement scores in the upper 90th percentiles. These high ability "refuseniks" are assigned the same low grades that are given to low ability students who score poorly but try hard. The message that these bright students get is that it is important to conform and be like everyone else, even if conformity is—for them—separate from learning.

Societal Priorities and Funding

The Federal *No Child Left Behind Act* capped off an approximate 30-year period when the nation went from an acceptance that we need to instruct all children at their own level to the motto "All Children Can Learn." Social class and racial barriers were significantly reduced in the 1960s and 70s. Policy makers then believed that environment and effort were primary factors in one's eventual achievement, both in school and in the workplace. Of course all children can learn, but can they all learn the same things at the same pace and to the same levels?

It is currently more politically acceptable to give all children the same instruction rather than make the error of prejudging someone's ultimate learning attainment and putting them in the wrong ability group. The popular explanation for why tracking and ability grouping have been largely abandoned in the United States is that there is a fear that we might put someone in a low group who shouldn't be there, that we might overlook children who would benefit from advanced course-work or instruction, or that a student might get "locked" in a track and not be given the opportunity to later test out or move to a higher track.

Children who learn slowly and struggle academically are routinely given extra support, including small groups at their own readiness levels, in order to maximize their chances of keeping up with the average for their grade level. Apparently it is not viewed as unfair that the brightest students who need additional challenge are left to learn at the same pace as the average students. This assumption is implicit in the decision to group children heterogeneously (mixed-ability) by age in which the most capable learners' potential is not seen as lost, squandered, or sacrificed.

As the chapters on the different giftedness levels in Part II spelled out, active learning and achievement grind to a near halt for bright children when they enter school. Prior to that, they learned at their own pace at home through reading, listening, and asking questions. But at school, they are held back to varying degrees by the strict age grouping of classrooms and a curriculum designed for slower learners. Sometimes a gifted child held back like this becomes depressed and angry about endless uninteresting schooldays.

Throughout the intellectual range, children face learning challenges; a variety of learning disabilities are recognized and accommodated in our schools. Parents who have two special needs children—one a learning-disabled child and the other a gifted child—are often amazed at how much easier it is to get help for the disabled child while their gifted child loses interest in school.

Children with learning disabilities are by law provided specialists to work with them on a regular basis, and if necessary, they are transported at school district expense to locations where they work with specialists and get instruction at their own level and pace. By comparison, intellectually gifted children almost never receive such consideration and accommodation and are seldom given instruction at their own level and pace. In districts that do provide something for gifted children, the programs are minimal, usually part-time—one hour a week in a class with other gifted children—with a specialist teacher traveling between two or more schools.

Mainstreaming is a term for putting all children, including children with learning disabilities or other special needs, into the "main stream," or the same general classroom. Mainstreaming, also called "inclusion"—i.e., mixing slow learners and learning disabled children into the regular classroom setting for as much of their day as possible—was legally mandated some years ago in order for children with disabilities to experience a normal classroom environment and mix with other children so that they will feel better about themselves and learn better, thus giving them the opportunity to experience a normal childhood. Many educators extended this thinking to gifted children. It seemed that if social and emotional development and learning to work and get along with others are a priority for special needs children, then they should also be a priority for gifted children.

Unfortunately, while mainstreaming helps disabled children, this practice has negative consequences for gifted children. Although it can help to motivate slow learners, it discourages rapid learners by holding them back; they aren't allowed to learn as fast or as far as they might. Many times, gifted children are placed in cooperative learning groups with other children in which the gifted children do the majority of the work and help others in the group rather than learn at the level that would fit their intellect.

Gifted programs and other options for gifted learners continue to decline in the United States. Full-time mainstreamed gifted children have few ways to show their abilities and knowledge when placed in classrooms that teach the basics. Because gifted students score well on achievement tests regardless of what they study in school, many school districts greatly underestimate how many of their brightest students are underachieving compared to what they could be achieving with the right instruction.

Schools may conduct simple screenings to see how many of their students already know some of the grade-level material, but they rarely look more closely to discover just how far beyond grade level these children might perform. Since children performing below grade level attract substantial public funding, programming, personnel, and support, it is reasonable to expect that teachers will be more aware of the issues related to their learning needs. If there were mandates—state[6] and federal funds—specifically for gifted children as there are for other special needs children, there would be improvement in the nation's schools for meeting gifted children's learning needs. The actual costs of supporting the educational needs of gifted children are far less than those of other special needs children.

Teachers Are Not Trained to Recognize Individual Differences

Many parents of gifted children are dismayed by the general lack of awareness of the wide intellectual ability ranges in their children's classrooms. They are surprised to learn that most teachers are never taught how to recognize or work with individual differences. Teacher preparation programs might include one course or possibly just a chapter on "exceptional" children, but the material generally focuses on disabilities, not learning strengths. While other exceptionalities are described in some detail, gifted children are usually portrayed as all being more or less alike, without mention of the wide range of gifted abilities and behaviors. The continuum of intellectual ability across same-age children is not emphasized in helping teachers understand the variations in educational responses that they see in their classrooms.

Interpreting available assessments is another potential weak spot within schools. Teachers, administrators, and even school psychologists are often inexperienced or otherwise unqualified to interpret standardized test data for children who are at the high end of the ability range. Even when ability and achievement test results are available, most educators, and even many private psychologists, do not have the background to estimate levels of giftedness or their accompanying needs.

Most teachers have erroneously been taught that grade equivalencies on grade-level achievement tests do not reflect the grade-level education that a student can actually handle. But such tests do indeed indicate the child's true academic level. When a fifth grader receives a tenth-grade equivalency score, it means that the child is ready for the same curriculum as a typical tenth-grade student—not an *advanced* tenth-grade student. Grade equivalencies reveal a wide range within each class as well. Achievement levels of lower functioning students are averaged with those of the brightest students when reporting composite equivalencies, so the class average becomes the important score to the teacher. When students score high, the teacher is satisfied that the students are doing well, but they don't realize that these children could be learning more.

Despite wide-ranging grade equivalencies within each classroom, rapid learning students continue to spend the majority of every school day being instructed at the level of other students their same age. When higher ability students can easily deal with higher grade-level instruction, simply piling on more lower level work is not an appropriate accommodation.

Fortunately, SAT[7] results have commanded some interest. When educators see SAT results for elementary students that are commensurate with high school juniors' scores, they are more likely to accept that these children have unusual abilities. Young gifted students who score high school equivalency on SAT tests as sixth and seventh graders are "discovered" through various Talent Search programs. They are then invited to special summer programs, usually on university campuses, where they can take accelerated math or language classes with other similar students. Thus, while public and private schools rarely provide significant advanced learning opportunities before senior high school, universities in some of the larger metropolitan areas have created weekend and summer programs for these exceptional students.

Negative Effects of the Same Pace for Everyone

Children Learn to Underachieve

Elementary school curriculum spirals and repeats throughout elementary school. There are seven to eight repetitions of the material in the typical six years to allow a child of average ability to learn the material. A Level One child generally needs three repetitions—roughly four years—while a Level Two child will need only one or two repetitions—about half the time in school needed by an average child. Level Three children could easily complete the entire elementary school curriculum in less than two years if it were appropriately compacted, and Levels Four and Five start school already knowing most of what is taught in elementary school. Putting these advanced children in regular elementary classes virtually forces them to learn to underachieve. Gifted children cannot learn study skills or time management in such a classroom, and they may also get a distorted, unrealistic impression of how smart they are, where they fit in, and which behaviors and kinds of performance indicate high intelligence. Additionally, if the material is perpetually easy, they may resist challenge when it is finally provided in high school or college.

Although the children in the lowest one-third of the class may achieve below grade level, instruction is aimed at them, and they are given constant opportunities to learn more and achieve at higher levels. This is good and makes sense—unless the learning needs of others in the class are ignored as a result, as is often the case. Throughout the first eight years of school, most bright students learn far less than they are capable of learning because the instruction is aimed at the learning needs of the lower two-thirds of the class.

One free, or at least inexpensive, option that schools have readily available to them is that of allowing faster paced children to move to higher grade levels for a few, or all, of their subjects—at least when these students are in the same building as the courses they are ready for and might enjoy. Schools rarely do this, though it can be an easy solution. If a Level Three child, for example, starts kindergarten reading at a second-grade level and progresses at a pace common to Level Three children, that child will be ready for fourth-grade reading instruction by the time she is in first grade. Her teacher and principal could allow her to take her reading instruction with the fourth-grade class down the hall. The problem comes when she is in second grade and reading and comprehending at a level similar to sixth graders; she will run out of classrooms that are teaching at her level before she finishes second grade. The building stopped her. Now she has to wait for middle school. Once there, she has to wait again. Finally in high school, this Level Three student will get to take coursework that is suited to her ability, she can learn with others her age, and the other Level Three and Four children from all over the district will be right there with her, having finally escaped from middle school into high school. When elementary, middle, and high school are within easy walking distance of one another, the simple acceleration strategy of moving ahead works well.

Social and Emotional Ramifications

There are negative effects for the entire range of learners when they receive group instruction with children whose learning needs and abilities are very different from their own. The repetitive curriculum leaves the brightest children a great deal of extra time. Consequently, they often tune out, act out, or grow either hostile or overly compliant, and they inevitably learn far less than they could have learned in those six years. Depending on the level of giftedness, a child like this may also be the only youngster in her class who thinks the way she does; she may be treated as odd, and she may very likely be lonely, too. Sometimes a gifted child will become a perfectionist. Many under-challenged gifted children erroneously conclude that being perfect or always being right is who they are. As a result, they perceive it as necessary to continue being the fastest or the best so that others will still love and admire them. Much of their self-concept is shaped by their reflected school experiences.

Mixed-ability grouping has negative effects for the slow students as well. When the majority of the slower students' classmates are always ahead, the slower learner rarely gets the chance to be the best, be a leader, or feel comfortable with his own learning pace. Unfortunately, gifted children who must work with and wait for slower children on a regular basis often become less tolerant, less helpful, or less empathetic to individual differences than those children placed in mixed-ability groups intermittently for non–academic activities.

Many educators say that children need to be with people their own age in order to learn social skills and to "just be a kid." "They need to learn to get along with others," is a phrase that is frequently heard coming from teachers. Mixed-ability grouping, however, puts children together who have very different interests, senses of humor, and perceptions. Coupled with the natural immaturity that accompanies childhood, this situation is not a good recipe for learning how to enjoy other people. We learn social skills from people who *have* social skills, usually the adults in our lives, not other children. When children have little beyond their age in common, they can be very intolerant, even cruel. Because highly intelligent children tend to have different interests and abilities than the majority of their classmates, they are often rejected, teased, or bullied by age peers.

Gifted children, like any children who are noticeably different from their classmates, require an emotionally safe and supportive environment while they are young and still learning about their place in the world. If parents can arrange things so that their children have the chance to experience regularly accepting and supportive environments when they are young, these children will gain the wisdom and experience to deal with and enjoy people from a variety of backgrounds and interests as they mature.

The Way Gifted Children Are

Gender, intellectual levels, and personality differences between children, their parents, and their teachers all make a difference in how gifted children adapt or adjust to school experiences.

Gender Differences

Boys and girls are very different in the ways they approach school.[8] Most often, they have different activity levels and interests no matter how we rear them, as most parents quickly discover. Whatever the reasons are for persistent differences between males and females, these differences have behavioral consequences for children in school.

In my experience, most girls and women, as a group, tend to see shades of meaning and concepts more easily and are more general in their interests than most boys and men. Many girls and women also enjoy learning about a variety of topics to a fairly high level more than they tend to enjoy specializing in something that they feel would restrict them in any way. When both people in a couple have equally high intellectual ability, it is not unusual for them to assume that the male is smarter because he can dominate in his one subject. I point this out because women often underestimate themselves and their intellectual abilities (Kerr, 1994).

Gifted girls and boys approach and adapt to the school environment differently.[9] When gifted girls start school already knowing how to read and do most other tasks, they look around and decide how else to keep themselves busy and occupied. They make the most of it. By being quick and efficient at their assignments, they can use the extra time gained to read, talk with friends, help the teacher, or take on a leadership role. Most girls have the added benefit of a teacher and parents who think that she is cooperative and a good student.

When a little boy starts school, however, he almost immediately notices that what he wants to do is not happening in school. To make matters worse, what he wants to do isn't allowed or isn't even available. Therefore, boys are much more likely to act out and complain than girls. As a result, more boys than girls are diagnosed with attention deficit disorder (ADD) or hyperactivity. This is often because boys are more physically active, and when they have little to hold their interest, they move around. Their lack of attention to the teacher and their schoolwork is confusing to those parents who know that their sons have huge attention spans for things that interest them.

These gender differences set up additional problems down the road. The gifted girl fills her time with all of the different things that interest her and which please the adults in her life. She comes to define herself by how quickly and efficiently she can get her required work done and still juggle other activities and interests. This can set her up for perfectionism, as it is threatening to her self-image to fall short of what she sees as her appropriate level of performance.

Studies have indicated that girls often show a plummeting of self-esteem when they reach middle school age (American Association of University Women, 1991). It appears that when school is finally challenging and assignments require a great deal of time, gifted girls do not know how to manage their time for the greater demands on their intellect. Their sense of who they are starts to crumble; they become stressed and anxious, and they feel that they have lost control. They need help interpreting this change, where it came from, and how it happened so that they can let go of some activities and obligations for a while and give themselves the time needed to learn how to study, review, and take academic learning in stride.

Girls particularly tend to avoid the most difficult mathematics courses in high school, even though these are often necessary for better career opportunities (Lubinski & Benbow, 1992). Lubinski and Benbow reported that on the SAT-M (the mathematics portion of the *Scholastic Aptitude Test*), the ratio of males to females who score above 500 was 2/1; above 600, it was 4/1; and above 700 it is 13/1. Some persons have alleged that girls—as a group—are simply less intellectually able in various areas, such as math, and they cite studies showing general differences in ability between girls and boys. On virtually every ability or achievement test, there are more males than females at both the highest and the lowest ranges. Although the average ability level is the same, 100 IQ, approximately 20% more men than women score above IQ 140 and below IQ 60 (Seligman, 1992). Another study estimates that there are 37% more men than women above IQ 132 (Eysenck & Kamin, 1981. Despite these group differences, it is important to note that these disparities are relatively small, and that the abilities of any specific individual are far more important in educational planning. In fact, some of the group differences seem to be significantly declining as girls have more exposure to specific curriculum earlier in life (Monastersky, 2005).

It makes sense that—for some girls—cases of anorexia or bulimia may be related to this sudden change from no academic challenge for six to eight years to much more demanding coursework suddenly and without transition. It is also not at all surprising that many gifted girls deliberately opt for easier coursework in high school.

Boys have specific issues, too. Parents and teachers may start to worry about gifted boys fairly early in their school careers because so many of them demonstrate defiant or oppositional behavior, lose their motivation, and underachieve. In truth, many boys become more and more angry about all of the things that they are expected to do in school—things that make no sense to them and seem like a waste of time. No one validates their intuition—their accurate gut feelings—that the school environment and curriculum are wrong for them, too confining, and not teaching them anything new or useful. Instead, everyone bands together to force their compliance to this system. Hostility builds, as they correctly perceive that adults have the power to force them to do assignments that don't teach them anything new.

Some boys, far more than girls—although girls sometimes do this, too—refuse to turn in assignments or complete their work. They are then accused of being disorganized, not paying attention, and underachieving. It is ironic that they are so often accused of underachieving, when the one guarantee of their underachievement is to force them to totally comply with instruction so far below their capacity to learn and perform. It is this lack of compliance that gets gifted boys into trouble. Unfortunately, it also keeps them from being recommended for opportunities that might work for them, like the occasionally available gifted class.

Of course, not *all* boys or *all* girls fit the profile described above. But this information is crucial to an understanding of normal behavior and interest profiles that are different for most gifted boys and girls. It also has ramifications for the social lives of both sexes because it means that the most intelligent males might have more difficulty finding a partner or spouse who is on an equal intellectual level with them. The most intelligent females have a larger pool of highly intelligent males from which to choose, but they are at considerable risk for feelings of isolation and differentness because there are fewer females like themselves. There are additional issues that gifted young women face that complicate their own achievement and goals—issues most related to the differential way that marriage and parenthood affect females as compared to males.[10]

Parents find it enlightening to learn a bit more about how male and female preferences affect choices in our lives. For example, a number of years ago, researchers tried to figure out why so few capable women enter hard science and math (Lubinski & Benbow, 1992). The salary difference between males and females in science and medicine is largely explained by the specific discipline choices within a field that each sex makes (National Science Board, 1991).

> *Mathematically talented males...are more theoretically oriented...their primary interests lie in the investigative and realistic sectors (working with mechanical gadgets). Mathematically talented females are more socially and aesthetically oriented and have interests that are more evenly divided among investigative, social, and artistic pursuits. It appears that females as a group are more balanced and less narrowly focused in terms of their interests and values. Females...have greater competing interests and abilities, which draw them into a broader spectrum of educational and vocational pursuits. Gifted males, in contrast, are more narrowly focused and congruent with the pursuit of careers in the physical sciences* (Benbow & Lubinski, 1993, p. 94).

Benbow and Lubinski have written numerous articles on how SAT or College Board test profiles correlate with eventual career choices for individuals. When students achieve higher quantitative than verbal scores, they are very likely to aim for and remain in careers that involve science, mathematics, or engineering. When their scores are nearly the same or lean more toward the verbal side, they usually prefer careers that capitalize on their verbal strengths. Mathematically gifted girls score high in verbal abilities more often than boys. This male-female difference is important for parents to understand because it helps them to know why their daughters might not select courses and careers that are more mathematically or scientifically based, even when they have the ability to do so.

There is one more point on gender issues that should be addressed here. The farther out on the ability continuum one travels, the more androgynous are the interests and behaviors of both boys and girls. A Level Three girl, for example, is less likely to enjoy the games and social interactions that most girls her age enjoy. A Level Three boy is less likely to be as rough-and-tumble as his typical age-mates. In fact, this more highly gifted population tends to select companions and friends from both sexes, while their classmates rarely do so until they are much older. This tendency toward androgyny continues into adulthood and makes stereotypically masculine or feminine interests less common among the gifted. Knowing this has been a comfort to many parents.

Intellectual Differences

As complexity increases within a specialty field, so does the average IQ (Gottfredson, 1994). For example, the average surgeon's IQ is higher than the average general practitioner's, and the average high school teacher's IQ is higher than the average primary-grade teacher's. People of higher intellect are attracted to the challenge or complexity of certain fields. We cannot assume to know someone's abilities just by the job they perform (in other words, although the average IQ of teachers may be 120, there can easily be a teacher with an IQ of 145), but we can assume that they possess at least a certain minimum level of intelligence.

All of this information leads up to the likelihood that the Level One gifted kindergartner or the Level Three first grader has a very different reasoning approach than his or her teacher, and perhaps a higher IQ. It is important to remember that, even though the child's IQ may be higher, the teacher's mental age is still ahead of that of even a Level Five six-year-old. Gifted students and their teachers are often not on the same wavelength.

Just as gifted children usually have gifted siblings and parents, teachers' children are typically intellectually like them. If the average IQ of teachers is 120, it is likely that their own children are bright and that they are good students, even though they may just miss the cut-off for gifted identification. When one considers that the teacher's children generally do as well in school as the identified gifted children in the mixed-ability classroom, it is not surprising that the teachers might be skeptical or even resentful of standardized tests and cut-off scores that exclude their own children. This dilemma highlights one of the biggest problems with using a strict cut-off score, a classification that views children as either "gifted" or "not gifted." Many Level One gifted children are often missed by an in-or-out program mentality.

Just as teachers' children are often intellectually similar to the teachers, gifted children's parents are usually gifted themselves and often have professional level careers. Some teachers assume that these parents feel superior to them. In addition, these parents are often new at parenting a school–age gifted child and are unprepared for how to tactfully approach teachers without offending them. In these days of higher teacher accountability for standardized test scores, teachers have little flexibility to work with children who are already ahead of their classmates, yet they still want to be appreciated for their professional stature and their efforts on behalf of their students. If there is an intellectual discrepancy between the teacher and the parents and both parties are already somewhat on the defensive, effective communication and problem solving can be very difficult.

Personality Differences

The personality of the child also plays a role in whether or not the typical school environment will lead to problems. A personality assessment can help families understand how to work with the school to set up a plan for their child's academic success. The *Myers-Briggs Type Preferences* and the children's equivalent, the *Murphy-Meisgeier Type Indicator for Children,* are two helpful instruments for this purpose.

One of the most common problems parents ask about is how to get their gifted child to finish her assignments. This is often an issue of parent–child personality differences. Information about personality type differences can help parents understand that what is important to them may not be important to their child. Their child, for example, may have accurately determined that the assignment was essentially busywork for her; she just didn't have the maturity, tact, or power to arrange for something more appropriate. Once the problem is reframed, the parents need to understand that not finishing the assignment is the child's way of saying that the classroom expectations are not working for her. Parents need to work to move the child into an environment where it becomes clear that the assignments, time management, and organizational skills are relevant because they are necessary to learn the material, rather than try to force the child to comply with the setting. Children who are forced to comply against their own values about what is right for them can become depressed, defiant, generally oppositional, hostile, and can acquire long-term issues with authority.

Another personality aspect that affects the gifted child's or adolescent's adjustment to the mixed-ability classroom is the extraversion-introversion dichotomy. It is easier to arrange for a gifted introvert to work alone or independently than it is to expect an extroverted child to leave whole-class activities to work alone. The primary recommendation for an introvert whose school uses mixed-ability classrooms is to work with independent continuous progress,[11] online instruction, or full or partial home school. The most acceptable approach for an extroverted gifted child is regular placement in a higher-level class with older students for the subjects in which he or she excels, or a full-time immersion gifted program or school. Although it is harder to meet the learning needs of a gifted extrovert in the regular school, extroverts are not good home schooling candidates because they get restless and lonely if they are not with other people for most of their day.

A final observation related to the personalities of gifted people involves the stereotype that highly intelligent people are socially challenged nerds and geeks. Actually, only *some* highly intelligent people are what we would call nerds and geeks who are uncomfortable in social settings. Levels Three, Four, or Five gifted people usually find social interactions to be fairly easy if they are verbally strong or possess an "evenness" between their verbal and nonverbal abilities. Smart children and adults with this more balanced profile may hear people exclaim with surprised pleasure, "You seem so normal!" Many people expect highly intelligent people to be socially awkward, but that is less a factor of their intellectual level than of their personality.

Other Important Factors

Other characteristics of giftedness may go beyond merely the intellectual, and these are discussed in other chapters. Some characteristics, behaviors, qualities, and tendencies are common among *all* levels of giftedness, and some are more prevalent in the lower or higher levels. Common concerns of parents are issues with competitiveness, sensitivity, intolerance, perfectionism, hostility toward authority, underachievement, poor motivation, depression, issues with writing and math, teacher resistance, school inflexibility, and more.

Crash Course Summary

There are numerous reasons why schools are problematic for gifted students. Particularly important are the very structure of the schools, mixed-ability same-age grouping for instruction, the recent strong focus on bringing slower learners to mastery while ignoring the needs of other students, and an accompanying lack of training or awareness among teachers about individual differences in learning ability that exist in a mixed-ability classroom. The current system has several specific and common negative effects. Gifted children learn to underachieve, they have difficulty fitting in and forming satisfying friendships, and they become confused over who they really are and what they can do in the real world. Gifted children vary by level of giftedness, intellectual profile, gender, and personality. All of these factors intersect with their parents' and teachers' attempts to understand and support them.

Chapter 11
School Years and Ongoing Issues

*My child didn't broadcast how much she knew, so most people
at school thought she was just like the other children. She voiced
her dissatisfaction with school by saying things at home like,
"I don't want to go to school today," "It goes too slow," and
"There's too much time waiting for everyone else to finish
their work." She thought that all of the work was pointless
and spent much of her time daydreaming.*
~ Mother of a Level Five girl

Many people assume that all children can (and do) learn in school and that the smartest children are the best students in their class, but neither assumption is necessarily true. Regrettably, families often encounter rigidity when they first talk to the school about the possibility of making changes to accommodate the child's advanced learning level.

This chapter describes the many ways that schools and the nation's brightest children clash with one another. Gifted children have fairly universal, predictable problems in school, caused largely by the ways in which schools group children—by age rather than ability or level of performance—which makes school too slow and repetitive for those who are highly intelligent. The children's level of giftedness contributes to their degree of social and emotional adjustment problems—the higher the level, the more emotional adjustment becomes a factor.

Schools Resist Making Changes

Few educators are aware of the vast differences in learning that can exist among children who are the same age. Teacher training stresses typical development rather than unusual development. Teachers or administrators are rarely required to take courses on individual differences in learning abilities or on characteristics and needs of gifted children. Continuing education and in-service training for teachers seldom address the characteristics of gifted children, either, and when they do, teachers receive ideas only for occasional, modest adaptations for the education of gifted children, such as enrichment or extension of already existing curriculum. Rarely do they hear about any form of radical acceleration into more challenging material.

Yet just a few decades back in time, children were ability-grouped for instruction—in high, middle, and low groups for reading and math, for example—and until the 1950s and 1960s, grade skipping and other forms of academic acceleration were common (Colangelo, Assouline, & Gross, 2004). What changed? The Civil Rights Movement and President Johnson's Great Society in the late 1960s directed our country's attention toward educating everyone—a laudable goal. Minority children had been disproportionately found in lower ability school groupings. Researchers seriously examined whether prejudice or racism was at the root of this, and activists concluded that any form of instructional grouping other than age grouping was wrong for an equal opportunity society (Yecke, 2003).

In 1991, John Feldhusen, a leader in the field of high intelligence and gifted education, pointed out that removing ability grouping as an instructional method was to ignore the educational research that shows its usefulness and validity for all children, not just for gifted and talented children. He said, "The question we now face is how to call a halt to a national reform agenda in which some school reformers have arrogated unto themselves a political-social agenda that is based on misinterpretation of current research evidence" (p.67).

Despite considerable information from proponents of gifted education about good educational practices, numerous education reformers heralded identical classroom treatment and instruction for all as the best way to guarantee equal outcomes in achievement and lifetime success.[1] It was an appealing and powerful message to say that we could all achieve to the same high levels if we were only given the same opportunities. Unfortunately, many educators took equal treatment to mean the exact same instruction for children who are the same age, regardless of their general readiness or their ability to learn from it. One has only to look at the requirements of the current *No Child Left Behind Act* to see that lawmakers still believe that equal treatment in schools will lead to the outcomes of high level school achievement and career success for all.

These educational reforms have harmed all students, not just those who are gifted. Joyce VanTassel-Baska, another prominent researcher, wrote, "Only a small percentage of schools…[or] teachers across the

United States currently employ instructional plans for *any* learner based on a diagnosed assessment of individual learning needs. How can we believe that less grouping and more heterogeneous—mixed-ability— classrooms will enhance the learning process for *any* student with special needs?" (1992, p. 13).

Parents of gifted children, who have already spent several preschool years witnessing their children's advanced skill level, usually assume that schools will recognize and respond to their children's abilities. These parents have no way of knowing ahead of time that being ahead of others simply means that teachers will see their children as doing well enough. They don't realize that it runs counter to most educators' value systems to give "special treatment" to children who are perceived as already having advantages when compared to slower classmates.

Anecdotes from the parents in this chapter feature children from Levels Three through Five. All were extremely advanced in their academic mastery when they started school and needed special educational modifications if they were to thrive in any kind of school environment. Note that the actual abilities of the children were usually not a factor in the school's response.

Social Adaptation Trumps Academic Abilities

When parents go to a school to suggest that their child is not being adequately challenged—an observation that offends most teachers— one of the responses that they often hear is "What about social skills?" The belief that social skills should take precedence over academic progress is widespread among educators, counselors, and others. There is also a tacit belief that social skills can only be learned among groups of same-age individuals. The issue of social development often becomes the leading obstacle to making changes in a child's school program that might allow work at a higher level with older students.

Certainly it is important for all of us to learn to work with others, to be taught manners and common courtesy, and to feel social responsibility—skills which take time, maturity, good modeling from people who have those skills, and an emotionally healthy environment. But classrooms of 20-35 mixed-ability, immature young people do not provide an ideal environment for acquiring social skills. Virtually every expert in gifted education since the 1920s has noted that the more dissimilar gifted children are to their classmates, the more difficulty they have communicating and interacting in a positive manner.

It is very hard for highly intelligent—but immature and inexperienced—young people to be patient with others who are on a completely different intellectual plane. Appropriate group interaction is very difficult for highly advanced children under the age of 14—the age at which experience and maturity begin to get closer to their reasoning.

Teachers want to meet the needs of all of the children in their classes, but they worry that a change from the regular classroom routine won't be socially or emotionally good for children. Many parents find that teachers are so concerned about gifted children's social difficulties in group activities that they are unwilling to discuss advanced coursework at all. Yet research tells us that social problems often improve when a gifted child receives accelerated coursework. Even if the problems don't improve, they rarely get worse (Assouline, Colangelo, Lupkowski-Shoplik, Lipscomb, & Forstadt, 2003), and at least the child has the benefit of being educated at a level appropriate to him or her.

Teachers and administrators often lack even the most basic information and understanding of the needs of gifted learners. One second-grade teacher (who was awarded "Teacher of the Year" in her upper middle class, well-educated district) used a lengthy, detailed reading assessment that she designed for grades one to three but which did not go past the third-grade level for those children whose reading achievement level might be higher. She freely acknowledged that although a third of her beginning second-grade students could read with full comprehension to the end of the third-grade level—two years above grade level—those students were not instructed at a higher level. She said that this just gave her more time to work with those children who were most at risk for not reading at grade level. She believed that although young children may be able to read well beyond grade level, they couldn't possibly grasp high-level material because they still didn't have enough "life experience." In her opinion, it was far more important that advanced children gain appropriate life experiences with age-mates than move forward academically. This teacher, like so many others, knew very little about the needs of gifted students.

Bill Arnesen—Bill took a battery of group and individual tests with other prospective first graders to get into a private school. When I asked how things had gone, the test administrator told me that Bill had become frustrated at one point and had cried. She said that he was "the right age" for kindergarten and that I was pushing to have him placed a year ahead in first grade. She also told me, "He's just too little." The bottom line was that the school wouldn't consider allowing Bill to skip kindergarten, even though all of his achievement scores were at or above third-grade level.

Keith Sands—Keith's second-grade teacher wrote that he was an exemplary student, especially in math, but she was concerned that he needed to work on appropriate group interaction because he was sometimes rude when other students tried to express their ideas.

Brennan Ahlers—By the time he was in second grade, Brennan said that he was tired of being frustrated all of the time and wanted to be home schooled, even though he would miss the other kids. His teacher seemed sympathetic to our situation and suggested that she write up a half-day ILP[2] (Individual Learning Plan), and I could work with him in the library each day. I talked with Brennan over the weekend while she tried to get approval from the principal and the librarian before we met again. But by Monday, she had changed her mind—after all, he would miss out on too much "fun" in the classroom, and really, school wasn't just about academics but about being with others and making friends. She told Brennan that he would be lonely if he was home schooled and to just come to school and "try to have fun."

Stephen Williams—Stephen's third-grade teacher thought that it was important to focus on Stephen's social/emotional development, as this was an area that created great frustration to him and didn't come as naturally as his academic ability. Stephen worked with a variety of adults to learn how to self-monitor his actions, as well as how to respond to and cope with conflict among his peers.

> *Author note: Age-mates are not necessarily peers. True peers are people whom you share interests or abilities with, and they can come from various age groups and places in an individual's life. At least Stephen was allowed to work with adults on effective social strategies. Gifted children who get the chance to develop good self-concepts—i.e., get a good sense of who they are and what they are capable of doing in surroundings that accept them for the way they are—usually become very adaptable and tolerant of a wide variety of others as they mature.*

Rick Arnesen—When Rick started school and I suggested changes for him to learn at a more advanced level, all I heard was how important it was to let him be a child and not to push him. They said that he needed to learn his social skills and how to play with other children.

They'll Help My Child

Most parents find that schools promise at least some changes, but those changes are usually either insufficient or short lived. Lack of funding is a common excuse, but flexibility and creativity, more than money, are what are important in meeting the needs of gifted students. For example, gifted students might have single-subject acceleration in an area of strength, independent study in a topic of interest, and work on a learning contract with one teacher as a supervisor. Stories like the ones below are familiar to those who work with gifted children and their families.

Jacob Jones—When Jacob first started school after we had him tested, we expected him to have access to high quality curriculum, instructors, and facilities and that his needs would be analyzed and met. Instead, he was put in a room with other children who were bright but nowhere near the level where he was. What we found out was that, for the most part, the school was quite comfortable teaching the way they always had.

There were so many things we didn't know; we felt so alone in making big decisions. Frankly, the thought of resorting to home schooling was overwhelming, but we were running out of other options. When Jacob turned 12, we thought that maybe he should take high school courses the next year, but we were unsure of how to facilitate that. We wondered if, like handicapped young children who needed special consideration, the school could provide a paraprofessional for Jacob to accompany him if he attended high school classes. The ILP and occasional contact with a high school teacher hadn't worked well the year before because the weekly time for Jacob to be with the teacher hadn't work for her, so Jacob went weeks without any contact and spent most of the time working on his own. He could attend community college classes, but we didn't know if he could go straight there without fulfilling high school requirements first.

Rick Arnesen—When Rick started kindergarten, I talked with the Assistant Superintendent for Instruction, and I told him that both of my children already read very well, but the curriculum didn't allow for them to do any independent reading until at least second grade. I expressed concern that my children had to memorize poems for each alphabet letter when they were already reading chapter books with excellent comprehension and interest. He said soothingly, "Oh, I wouldn't worry Mrs. Arnesen. We find that by fourth grade, you can't even tell who the early readers were."

Brennan Ahlers—We placed Brennan in a private school where they first said that they were unable to handle a child with his abilities, but after I begged, they said that they would accept him as a student on a trial basis for one year and would do their best. I gave the principal Brennan's test scores and analysis and samples of his previous work, and I talked with her about the problems that we had faced at his previous school. I asked if she would let me meet with Brennan's teacher. She refused, saying that I should wait a few weeks to let his teacher form her own opinions. I finally met with his teacher the third week of school and was shocked to find out that she had not seen the tests, nor had she seen the samples of his previous work. When I explained the situation, she said that she would stay on top of it and be sure to monitor his work. But nothing changed.

Author note: Valuable information and learning time was lost with this approach—especially since professional recommendations were already part of the child's cumulative file.

Phil Burns—When we told the local school system about Phil's test results, they were sympathetic but said that they could do nothing for us that required any additional funding; they couldn't afford to start any sort of gifted program and couldn't give him special services. All they could offer was another grade skip for the next school year. We seriously considered this but decided against it for several reasons. Third grade is when a lot of petty and unkind behaviors and peer pressure begin, and Phil was especially vulnerable to teasing. Where we live, middle school begins with fourth grade, and the thought of him in middle school at the age of seven seemed absurd. Skipping another grade wouldn't fix the problem of material being presented too slowly, either—Phil would undoubtedly catch up quickly and then languish the rest of the year. We ultimately decided to home school, which made Phil much happier and far less stressed.

Samantha Forrest—We expressed concern to the school that Samantha wasn't being challenged enough. The elementary school principal said that he had seen plenty of others with Samantha's ability and that she was not unique. This was extremely frustrating, because the district's head psychologist who administered the IQ test told us that she'd *never* seen a score that high and that our daughter's *was* a unique situation. Despite this, the school psychologist from Samantha's own school claimed that she was well adjusted and "just interested in being a kindergartener."

<blockquote>
Author note: This was a double bind for Samantha's family—because she appeared to be adjusting well, the teacher assumed that Samantha's intellectual needs were not an issue.
</blockquote>

Parents Assume that They Can Work with the Schools

Once parents know that their children are intellectually advanced, they generally approach the school hoping that the instructional pace can be speeded up or that the child can work at a higher level with others—either the same age or older—whose intellectual levels are similar. However, most schools today offer a list of reasons why they can't or won't do what the parents want. It is often difficult for the parents of highly intelligent children to believe that their children's emotional and intellectual well-being is either misunderstood or relatively unimportant to the educational establishment. Parents' initial faith in the ability—and desire—of the schools to help generally adds one to two years to the time period in which the child is in the wrong educational environment before the parents give up and decide to work outside of the system.

Although this book only shows examples of families who wanted to make changes for their children, there are many parents of gifted children who do not advocate for educational modifications. In fact, their lack of advocacy sometimes undermines the efforts of others to obtain educational accommodations.

There are a number of reasons why some parents simply accept how the schools are educating their advanced learners: (1) their child does very well, and the entire family enjoys the child's school excellence, (2) their child is compliant and doesn't express any dissatisfaction, (3) the parents' concern for their child fitting in and being cooperative outweighs their concern about his or her possible underachievement, (4) the parents are unaware that they could reasonably expect the child to learn more than the school is providing, and (5) the parents tried but were persuaded by the school that no changes needed to be made.

Despite the difficulties involved, it is usually best for families to try to work as much as possible with the school and to seek educational accommodations there. There are several reasons for this: (1) it can minimize the disconnect between the child and "normal" life, (2) it supports our public, tax-supported educational system so that it remains available for everyone, and (3) it spares the time and monetary expenses that will otherwise fall on the individual families. Everything that a gifted child needs is available somewhere in the typical school system. If a school can be flexible enough to allow a child to go to another teacher, building, or group of other learners who are ready to learn at his or her same level and pace, the child's needs can be met. Unfortunately, the schools themselves often make reaching these goals next to impossible.

Many gifted children's parents volunteer at the school in the hopes that the school will see them as partners, not adversaries, and that their donated time will give the teachers more time for some individualized instruction. However, for some highly gifted children, no amount of individualization at grade level will help them feel at home in a same-age mixed-ability classroom.

It is worth mentioning that some states have statutory language defining a gifted child and then mandating that "a gifted child must be provided with curriculum that is commensurate with his or her ability and potential." Parents who live in states with a strong legal directive can seek help through due process, mediation, or even the court system if the school is not willing to provide accommodations. The downside of this for parents is that the process can be lengthy, and the issues may not be resolved for several years.[3] Parents can contact their local state department of education to see whether a mandate exists and, if so, to request a copy.

Keith Sands—I was very naïve in believing that once Keith started school, the school would take over. They were totally unprepared for him. I had to meet with his teacher and principal on a regular basis to develop strategies for him. Although he went to a weekly gifted pullout program, Keith primarily believed that school was for fun and games and to have a good time.

Ross Oliver—Ross was allowed to skip from third to fifth grade, but the only modification he received to his programming there was intermittent EPGY algebra. I'm a high school math teacher, so I was "allowed" to mentor him during my prep period. His teachers reported moderate to severe underachievement because he simply lost interest in school altogether. He was so out of place in his school due to his extremely high giftedness that even the special online courses left him feeling alone and frustrated.

Emily Newton—I asked the district if we could personally hire a tutor to work with Emily at school, but they said no. We suggested that there might be a substitute teacher, approved by them, who could work with her, paid by either the district or by us, and they said no to that as well. Some of our relatives said that we should get a lawyer and push the district to supply an in-school tutor for her, as her educational needs were not being met.

Author note: This family knew a deaf child who had a full-time interpreter all day every day throughout his elementary school years. School systems are legally required to provide resources to help children with learning disabilities or handicaps, including paying for full-time aides to help students who are physically disabled so that they can be mainstreamed and benefit from the least restrictive environment.[4] There is no similar Federal mandate for gifted learners, but some states have strong legal language in their education law for provisions for them.

Jacob Jones—We attended meetings with Jacob's teachers, but they were defensive in even considering ideas of how best to meet his needs. One teacher actually said, "Give me two weeks and I'll make him into the student I want him to be." During our first meeting with the principal and district gifted coordinator, they seemed to agree that he needed enrichment, but they were very hesitant about having him take high school courses. They felt that an 11-year-old would not fit in a classroom with high school students and wondered how it would affect him socially and emotionally—something we heard continually. They also worried about gaps in his curriculum if we started skipping. They thought that acceleration in math would be a good place to start and that his current seventh-grade teachers should be able to enrich his curriculum in the regular classroom. During all of this, Jacob grew more and more restless and discouraged, wondering if anything would ever get settled.

Author note: Jacob's parents experienced a version of the "it's your child's atti- tude that's the problem" refrain when the teacher said that she could "make him into the student" she wanted him to be. In school meetings with parents, it is not unusual to have at least one educator in attendance who speaks authoritatively about how something is wrong with the child's behavior, atti- tude, maturity, or handwriting, and therefore it would be a mistake to make any changes. The issue of gaps in the child's learning is also common, but Levels Two through Five gifted children can easily learn on their own when they detect a need to fill in information gaps.

260

Samantha Forrest—We talked with the district gifted supervisor who said that because our school was so large, the gifted teacher didn't have time to design individual learning programs for students who need them. We felt that partial home schooling would be excellent for Samantha, but convincing the district was like climbing Mt. Everest. We found no one else in the district who had a partially enrolled grade school child. The home school support group suggested that we simply tell the school we'd be pulling Samantha out a few mornings a week and then let them react, rather than asking permission.

Author note: The fact that Samantha was in such a large school system should have made it easier, not harder, to pull together a group of children similar to her.

Carol Johnston—We found that administrators promised the world but wouldn't follow through with adjustments to the curriculum. It was a constant battle to get Carol what she needed, and it was totally exhausting. We volunteered at the school as much as we could and initiated programs such as Junior Great Books—which helped all of the kids, not just the gifted—hoping that the school would realize that our intentions were good. The bottom line, however, was that we didn't succeed.

Problems for the Gifted in School

Boredom

Certainly many students throughout history have experienced occasional boredom in school. However, recent reforms designed to "level the playing field" for all children and put more attention toward helping slower learners have left gifted children with too little to learn and do all day long. Even more dismaying, children of other ability levels—not just gifted students—frequently have their learning needs unmet under this system as well. Experienced teachers know that an excellent way to manage children's behavior in the classroom is with instruction and assignments that grab and maintain the students' interest. When schools fail to provide a time and place for children to continue their natural love of learning, the school itself becomes a source of problems.

Why are so many bright children bored in school? Gifted children have long attention spans, and the length of the span increases with the level of giftedness. Average elementary grade children have attention spans of 15-20 minutes, and teachers keep lessons to that length for this reason. This is also the reason that children's television programs move quickly from one topic to another. But for gifted children, 15-20 minutes on a subject is completely wrong, irritating, and even disrespectful; gifted children want to learn more before moving on. It is not surprising that children who are eager, absorbed learners at home quickly lose their enthusiasm for school in the primary grades.

Stephen Williams—We expected that a respected private school would provide a good, challenging educational experience. We were disappointed, as Stephen's knowledge was more advanced than other children in his class—he learned new concepts faster.

Phil Burns—In first grade, the reading teacher insisted that the children use their pointer finger to follow along in their own books. The class slowly and laboriously enunciated each word as they read aloud together. Phil (who read at a fifth-grade level) was clearly bored. He quickly flipped through the pages to count how many there were, turned to the correct page and read silently, and then searched for other things to do. Each time the class turned to a new page, he read quickly and then lost interest. Because of this, the school told us that something was wrong with Phil and that he might have an emotional disorder. He was graded and judged completely on his behavior and compliance.

Author note: Teachers must consider whether they are expecting compliance and attention under circumstances that are completely wrong for the child. Adults in authority in this case needed to respond to Phil's needs, place him in classrooms where he could learn new material, and show him that his needs and interests mattered.

Charles Engquist—One day, I was walking home with the kids from the kindergarten bus. I asked them, "What did you learn today?" They started laughing and said, "Mom, this is *school*," in a tone that told me that they thought my question absurd. It was clear that they had no association of school with learning. It was just for play for 2½ hours a day.

Abilities Surpass Maturity

Closely related to the issue of boredom is the question of the child's maturity and ability to pay attention in class. It's not surprising that a five- or six-year-old who enjoys reading chapter books doesn't want to pay attention to learning letter sounds. It should not be shocking that children who are advanced in their mathematical reasoning don't want to join a small group learning to count by twos with poker chips. Intellectually advanced children who have become frustrated with the classroom's daily expectations may show their aggravation in age-normal ways like crying or acting out. This is a natural reaction in children who find their environment boring or intolerable.

It is difficult for gifted children to demonstrate their advanced abilities while slogging through regular classroom activities. How can a gifted child demonstrate special aptitude during a simple counting exercise? Instead, the child is likely to lose interest and either act out or stop paying attention. Rather than thinking that the child is especially capable and should be accelerated, teachers and administrators see the lack of attention as stemming from a short attention span, and they interpret this as a sign of immaturity. They work on forcing the child to comply with grade-level expectations instead of providing more appropriate accelerated instruction.

Far too many adults attribute a young child's poor reaction to school to immaturity. The reality is that a five- or six-year-old child is *always* immature, and this makes it difficult for the child to figure out how to cope with what isn't working for him or her. Such a child is not *less* mature than a same-age child for whom no big adjustment is required. *Any* child who is in a grossly inappropriate setting will react badly.

Blake Hauge—In first grade, the school told us to have Blake assessed for ADHD. He tended to lose interest in school-related tasks like counting and learning words he already knew, and he was reported to flit about his classroom. They thought that he needed more time to mature rather than advance through the lessons more rapidly.

Author note: Some gifted children are suspected of having learning disorders like ADHD or ADD,[5] when in reality, these children are simply in an environment that doesn't keep them engaged. Bright youngsters quickly learn to tune out what they've heard before and then are caught not paying attention. A book titled Misdiagnosis and Dual Diagnoses of Gifted Children and Adults *(Webb, Amend, Webb, Goerss, & Olenchak, 2005) explains how sometimes children are diagnosed as ADD, ADHD, or another disorder when in fact the problem is a poor fit with the educational environment and subsequent frustration.*

Brennan Ahlers—Because he loved talking with adults and didn't mix well with most of his classmates, Brennan preferred to sit with an adult at lunch. He chose teachers, the assistant principal, a specialist teacher, or any parent who happened to be visiting. The school counselor decided that because he didn't look for other kids to sit with, he was socially immature, and she implemented a "behavior modification" plan for him without my knowledge. Each day, he had a sheet that stated that his goal was to sit at a table with other children and no adults. Because he was a compliant child, he did this.

> *Author note: Bright children are often accused of being immature when they don't want to interact with other children. Children who are interested in topics that are several years beyond their own age group rarely find classmates who are interested in the same things. It is common for children like this to prefer talking with adults instead. School personnel, however, often see this as a sign that the child is socially immature. However, if these children are provided the opportunity to spend time with others their age who share their intellectual level and some of their interests, they typically prefer their company to that of adults.*

Rick Arnesen—Because Rick had a summer birthday and was small for his age, the school tried to talk us out of sending him to kindergarten at age five. They said that he was distractible and immature. Rick was not distractible at home or any time when he actually got to learn and do things.

Teachers Overlook High Abilities

Teachers who lack even the most basic knowledge about gifted children are also totally unaware that there are different *levels* of giftedness. Even when teachers give assessment and achievement tests, they often ignore or don't quite believe the results. They also fail to understand the extraordinarily advanced behaviors exhibited by some of these exceptional children. And while many parents are aware that their child could learn more, they seldom know how the child actually compares to others in the class.

Many teachers try to placate concerned parents of gifted children by telling them, "We have lots of children as bright as yours." This statement stems from two different foundations. First, it might actually be true that there are children who are equally as bright as the child in question, but the other parents haven't complained, or the children's personalities are such that they go along without making any trouble. Alternately, teachers don't really know who is smarter than others because the low level of class assignments limits children's ability to show what they know and can do. When the top one-third of the class can all perform perfectly or nearly so on whatever is required, differentiating between their abilities is very difficult.

Educators also try to appease parents of gifted children who press for advanced educational opportunities for their children with the reasoning that above average abilities usually level off after a few years. This argument is so common and yet so wrong that it almost defies explanation. How can anyone believe that an early reader will simply "tread water" while others catch up, and they won't make any progress in the meantime? As discussed earlier, any school subject that has reading as a major component is one in which gifted children self-instruct and advance, despite the school's slow pace.

School achievement test results of high ability children reveal that their reading and comprehension scores not only are high, but they tend to go up more than two grade levels each year. Social studies and science scores often go up nearly as fast, probably because gifted children do a lot of reading and assimilate facts on their own.

Despite all of this resistance from school personnel, schools *can* make adjustments that require no specialist, no extra money, and no extra work for the teacher. Even though an adjustment may be slight, it can make a big difference in the child's sense of what he or she can do.

Brennan Ahlers—When I talked to the teachers and the school counselor about Brennan, I repeatedly heard phrases like these: "We have a lot of smart kids here." "The *Stanford-Binet (Form L-M)* scores kids too high—Brennan isn't really *that* smart." "We haven't done grade skipping in 25 years and we aren't going to start now." "He's so socially immature that you should be happy that academically he doesn't have to work so he can concentrate on his social skills."

Debra Sund—When Debra started kindergarten, she was already reading, so I told the teacher this the first day. As soon as the words were out of my mouth, I could tell that she had heard this before from other parents, so I didn't press. Within a month, the teacher told me (a little apologetically), "Debra really *can* read!" She said that she wanted the reading specialist to test her, and it was during this testing that we got a clearer picture of Debra's giftedness—she was reading at a fourth-grade level.

They let us put Debra in the third-grade reading group for a half an hour every day, where she did well and fit in fine with the older kids.

Janet Lewis—By first grade, Janet was reading third-grade books at home, but the teacher placed her in a middle reading group, interpreting her shyness and her mimicking the halting reading style of the other group members as an indication of only average ability. At our first conference, the teacher suggested that Janet had simply memorized books that we had repeatedly read to her. So the next day, I sent Janet to school with a challenging new shrink-wrapped book and a note asking the teacher to have Janet read it to her for the first time. After that, the teacher moved Janet to the top reading group and admitted that she was the best reader in the class.

Justin Janacek—We were confused by the lack of response from Justin's preschool and kindergarten teachers. Both said that many kids had Justin's abilities, and they brushed aside any special consideration of his academic or social needs. They said that he was a good listener, a good participant, and that he was well liked, but they were completely unwilling to see anything above average in him. The principal said that above average abilities usually level off by third grade anyway.

Behavior Problems

Many parents find themselves in an awkward position because their children do not cooperate with what is required by the school for an average student, and the teachers use that behavior as the criterion for access to more advanced curriculum. It's the old chicken and egg dilemma. Gifted children don't want to work on things they already know how to do, but until they dutifully demonstrate excellent completion of grade-level work, the children can't "earn their way" into more advanced, appropriate, and interesting coursework.

Teachers complain about several behaviors with gifted children—particularly talkativeness and not paying attention. Other complaints are about distracting or disruptive behaviors, particularly among gifted boys. Some gifted children, often boys, are class clowns. The normal elementary school classroom environment is probably too restrictive for most boys.[6] When they are expected to sit still for instruction that is years below their knowledge or ability level, behavior problems are exacerbated.

Teacher expectations for good behavior usually include the following: (1) be quiet when asked, (2) remain seated, (3) no fooling around during class, (4) participate actively in class activities, (5) be cooperative and respectful, and (6) complete assignments fully. When students experience appropriate classroom expectations and environments— classrooms that teach to their own level and pace—problems with the above expectations disappear. When there is enough real learning to do, gifted children appear more cooperative, feel more respect for their teachers, and find their natural talkative and humorous propensities appreciated rather than viewed as behavioral problems. Fortunately, some teachers are flexible and tolerant enough to not only enjoy gifted students, but also to keep them happily busy and learning.

Gary Lundquist—Gary was in a wonderful full-time gifted program for all of fifth and sixth grade, but when he went to seventh grade, there was absolutely nothing for him—classes were general education with the entire ability range in each class. By the end of seventh grade, he was totally uninterested and uncooperative in school. When we asked for some single-subject acceleration, the school insisted that he comply with the regular requirements first, which he refused to do.

Debra Sund—I was concerned about what might be underachievement for Debra. She was doing all right in math, and as she listened to what the second and third graders in her Montessori School were doing, she'd do it in her head. There was already another child in her class working at a higher grade level, but her teacher said that because Debra got distracted and didn't finish her work, she wasn't ready to move ahead—she lacked focus. She could easily do her homework, but she sometimes whined about it so much and then looked around at everything else that was going on so that it took her four times longer than necessary to get the homework done. This was also a pattern in school; they didn't see that she could work ahead because it took her so long to get her regular work done.

William Jones—Will dreaded going back to school to begin third grade, except for the fact that he'd see his friends. He hurried through his schoolwork and didn't give his full attention to it, and his teachers said that he was capable of so much more. We asked for a whole-grade skip, or at least single-subject acceleration in his strongest subjects, but the teachers held back doing anything for him because his grades included a few B's instead of all A's.

Poor Fit between Some Teachers and Gifted Children

As in any profession, people who teach school vary tremendously in their personalities, styles, and abilities. Most schools are not set up to match teacher style to a student's learning style, even though much is known about which teacher approaches work best for which learners.[7]

Phil Burns—On parents' visiting day, I watched Phil's preschool teacher asking the children various questions. When Phil didn't raise his hand, I asked him why he didn't. After continued prodding, he finally raised his hand, and when the teacher didn't call on him, he got upset, tried to hide his head under the table behind him, and then pulled on and rocked the table. The teacher told Phil that if he couldn't get control of himself, he would need to go out into the hall. She didn't ask what the problem was. I took him out into the hall myself so as not to interrupt the other parents and found out that he had raised his hand often at the beginning of the school year, but he didn't anymore. He thought that if the teacher didn't call on him, it meant she didn't like him. When she didn't call on him in front of his mother, he was hurt and embarrassed.

Author note: Highly intelligent children have the answers so frequently that the teacher often has to ignore them in order to give other children an opportunity to participate. But the gifted child enjoys attention as much as any other child. The intelligence of the gifted child does not translate into maturity, patience, or discernment when it comes to interpreting the big picture or the teacher's motives. If Phil were in a classroom with more children near his age who were very bright, his teacher would not have to selectively ignore and become impatient with him. This issue is so common and so emotionally important to the mental health of our highly gifted children that it is imperative that districts make changes. Magnet schools are one solution; they provide opportunities for grouping, instruction, and social interactions with other bright children who can understand and accept them. Magnet schools can answer many needs and cost little to organize and run.

Ross Oliver—Some teachers looked at Ross's unwillingness to do certain things over and over again as laziness or as him thinking that he was better than everyone else in his class. One said, "Let's color in the letter 'J' so you can learn it, Ross," yet he read at a sixth-grade reading level. When he was in third grade, he got in trouble frequently and was given lunch detentions for reading when he shouldn't and for asking too many questions.

Author note: These qualities in Ross should be nurtured, not punished. If he had been grouped with others of his intellectual ability, he would have been more normal among his classmates—most of whom would read and ask lots of questions every chance they got.

Rebecca Resnick—During middle school, Rebecca got to attend some special seminars for high achieving students. She complained that some of the teachers simply wasted her time, she didn't learn anything new, and they weren't very good at what they did. In a tenth-grade Enriched Biology course, the teacher did a broad overview of the different disciplines that encompass the field of biology. Rebecca asked some in-depth questions. He told her to look them up on the Internet or gave her answers that barely scratched the surface. I asked him about this, and he said that biology wasn't his area of expertise and that he couldn't spend class time going into a more thorough study of one sub-specialty area.

Emily Newton—Our "experiment" of grade-level advancing Emily in the private school for several subjects didn't go very well. A contributing factor was that her second-grade teacher was never enthusiastic about the plan to begin with. Emily decided to return to her old public school near our home.

Author note: Many teachers disagree with any grade skipping or subject acceleration and actively undermine the process. Often, the child herself will ask to give up on the plan rather than experience obvious lack of support or even open hostility from the teacher. The Templeton Report[8] cites research of the past 70 years to show that subject acceleration and grade skipping work very well for highly intelligent children.

Gifted Students Learn Poor Study Habits

When gifted children don't develop good study skills and habits, parents and teachers fear that they will underachieve as a result. Underachievement is very different, however, from not doing what is expected. When children score well on achievement tests but don't finish and turn in high quality assignments, they are not exhibiting underachievement; they are displaying noncompliance. Teacher and parent complaints related to underachievement or noncompliance include the following: (1) not doing or turning in homework, (2) doing the bare minimum rather than selecting challenging projects, (3) being disorganized, (4) not paying attention in class, and (5) distracting others. Whenever any of these issues are present, there is a strong likelihood that the academic environment is wrong for the child. Children whose work is either too easy or too difficult will often exhibit these kinds of behaviors.

Mixed-ability classrooms are poor venues for the development of good study skills. Slow learners are not interested in material they cannot understand, and faster learners are not interested in material they learned years ago. The point of studying is to teach or reinforce new learning. It is impossible to develop good study skills if no studying is needed. Teachers and parents alike frequently lose sight of this point. When the pace and curriculum are at an appropriate level for students, paying attention and completing assignments becomes meaningful and truly allows them to develop study skills.

Not Completing or Turning in Homework

Nothing seems to bother teachers and parents more than having a bright child who will not complete assignments. In Level Two to Level Five students, this refusal is often interpreted as arrogance, passive-aggressiveness, or even oppositional behavior. Some personality types are more prone to exhibit these behaviors, which is why families should consider temperament and personality when they try to determine the best course of action for their child in school.

Parents who try to get the schools to make lessons and assignments more relevant and meaningful for their children often run into roadblocks. What they find, among other things, is that teachers award grades based on assignment completion rather than on subject mastery. Thus, many parents worry that their children are "failing," when what the children are actually doing is refusing to comply with teacher demands.

Other than taking the child out of the school, one remedy for parents is to remove themselves from the situation and allow the student to earn poor grades for a while. The homework problem usually corrects itself by the time the gifted child reaches high school, because the courses are more intellectually challenging and the student can see a connection between assignments, learning, mastery, and grades, as well as a correlation to future goals such as college and career.

Some highly intelligent children will do their homework—but not the way that the teacher has instructed. When gifted students protest showing their work or giving detail (such as with math problems), adults need to explain why these things matter. If these children are given sensible reasons *why* it is important to show their work, they are much more likely to do it.

Teachers can explain that as you get older, you get to work on progressively longer and more detailed problems. If you don't get the answer that you expect, or if the answer is wrong, you need to be able to go back through your steps to see where you made an error. If you need help from anyone else, then they need to be able to follow your process in order to know where you made an error—only then can they help you. Finally—and this works well with Level Four and Five high school kids—teachers can pose this question: What if one day you are a famous researcher and you are very close to a cure or an elusive solution to a problem that has troubled humankind for centuries, but you die before you can get the patent or get it published? You would certainly want someone to be able to read through your work and put it to good use. These are the reasons why it is important to learn how to organize and show your work.

Samantha Forrest—From the time Samantha started school, we had trouble getting her to do homework. Even in kindergarten, she told us that she was not learning enough and that the assignments were pointless.

Gary Lundquist—Gary's second-grade teacher wrote that he worked slowly. He read 153 books independently that year, and she didn't understand why he didn't bring the same level of motivation to all of his school assignments.

Greg Cooper—We finally persuaded the teacher to agree to send all of Greg's unfinished assignments home and not keep him from recess, music, or gym anymore when he didn't finish his work.

Author note: Young children need a physical outlet. For many gifted children, it is lunch, recess, and special subjects like art, music, and gym class which make their days tolerable.

Tyler Lundquist—Once Tyler was exposed to a topic and thought he understood it, he tended to lose interest. He earned low grades on his homework due to lack of organization and logical progression in his solutions. There was no doubt that he had the capability of being an excellent student; he just needed to work harder on his homework. By the time he finally had access to instruction at a leve   l that was appropriate for him, he'd already developed bad habits that made it hard for him to transition to more difficult material.

Not Showing Enough Effort

By the time parents begin seeking help for their gifted children outside of the schools, they have usually had complaints from teachers and are concerned that their children are underachieving and developing poor habits. Teachers commonly complain that gifted students only show effort for what interests them, as though this is a terrible thing. However, when you stop to think about it, most of us exhibit little enthusiasm for repetitive or meaningless work. Gifted children would be far more likely to show interest in and motivation for assignments that are challenging and make sense to them. Teachers will have better success if they discuss the overall goals of the assignment with the children and let them make choices for how they will meet those goals, as well as how they will demonstrate that the goals have been met.

The *Harter Scales of Intrinsic versus Extrinsic Motivation in the Classroom* (Harter, 1985) showed that all of the children in this book were well above average for their age in intrinsic motivation. However, students like these are rarely motivated to do something simply because someone else tells them they should. Why should they want to do their best on every assignment or project that comes along? In addition, being in a mainstreamed regular classroom can squelch these children's motivation to learn. A long day of school, even when non-challenging, can still exhaust one's energy. Materials and topics that are motivating should be provided during—not after—the school day in order to be effective.

Sometimes teachers offer bright children the opportunity to come up with their own projects, but students shouldn't be expected to develop their own curriculum, particularly before middle or high school ages. Instead, the teacher might ask these children what they are reading, watching, or doing in their spare time and then use that information to tap into what might constitute an appropriate project. Expecting a nine-year-old to design his own course of study, no matter how bright, is unrealistic.

Charles Engquist—With Charles, our challenge was trying to find an interest area amongst normal school subjects and career fields. The only thing that he was passionate about was movies and computer games with simulated civilizations at war and in need of battle strategies. His best school subjects were history and languages. Charles loved to learn by absorbing information, but he never liked to put in a lot of effort. He was not big on problem solving or thinking—that took too much effort.

Tyler Lundquist—In fourth grade, Tyler's teacher said that he needed adult supervision in order to complete assignments and that he was a strong-willed boy who "marches to the beat of a different drummer." When Tyler got into high school and a number of ability-grouped classes, his grades improved. He contributed in class and tested well, but he still didn't turn his work in.

Bill Arnesen—Bill completed all of his homework, but it wasn't always done very well. When students were asked to "actively" read a series of pages in the text—underlining and taking notes—the teacher got the impression that Bill felt that this was a complete waste of his time.

Patricia Walker—I spoke with Patty's teacher just before Christmas because I was seeing signs of her being afraid to challenge herself. If something wasn't a breeze for her, she resisted even trying it. I didn't think it was laziness, but more likely perfectionism and fear of failure.

Author note: Some children think that others admire or respect them due to how quickly and well they can do their work. If there is a chance that it will be too hard, they can become paralyzed with fear that they will lose the acceptance and admiration of others, and they don't dare risk it. These children need to be eased into a steadily more challenging and interesting learning environment.

Disorganization

Different personality types handle organization in different ways. Some highly intelligent individuals appear to be disorganized when they are actually completely aware of where everything is and when everything needs to be done. However, too often, adults over-manage children so that the children don't have a need to organize themselves. Adults need to let children develop their own organization skills, but they can also make sure that the children know why it is important to organize themselves.

Colin Richards—I was surprised, and somewhat disappointed, to find that Colin became so disorganized and lackadaisical in his schoolwork in high school. He did rather poorly in subjects such as calculus and writing, for which he had once showed such aptitude. He also had trouble with his attitude toward his teachers—it was almost an arrogance, as though he thought that the work was too easy and so he shouldn't have to do it. On the other hand, some of the advanced classes were too hard for him to keep up with because of his lower maturity level and lack of organizational skills.

Author note: Colin was home schooled for most of his school years, and when he joined regular classes, he was not prepared to observe the more rigid requirements. He needed time to work out his own system for getting his work done.

Not Paying Attention in Class—Being Distracted and Distractible

Children learn to tune out extraneous information in classrooms that go too slowly and repetitively for them. They learn that it is rare that anything new is discussed, so they lose themselves in their own thoughts and then catch up quickly when necessary. Unfortunately, if this becomes a habit, these children may miss important information when the demands become greater in later school years.

Phil Burns—When Phil was listening and attending, he had excellent recall. Sometimes, though, his mind wandered, and he had no idea what the teacher was looking for.

Daniel Schmidt—Daniel's teacher said that he tried hard to stay focused, but he rushed through his work and made too many errors.

Blake Hauge—Teachers reported that, although Blake showed excellent concentration when he seemed confident and comfortable, he was often socially distracted and tended to lose focus, particularly in large group settings. He often seemed to be daydreaming or preoccupied, and he tended to avoid areas of challenge. His impulsivity interfered with his ability to establish friendships because other children became wary and defensive. In addition, he was reported to pester others for attention. His academic achievement varied from day to day. Although he often started out reflectively when working, he'd end up rushing through without thinking. His motivation varied from highly motivated to needing urging, depending upon the task and circumstances at hand.

Emotional Changes in the Child

Teachers may believe that advanced learners are okay in the mixed-ability classroom because they continue to do well on achievement tests and because so many of them appear to adapt well. But much of the damage is hidden or camouflaged. Gifted children can develop common emotional patterns—such as a confused self-concept, depression, and loneliness—when they are in the wrong educational environment.

Confused Self-Concept

Many bright children can't figure out what they are truly capable of doing because they are often the only one in their class, especially throughout elementary and middle school, who learns as fast or knows as much as they do. They come to believe that they are far more unique than is actually the case, and they become overtly impatient with the relatively impaired-looking abilities of their classmates.

A number of the children featured in this book exhibited anger, hostility, and condescension toward their teachers. Highly intelligent children need teachers who are also intelligent and who can appreciate them, who know how and when to be flexible, and who have the confidence and wherewithal to respond in a mature manner to model for the child appropriate ways to express needs and opinions.

Ronald Cooper—Ronald had a stimulating but somewhat frustrating year in sixth grade, when he was grouped for the first time with other gifted kids. Before that, when he had done coursework geared for average children, he had always been one of the brightest students. During those years, he experienced great success and ease and got a distorted view of his own abilities. But when he was grouped in math with kids who were more highly gifted than he, his self-esteem suffered a tremendous blow. His teacher assumed that his class had learned a lot of the math work previously, but it was all new to Ronald. He went from curriculum that was rudimentary to quite advanced with absolutely no transition time. The teacher expected students to know the answers and not need to ask for clarification. Ronald started to think that he wasn't so smart, and he was struggling and not producing a "quality job" like the teacher wanted. His self-esteem plummeted. He also felt the insults of the other children who were doing better than he.

Bill Arnesen—Almost every year, Bill got stressed because he felt that he didn't understand anything and was doing miserably in school. He tended to panic and worry until he became familiar with the teacher, the expectations, and his own ability to do fine. He needed steady reassurance. It was extremely helpful to know his ability level ahead of time—his behavior and fears would have led me to back way off for fear of pushing him too much if I had not known that he could do it.

Candice Richardson—Candice participated in a couple of pullout programs for reading and enjoyed them, but it was hard for her to switch gears, and she viewed the pullout classes as an interruption. She got frustrated because other kids in the class recognized her reading ability and came to her for help, and this made it difficult for her to complete her own assignments. She complained, "People don't understand that just because I'm smart, it doesn't mean I'm fast!"

Author note: Pullout programs can cause a number of difficulties for gifted children and for the school. First, the regular classroom teacher must decide whether or not to have the children make up the work they missed while at the gifted class, and most do require this. Second, many children are uncomfortable with being different and having to leave the room for these opportunities. If a pullout program is the only option, many aren't sure it's worth the price.

Depression

The problem of growing depressed or angry after starting school is extremely common among gifted children, particularly Levels Three through Five. Levels One and Two are less affected. Stories about feigning illness in order to skip school are also common among gifted individuals. Many of these children develop legitimate aches and pains as a result of the stress that they experience when trying to fit into a system that isn't working for them.

Justin Janacek—Until he was about seven, Justin was a very joyful child. Not just happy—joyful. The joyful times outnumbered the angry times by far. But by the end of first grade, he expressed happiness more often than joyful enthusiasm, and the angry times were more frequent. Since most things came so easily to him, being unable to meet a challenge frustrated and angered him, and he acted bored if the challenge was too great. He expended a great deal of emotional energy trying to figure out how to interact with other kids, especially when they were not thinking or feeling as he was. He had a definite set of standards, values, and rules for behavior and respect. He couldn't understand why all of the kids didn't simply do what the teacher said the first time. He wanted to fit in without really compromising what he felt was right. It was an exhausting balancing act.

Daniel Schmidt—When Daniel was in tenth grade, he saw a counselor who gave him an emotional assessment that indicated pretty significant depression and anxiety, and on a couple of occasions, it came to our attention (through school friends who spoke to the school counselor) that Daniel was thinking of suicide. Apparently, he didn't want to burden us, so he effectively hid his inner pain from us. Even when we were keeping very close tabs on his emotional state, we had no idea that he was so depressed that he was contemplating suicide. The encouraging thing in all of this was that he truly wanted to feel better. He was very open and cooperative with his therapist and school counselor.

Ross Oliver—Ross was referred for gifted evaluation in kindergarten, and although the test results indicated that he would qualify for an individualized plan, what the school provided was minimal. He was allowed to participate in a first-grade reading group for a while, but then he was sent back to kindergarten because, according to the school's learning specialist, "He's already more advanced than all of the other first graders, so he might as well stay with his class because we don't want to place him any higher." It made no sense. This was just the beginning—it was also the time we started seeing signs of depression from him.

Author note: Ross's parents were dumbfounded to see that the school needed no reason to keep their son from being instructed at his own level. The repercussions of thwarting Ross's progress over the years were that, although his ability was Level Five, his achievement fell seriously behind what he could have learned due to the school's casual decisions regarding staying with age-mates. He was unable to find friends among his same-age classmates, he grew to believe that there was something wrong with him, and he developed severe depression by the time he was 10 years old.

Brennan Ahlers—By January of first grade, Brennan complained of headaches and upset stomach, went to bed at night not wanting to go to school, and woke up in the morning sure that he was ill and unable to go. He became anxious, developed insomnia, had issues with food— gagging if he didn't like the texture and refusing to eat—and acted out in anger and frustration upon arriving home from school. He said he "just couldn't do it anymore." He was incredibly angry at having to sit through hours of repetitive work he already knew.

Loneliness and Feeling Different

When children are the only ones like them in their classes, it's hard to find friends and comfortable companions. It is important for adults to understand that children will sometimes resist appropriate instructional opportunities, such as going to another classroom, because it makes them appear very different from their classmates.

Debra Sund—Debra was still in second grade, but she was in the third-grade reading program and was learning at her own pace in many areas. Even though she'd been told that she was welcome to join in other third-grade lessons such as in math, she was shy about it. She worried that she wouldn't fit in.

Janet Lewis—After receiving Janet's evaluation, I took on a very resistant principal and teaching staff to skip her from second grade into middle school (sixth grade) and eighth-grade general math. They were converted to the merits of the plan after witnessing her intellectual capability, but she did feel very lonely. She was regarded as a curiosity, not as a potential friend. She liked her coursework but felt like a social pariah. It didn't help that she was much smaller than even kids her own age, not to mention far less physically developed, of course, than the other middle school girls.

Author note: If school systems grouped children according to what they were ready to learn, issues of being too young or too small would not exist. Many different ages and sizes would be represented within such classrooms.

Brennan Ahlers—Brennan struggled with friends. His best friend, a girl named Hope, decided that she would rather spend time with her girlfriends, which made him sad. He became frustrated during group projects when he could see a better or faster way of doing things but had to work at the pace of the group, and this behavior didn't win him friends, either.

Frank Price—We wondered if getting no special treatment at school was damaging Frank. However, this was his preference; he was embarrassed when I talked with his teacher about getting something more challenging for him in math. She developed a more interesting assignment for him, but he responded with tears because it was different from his friends' assignments.

Carol Johnston—Carol was early entranced to kindergarten when she was not quite five, and she began to notice that she was different. The other kids couldn't do the things that she could do, and she began having trouble finding friends. We found that she tried more and more to blend in with the other children and was afraid of being singled out or of being different.

Michael Cortez—At age 5½, when Michael began spending most of his time with his age-mates during the second half of the school year, we noticed that his speech became very simple and that he started making grammatical errors. Even his voice articulation changed to one that rose at the end of a sentence. He started using the word "like" a lot. He wanted to fit in.

Author note: Several parents mentioned that their children changed their speech patterns and slowed their oral reading to match that of classmates.

Additional Problem Areas

The repetitive nature of the work, the need to fit in and not feel too different, the difficulty showing enough effort, the growing reluctance to comply with assignments that make no sense—all of these obstacles can make gifted children look as though they either have attitude problems or aren't really any more advanced than their more typical classmates. Then, however, there are some academic subjects that really do give many gifted children difficulty—for example, spelling, which appears to be more of a talent or special aptitude than other subjects. Some people are naturally good at spelling, and some equally intelligent people are not. All gifted children—and most non-gifted children—can master weekly spelling lists, but this doesn't mean that they will be good spellers later.

Writing and math are two areas that cause problems for the majority of highly intelligent students throughout the first eight or nine years of school.

Math

Children who are gifted in quantitative reasoning—math—often find that their actual learning is stopped in its tracks compared to the children for whom the instruction is aimed. Even when schools provide an accelerated math sequence, it is usually not available until fifth grade or later, and then it is often only one year ahead of the regular grade level. Rote memorization of arithmetic facts is a constant issue; children are accused of being unmotivated, lazy, stubborn, or bad at math when they fail to memorize their math facts.

Many gifted children benefit from jumping ahead in math to a level where the need for the memorized facts becomes apparent. In other words, instead of insisting that they master—i.e., memorize—math facts before they are allowed to progress into more interesting material, I recommend going ahead to long division and multiplication. As the children repeatedly experience the inconvenience of having to "count out" the same number facts over and over again, they either automatically commit them to memory or they understand that learning these math facts would be useful after all.

Some children underachieve by not being instructed at their level. In first grade, schools generally don't teach numerical reasoning or mathematics. They do very concrete hands-on activities designed to make children familiar with relationships between sizes and quantities. These are concepts that most gifted children figure out long before they start school. They then become confused over what they are supposed to be doing, and they make careless errors because it is difficult to pay close attention over and over again. If these children miss one or two questions, they often conclude—as does the teacher—that they are not very good at math. Children like this would be much better off going straight to a higher grade-level class for math, skipping the repetition and allowing them to get into real concepts.

Debra Sund—There were times when Debra said, "I'm not very smart in math," which really disturbed me. She expected herself to be immediately as good at math as she'd always been at reading—and she got a lot of attention for her good reading.

Franklin Hayes—Franklin's calculation and computational skills lagged behind his conceptual understanding. He had some disturbing relapses in skills in the third grade. He was able to do long division well in second grade, but as a third grader, he had trouble on the pre-test for that unit. He had not used his skills for a while and was confused on the process. The new curriculum put more emphasis on concepts, which he already understood, than on calculation and computation.

Author note: Ability tests assess conceptual understanding and quantitative reasoning more than calculation skills. When teachers and parents see achievement and classroom test results that show poor calculation skills, they are often confused by the discrepancy. It is so easy to teach a very gifted child the mathematical processes of calculation that it is tempting to go forward

> *without providing enough occasional review. At the same time, memorization of math facts is inappropriate for gifted students and is not what is meant by review of processes.*

Layne Freeman—In the fall of third grade at Layne's school for highly gifted children, the teacher was concerned because Layne hadn't memorized her subtraction facts. I suggested that she be shown how to do multiplication and division out of sequence. She learned those in a snap and then understood subtraction.

Ross Oliver—Ross won the state's Knight's of Columbus Math Award and tested into algebra after completing the fifth-grade EPGY program. Despite all of this, his fifth-grade math teacher required him to attend classes for group work instead of with a math mentor. When working with classmates, his teacher wouldn't allow him to use algebra because "it would be an unfair advantage."

Writing

Parents worry when their gifted child's teacher says that the child is not doing well in writing. Gifted children's writing difficulties take numerous forms, but no matter the particular issue, teachers usually view it too seriously. It is as though they believe that there is no way that the child should receive instruction at an appropriate level in any other subjects until his or her writing is also at a more advanced level.

There are several reasons why gifted children are frequently behind in their writing ability. First, writing is inefficient when compared to speaking and reading skills. When most children are young, their writing is so slow and physically arduous that they resist writing anything until they know that they will not have to change it or redo it. Second, many highly intelligent people do not do "first drafts," and yet this is a process that schools encourage. Gifted children may appear to wait until the last minute to get assignments done, but many actually think about what they are going to write until the concept is well developed in their heads. Third, these students may have difficulty deciding which of their abundant thoughts and ideas should be selected for writing down. If the teacher doesn't like what they've chosen, they may have to do it over—and since the assignment didn't interest them in the first place, they decide that perhaps it's better to avoid it altogether. Fourth, they see little point in the art of writing since, in their minds, writing is simply a tool to communicate that only has to be minimally legible. Besides, typing on a computer is faster.

Boys are far more likely than girls to have these issues with writing. Adults need to guide the gifted child one step at a time by keeping assignments short and specific. Patient and kind persistence eventually helps most gifted students become excellent writers.

When writing reports or answering test questions, many Level Three and higher gifted children are on a different wavelength than their teachers and aren't sure what their teacher really wants them to write. One way to address this is to make sure that the child knows the purpose of the lesson, the purpose of the class, and the big picture for any of the skills or concepts being taught. In addition, some gifted children, particularly Level Four and Five boys, are excellent synthesizers and need to be coaxed to give detailed answers.

Frank Price—Frank's teachers noticed that he had difficulty writing. It wasn't for lack of ideas; his creativity was amazing, and he told great stories. It helped when one of his teachers suggested, as remedial work, that every night, Frank write down two characters, a setting, and a problem as preparation for writing a story. He would jot down characters like "an apple and the letter 'y'" and then proceed to tell me a story about them.

Layne Freeman—Layne was upset when compelled to do something that she thought was stupid, such as webbing (i.e., exploring numerous related subjects by drawing lines between them on a piece of paper). The writing process stuff, which works fine for some kids, didn't work for her. She usually had the entire report written in her head before she put it on paper. She got irritated and angry when forced to do the webbing, or notes on 3x5 cards, etc. The teacher said that Layne would have to be able to do webbing the following fall when all fifth graders take benchmark tests—the entire first day of the writing test is devoted to this webbing process.

Bill Arnesen—Bill put more depth and effort into his writing when the parameters were set for him. A naturally good speller, he was willing to study and memorize vocabulary because he enjoyed how good he was at it. He struggled with how to answer essay questions—his teachers complained that he was too concise and didn't write enough.

Author note: Synthesis is a natural component of high intelligence. The problem with essay questions is that the teacher is looking for a regurgitation and

> *elaboration of what was covered, and the gifted student is adept at synthesis—quickly getting to the point. Teachers need to understand that this is what is occurring.*

Rick Arnesen—In fourth grade, the teacher said that Rick's writing skills had developed in terms of content, organization, and mechanics, but he still needed to spend more time revising and polishing his work—he wanted to arrive at the end product too quickly. He needed to recognize that writing is a process. By middle school, Rick hated to write and resisted it strongly. As a university student, however, it was one of his greatest strengths and an ability of which he was very proud.

Summary of School Issues

All of the issues in this chapter are common for the families of gifted children. The typical home environment or flexible preschool are usually fine for keeping all levels of gifted youngsters stimulated, but when the children start regular school, most parents are shocked and unprepared for the struggles that they so often encounter.

No matter where they live and attend school, bright children encounter similar hurdles as they progress through the school years. The regular school curriculum is usually all that is offered to any child, regardless of ability. Most educators value play and social skill development over learning at one's own ability level. If teachers are asked which is more important—intellectual growth and making continual progress in one's learning, or learning and practicing social skills—they almost universally answer social skills.

Chapter 12
Educational Needs for Each Level

I keep asking myself, "How smart is my daughter?
Does knowing really matter?" I feel confused, but I think
that if I have her tested, then both she and I will know,
and I can do a better job of placing her in appropriate programs
and guiding her academically. Right now, I don't really
know where she fits and what would be best for her.
~ Mother of a sixth-grade girl

General School Placement Goals

When selecting a school for a gifted child, the primary goal is to find a good match so that the child can progress at a pace that fits his or her readiness, as well as to find friends and intellectual compatibility with adults and children there. Also important is the goal of providing a good chance at a normal life.

Until school systems radically change their approach to educating children of different intellectual levels—by doing away with strict age grouping in classrooms, for instance—parents will need to look at how to piece together options and opportunities that will contribute to: (1) accelerated learning, (2) the development of study and time management skills, (3) a continuing intrinsic love of learning, (4) opportunities to experience normal school and social activities like school plays, band, sports, yearbook, math league, and spending time with friends, and (5) ultimately leaving home for a satisfying university experience. The good news is that, with some advocacy, all of this is possible.

For a gifted child to become a self-actualized, resilient gifted adult, it is important for that child to have:

- Parents or others who make the child feel loved and valued for the essence of his or her being.
- Many opportunities to learn at the child's own pace and depth.

- Frequent occasions to spend time with others—adults or age-mates—who enjoy and understand the child's jokes and observations about the world—literature, politics, philosophy, religion, etc.

There is no one best program or approach that will effectively address the numerous issues that the wide ability ranges in the five levels of giftedness present, and compromises may be needed to achieve a balance. Several types of schools are available to address the needs of children at each level of giftedness. These schools use a variety of instructional and grouping options that educators and parents can consider when taking children's different learning abilities into account.

Types of Schools

Just as there are different levels of giftedness, there are different types of schools. To make it simpler to explain what each level of giftedness needs, I have designated school options as Type I through Type V. As with the levels of giftedness, Types I through V are general categories of schools—not exact, strict criteria.

Daycare Centers and Preschool Programs

Daycare centers and preschools usually gear their programs toward the average developmental level of the children who attend them. When a center or a school advertises that it uses "developmentally appropriate curriculum," parents should visit the school and see how it feels to them. Sometimes "developmentally appropriate" refers to the average or typical child's development, without sufficient flexibility for a gifted child. If the fit is poor, a child is more likely to exhibit—or be accused of—poor social skills and misbehavior. Parents should choose a place where they feel natural and comfortable with other parents and teachers.

Type I Schools

These are usually public schools that serve the general population with a wide range of student socioeconomic backgrounds. This school might include recent immigrants still learning English, residents who are highly mobile, and sometimes a moderate to high proportion of culturally disadvantaged or poverty-level individuals, with many students who qualify for the federal subsidy of free or reduced price lunches.

Type II Schools

These are public, private, or parochial schools, small rural school systems, or specialty magnet schools that accept children on criteria other than just ability and achievement scores—perhaps a portfolio of previous work or demonstrated talent and interest. This type of school usually draws from a strongly middle class population with few students from families in either poverty or wealth.

Type III Schools

This type of school has a reputation for high standardized test scores, a large percentage of students going on to colleges and universities, and no dropouts. It can be public or private. Parents are often from a high educational and socioeconomic background, and the school generally draws from a population with little or no poverty.

Type IV Schools

These are magnet schools—public or private—for highly gifted students in which admissions are based primarily on standardized test scores and demonstrated achievement. Teachers are highly qualified, and the learning environment is challenging and somewhat competitive.

Type V Schools

These are any schools, anywhere, that facilitate continuous progress throughout the subject levels without regard for the children's ages. This type of school or school system instructs all children at their own ability and readiness levels without regard to age or typical grade-level designations. This is sometimes described as cross-age grouping or cross-grade grouping. This means that students of varying ages and abilities will be moving at different rates through the school's coursework. Student feelings of isolation or strangeness are minimized because students are grouped flexibly in mixed-age classes. Schools based on the Montessori method do this type of grouping well, but few Montessori programs are available after the primary grades, which means that the opportunity for similarly-minded classmates diminishes in the later grades.

Educational Options that Work for Gifted Students

Children who learn faster and in more depth and complexity than others their same age require different educational opportunities. Unless the instructional depth and pace are a good fit for the ability and preparation of each student, underachievement occurs, and many advanced learners may suffer significant social and emotional difficulties. There is nothing as effective as accelerating instruction for gifted learners (Colangelo, Assouline, & Gross, 2004), and there are numerous ways to accomplish this goal through a variety of educational options that are useful for different levels of giftedness. Rogers (2002) is an excellent resource, and additional information can be found in the gifted education literature.

The 15 different curriculum programs or options that follow are presented in order from the simplest to the most difficult to arrange. Some schools routinely offer one or more of the suggested options; others may be opposed to even the least costly plan. Every school, however, is capable of offering some—if not most—of them, and working with the schools is always the best first option.

Parents should check to see what the school's gifted program involves to decide if the program will be adequate for meeting any or all of their child's needs. Gifted programs—through schools or in the community—can have any or all of the 15 educational options that follow. Frequently, programs focus on enrichment alone, particularly "lateral enrichment,"[1] or on a pullout program for only one hour each week. These two approaches are misleading as gifted programs; they are often shallow and do little to advance gifted children's learning. Additionally, parents should be aware that many school gifted programs start very late—at third grade.

Early Entrance

Parents may be able to arrange for their bright child to start kindergarten before age five, though many schools require intelligence testing at the 98th percentile in order to consider a child for early entrance. Early entrance gives children the opportunity to be closer to the mental age of other children in their class.

Ability-Grouped Instruction

In ability-grouped instruction, children of similar learning ability—from an otherwise mixed-ability class—are placed together within the classroom for instruction in one or more subjects. Parents need to ask if ability grouping is used for all subjects or only a few, and whether it occurs daily or is only occasional. They also need to know whether, and how, the instructional level differs for each group.

This kind of flexible grouping is usually done at grade level, and there are many variations. Some schools offer a daily re-grouping in math or reading or both, in which the faster learners go to a different teacher for that subject, while slower students are grouped together, and average students are grouped together.

A variation of this is clustering, in which six or eight gifted students within the same grade level are all placed in one teacher's classroom—generally the teacher who has the most training in how to work with gifted students. This arrangement allows gifted students to be with others who are like them and, if the teacher differentiates the instructional activities well, to be challenged.

Differentiated Instruction

In this instructional strategy, the teacher modifies or tiers the instruction and assignments so that children can learn at the pace that matches their ability and readiness for different levels of assignments. Students in the same-age mixed-ability class might study the same topic at the same time with the same basal textbook and materials, but the extensions, enrichment, and practice assignments are modified according to each child's needs.

This approach is very popular as an attempt to meet the needs of gifted learners while keeping them in mixed-ability classrooms. Some experts describe the differentiation process as creating a parallel curriculum.[2] The utility of this approach is limited for children who are already too advanced for the material. Levels Three, Four, and Five students will often spend the majority of their time working alone, waiting for the teacher to design or assign something for them.

Single-Subject Acceleration

In this option, a child stays at his own grade level with age-mates for the majority of the day but moves up one or more grade levels in specific subjects where he shows high ability and needs to learn at a more advanced pace. This requires coordination of teachers' classroom schedules and decisions about what the child can miss at grade level while attending the more advanced class. How well this works depends on the child's personality—i.e., whether the child is independent and confident and doesn't mind looking different from others—and support from the teachers for the child's schedule needs.

Online and Correspondence Courses

Online courses have recently mushroomed, and correspondence courses have been available for years. Students may get permission to use school time for either method, or the courses can be part of a full or partial home school arrangement. Such courses provide an alternative to age-level instruction and also avoid placing the youngster in situations before he or she is ready, such as in college classes with 19-year-olds. Students may take these classes independently, or they can have a tutor, parent, or mentor to guide them and keep them on track.

Whole-Grade Acceleration

This option involves moving a child ahead of age-mates by skipping a full grade and receiving instruction with older students. The book *A Nation Deceived: How Schools Hold Back America's Brightest Students* (Colangelo, Assouline, & Gross, 2004) analyzes more than 100 years of acceleration research and concludes that acceleration is the most effective approach to maximizing children's learning. *The Iowa Acceleration Scale* (Assouline, Colangelo, Lupkowski-Shoplik, Lipscomb, & Forstadt, 2003) can be used to guide a child study team through indicators regarding whether a child is a good candidate for a full grade skip or whether some other option, such as single-subject acceleration or mentoring, should be considered instead.

Partial Home Schooling

In this arrangement, parents instruct their child at home or on the school campus separately from the regular class for a portion of each day. The student can rejoin classmates for regular grade-level lessons and activities for the remainder of the day. The parent should negotiate with the teacher so that these parent-established, home-taught subjects supplant a specific subject or two rather than add to the child's normal workload. Interested parents can work together to share this obligation and offer advanced learning opportunities to several children. Parents who aren't available to teach or coordinate lessons may pay a tutor to work separately with a group of children for part of the school day—on or off the school campus. Parents should avoid offering this extra instruction at the end of the school day, however, because children also need time to relax and play.

Partial home schooling has the advantage of allowing the child to stay in touch (through part-time school) with other children and activities that children their age enjoy or need, and it allows the parent to continue his or her own work or career for part of the day as well.

Full-Time Home Schooling

Families may decide that one or both parents will instruct their children at home full time. Home schooling is legal in every state, and there are numerous materials available about it, such as books like *Creative Home Schooling: A Resource Guide for Smart Families* (Rivero, 2002). Support groups for parents are also available. Such schooling at home works quite well when supplemented by community activities and involvement, but home schooling is a full-time commitment for the parents, often necessitating at least one parent leaving the work force. However, the advantage of children learning at their own pace and covering far more material during their school years than children in the regular classroom is an obvious benefit.

Full-Time Ability-Grouped Classroom

In a full-time ability-grouped class, children of similar stages of intellectual development are placed together for instruction in all of their subjects all day, every day. There are both social and academic advantages when children of the same age and ability range are grouped together, although a several year spread in age is also good. This option can be part of a magnet school, a gifted magnet program within a school, or simply a cross-section of the students in one school who are ready to learn together at a specific, identified level of instruction.

Tutoring or Mentoring

In tutoring or mentoring, arrangements are made for an adult to work alone with the gifted student for one or more subjects that match the student's interest and ability level. This can occur during the school day or at another time. Sometimes a teacher or librarian within a school can act as a tutor or mentor for a child, or parents may need to hire a tutor outside the school system.

Summer Institutes and Outside Supplemental Advanced Classes

Courses for gifted students whose schools do not meet their needs have been burgeoning since the early 1970s. Many Talent Searches,[3] weekend and summer institutes, and advanced math and science courses for middle school gifted students are now available. Some schools give high school credit for these classes.

Radical Acceleration

This is a process of promoting or grade skipping a child more than one grade at a time, possibly more than once, so that the gifted child takes progressively more complex and advanced subjects with progressively older and older classmates, graduating from high school early and entering a university anywhere from two to six years younger than usual.

Advanced Coursework

Honors courses, Advanced Placement (AP), and International Baccalaureate (IB)[4] programs are options that are available in some high schools. Honors courses are special classes that an individual school designs and offers for advanced students. Some schools have honors courses available from sixth grade through high school, and many have criteria for taking them, such as grades, past performance in the subject, or teacher recommendation.

AP courses are actually college-level courses with exams that qualify students for concurrent high school and college credit. IB is a rigorous international program that follows a specific course and is less flexible than AP class choices. The IB diploma requires fluency in one foreign language and four years of lab science. A benefit for some students is that the IB diploma is honored by all international universities and would allow a student to apply to the Sorbonne in Paris, for example. Teachers of AP and IB courses receive special training and curriculum material and must hold their courses to the strict standards of the program. Exams for both AP and IB are standardized, and credit is given by many colleges for AP or IB coursework.

Concurrent Enrollment

Concurrent enrollment generally refers to the practice of attending both college and high school classes at the same time. Some states actually pay tuition for advanced, qualifying high school students to take university courses. The students attend high school and live at home but take one or more courses at a nearby institution of higher learning. They receive credit for the class in both high school and college. A middle school student who attends one or more high school classes and receives high school credit is also using the concurrent enrollment option.

Individualized Approach

Depending on a child's level of giftedness and the options available, an individualized approach often works best. Parents can use a combination of home schooling, tutoring, independent study, online learning, community resources, family travel, and part-time or intermittent school attendance.

Summary

Regardless of the methods or options used, each level of giftedness has particular needs for optimum intellectual, social, emotional, and self-actualizing growth. Ultimately, the goal is to provide some form of accelerated instructional opportunity for advanced learners while maintaining as many normal social interaction opportunities as possible.

Level One Needs

Early Childhood—Birth to Kindergarten

Level One children's early childhood needs are best served at home or at daycare where they can interact freely with their environment, exploring and choosing their own playthings with little specific guidance. Parents often seek out recommendations for toys and activities that will "stimulate" their children's intelligence, but young children of all intellectual abilities only pay attention to that which interests them, despite parents' best efforts to encourage any particular interests.

When selecting toys or books to appeal to Level One children's interests, choose items that are labeled about a third ahead of their actual ages. Of course, many children put small objects in their mouths, so it is important not to give them things that might cause choking before they are old enough to understand this.

Most childcare books and magazine articles are written with bright Level One children in mind and are geared toward mothers who are educated and want to read articles about how to raise their children.

Early Grade School Years

Level One children are generally already ahead of Type I school curriculum goals, but a Type II or III school will likely have primary-grade goals that are more advanced. It is ideal if Level One children can attend academically challenging schools during the primary and middle school grade years. If they can, further adjustment is rarely needed. Most Level One students won't qualify for most Type IV schools—magnet schools for gifted students—unless they are from a recognized underrepresented group. It is not advisable for parents to send Level One children to schools where the academic level and pace is too strenuous; it can be demoralizing and does not lead to better learning. A Type V school—a school that facilitates continuous progress for each child—would be ideal, if such a school is available.

If the Type I school is not sufficiently stimulating and there are no better options to switch to, parents might consider using early entrance, single-subject acceleration, or a whole-grade skip. A whole-grade skip will take care of advanced learning needs of Level One students without putting their social and emotional interactions too out-of-sync with their classmates. Cluster grouping, in-class ability grouping, and instructional differentiation also meet the needs of many Level One students, but it is important that the other children in the group are as capable as the child in question. If your school provides none of this, you can consider full- or part-time home schooling.

Middle School Years

Middle schools, like elementary schools, almost always group students solely by age. Since the achievement gap between the slowest learners and the fastest learners gets larger every year, the gap between the classroom instructional level and the Level One child's achievement and ability level is large by the time a child reaches middle school. It is a fallacy that the typical middle school environment—which focuses on the social interests and needs of adolescents while maintaining little or no ability grouping or academic acceleration—is socially good for gifted students, particularly Level 2 and above.

Parents can request ability-grouped or accelerated courses in the school, but if that doesn't happen, Level One students can benefit from accelerated instruction by taking one or two subjects at the high school, working with a tutor on advanced curriculum to replace one or two regular classes, taking an online or correspondence course, or participating in accelerated summer or weekend courses.

High School Years

Most high schools are fine for Level One students because coursework is offered for different ability levels. Level One students should register for all of the required courses, some Honors courses, and at least one Advanced Placement (AP) course per semester. They should take advantage of high school activities to round out their experiences and their high school transcript. This will also give them more materials for their portfolio for college admissions, as well as opportunities to associate with adults who can write recommendation letters. Parents find it hard to believe, but colleges look less for perfect grades than for students who have taken difficult courses while still participating in athletics, arts, and community opportunities during their high school years.

If the Type I high school has no AP or other advanced courses, parents should arrange for their child to take at least one demanding, higher-level course each year to give the student the opportunity to practice study skills and experience academic rigor. This can be accomplished with online or university correspondence courses or through a university-affiliated summer institute for advanced students. Level One students should be careful, however, not to enroll in too many AP or Honors courses at the same time.

College Life and Career Planning

Level One students are in the general ability range from which most political and community leaders emerge. Because they are close enough to the majority of the population in their viewpoints and language, they tend to communicate well and be acceptable to those they might later lead or supervise.

When planning for and selecting a college, it is important to look for the best overall fit for the student. A school with a good fit is one where the work is challenging but doable and the other students' intellectual levels and interests are in the same general range as the child. College freshman can experience tremendous adjustment problems when they go to college, and it is important that they quickly find compatible friends and not feel overwhelmed by their classes.

A student with an obvious area of strength should look for a school with a broad range of subjects and majors in that domain. Students should send one application to a school that they would be extremely proud to get into, another to one that would be a fall-back option, and two or three to schools that have everything that the student likes—right down to the weather. For each of these colleges, the student's college entrance examination scores should be slightly above the average for the institution. The schools report these averages, and they are also published in college resource manuals.

Social Life for Level One Children

Level One children appear frequently enough in most school populations, so it easy to group them for social interactions and friendships. The social life for the Level One child is often enhanced if their place in the mix is slightly above average for the group. However, Level One children who attend Type I schools sometimes experience great loneliness and may find it difficult to tolerate the interests and activities of their classmates. A Type II school usually provides a good social fit because of Level One children's similarity to their classmates in maturity, interests, and abilities, so that they find it easy and natural to get along with the other students with whom they spend their days.

On the other hand, Level One children who attend Type III schools may find themselves in the lower half of the group as far as their learning abilities are concerned. As a result, they may develop an inaccurate self-concept that their ability and potential are lower than is the case. This can lead to bitterness, hostility toward the perceived advantages of others, or efforts to compete too hard or not at all.

Level Two Needs

Early Childhood—Birth to Kindergarten

Books, articles, and websites that talk about gifted preschoolers are usually talking about Level Two gifted children. Level Two children need the same basic environment as Level One children except that their interest in books and toys will be slightly more advanced. They often hold stronger opinions and personal preferences earlier, too, making it necessary to consider their thoughts when designing rules and disciplinary approaches. By age 18 months or younger, they easily understand that books need to be handled with care, small items don't go in their mouth, and some things must be treated gently. Before they are even two years old, Level Two children can enjoy computers and other electronic equipment, play with puzzles and toys with small pieces, and start to play simple games with older children and adults—activities often associated with children who are at least four years old. They enjoy opportunities to talk, interact, and play games with older children and adults.

Daycare and preschool can be a problem unless those in charge understand that Level Two children need frequent interaction with adults, that they can appear bossy or strong-willed, and that they usually have a deep concern that everyone follow the rules and routines that they are learning. This is the time when adults must patiently start explaining how different people sometimes see things differently. Level Two children can begin to learn patience and tolerance for others who don't understand rules or game strategies or who may not read yet.

Level Two children have longer attention spans and better memories than most children and thus can benefit greatly from family field trips to places like zoos and museums far earlier than many children. While all children enjoy a trip to the zoo, by the time they are about three years old, young Level Two children actually want to know about the animals and will remember what they've learned. The difference is in the *degree* of interest and attention that Level Two young children can give to the experience.

In deciding when a child is ready for an activity, parents should know that when a child whines, complains, or doesn't really pay attention to what is going on (assuming, of course, that the child is not just tired or hungry), then the child isn't ready for the experience. It is normal for a young child who isn't able to comprehend very much information about particular zoo animals, for instance, to whine and complain rather than focus on the activity at hand. This doesn't mean that something is wrong with the child or the child's behavior—only that the parents have misjudged the child's readiness for the experience and should try again when he or she is a little older.

Early Grade School Years

Most Level Two children could complete the basic K-6 curriculum in about three years if it were compacted or telescoped. The best education solution for them is placement in Type III, IV, or V schools. They will easily qualify for gifted programs, but unless the program provides full-time ability grouping, acceleration, or continuous progress, these programs won't be enough to stimulate their potential. When Level Two students attend Type I schools, they desperately need grade acceleration or ability grouping across grade levels in order to have their social and academic needs met.

If the child cannot go to a Type III, IV, or V school and the available gifted program is just an infrequent pullout, then subject or grade-level acceleration should be considered. A good ability assessment can indicate which subjects need acceleration, and the child should be facilitated to skip as many grades as necessary to get appropriate instruction.

It is not unusual for a Level Two child to need to move up two or more grades in several subjects to receive appropriate pace and content. Generally, the student can continue with that particular group, rather than skip any more grades, after the initial acceleration. School systems could provide the same transportation assistance for accelerated students that they currently do for special education students to go to instruction and therapies in other buildings. If transportation is available, or if buildings are within walking distance, depending on the size of the school district, students from numerous grade levels could be grouped at one location for instruction at their own readiness levels.

As Level Two children approach fifth or sixth grade, parents can enter them in academic Talent Searches and accelerated summer opportunities—not just fun classes, but true learning experiences for gifted youth. In sixth or seventh grade, Level Two students can take an online or correspondence course to replace a grade-level course during the school year. At this age, do not insist upon total compliance with school grade-level expectations, but instead help these children to recognize when typical expectations are wrong or inappropriate for them and how they might tactfully approach the teacher to negotiate alternative assignments or coursework. Negotiation skills will be important to gifted children throughout their life.

Middle School Years

Someday, middle schools may return to an emphasis on academics, but for the present, they focus primarily on socialization. Until middle schools start grouping and accelerating students by their ability to learn, parents may need to find educational activities to substitute for or supplement the middle school years. Level Two children who attend a Type I or II middle school will find that not all of the classes and assignments will be good for them. Compliant children may adapt to grade-level instruction but are actually underachieving and losing precious learning opportunities. Parents of non-compliant students should recognize the resistance as a clear sign that the school environment is inappropriate, and they must make changes for their children. These adolescents need to know that their parents understand that most of what is required of them in middle school neither fits their needs nor makes them better people for the experience.

Level Two children in Type I and II schools may find that Talent Searches and university summer institutes supplement—and in some cases directly replace—the middle school general education mixed-ability classes. Even when course credit for these classes is not granted by the school district, the experience is invaluable for such students. For some, it will be the first time that they have ever been academically challenged. For others, it is the first time that they meet another student with the same ability level.

The achievement range within a typical middle school mixed-ability seventh-grade class goes from approximately third-grade equivalency to post-graduate college level (Lohman, 1999). The most that typical middle schools offer is an acceleration of one grade; Level Two gifted students may need more acceleration than that. If a family can afford the high cost, Type III schools are often the best option for Level Two children because all of the students there will be college bound, and additional academic arrangements are seldom required. Other options are full- or part-time home school, family trips, and independent study with a tutor or mentor. Even when the children crave social interaction and opportunities, Level Two learners are too different from the instructional level of most mixed-ability classrooms to benefit significantly in the typical middle school's social or academic arena.

High School Years

High schools traditionally provide ability-grouped classes and can be a refuge for gifted students not burned out by years of forced underachievement. Because middle schools do not ability group— something junior high schools formerly did—the ability grouping in high school can be a shock to some gifted children. If Level Two students have received appropriate academic opportunities prior to high school, each of their ninth-grade semesters could contain at least three courses taught at a rigorous level—Honors, Advanced Placement, or International Baccalaureate classes. Professional or individual tutoring services might be necessary for developing the now-needed study skills that many Level Two students failed to acquire earlier. Students should sign up for activities like sports, music, drama, visual arts, and different organizations that interest them so that they can meet others who share similar interests and so that they can explore interests that are important for later career choices.

Level Two students need to allow themselves time to learn difficult new material without losing confidence that they are smart enough. This will usually be a new experience for them. By the time they are ability grouped for difficult courses, they will meet students who are smarter than they are—Level Three and Four students in a large high school, or maybe even one Level Five. Someone needs to explain this to them, and maybe to their parents, so that they don't automatically assume that they aren't good enough or aren't trying hard enough when they encounter this new level of competition.

Many Type I school districts have high schools that will meet the needs of Level Two students. The exception may be the small rural school. In a school that does not offer advanced classes, concurrent college enrollment or online courses are essential. If the student can't afford the cost, financial aid is available.

College Life and Career Planning

Level Two individuals, those who score in the 98th and 99th percentiles all along the way, usually become part of the professional class in the United States. Intellectual level does not guarantee a particular kind of success, and personal interests and drives are quite important in determining what individuals choose to do as adults. Nonetheless, Level Two individuals need to know that they can do nearly anything they want to do in terms of career, and they also need to get appropriate training.

Although many doctors, lawyers, business CEOs, and entrepreneurs come from Level Two, individuals in Levels Three through Five also choose these careers. Level Two learners will need to focus a bit longer and harder to compete with individuals in the higher levels. If they don't understand their abilities ahead of time, Level Two students may become overwhelmed by the competition when they encounter others in graduate school or other advanced learning situations who learn more rapidly than they. If they don't come from a background where a college education and professional career are traditional, it will help them to know what they are capable of when they are making choices for their future.

When selecting a college, it is important to realize that although these students are "good enough" to go to Harvard, the number of applicants to such universities is great; about 20,000 students a year apply to Harvard, and nearly as many apply to other elite colleges and universities. It is wise to have alternative choices.

Unless the family knows a great deal about college selection or the student attends a Type III high school with a full-time college counselor, it is a worthwhile investment to hire a professional college placement advisor. Otherwise, students at any level might fail to realize their potential and miss making satisfying and helpful social connections.

Social Life for Level Two Children

Whether or not Level Two students will feel particularly odd, different, or lonely depends upon which type of school setting they experience. Intellectual compatibility is ultimately more important to social relationships and interactions than socioeconomic class. If they are in a school where there are many others like themselves intellectually—some Type II and most Type III and IV schools—these students will experience more positive feedback and acceptance than if they are with others who don't understand what they are talking about. Most high schools work well socially for Level Two children, and these are the students who often enjoy taking on leadership roles.

Level Three Needs

Early Childhood—Birth to Kindergarten

Most Level Three children are very active, inquisitive, and alert babies and toddlers. If someone reads to them, especially with animation and play or rhythm and rhyme, they show enjoyment and attention when just a few months old. Although all parents should read with their children, children who are less intellectually precocious won't respond with the same degree of interest or attention. Most Level Three children are careful with things like books or computers when shown how to use them and given the chance to try.

The most significant need for Level Three children is direct conversation and interaction with adults. Most of these children are early talkers, questioners, observers, commenters, and arguers. With their early love of learning, they delight in magnetic letters, shape sorters, and puzzles when still less than two years old. They thrive and blossom when given activities that most people think of as appropriate for children twice their age. In sports, though, their ability is usually based on physical development, which may be normal for typical children their age.

Although most private preschools and daycare centers are set up to be developmentally appropriate for Levels One and Two children, good preschool programs are usually very enjoyable and workable for Level Three children and are less restrictive of their learning than typical kindergartens, so there should be no hurry to leave preschool. If your toddler likes to do 50-piece puzzles, print letters, and carry on detailed conversations with adults, you should select an early childhood program where he or she will be able to do some of that.

Early Grade School Years

Level Three children need to be in primary grades where what they are already able to do is not drilled over and over again. At their own pace, most Level Three children could complete all six grades in about two years. If they continually need to wait for the slower pace of the rest of the class, they learn to underachieve, have difficulty paying attention, and even feel hostility toward the teacher who has the power to make them do things they already know how to do. They can also feel like social isolates among same-age children whose interests and abilities are very different from their own.

Magnet schools and gifted programming are seldom available for the earliest school grades because gifted identification typically takes place after children have been in school for at least two to three years. As a result, the child's first school must be chosen on other factors. Because most kindergarten programs will be more enjoyable and acceptable to Level Three children than a more structured first grade, I usually recommend *against* early entrance for Level Three children. Instead, they can start kindergarten with age-mates and then skip first grade.

If the school won't consider a skip to second grade, then early entrance is the next best option. Being younger than most of their first-grade classmates will take away a slight bit of these students' intellectual advantage and will make the slower pace tolerable for a while. Level Three children who start early or skip a grade will still be the smartest kids in their classes under most circumstances, but they will certainly be better off than if they had stayed with their age-mates.

The best place for elementary-age Level Three children is a Type III, IV, or V school that has flexibility and allows for subject-level acceleration and some ability grouping across ages. Private school elementary classes are no more challenging than those in public schools, though this is not true in the upper grades. Perhaps this is because private schools typically attract larger numbers of students for the elementary years than for the upper grades. For this reason, I discourage parents from spending the extra money to send their children to private schools during the elementary grades if academic rigor is more their goal than the private school atmosphere in general.

Once early entrance or an early grade skip has been accomplished, there is little short of a special school for the highly gifted that will meet the needs of a Level Three elementary-age child. A gifted magnet school or a self-contained classroom for gifted students is a good start. It is important to know the acceptance criteria, however, because if the group is still too intellectually diverse or weighted toward Level One students, Level Three children will spend too much time waiting and learning to underachieve. Subject-level acceleration in all of the core subjects is a good option, if the school will allow it. Most will not. If not, parents may need to supplement through partial or full-time home schooling during the years leading up to high school. Talent Searches and summer programs are essential if these children are to learn what it's like to work at their own level and interact with others who think the way they do.

Middle School Years

Because of the learning disparity within most mixed-ability classes, little meaningful learning takes place in middle school for Level Three students. If the Level Three student is in a Type I school, the slowest middle school learners are struggling at very basic reading and math skill levels—some as low as second and third grade—while the highest can already read, interpret, and analyze material at college levels. Even Type II schools can still be troublesome for Level Three students because there is insufficient focus on highly achieving students. Type III, IV, and V schools are a good start for Level Three children.

When middle schools are located close to high school buildings, advanced middle school students can easily attend high school classes in core subjects. Online courses, correspondence courses, tutors or mentors, and independent progress designed by parents to be completed at school or at home can all enhance the middle school years while still allowing the student to benefit from the activities and social interactions at school. Level Three students can successfully take community college courses by the time they are about 11 or 12 years old, but socially and emotionally, this option is less than ideal.

Another solution for the middle school years is for one or both parents to accept a sabbatical trip to another part of the country or to move overseas for a year or two. Although it is difficult to believe, Level Three students learn so little that is new during regular middle school classes and develop so many poor attitudes and study habits that skipping those school years altogether is actually a good idea. The family can arrange for a more individualized learning plan for their children to complete while abroad. Parents should check the attendance requirements of their chosen country, however, because some countries have mandatory attendance rules and do not allow home schooling of any kind—even for visitors.

Families who choose this option shouldn't worry about grades. It is far more important that bright students get opportunities to work up to their potential and develop time management and study skills than that they earn all A's. Another advantage of attending school abroad is that the whole family experiences another country together, another culture, and often another language. Children typically come back from such an experience with new confidence and new skills. For helpful tips, parents can read *A Family Year Abroad* (Westphal, 2001).

High School Years

Most high schools provide options that Level Three students need for academic and social success. Type I school systems are the exception. If a student is in a rural area or a school with a high level of poverty and a majority of students who are well below the national average in achievement, then early college is almost a necessary choice.

Many areas offer concurrent enrollment in high school and college, and some provide funding for high school age students to take university courses. Level Three students who attend high schools that offer AP or IB courses should be sure to take a wide variety of courses and should expect to handle two or three advanced courses per semester while also participating in other school activities. Both AP and IB are challenging options. The International Baccalaureate program is prescribed and works well for students who simply want to follow a pre-designed program. Some Level Three students will prefer the flexibility of Advanced Placement courses because they may want to specialize or pace their course load to work with the rest of their activities and schedule— sometimes light, and sometimes more intensive.

College Life and Career Planning

Level Three students need information about themselves to fully realize how capable they are relative to the rest of the population. They have the potential to be true specialists and innovators in their chosen fields (Gottfredson, 1998). For much of their school life prior to college, they have been the smartest one in the class, often feeling different or odd and perhaps lacking true soul mates as friends, but college will change all of that. In an ideal college for the Level Three student, there will be opportunities for deep discussions and debates that are exhilarating and affirming.

Parents should look for a school with College Board scores that match or are near that of the Level Three applicant. Look for a college or university that has specialties that have always intrigued the student so that even if she changes her major, she will still be in the right place.

Level Three students are so talented in multiple areas that selecting a major is often difficult. Many Level Three college students feel shame over their inability to find and stick with a major or commit to a career choice. Aside from working with a college career counselor, I suggest that these students keep a notebook in which they write a main interest at the top of each page. This task can be started any time; it's never too early or too late. Then, during their regular daily life, they should reflect on what they have been doing lately, the components of the activity, what they really enjoyed, which of their talents were involved, and so on. Next, they can list the event or activity under that heading in the note-book—or add a new heading as necessary. Eventually, these students will have some pages containing many talents, strengths, and skills and some with very few or none. Sharing their notebook lists with others can also help them identify prospective jobs and careers. A student might even create a new career specialty. Parents should advise young Level Three college students to keep an open mind about how to integrate the things they enjoy into the classes they select and the career they choose. Careers tend to evolve over time; one's first career decision need not be the last.

Social Life for Level Three Children

People in Level Three can experience social difficulties because they are seldom with others like themselves. The key for good social interactions and friendships is to arrange classes and activities in which other Level Two, Three, Four, and Five people are involved. Young people learn good social skills when they spend time with others who get their jokes and who share many of the same interests and abilities.

Level Four Needs

Early Childhood—Birth to Kindergarten

Level Four children are so far ahead of most children, either in all areas or profoundly so in one or two, that most parents know quite early that these children are exceptional. They require constant stimulation to satisfy their curiosity, interests, and need for interaction with their environment, and they initiate activities themselves. Level Four babies react to music, reading, conversation, television, and whatever is going on around them with great interest and early understanding.

By the time Level Four children are toddlers, they can handle books, electronic equipment, and toys more like children who are already four or five years old. Parents need to be alert and find toys and interactions that fit their children's incredible early abilities and interests. When they provide advanced materials, parents sometimes worry that they are pushing their children, but this is exactly the way to respond. Talking to the children at a more advanced and mature level, spending time reading to them, and taking them to zoos, museums, and children's activities are just the things they need. I don't recommend signing them up for music or gymnastics lessons when they are only 2½, but exposing them to things like good play equipment and music is ideal.

The best daycare centers and preschools for Level Four children are those that allow them to pursue their interests. For example, if a three-year-old wants to work on complex puzzles and primary-grade workbooks, he should not only be allowed to do so, but those materials should be readily available. Some preschools stress "developmentally appropriate" environments to such a degree that they mistakenly leave out any opportunity for bright children to do anything academic at all. Many Level Four children truly enjoy writing letters and reading when they are just three and four years old. Look for a center or school that offers what you already know your child likes and wants to do.

Early Grade School Years

Level Four children could complete the typical elementary school curriculum in about a year. Consequently, it will be difficult to find any school that can meet these children's needs without significant adjustment. Type I schools rarely have any Level Four children in them, Type II schools usually have at least one per grade level, Type III schools might have at least one in each class, and Type IV gifted magnet schools will have several, though it depends upon the demographics of the area.

The fit is so poor for a Level Four child in a Type I school that parents must quickly search for other options and try to integrate alternatives into the child's schedule as often as possible. In a Type I school, individualizing and ability grouping for such a child would be difficult except through a form of radical acceleration.[5]

These children are more than highly gifted, and even a Type IV or V school will need to provide some subject-level acceleration and ability grouping across age levels. How much adjustment is needed will depend upon the type of school the child attends. Some Level Four children are significantly advanced in all subject areas, but some are gifted in only one subject area. Educators and parents should not expect uniform achievement. They must also keep in mind that Level Four students may balk at inappropriate assignments or classroom situations and get poor grades as a result.

The goal is to give Level Four children a chance to take as many subjects as they can at their actual ability level while they are in their elementary-grade years. These children are capable of moving through the curriculum so fast that parents need to decide how they want to balance social, emotional, and academic aspects of their children's childhoods. A large metropolitan area might establish a school and provide transportation for all students who are this bright, as has been done in the Seattle area.[6] With this as an option, Level Four students can develop acceptance of challenging material, are less likely to develop habits of underachievement, can develop organizational and study skills, and can learn at least a portion of what they are capable of learning during these early years.

Without access to this kind of a school, home schooling is probably the next best academic option for meeting the needs of Level Four children. Sometimes it works well to home school the child in the morning for core subjects and then have him or her rejoin age-mates for the more social classes in the afternoon—including lunch and recess—to minimize feelings of isolation and loneliness.

Middle School Years

The only middle school options that work well for Level Four children are: (1) a highly flexible Type III or IV school that is willing to accelerate a child or to group children in subjects by ability, (2) a Type V school, (3) radical acceleration right into high school, or (4) home schooling. The long-term effects of inappropriate curriculum on these children can be significant. The middle school years are where the most emotional damage is done to Level Four students if they are left to fend for themselves. These students can easily handle high school courses and should be allowed to either go to where the courses are or take correspondence or online courses instead. Academic Talent Search evening or summer courses should supplant middle school coursework rather than be added to it.

High School Years

Level Four high school students must have regular access to advanced courses through Advanced Placement, International Baccalaureate, college courses, or concurrent enrollment in both high school and college. Sometimes Level Four students should simply leave high school without graduating. A GED (Graduate Equivalency Diploma) is possible and easy to obtain, but it isn't necessary for gaining admission to college programs. Level Four students should weigh carefully whether or not the available high school programs are adequate and appropriate for their learning needs, although they should seriously consider at least part-time enrollment in order to enjoy some of the social or athletic benefits of high school while pursuing other learning elsewhere.

As mentioned earlier, concurrent enrollment programs exist that allow highly or exceptionally gifted youngsters to complete high school and college at the same time on a college campus. However, living away from home so young doesn't suit everyone, and some of the programs specifically designed for concurrent enrollment are actually not challenging enough for Level Four students.

College Life and Career Planning

Level Four students attend every kind of college and university, but if they do not aim high enough, they may still be the only ones like them at their school. They can still be under-challenged, unfulfilled, and lonely. When Level Four students attend the most challenging institutions of higher education in this country, many of them find themselves struggling to compete—especially with foreign students who come from much more academically well-prepared backgrounds than their American counterparts. If the highly gifted students have enough confidence, however, they will catch up and do well, but if they lack the understanding that their academic backgrounds were less than they might have been and that it is not their fault that they are struggling, they may drop out.

Students who have been led to believe that they are the most amazing and wonderful intellects in their less-than-challenging local school situations may feel disappointed and ashamed of their struggles in highly competitive colleges. Level Four students need to know their level of intelligence so that they can develop perspective on their potential and how it affects so many aspects of their lives, including their choices and their feelings about themselves.

Many Level Four people experience depression. They are existentialists at a young age, and they truly need to find their purpose in life. They are also so amazingly multi-potentialed that they need help sorting out what will be fulfilling and give their lives purpose. I recommend the same notebook device for Level Four individuals as discussed for Level Three. Career counseling, mentors, internships, and summer and vacation jobs in a variety of fields are all important to weeding out what works and what doesn't. These students should get a broad background and keep options open unless they are absolutely certain that they know what they want to do. Even then, they should be flexible enough to change their mind.

Social Life for Level Four Children

Level Four individuals spend a great deal of their time in childhood with people who don't always understand them or appreciate their interests. Because of their early and persistent existentialism, their awareness of what could be, and their general inability to be less cerebral than they really are, Level Four people often have trouble making casual social connections. Social awkwardness can be painful.

During childhood, parents and other relatives can be good friends for Level Four individuals, and parents can try to place them in special programs with other very advanced children as often as possible. Adults can then work on friendship skills with the youngsters. It makes no sense to force Level Four children to work on any but the most rudimentary friendship skills with others who are intellectually very different from them. They do, of course, need to learn to be polite and sensitive to others' needs.

In high school, because the brightest students from an entire district are pulled together for advanced courses, Level Four students may finally have the opportunity to enjoy class time with others who appreciate their insights and truly enjoy their company. If they are fortunate, they will meet others like themselves in a challenging college or university environment.

Level Five Needs

Early Childhood—Birth to Kindergarten

Level Five children are so advanced that most parents know quite early that their children are exceptional. All of the intensities, interests, and temperamental idiosyncrasies common among Level Four children are also present in Level Five children—but are a little more intense and appear even earlier. Comprehension of what their parents are talking about starts so early for Level Five children that parents find them somewhat frightening. These children thrive on conversation and direct attention. They want to be included in everything. They watch TV and listen to music, respond to familiar events appropriately, and can be soothed by words of explanation because they know what adults are talking about.

The best daycare centers and preschools for Level Five children allow them to do what they are interested in doing. Most Level Five children are quite independent and don't see the reason for doing what everyone else does, especially when it seems too babyish for them. Advanced activities and materials should be made readily available to them.

The preschool environment is generally where parents first begin to suspect that they may have a problem on their hands because many Level Five children do not enjoy spending time with age-mates or doing typical activities that children their age often engage in. If the family can afford it and one parent is willing to delay career advancement, Level Five children should be left in daycare as little as possible until they are at least three years old. If your available options still do not fit your child's personality and she is clearly not getting along with others or enjoying daycare or preschool, keep looking, or try to keep her home for one more year. Level Five children ages four and under simply do not have the experience or maturity to cope if there is a bad fit between themselves and the other children or their teachers. As an alternative to group daycare, these children will do better in home daycare environments with one adult and one or two other children.

Early Grade School Years

Level Five children could easily complete the typical elementary curriculum in less than one year, largely because most Level Five children start school already knowing more than the typical fifth or sixth grader. School Types I, II, III, and V do not regularly have any Level Five children in them. Type IV gifted magnet schools may attract Level Five children, but unless the school has enough grade levels to provide great flexibility and continuous progress, the situation will still be problematic for the family of a Level Five student. Gifted magnet schools are usually found only in large metropolitan areas, and they may not serve all of the school systems within the area. This lessens the chances that more than one or two Level Five students will ever be in any one school at the same time.

Level Five children need subject-level acceleration and ability grouping across age levels. Under no circumstances is it appropriate to keep a

Level Five student with age-mates at grade level for more than socialization-type activities during the elementary years. As with Level Four students, the goal should be to give Level Five children a chance to take as many subjects as they can at their actual ability level while they are still in their elementary years. This means that even though they can stay in elementary school for gym, recess, lunch, and field trips, they should skip quickly through most subjects to middle school level, do Talent Search programs by age eight or nine, and have tutoring at their level for a variety of subjects until they are independent enough to work in a classroom with children who are in seventh grade and older. The only appropriate academic subject at grade level for a Level Five child is handwriting, and then only for a year or two. Whether or not home school options will work best will depend on the child's personality, but in either case, parents should also find mentors, special classes, tutors, and activities to increase exposure to others who can provide social as well as intellectual opportunities.

Level Five children are capable of moving through the curriculum so fast that parents need to discuss and decide how they want to balance social, emotional, and academic aspects of childhood. Ideally, children should simply go at their own pace, learning in depth with others who learn like they do, but Level Five children are truly too unusual for this to happen easily.

Middle School Years

Even the best, most advanced middle schools cannot meet the academic and learning needs of Level Five children. By the time they are 10 or 11, the age for middle school, Level Five children are ready for the challenges of college courses. Although some parents start their children in college at this point, considerable longitudinal and observational feedback from people who have done this indicates that it works fairly well at the time, but the students often end up wondering what they missed by skipping high school. For that reason, I generally recommend a combination of correspondence courses along with high school and accelerated program attendance during the middle school years.

Even home schooling families can start to take advantage of high school in their children's middle school years—in addition to college-level correspondence or online courses—by enrolling their children in a couple of classes a day on the high school campus. Many Level Five students complete most of the high school coursework and get a good start on college courses by the time they are 12 or 13; some are happy to do this when they are even younger. Although Level Five—and many Level Four—children could start college coursework in their strongest academic areas by age nine or 10, this works best when the child does not actually attend classes with college-age students.

High School Years

The high school "coming of age" years are such a strong part of our nation's identity that many Level Five students will want to experience it, at least for a while. Parents who have worked hard for years to provide flexible environments and accelerated opportunities for their Level Four and Five children should not feel too disappointed if their youngsters opt for something more normal and traditional during the high school years. These students should take all of the advanced courses available and participate in whatever academic competitions, arts, sports, and social opportunities interest them. Many Level Five students start college with their first year or two completed, thanks to Advanced Placement course exams taken in high school and a number of the other previously mentioned college credit options, but they can still join others their age in the freshman dorms.

There are some special programs around the country—designed for highly gifted youngsters—that combine high school and college into one well-supervised, nurturing, and intellectually challenging experience. An accelerated program of this kind can save advanced students a lot of time, and they can start graduate school when their age-mates are just starting undergraduate school. Among the advantages are more time to travel, read, and grow up at some point when the student feels that it is time to slow down and figure out what comes next. Many of these programs are designed for Level Three students, but of course they will accept Levels Four and Five. As has been the case all along, though, there may not be any other Level Five students there at the same time, and unless the institution itself is highly competitive and advanced, the coursework and classmates may not be as satisfying as waiting for the opportunity to attend a more competitive institution later, even as a 16-year-old. Again, parents must look for the blend of experiences for their Level Five child that will offer the most normal social and emotional adjustment.

College Life and Career Planning

It is imperative that Level Five students attend the kind of college that is most likely to attract others like themselves. Someone needs to explain to them that they are intellectually unusual and that they won't often find others who think the way they do or have the intensity of interests that they have. If they don't understand this, they might not see why it is so important that they work toward later opportunities that will bring them into contact with others more like themselves. For Level Five students in particular, a good portfolio or résumé and high test scores are more important than perfect grades. Level Five students have trouble complying with or understanding many teacher directives in the earlier school years, so rather than obsess over grades, they should take complex and challenging courses wherever they can find them. Even Level Five students can struggle initially if they haven't had the opportunity to develop study and time management skills, but they are so intelligent they are able to succeed.

Level Five American students typically observe that many foreign students are often much better prepared than they for the challenging coursework at America's most prestigious colleges and universities, but they also notice fairly quickly that they are smarter than most of the foreign students, too. If Level Five students understand their abilities, they can adjust quickly to the demands of a difficult school. Those who were never told how unusually intelligent they are may struggle and lose confidence in their abilities.

Level Five people get depressed, of course; they worry about whether they can live up to everyone else's expectations, and they wonder if they will ever find purpose and personal connections that are fulfilling and meaningful for them. Finding a purpose helps, and finding a soul mate helps.

Level Five people should not lock themselves into a professional path too early with the expectation that they should fill some preordained role as, for example, an attorney, scientist, doctor, or engineer. If they go for a safe career, they may never find out what they are really capable of. They may want to be a composer, playwright, or psychologist. Level Five individuals also have an advantage over the other levels in that they have more time to try different career paths and still start over.

Social Life for Level Five Children

More than any other level, it is important to help Level Five children look for and be around people of all ages who share their interests. It is possible to have many different peers—one for chess, one for video games, one for trivia contests, and still another for hiking or bike riding, for example. If the child's schedule is flexible and the parents are open to many different programs and opportunities, Level Five children will find friends and enjoyable companions everywhere they go. When someone is very different from others, parents need to talk honestly about these differences and help their children to navigate socially and look for ways to connect with and show interest in others. There is no need for any of us to get along with everyone we meet, but we can learn how to look for the best in others, be polite, and keep looking for those with whom we want to spend more time. Level Five people can make good, fulfilling social connections, especially if they have been shown how during their formative years.

What Parents Can Do for Level Five Children

Parents can develop the confidence and courage it takes to stand up to those who might make them and their children feel guilty for wanting something different than what works for most people. Parents can convey a similar confidence and courage as they offer support to their children. They can allow their children the freedom to explore and learn, make mistakes, flounder along the way, and not know for sure what they want to do or how to do it. Being incredibly smart does not mean that these children will have all of the answers; parents should never expect that from their growing children.

Parents should try to maintain as normal a family life as possible. They should follow their own interests and career paths again as soon as possible so that no one—not their child, nor anyone else—thinks that they are living through the child. They should actively resist turning their children into their own best friends. They should raise them to become independent, self-reliant, confident individuals who love their parents but know when it's time to leave. Parents should accept that, even after all the time and sacrifices their children required, few children really appreciate their parents for a great many years—say from ages 13 or so to around 40. This is okay.

Conclusion

It is time for educators, parents, government officials, and policy makers to accept that people are not all the same and that teaching everyone the same material in the same way will never make all people the same. Children learn at different rates, depths, and with different levels of complexity, and they retain and understand information differently as well. In order to meet the needs of children of all ability levels, schools themselves—and the organization of children within schools—

must change. Colleges of education that train our nation's teachers must change. Communities must change in their attitudes and support of schools. All of these changes are necessary if we are to meet the needs of children who will one day contribute to the areas of business and industry, science and technology, as well as to the creative arts and all of the various career fields.

Business leaders question why our workforce seems unprepared for today's economy and job market. They know that it's poor use of taxpayer's money to keep students in school for 12 years or more and yet have them graduate still needing job training. It isn't that the schools don't have enough money or good teachers; it's that the instructional configuration—lumping everyone together in the same classes—is ineffective.

This American system of education is now a strong tradition. But it may be a tradition that no longer works for society or for our future. How can things change? Business and community leaders can insist that schools train and educate students according to what they are ready and able to learn. School boards, often elected from the business community, can insist that students be taught what they are capable of learning when they are ready to learn it. Such insistence by stakeholders and policy makers would go a long way toward making it possible to meet the needs of all students—including gifted learners—without sacrificing the needs of average or below average learners who would also be learning at the appropriate pace for their abilities.

School and community expectations have to adjust to reflect this reality. Our current education systems and approaches waste precious time and energy. They only work for the children who are not too different from those in the middle of each class. This does a disservice to the nation's brightest children, in particular, because it puts a lid on their learning. They are locked into systems that leave them no time or freedom to learn what they could.

Communities could elect school board members who write policies that include the recognition that different students learn at different speeds and to different levels. They could provide funding to pay for online, college, and correspondence courses or special program attendance for their most advanced learners. These communities often supply athletic scholarships for talented athletes to attend special summer training camps or competitions; they could similarly support special programs for gifted students. They could also support greater flexibility in school attendance rules so that Level Three and Four children could work with mentors, study subjects in depth at home or elsewhere, test out of subjects that they comprehend well, and travel with their families and still earn credits—without facing truancy sanctions.

In learning about the levels of giftedness, one can see just how different even the most intelligent children are, even from one another. It is time to free up our brightest children so that they can go to the places in schools and in the greater community where what they are ready to learn is already happening. We must stop making bright children wait for 10 years or more to learn what they are ready to learn!

It will take a great change of perspective and a letting go of the traditional and the familiar, but we owe it to our nation's children and to ourselves to make significant changes in how we educate all children, including our brightest children. We must provide for more flexibility for all learners. Regardless of level of intelligence, children cannot and will not grow up to be their best possible selves without an education that provides for their particular needs and abilities. If we provide family and educational support that is appropriate for their level of ability, our brightest learners can thrive.

Appendix A
Developmental Guidelines for Identifying Gifted Preschoolers

Task	Normal Months	30% More Advanced
Smiles socially at people	1.5	1.05
Searches with eyes for sound	2.2	1.54
Vocalizes four different syllables	7	4.9
Says "dada" or equivalent	7.9	5.53
Responds to name and "no"	9	6.3
Holds an object between finger and thumb	9	6.3
Looks at pictures in a book	10	7
Babbles with intonation	12	8.4
Scribbles spontaneously	13	9.1
Has a speaking vocabulary of three words other than "mama" and "dada"	14	9.8
Has a vocabulary of four to six words including names	15	10.5
Points to one named body part	17	11.9
Names one object ("What is this?")	17.8	12.7
Follows direction to put an object on a chair	17.8	12.7
Turns pages of a book	18	12.6
Has a vocabulary of 20 words	21	14.7
Combines several words spontaneously	21	14.7
Uses the personal pronouns "I," "we," "me"	24	16.8
Names three or more objects in a picture	24	16.8
Uses three-word sentences	24	16.8
Can draw imitating V stroke and circular stroke	24	16.8

Task	Normal Months	30% More Advanced
Is able to tell what various objects are used for	30	21.0
Imitates bridge with blocks	36	25.2
Counts (enumerates) objects to three	36	25.2
Draws person with two parts	48	33.6
Draws person with neck, hands, and clothes	72	50.4

Derived from Hall, E. G. & Skinner, N. (1980). *Somewhere to turn: Strategies for parents of gifted and talented children.* Reprinted by permission of Teachers College Press.

Appendix B
Public School Curriculum Expectations by Grade Levels

This list includes only reading and math curriculum expectations, although most schools also teach social studies, science, technology and computer skills, etc.

Grade-Level Expectations for Kindergarten

Language Arts—Reading

Teachers help kindergarten students learn letters and words and to read short, simple books with many pictures. Kindergarten students learn:

- the alphabet.
- the sounds that consonant letters make.
- to hear the sounds in words.
- important words.
- to talk about the stories that their teacher has read to them.
- that print goes from left to right.
- to enjoy books.

Kindergarten students learn to:

- order the numbers from 0 to 21.
- read and write the numbers from 0 to 31.
- count aloud to 100, by 10s to 100, and backward from 10.
- build addition and subtraction number families to 5 (i.e., 2+3=5, 3+2=5, 5-3=2, and 5-2=3).
- recognize and name common geometric shapes (square, rectangle, circle, and triangle).
- Measure objects with non-standard units (i.e., the table is four teddy bears high).
- use the terms "longer," "shorter," "equal," "more," and "less" to compare lengths, heights, weights, and capacity.

- recognize and name coins (penny, nickel, dime, and quarter).
- know that a clock tells the time of day.
- know the names of the days of the week and the months of the year.
- recognize, create, describe, and continue a simple pattern (i.e. a/b/a/b/a/b, red/yellow/red/yellow, or bear/truck/bear/truck).
- sort objects using one attribute (i.e., sorting blocks by color, size, or shape).
- read and interpret a real object or picture graph.
- explore concepts of fairness in relationship to games (i.e., using spinners and dice).

Grade-Level Expectations for First Grade

Language Arts—Reading

First graders read 60 short stories or little books during the year. In addition, first-grade students learn:

- the sounds that letters make.
- word families, such as the -at family of cat, rat, bat, hat, sat.
- to sound out short words.
- to recognize many words quickly.
- ways to figure out new words.
- to notice when they have made a mistake.
- to look through a book before they read it to get an idea of what it's about.
- to think ahead about what might happen in a story.
- to tell what happened in a story after they have read it.

Mathematics

First-grade students learn to:

- count by 1s to 130 (or greater).
- read and write numbers to 999.
- count aloud by 2s, 5s, and 10s to 100 (or greater).
- build addition and subtraction number families to 13 (i.e., $8+5=13$, $5+8=13$, $13-5=8$, $13-8=5$).
- recognize the less than ($<$), greater than ($>$), and equal to ($=$) symbols.
- divide things into equal parts (i.e., a pizza or a bag of cookies).
- name and draw two-dimensional shapes (i.e., triangles and circles).

- count pennies, nickels, dimes, and quarters and know coin exchange values (i.e., 1 dime=2 nickels=10 pennies).
- read and use a calendar.
- write and tell time to the hour and half-hour.
- measure the lengths, heights, area, and capacity of everyday objects using non-standard units (i.e., it takes 45 beans to cover the picture of the dog).
- identify an output based on a given rule and input (i.e., when the rule is +2 and the input is 6, the output is 8).
- name odd and even numbers.
- conduct a simple survey using tally marks.
- read and interpret a real object or picture graph.
- sort, classify, count, and arrange real objects and/or pictures.
- describe events whose outcomes are not likely to occur equally (i.e., when two dice are thrown, a "7" is more likely to occur than a "2").

Grade-Level Expectations for Second Grade

Language Arts—Reading

Second graders read 35 short books or stories during the year. In addition, second-grade students learn:

- sounds that groups of letters make, like bl-, str-, or -igh.
- word families, like the -ail family of pail, snail, trail.
- ways to figure out new words and what they mean.
- plurals, opposites, and compound words.
- ways to correct mistakes they make when they read.
- to read out loud with expression.
- to read silently.
- to think about what they already know that will help them understand what they are reading.
- to find the main idea of a story.
- to remember important details.

Mathematics

Second-grade students learn to:

- count aloud by 2s and 10s, forward and backward, from any two-digit or three-digit number.
- know addition and subtraction facts to 18.
- correctly add and subtract one-, two-, and three-digit numbers (no regrouping).
- read and write numbers to 9,999.
- use comparison symbols (<, >, =) correctly.
- identify place values for numbers up to thousands.
- name parts of regions with fractions (i.e., folding a paper into four equal parts and labeling each part "¼").
- name two-dimensional shapes (i.e., rectangle, hexagon) and three-dimensional shapes (i.e., sphere, cone, cylinder, cube).
- count, write, and say money amounts with pennies, nickels, dimes, quarters, and dollars.
- use equivalent coins to show money amounts.
- tell and write time to within five minutes.
- measure to the nearest inch or centimeter.
- read and write Fahrenheit or Celsius temperatures on a thermometer.
- review odd and even number patterns.
- complete and describe number patterns from one given rule (i.e., rule: add 5; number pattern starting with 10: 10,15, 20, 25, 30, 35).
- conduct a simple survey.
- interpret a bar graph.
- have an awareness of why some events are more likely to occur than others.

Grade-Level Expectations for Third Grade

Language Arts—Reading

Third graders read 20 books during the school year. They read some of these at home and some at school. In addition, third-grade students learn:

- ways to figure out new words and what they mean.
- root words and endings, like -ing or -ed.
- prefixes, like un-, and suffixes, like -er.

- to find the main idea of a story.
- to use charts, tables, and graphs.
- to summarize what they have read.
- to understand ideas that were implied but not said.
- to draw conclusions from what they have read.
- to tell the difference between facts and opinions.
- to compare characters, settings, or stories they have read.

Mathematics

Third-grade students learn to:

- count forward and backward by 1s, 10s, 100s, and 1,000s, including four-digit numbers.
- correctly add and subtract one-, two-, or three-digit numbers (with regrouping).
- know multiplication and division facts through 5s.
- understand multiplication using arrays.
- know square number facts through 10x10 (i.e., 3x3= 9, 5x5=25, 9x9=81).
- use various procedures for adding, subtracting, and multiplying multi-digit numbers, including using calculators.
- name the numerator and denominator in fractions, and understand fractions as equal parts of a whole.
- name and construct polygons through hexagons.
- identify congruent shapes.
- make change by counting up with coins.
- know dollars-and-cents notation, and use that to solve problems.
- measure everyday objects to the nearest half-inch or half-centimeter.
- measure the perimeter of everyday objects and polygons.
- explore finding the area of a rectangle using a concrete model.
- complete and describe number patterns from one or two given rules (rules: add 5, subtract 2; number pattern starting with 10: 10, 15, 13, 18, 16, 21, 19, 24, 22, 27, 25).
- identify an output based on an unknown rule and input.
- find the solutions to simple number sentences.
- collect data, use it to make predictions, and answer questions accurately.
- put data in order.

- plot and interpret data on a bar graph.
- tell why some events are more likely to occur than others.
- identify events as certain or uncertain.
- create Venn diagrams with three categories.

Grade-Level Expectations for Fourth Grade

Language Arts—Reading

Fourth graders read 25 books during the school year. They read some of these at home and some at school. In addition, fourth-grade students learn:

- ways to figure out how to say new words and what they mean.
- dictionary skills and grammar.
- to use what they already know to help them understand what they are reading.
- to predict, summarize, and ask questions about what they read.
- to find main ideas in stories and articles.
- to remember important details.
- to remember the order of events or ideas in selections they have read.
- to tell the difference between facts and opinions.
- to describe parts of a story such as characters, setting, and plot.
- to read between the lines.

Mathematics

Fourth-grade students learn to:

- add and subtract multi-digit numbers, with and without regrouping.
- know multiplication and division facts through 10s (10x10=100, 100/10=10).
- multiply and divide two-digit numbers by 10, 100, and 1,000.
- know place value to millions in whole numbers and read decimals to hundredths.
- use a calculator to convert fractions to decimals and fractions to percents.
- use equivalent names for fractional parts of a region (i.e., 1/4=2/8=4/16=8/32).
- construct and classify polygons through decagons.

- use ordered pairs of numbers to locate points on a two-dimensional grid.
- find lines of symmetry in a drawing or figure.
- find the areas of rectangles.
- understand area concepts.
- find the latitude and longitude of various places on a globe or world map.
- solve simple number sentences based on real-world situations.
- collect data using different methods (i.e., tallies, measurements, and experiments).
- find the range, mode, and median of a set of data.
- create tables, charts, line plots, bar graphs, and tally charts to collect, organize, and compare information.
- predict the outcome of a chance experiment as being more or less likely.
- use Venn diagrams to record information and make observations about a group.

Grade-Level Expectations for Fifth Grade

Language Arts—Reading

Fifth graders read 25 books during the school year. They read some of these at home and some at school. In addition, fifth-grade students learn:

- ways to figure out how to say new words and what the words mean.
- dictionary skills and grammar.
- to summarize what they have read.
- to read and follow directions.
- to think about why the author wrote a story or article.
- to understand ideas that are implied but not said.
- to make predictions based on what they have read.
- to recognize ways that a writer tries to persuade people.
- ways that stories and articles are organized.
- ways that different cultures appear in stories and articles.
- to recognize figurative language, like "a frog in one's throat."

Mathematics

Fifth-grade students learn to:

- use addition, subtraction, multiplication, and division of whole numbers to solve problems.
- find equivalent fractions.
- solve parts-and-wholes problems using fractions.
- use calculators to convert fractions to decimals and decimals to percents.
- use calculators to add, subtract, multiply, and divide whole numbers and decimals.
- understand the difference between prime and composite numbers.
- round numbers to selected place value.
- know the properties of three-dimensional shapes (geometric solids).
- identify and measure different types of angles (i.e., right, acute, obtuse).
- identify congruent figures.
- explore tessellations, transformations, translations, and reflections of shapes.
- find the measure of each angle in a polygon.
- solve perimeter, circumference, area, and volume problems.
- measure and draw angles using a circle protractor.
- find the perimeter of a polygon.
- find the latitude and longitude of various places on a globe or world map.
- solve simple equations.
- match graph shapes with events that happen over time.
- collect data using several methods (tallies, measurements, or experiments).
- find the range, mode, median, and mean of a set of data.
- create and compare bar graphs, circle graphs (up to three categories), stem-and-leaf plots, and side-by-side line plots.
- organize and interpret data and use it to make predictions.
- conduct experiments to find the probability of an event happening.

Appendix C
Levels of Giftedness for Some Historical Figures

To provide perspective, I have selected some historical figures from Catherine Cox's book *The Early Mental Traits of Three Hundred Geniuses* (1926) whose childhood abilities, behaviors, and accomplishments roughly mirror those of the children in each level. Based on her research, Cox estimated the IQ scores of each of these and many other prominent individuals from history; no other references are available that give either actual IQ scores or estimated IQ scores for these eminent people. Two other excellent resources, however, that describe highly intelligent and creative people of eminence include Goertzel and Hansen (2004) and Simonton (1994).

There are no female examples in the 1926 Cox volume. There are many reasons why women have historically lagged behind men in attaining eminence (Simonton, 1994). Even without women as examples, though, it is useful to compare Cox's IQ estimates with the IQ scores of the children in this current study.

The majority of persons described by Cox endured school but were not especially fond of or remarkable at it. Most showed strong and specific interests very early in their development. Many were poor students because they were single-minded in their interests and uncooperative in school settings as a result. These are people who did not manifest their talents until they were allowed to enter their own appropriate environment. Talent and ability may not always have been evident for these individuals, but they were always present.

Level	Historical Figure
One	Hernando Cortez
	Oliver Goldsmith
	Ulysses S. Grant
	Andrew Jackson
	Martin Luther
	Rembrandt Van Rijn

Level	**Historical Figure**
Two	John Adams
	Johann Sebastian Bach
	Napoleon Bonaparte
	Charles Darwin
	Daniel Defoe
	Joseph Louis Gay-Lussac
	Jakob Grimm
	Alexander Hamilton
	Franz Joseph Haydn
	Abraham Lincoln
	John Locke
	George Washington
Three	Michelangelo Buonarroti
	Thomas Carlyle
	Leonardo da Vinci
	René Descartes
	Charles Dickens
	Benjamin Disraeli
	Ralph Waldo Emerson
	Benjamin Franklin
	Galileo Galilei
	George Frederick Handel
	Thomas Jefferson
	Johann Kepler
	John Milton
	Daniel Webster
Four	Samuel Coleridge
	Francois-Marie Arouet Voltaire
Five	Jeremy Bentham
	Johann Wolfgang Goethe
	Gottfried Leibniz
	Blaise Pascal

References

American Association of University Women. (1991). *Shortchanging girls, shortchanging America*. Washington, DC: AAUW.

Assouline, S. G., Colangelo, N., Lupkowski-Shoplik, A., Lipscomb, J., & Forstadt, L. (2003). *Iowa acceleration scale, 2nd ed*. Scottsdale, AZ: Great Potential Press.

Benbow, C. P., & Lubinski, D. (1993). Individual differences amongst the mathematically gifted: Their educational and vocational implications. In N. Colangelo, S. G. Assouline, & D. L. Ambroson (Eds.), *Talent development: Proceedings from the 1993 Henry B. and Jocelyn Wallace National Research Symposium on Talent Development* (pp. 83-100). Scottsdale, AZ: Gifted Psychology Press.

Bloom, B. S. (Ed.). (1985). *Developing talent in young people*. New York: Ballantine Books.

Bouchard, T. J. (1997). IQ similarity in twins reared apart: Findings and responses to critics. In R. J. Sternberg & E. L. Grigorenko (Eds.), *Intelligence: Heredity and environment* (pp. 126-161). New York: Cambridge University Press.

Carson, A. D., & Lowman, R. L. (2002). Individual-level variables in organizational consultation. In R. L. Lowman (Ed.), *The California School of Organizational Studies handbook of organizational consulting psychology: A comprehensive guide to theory, skills, and techniques* (pp. 5-26). San Francisco: Jossey-Bass.

Clark, B. (2002, Winter). No wonder they behave differently. *Gifted Education Communicator*. Retrieved from www.cagifted.org/Pages/Publications/ ★communicator/commPastIssues/comm2002.html.

Colangelo, N., Assouline, S. G., & Gross, M. U. M. (2004). *A nation deceived: How schools hold back America's brightest students*. (The Templeton National Report on Acceleration). Iowa City, IA: University of Iowa Press.

Cox, C. M. (1926). *Genetic studies of genius, vol. II: The early mental traits of three hundred geniuses*. Stanford, CA: Stanford University Press.

Cox, J., Daniel, N., & Boston, B. (1985). *The Richardson study: Educating able learners*. Austin, TX: University of Texas Press.

Dabrowski, K. (1972). *Psychoneurosis is not an illness*. London: Gryf.

Davidson, J., & Davidson, B. (2004). *Genius denied: How to stop wasting our brightest young minds*. New York: Simon & Schuster.

Eysenck, H. J., & Kamin, L. (1981). *The intelligence controversy.* New York: Wiley-Interscience.

Feldhusen, J. F. (1991, March). Susan Allan sets the record straight: Response to Allan. *Educational Leadership, 48(6),* 66.

Feldman, D. H. (1986). *Nature's gambit: Child prodigies and the development of human potential.* New York: Basic Books.

Flanders, J. R. (1987). How much of the content of mathematics textbooks is new? *Arithmetic Teacher, 35,* 18-23.

Flynn, J. R. (1984). The mean IQ of Americans: Massive gains 1932 to 1978. *Psychological Bulletin, 95,* 29-51.

Flynn, J. R. (1987). Massive gains in 14 nations: What IQ tests really measure. *Psychological Bulletin, 101,* 171-191.

Gagné, F. (1985). Giftedness and talent. *Gifted Child Quarterly, 29,* 103-112.

Gagné, F. (1993). Constructs and models pertaining to exceptional human abilities. In K. A. Heller, F. J. Monks, & A. H. Passow (Eds.), *International handbook of research and development of giftedness and talent* (pp. 69-87). Oxford, MA: Pergamon Press.

Gardner, H. (1983). *Frames of mind: The theory of multiple intelligences.* New York: Basic Books.

Geschwind, N., & Galaburda, A. M. (1987). *Cerebral lateralization.* Cambridge, MA: MIT Press.

Gilman, B. J. (2003). *Empowering gifted minds: Educational advocacy that works.* Denver, CO: DeLeon Publishing.

Gleick, J. (1993). *Genius: The life and science of Richard Feynman.* New York: Vintage Books.

Goertzel, T. G., & Hansen, A. M. W. (2004). *Cradles of eminence, 2nd ed.: Childhoods of more than 700 famous men and women.* Scottsdale, AZ: Great Potential Press.

Goleman, D. (1995). *Emotional intelligence.* New York: Bantam Books.

Gottfredson, L. S. (1994, December 13). Mainstream science on intelligence. *The Wall Street Journal,* p. A18.

Gottfredson, L. S. (1998, Winter). The general intelligence factor. *Scientific American Presents, 9(4),* 24-29.

Gottfried, A. W., Gottfried, A. E., Bathurst, K., & Guerin, D. W. (1994). *Gifted IQ: Early developmental aspects.* (The Fullerton Longitudinal study). New York: Plenum.

Greenspon, T. S. (2002). *Freeing our families from perfectionism.* Minneapolis, MN: Free Spirit.

Gross, M. U. M. (1992). The use of radical acceleration in cases of extreme intellectual precocity. *Gifted Child Quarterly, 36(2),* 90-98.

Gross, M. U. M. (1993). *Exceptionally gifted children.* New York: Routledge.

Gross, M. U. M. (2003). *Exceptionally gifted children, 2nd ed.* New York: Falmer Press.

Hall, E. G., & Skinner, N. (1980). *Somewhere to turn: Strategies for parents of gifted and talented children.* New York: Teachers College Press.

Halsted, J. W. (2002). *Some of my best friends are books, 2nd ed.* Scottsdale, AZ: Great Potential Press.

Harter, S. (1985). *The Harter Scales.* Denver, CO: The University of Denver.

Heacox, D. (2002). *Differentiating instruction in the regular classroom.* Minneapolis, MN: Free Spirit.

Herrnstein, R. J., & Murray, C. (1994). *The bell curve: Intelligence and class structure in American life.* New York: The Free Press.

Hollingworth, L. S. (1926). *Gifted children: Their nature and nurture.* New York: Macmillan.

Hollingworth, L. S. (1931). The child of very superior intelligence as a special problem in social adjustment. *Mental Hygiene, 15(1),* 3-16.

Hollingworth, L. S. (1942). *Children above 180 IQ Stanford-Binet: Origin and development.* Yonkers-on-Hudson, NY: World Book.

Janos, P. M., & Robinson, N. M. (1985a). The performance of students in a program of radical acceleration at the university level. *Gifted Child Quarterly, 29(4),* 175-179.

Janos, P. M., & Robinson, N. M. (1985b). Psychosocial development in intellectually gifted children. In F. D. Horowitz & M. O'Brien (Eds.), *The gifted and talented: Developmental perspectives* (pp. 149-195). Washington, DC: American Psychological Association.

Jensen, A. R. (1998). *The g factor: The science of mental ability.* Westport, CT: Praeger.

Karnes, F. A. & Marquardt, R. G. (1999). *Gifted children and legal issues: An update.* Scottsdale, AZ: Great Potential Press.

Kearney, K. (personal communication, August 12, 2003).

Kerr, B. A. (1994). *Smart girls: A new psychology of girls, women, and giftedness, rev. ed.* Scottsdale, AZ: Great Potential Press.

Kerr, B. A., & Cohn, S. J. (2001). *Smart boys: Talent, manhood, and the search for meaning.* Scottsdale, AZ: Great Potential Press.

Klein, A. (2002). *A forgotten voice: A biography of Leta Stetter Hollingworth.* Scottsdale, AZ: Great Potential Press.

Kline, B. E., & Meckstroth, E. A. (1985). Understanding and encouraging the highly gifted. *Roeper Review, 8(1),* 24-30.

Kohlberg, L. (1984). *The psychology of moral development.* New York: Harper & Row.

Kulik, C. L. C., & Kulik, J. (1984). *Effects of ability grouping on elementary school pupils: A meta-analysis.* Paper presented at the annual meeting of the American Psychological Association, Ontario, Canada.

Kulik, J., & Kulik, C. L. C. (1990). Ability grouping and gifted students. In N. Colangelo & G. A. Davis (Eds.), *Handbook of gifted education* (pp. 178-196). Boston: Allyn & Bacon.

Lohman, D. F. (1999). Minding our p's and q's: On finding relationships between learning and intelligence. In P. L. Ackerman, P. C. Kyllonen, & R. D. Roberts (Eds.), *Learning and individual differences: Process, trait, and content determinants.* (pp. 55-76). Washington, DC: American Psychological Association.

Lovecky, D. V. (1993). The quest for meaning: Counseling issues with gifted children and adolescents. In L. K. Silverman (Ed.), *Counseling the gifted and talented* (pp. 29-50). Denver, CO: Love Publishing.

Lubinski, D., & Benbow, C. P. (1992). Gender differences in abilities and preferences among the gifted: Implications for the math/science pipeline. *Current Directions in Psychological Science, 1,* 61-66.

Mackintosh, N. J. (1998). *IQ and human intelligence.* Oxford, MA: Oxford University Press.

Matarazzo, J. D. (1972). *Wechsler's measure and appraisal of adult intelligence, 5th ed.* Oxford, MA: Oxford University Press.

McCoach, D. B. (2003). *Waiting to learn: A longitudinal analysis of reading growth trajectories of students who enter school at various proficiency levels.* Paper presented at the annual meeting of the National Association for Gifted Children, Indianapolis, IN.

Mills, C. J. (2003). Characteristics of effective teachers of gifted students: Teacher background and personality styles of students. *Gifted Child Quarterly, 47(4),* 272-281.

Monastersky, R. (2005). Studies show biological differences in how boys and girls learn about math, but social factors play a big role, too. *Chronicle of Higher Education, LI (26),* A1-A17.

Morelock, M. (1991, July). Unpublished transcript of the meeting of the Columbus Group, Columbus, OH.

National Commission on Excellence in Education. (1983). *A nation at risk: The imperative for educational reform.* Retrieved from www.ed.gov/pubs/NatAtRisk.

National Science Board. (1991). *Science and engineering indicators, 1991.* Washington, DC: U.S. Government Printing Office.

Piechowski, M. M. (1991). Emotional development and emotional giftedness. In N. Colangelo & G. A. Davis (Eds.), *A handbook of gifted education* (pp. 285-306). Needham Heights, MA: Allyn & Bacon.

Rest, J. R. (1986). *Defining issues test*. Minneapolis, MN: University of Minnesota Press.

Reis, S. M. (2002, Winter). Internal barriers, personal issues, and decisions faced by gifted and talented females. *Gifted Child Today, 25(1)*, 14-28.

Reis, S. M., Westberg, K. L., Kulikowich, J., Caillard, F., Hebért, T. P., & Plucker, J. A. (1993). *Why not let high ability students start school in January? The curriculum compacting study*. Storrs, CT: National Research Center on the Gifted and Talented.

Rivero, L. (2002). *Creative home schooling: A resource guide for smart families*. Scottsdale, AZ: Great Potential Press.

Robinson, H. B. (1980). The uncommonly bright child. In M. Lewis & L. A. Rosenblum (Eds.), *The uncommon child*. New York: Plenum.

Robinson, N. M., & Noble, K. D. (1991). Social-emotional development and adjustment of gifted children. In M. C. Wang, M. C. Reynolds, & H. J. Walberg (Eds.), *Handbook of special education: Research and practice, vol. 4: Emerging programs* (pp. 57-76). New York: Pergamon Press.

Robinson, N. M., & Robinson, H. B. (1982). The optimal match: Devising the best compromise for the highly gifted student. In D. Feldman (Ed.), *New directions for child development: Developmental approaches to giftedness and creativity*. San Francisco: Jossey-Bass.

Roedell, W. C., Jackson, N. & Robinson, H. B. (1980). *Gifted young children*. New York: Teachers Press.

Roeper, A. (1982). How the gifted cope with their emotions. *Roeper Review, 5(2)*, 21-24.

Roeper, A. (1995). *Annemarie Roeper: Selected writings and speeches*. Minneapolis, MN: Free Spirit.

Rogers, K. B. (1986). Do the gifted think and learn differently? A review of research and its implications for instruction. *Journal for the Education of the Gifted, 10*, 17-41.

Rogers, K. B. (1991). *The relationship of grouping practices to the education of the gifted and talented learner*. Storrs, CT: National Research Center on the Gifted and Talented.

Rogers, K. B. (2002). *Re-forming gifted education: How parents and teachers can match the program to the child*. Scottsdale, AZ: Great Potential Press.

Roid, G. H. (2003). *Stanford-Binet intelligence scales, 5th ed.: Interpretive manual: Expanded guide to the interpretation of SB5 test results*. Itasca, IL: Riverside.

Ruf, D. L. (1998). Environmental, familial, and personal factors that affect the self-actualization of highly gifted adults: Case studies. Unpublished dissertation: University of Minnesota.

Ruf, D. L. (2003). *Use of the SB5 in the assessment of high abilities.* (Stanford–Binet intelligence scales, 5th ed. assessment service bulletin No. 3). Itasca, IL: Riverside.

Schmidt, F. (2002, Fall). The role of general cognitive ability and job performance: Why there cannot be a debate. *Human Performance, 15,* 187-210.

Seligman, D. (1992). *A question of intelligence.* New York: Carol Publishing Group.

Silverman, L. K. (1989). The highly gifted. In J. F. Feldhusen, J. VanTassel-Baska, & K. R. Seeley (Eds.), *Excellence in educating the gifted* (pp. 71-83). Denver, CO: Love.

Silverman, L. K. (Ed.). (1993). *Counseling the gifted and talented.* Denver, CO: Love.

Silverman, L. K. (2002). Asynchronous development. In M. Neihart, S. M. Reis, N. M. Robinson, & S. M. Moon (Eds.), *The social and emotional development of gifted children: What do we know?* (pp. 31-37). Waco, TX: Prufrock Press.

Silverman, L. K., & Kearney, K. (1989). Parents of the extraordinarily gifted. *Advanced Development, 1,* 41-56.

Silverman, L. K., & Kearney, K. (1992). The case for the Stanford-Binet L-M as a supplemental test. *Roeper Review, 15(1),* 34-37.

Simonton, D. K. (1984). *Genius, creativity, and leadership: Histriometric inquiries.* New Cambridge, MA: Harvard University Press.

Simonton, D. K. (1994). *Greatness: Who makes history and why.* New York: The Guilford Press.

Simonton, D. K. (1999). *Origins of genius: Darwinian perspectives on creativity.* New York: Oxford University Press.

Smutny, J. F. (2001). *Stand up for your gifted child: How to make the most of kids' strengths at school and at home.* Minneapolis, MN: Free Spirit.

Snow, C. E., Burns, S. M., & Griffin, P. (Eds.). (1998). Preventing reading difficulties in young children: Committee on the prevention of reading difficulties in young children. Washington, DC: National Academies Press.

Sommers, C. H. (2000, May). The war against boys. *The Atlantic Monthly,* 59-74.

Stanley, J. C. (1996). Educational trajectories: Radical accelerates provide insights. *Gifted Child Today, 19(2),* 18-20.

Starko, A. J. (1986). *It's about time: Inservice strategies for curriculum compacting.* Mansfield Center, CT: Creative Learning Press.

Sternberg, R. J. (1985). *Beyond IQ: A triarchic theory of intelligence.* Cambridge, MA: Cambridge University Press.

Terman, L. M. (1925). *Genetic studies of genius vol. I: Mental and physical traits of a thousand gifted children.* Stanford, CA: Stanford University Press.

Terman, L. M., & Oden, M. H. (1947). *Genetic studies of genius vol. IV: The gifted child grows up.* Stanford, CA: Stanford University Press.

Tolan, S. S. (1985, Nov.-Dec.). Stuck in another dimension: The exceptionally gifted child in school. *Gifted Child Today, 41,* 22-26.

Tolan, S. S. (1989). Special problems of young highly gifted children. *Understanding Our Gifted, 1(5),*1, 7-10.

Tomlinson, C. A., Kaplan, S. N., Renzulli, J. S., Purcell, J., Leppien, J., & Burns, D. (2002). *The parallel curriculum: A design to develop high potential and challenge high-ability learners.* Thousand Oaks, CA: Corwin Press.

Tucker, B., & Hafenstein, N. L. (1997). Psychological intensities in young gifted children. *Gifted Child Quarterly, 41(3),* 66-75.

U.S. Congress (2001). *No Child Left Behind Act of 2001, H. R. 1.* Retrieved from www.ed.gov/nclb/landing.jhtml?src=pb.

VanTassel-Baska, J. (1983). Profiles of precocity: The 1982 Midwest Talent Search finalists. *Gifted Child Quarterly, 27(3),* 139-144.

VanTassel-Baska, J. (1992). *Planning effective curriculum for gifted learners.* Denver, CO: Love.

Wallace, A. (1986). *The prodigy: A biography of William James Sidis, America's greatest child prodigy.* New York: E. P. Dutton.

Webb, J. T. (2000). *Parenting successful children.* (Video or CD Recording No. 0-910707-36-7). Scottsdale, AZ: Great Potential Press.

Webb, J. T., Meckstroth, E. A., & Tolan, S. S. (1982). *Guiding the gifted child.* Scottsdale, AZ: Great Potential Press (formerly Ohio Psychology Press).

Webb, J. T., Amend, E. R., Webb, N. E., Goerss, J., & Olenchak, F. R. (2005). *Misdiagnosis and dual diagnoses of gifted children and adults: ADHD, Bipolar, OCD, Asperger's, depression, and other disorders.* Scottsdale, AZ: Great Potential Press.

Westphal, C. (2001). *A family year abroad: How to live outside the borders.* Scottsdale, AZ: Great Potential Press.

Winebrenner, S. (2000). *Teaching gifted kids in the regular classroom.* Minneapolis, MN: Free Spirit.

Winner, E. (1996). *Gifted children: Myths and realities.* New York: Basic Books.

Wright, J. C., & Huston, A. C. (1995). *Effects of educational TV viewing of lower income preschoolers on academic skills, school readiness, and school adjustment one to three years later.* Lawrence, KS: University of Kansas Center for Research on the Influences of Television on Children.

Yecke, C. P. (2003). *War against excellence: The rising tide of mediocrity in America's middle schools.* Westport, CT: Praeger.

Endnotes

Chapter 1

[1] Chapter books have fewer illustrations than beginner books and are divided into chapters. They generally read at least at the first-grade level. *Frog and Toad Are Friends*, at 64 pages and with many illustrations, is a first-grade-level chapter book; *Charlotte's Web* is a third-grade-level chapter book with 184 pages; the *Harry Potter* books are typically 350 pages and sixth- to seventh-grade level.

Chapter 2

[1] Some people may notice how the advanced vocabulary of the parent stands out, and this might lead them to think that it would only be natural for the children of such people to be equally intelligent. The heritability of intelligence, although continually the subject of debate, is well documented. Estimates from twin studies suggest that about 60% to 65% of intelligence is inherited (Bouchard, 1997), but Mackintosh suggests a range of 10% to 55% (1998).

Chapter 3

[1] An outlier is a statistical term that refers to a score, data point, or person who scores very differently from anyone else in a group. If a ninth-grade class were to take a college-level vocabulary test, for example, most of the students would score low compared to the college students on whom the test was normed. If one person from the ninth-grade class scored like the highest-performing college students, though, this high-scoring student would be called an outlier and would not be considered a representative example of the ninth-grade class.

[2] Gifts and talents are both part of the U.S. Department of Education definition of the qualities that require special services in American schools. This list and description changes periodically but remains quite broad and inclusive.

[3] Howard Gardner introduced his Theory of Multiple Intelligences in 1983. It led to sweeping changes in how many American schools started to design and implement their programs for the gifted and talented. His definitions were so broad and covered so many ability domains and talents that many schools began to offer enrichment and opportunity rather than advanced courses to students younger than ninth grade.

4 Daniel Goleman made quite an impression in 1995 when he introduced the concept that emotional intelligence, or "social skills," possibly means more than high intellectual intelligence to adult success.

5 In 1985, Robert Sternberg's triarchic theory was groundbreaking in that it was among the first to go against the psychometric approach to intelligence (using tests) and takes a more cognitive definition of intelligence as "mental activity directed toward purposive adaptation to, selection and shaping of real-world environments relevant to one's life" (p. 45). Sternberg's theory has three parts: componential, experiential, and practical.

6 Many schools of education started to adopt the position that all children are gifted, and this view was strengthened by the work of Gardner (1983), Goleman (1995), and Sternberg (1985).

7 A standard deviation is based on a statistical method of calculating a score spread among test-takers. The larger the standard deviation, the larger the range among the test-takers.

8 Unless the term "ratio" is used, all IQ references are for modern, standard score, deviation IQ test results—all tests except the old *Stanford-Binet (Form L-M)*.

Part II

1 There is evidence that IQ scores drift up over time. This is explained by a phenomenon called the Flynn Effect. For more information, see Flynn, 1984; 1987.

2 The author's doctoral work was in Educational Psychology: Tests & Measurement. During the period when I transitioned from the old *SBLM* to a current test, I wrote the bulletin (2003) for how to use the instrument for high ability assessment.

3 The *Stanford-Binet 5*, in my experience, works well for brighter children and adults; it generally has plenty of "ceiling" in the sense of enough questions on each subtest to allow bright children not to "run out of test." The *SB5* does not award points for speed (like some of the other tests), and thus creates a more relaxed atmosphere for testing, as well as not penalizing children whose slower motor skills might otherwise cause an underestimate of ability. The Interpretive Manual delineates further methods for determining strengths and weaknesses and allows for a 'gifted composite' that removes specific subtests when advisable, an Abbreviated Battery score (useful for quicker screening), age equivalencies for each of five intellectual domain subtest results, and Change Sensitive Scores (using Rasch Item Response theory) that help create a comparison method of actual intellectual growth between people of different IQs and ages (useful for educational and training grouping decisions). Once a practitioner becomes familiar with which level of intelligence is associated with which profile of subtest scores, the normalized forced bell curve distribution—which causes the lower scores compared to the old SBLM—ceases to be a serious interpretation problem.

4 For children ages six to seven who are quite strong in their verbal reasoning, scores are often misleadingly high because that age range on the test does not

assess quantitative reasoning as much as other instruments or other sections of the same test. For older children, the *SBLM* is not difficult enough for very bright children; they "run out of ceiling," and their scores are artificially depressed.

5 This is largely due to the Flynn Effect (Flynn, 1984; 1987).

Chapter 4

1 The *Technical Manual* for the *Stanford-Binet Intelligence Scales 5th Edition* (Roid, 2003) explains that it is highly subjective and problematic to gather direct socioeconomic information from people, so in Riverside Publishing's normative sample for the *SB5*, "the chosen variable was years of education completed. Socioeconomic levels for adults were measured by their years of education completed, and for children under age 18 by the years of education completed by parents or guardians" (p. 51).

2 Schools that draw from disadvantaged neighborhoods where there is a high poverty concentration and a high proportion of parents who do not finish high school often have few children beyond the Level One gifted range. The relationship between cognitive level, educational attainment, and socioeconomic status is strong. This relationship is explained in some detail in Herrnstein and Murray (1994). For just a sample of further information and research on the relationship between poverty and cognitive ability, see Gottfredson (1994) and Schmidt (2002).

3 This estimate is not mathematically accurate, but it presents the idea that it will be rare to have more than one gifted child in each classroom, although sometimes there will be as many as two.

4 Interestingly, in the 120-125 score range, old ratio IQs and standard scores compare quite closely, so it is still reasonable to consider this score range optimal.

5 Joan Ganz Cooney, one of the creators of *Sesame Street*, said that one of her early goals was to give poor, especially inner city, children the same sort of access to letters and numbers and enriched learning opportunities that their suburban counterparts experienced. Longitudinal research (Snow, Burns, & Griffin, 1998)—research on the same children over many years—shows that watching educational programming, particularly *Sesame Street*, increases school and reading readiness in children who watch the program starting between ages two and four. An additional study discovered that many children who come from lower socioeconomic backgrounds prefer cartoons and adult programming to educational television, even when given the opportunity to watch programs such as *Sesame Street*. John C. Wright and Aletha C. Huston, a husband-and-wife team at the Center for Research on the Influences of Television on Children at the University of Kansas, conducted the five-year study of children from low-income families in the Kansas City, Missouri area (1995). The Children's Television Workshop, the New York City-based producer of *Sesame Street*, commissioned the study paid for by the

John D. and Catherine T. MacArthur Foundation. *Sesame Street* appears to be responsible for an increase in early readers from the very homes that have already historically produced the most able students. Many highly gifted parents of the children in this book were not themselves preschool readers, but they all finished their preschool years before *Sesame Street*'s airing. Perhaps they, too, would have read early if exposed to similar programming.

6 *JumpStart* refers to a series of educational computer software for children. Each title lists the normal expected age level for whom the software is intended, but parents of gifted children often purchase higher age levels because their children are ready for more complex games and tasks.

7 D. Betsy McCoach, working with data from the National Center for Educational Statistics (NCES), studied 4,071 children starting kindergarten by using four waves of IRT (Item Response Theory formatted questions) data collection to evaluate reading skills over several years (2003). In essence, children who start school already reading make as much progress in their skill attainment over the summer when they are not in school as they do during an entire school year. Children who start school at several levels of non-reading ability show a virtual halt in their skill attainment over the summer breaks while making significant strides during the school year. Despite the fact that the early readers are "Waiting to Learn," as McCoach titles her paper, the relative difference in the reading achievement gap between the early readers and both the typical and below average kindergarten students does not appreciably narrow over the course of several years' instruction. The study underscores the instructional time that is wasted for the early readers, however, in the typical primary-grade classroom.

8 *Hooked on Phonics*® is a program for parents to use with children eight and younger to teach them to read.

9 *Bob* books are a series of beginning reader books published by Scholastic that guide new and emerging readers through phonetics with colorful, child-oriented topics.

10 *Arthur* books, by Marc Brown, are part of the PBS Arthur series for preschool and primary-grade children. These are beginner books with very few words and lots of pictures on each page.

11 *Math Blaster*® is a series of children's educational software that uses a mystery format that requires answers to math problems at different difficulty levels as part of the child's progress through the game.

12 *Ramona* books, by Beverly Cleary, are early chapter books at about the fourth-grade reading level and have high interest for children in first through fifth grades.

13 The *Oregon Trail*® educational software game is typically introduced in the third or fourth grade. It is a role playing game that requires spelling and typing skills and teaches geography and problem-solving skills.

14 The *Hardy Boys* book series, by Franklin Dixon, is for children ages nine to 12.

15 Tangrams are popular puzzles that require moving pieces to duplicate different pictured patterns. It appeals to all ages.

16 *PowerPoint®* is a Microsoft® computer program for making presentations in front of groups.

17 *Redwall* books, by Brian Jacques, are adventure stories that appeal mostly to upper–elementary–level boys.

Chapter 5

1 Board books are picture books made of cardboard rather than paper or cloth and are sturdy for young hands—and mouths. (Many babies chew on books, although none of the gifted children in this study ever did that.) These books have very few words on each page, and parents read and point to pictures for the baby or toddler. The books are fairly indestructible, it's easy for young children to turn the pages, and they are the first books that many children memorize and read.

2 DUPLOs® are building blocks that are like LEGOs® but for younger children

3 BRIO® is the brand name of a wooden train system designed for young children.

4 *Reader Rabbit®* software, recommended for children ages four to six, contains interactive stories, activities, and reading lessons.

5 The *Narnia* books, by C. S. Lewis, are fantasy chapter books for children ages nine through 12.

6 J. K. Rowling's *Harry Potter* books are frequently mentioned as being widely read by children in each of the five levels. The magic and intrigue in them often captures the attention of very young, highly intelligent early readers. The largest audience for *Harry Potter* is upper elementary and middle school children, but the children in this book tend to read them at much earlier ages.

7 The *Berenstain Bears* book series is a parent read-aloud preschool book or a fairly advanced beginner book at about the first-grade reading level.

8 The *Power Boys* book series, by Mel Lyle, is aimed at pre-teens.

9 The *Magic School Bus* book series, by Joanna Cole, is for children ages four to eight.

10 The *American Girl* books are written by various authors and published by the Pleasant Company.

11 *Calvin and Hobbes*, by Bill Watterson, is a cartoon strip of sophisticated humor actually aimed at adult audiences.

Chapter 6

1 Some fairly recent IQ tests used deviation IQ scores, but with normative samples that were not normally distributed. Newer IQ tests consistently use deviation IQ scores in which the normative samples are forced into a normal distribution. For further information, see Ruf (2003).

2 The *Magic Tree House* series of books, by Mary Pope Osborne, are for children ages four through eight.

3 *Cam Jansen*, by David A. Adler, is a mystery series with a girl as the main character. It has a reading level of ages nine to 12.

4 While analyzing case studies of highly gifted adults, I discovered that early reading was not very common among my subjects. Most of them were not exposed to television in their preschool years because they were all born before 1960 (Ruf, 1998). Also, most of the subjects' mothers avoided exposing their children to reading before school because educators said it made their job more difficult. Until educational programming on television started, most gifted children in the United States—even Level Three or higher gifted children—did not start reading before first grade. Then, they, like the present gifted children, moved very quickly to advanced chapter books, usually by second grade, while their classmates still worked with easy readers.

5 The *Sweet Valley Twins* series are books by Francine Pascal for readers ages nine to 12.

6 AP refers to Advanced Placement courses that are college-level curriculum taught in high school for the possibility of concurrent high school and college credit upon successful final exam completion.

Chapter 7

1 *The Richardson Study* (Cox, Daniel, & Boston, 1985) and *A Nation at Risk* (National Commission on Excellence in Education, 1983) both asked superintendents how many gifted students were in their districts. In both reports, more than one-third of these superintendents reply that they didn't have any gifted students at all. Repeated polling continues to show that school officials greatly underestimate their numbers of gifted.

2 *Junie B. Jones* books, by Barbara Park, are beginner chapter books at about the first-grade reading level for ages four to eight.

3 *Jigsaw Jones*, by James Preller, is a series of mystery books for ages four to eight.

4 *Operation Neptune*™ is pre-algebra software by The Learning Company for children ages nine to 14. It uses an adventure game format.

5 *Nate the Great* children's books, by Marjorie Weinman Sharmat, are for children ages four to eight.

6 When Samantha was assessed at nearly six years old, she was not yet reading. Her IQ score was so very high that I suggested to her parents to have her screened for a possible vision coordination problem. She did not need glasses but rather vision therapy to make her eyes work together. Reading followed almost immediately. We cannot know for certain, of course, whether Samantha might have started reading at that point or if it was the vision therapy that made the difference, but it is worth checking in such cases.

7 UMTYMP stands for the University of Minnesota Talented Youth Math Program and is designed for math-gifted seventh to twelfth graders to complete high school and college math before they finish high school. It is patterned after the Johns Hopkins and Northwestern University Programs for gifted youngsters.

8 EPGY (Education Program for Gifted Youth) is online instruction for gifted students through Stanford University. Many families pay for such coursework for their children because they cannot get permission from their own school systems to move their child ahead in any subjects.

Chapter 8

1 For those who wish to explore this issue further, Simonton (1994, 1999) has investigated the internal and environmental influences of genius-level production and eminence.

2 For additional information on talent development, see Benjamin Bloom (1985).

3 Environments for siblings can never be completely identical due to ever-changing circumstances as the parents mature, moves are made, siblings interact with one another, and others react to each child differently.

4 For an update on what each state mandates, funds, and the extent of services each provides, see www.geniusdenied.com.

5 Rick Arnesen is the oldest subject in this book, and personal computers were not available until he was nearly six years old. Readers must make allowances for the different ways in which high ability can show itself—e.g., what is common to the times.

6 Mensa is a high IQ society and has a number of books and games available for purchase.

7 See www.hoagiesgifted.com for advocacy information for parents.

8 Rick Arnesen didn't have a computer until age five.

Chapter 9

1 As Greenspon notes, "Shame is not so much a single emotion as an overall sense of inferiority and unacceptability. It is a feeling of being judged and found lacking" (2002, p. 18).

2 Emotional sensitivity and emotional intensity are well documented in gifted children. Dabrowski (1972) proposed that sensitivity and intensity were part of these children's psychological makeup and, instead of being indicators of neurotic imbalances, were positive potentials for further growth. These characteristics were displayed in gifted children through five overexcitabilities: psychomotor, sensual, intellectual, imaginational, and emotional" (Tucker & Hafenstein, 1997, p. 66). See also Piechowski (1991) for extensive interpretation of intensities and overexcitabilities.

3 ADHD (Attention Deficit Hyperactivity Disorder) and ADD (Attention Deficit Disorder) are commonly suspected in gifted children, particularly boys. Before they start school, the possibility of ADHD is seldom brought up. Once gifted children enter school, however, they discover that they have little to pay attention to because they already know most of the curriculum, and they start getting into trouble. What results is sometimes a misdiagnosis

of ADHD or ADD. Such behaviors, however, are a normal pattern for Level Three and higher gifted children.

4 A good summary of this work can be found in Silverman (1993). See also Hollingworth (1926), Lovecky (1993), Piechowski (1991), and Roeper (1995).

5 Dabrowski (1972) hypothesized that many gifted people have a strong innate ability and drive for higher-level moral development. In Ruf (1998), 41 highly gifted adult subjects completed the *Defining Issues Test* (DIT) (Rest, 1986), based on Kohlberg's (1984) developmental scheme, and found that the levels of moral development were significantly higher than the average for the highest normed groups—the clergy and philosophy majors in college. As with Gross's (1993) study of exceptionally gifted Australian children, the scores of the children in the current study are significantly higher than those for the normal population. What is most noteworthy, however, is how high the scores are for many very young children who are Levels Three through Five. The most significant aspect of higher-level moral reasoning is a predisposition to seek what *should be* rather than what *is.*

Chapter 10

1 The *No Child Left Behind Act* is a federal mandate passed during the Bush administration in 2001 that requires all students to learn to a minimum standard. Schools where children do not meet these standards are sanctioned and lose funding, and teachers are penalized or dismissed. The government threatens to take over those schools that do not meet annual yearly progress expectations. More information is available at www.ed.gov/nclb/landing.jhtml?src=pb.

2 For a thorough description of how the middle school movement aggravated school problems for gifted children, read Yecke (2003).

3 Differentiation is an educational term that refers to planning and teaching something different for a child whose needs are different from others in the classroom.

4 Pullout instruction is an educational term that refers to a practice in which a group of children are "pulled out" of their regular classroom for a different level of instruction or for instruction on a different topic while the majority of their classmates remain in the regular classroom for regular instruction with their teacher. Slow learners are instructed during their pullout time in math and reading and do not have to make up the work that takes place while they are gone. These classes for slow learners take place an average of one to three hours per school day for children who are struggling to learn at grade level.

5 Most schools that offer any gifted programming offer "pullout programs," in which the children leave their classroom for unrelated enrichment with a specialist and then return to make up the grade-level work they missed while gone. Most programs meet an average of one hour per week. Research into the effects of pullout instruction reveal that it is the least beneficial approach to increasing achievement in gifted children.

6 For a current listing of which states mandate and fund gifted services, go to www.geniusdenied.com.

7 SAT (the *Scholastic Aptitude Test*), the familiar College Board examinations usually taken by high school juniors and seniors and used for admission to colleges, can be taken early by bright, high-achieving students. They are available through the Educational Testing Service.

8 For an excellent summary on this topic, read Sommers (2000).

9 For much more detail, see Clark (2002), Reis (2002), and Sommers (2000).

10 For an excellent article on this topic, read Reis (2002).

11 Independent continuous progress is a form of individual learning in which learners use pre-assigned or formatted curriculum so that they can move at their own pace largely on their own.

Chapter 11

1 The topic of equalizing opportunity and its outcomes is discussed in both Davidson and Davidson (2004) and Yecke (2003).

2 ILP stands for Individual Learning Plan. The teacher, and sometimes a team of educators, develops a lesson plan that requires frequent updating, monitoring, and signatures from parents, the child, and teachers. It is labor intensive, time-consuming, and frequently does not get any sustainable implementation because it is so cumbersome.

3 Karnes and Marquardt (1999) have compiled mediation, case law, and statues pertaining to legal aspects of the education of gifted children. They describe strategies that parents can use to advocate for appropriate education for their children.

4 Least restrictive environment is legal terminology that means that it is illegal to restrict any child from normal exposure to what non-handicapped children experience during their school days. Mainstreaming to the maximum extent appropriate was adopted by the U.S. Congress when it enacted the Education of All Handicapped Children Act of 1975 (P.L. 94-142), the precursor to the Individuals with Disabilities Education Act (IDEA).

5 ADHD and ADD are two learning disabilities that have seen a huge upswing in diagnoses whose time-frame corresponds rather well to the dropping of ability-grouping.

6 See Sommers (2000) for an excellent overview.

7 Carol Mills questioned whether some teachers of the gifted are "highly effective because they possess certain personality styles, or are some teachers effective because their personality styles more closely match their students' personality styles?" (2003, p. 279). Her study compared the *Myers-Briggs Type Indicator* preferences of student participants in the Center for Talented Youth (CTY) of Johns Hopkins University summer programs with a portion of the teachers whom the students identified as "exemplary." The results showed a strong style preference match between favorite admired teachers and the

gifted students. A normative sample of middle school teachers had a significantly different style preference when measured on the *Myers-Briggs Type Indicator.*

8 www.geniusdenied.com/Articles.aspx?ArticleID=46

Chapter 12

1 Lateral enrichment is an instructional method that adds depth of content to a subject rather than moving the students ahead of their age-mates. It is most acceptable in classes like literature and social studies, in which more reading, discussion, and fact learning with higher order thinking are possible. For example, the whole class may be studying communities and using just a grade-level textbook. But the advanced learners could also be assigned separate literature, such as biographies or nonfiction material that goes into more depth about some facet of community life. These students would then get an opportunity to discuss what they read, present it to the class, or develop some sort of product—a paper, a model, a series of labeled photos from the Internet—to add to their learning experience. The problem with lateral enrichment is that busy teachers often don't have enough time to sustain the separate group and instead add more worksheets or extra end-of-chapter questions rather than substantive material.

2 *The Parallel Curriculum* (Tomlinson et al., 2002), a National Association for Gifted Children (NAGC) publication, guides teachers through an approach to maintaining grade-level curriculum while providing learning depth and challenges at different student levels.

3 Talent Searches are usually university-sponsored screenings using out-of-level standardized tests on students who are considerably younger than the groups on which the tests were normed. Children who score very high are invited to participate in special university-sponsored summer school courses, usually at their parents' expense, with other highly intelligent students near their same ages. Simply do an Internet search of "Academic Talent Search" to find out more about these wonderful programs.

4 International Baccalaureate (IB) is a program designed to combine the educational goals of numerous countries covering specialization as well as breadth. Different schools provide this option for 16- to 19-year-olds within their high school setting.

5 Radical acceleration is moving the child up through as many grade levels as necessary to have him or her work at the right level and pace for his or her ability. This can put the child out of sync with classmates as far as size, dexterity, and maturity and can lead to social and emotional issues unless there is a lot of support for the child. See Gross (1992) and Stanley (1996).

6 Seattle's Accelerated Progress Program (APP), established by the late Halbert Robinson of the University of Washington, is at least two years ahead of typical curriculum and serves about 1,000 students from around the Seattle area in grades K–8 each year.

Index

About the Author

Deborah L. Ruf, Ph.D. evaluates different profiles and levels of high intelligence in children and adults. She is the founder of Educational Options, a private organization located in Minneapolis. Dr. Ruf has studied both gifted adults and children and has presented throughout the United States on topics related to tests and assessment, levels of giftedness, educational needs of highly intelligent children, and personality factors in gifted individuals.

Dr. Ruf has taught post-baccalaureate classes in gifted education for St. Mary's and St. Thomas Universities in the Minneapolis area. She taught undergraduate education courses for North Dakota State University and Moorhead State University, and she supervised elementary student teachers. She served as Cass County Superintendent of Schools, where she worked as an administrator between 11 local school districts and the North Dakota State Office of Education.

Dr. Ruf holds a Ph.D. in Psychological Foundations of Education from the University of Minnesota, with a double major in Tests and Measurement and Learning and Cognition. She holds an M.Ed. degree in Elementary Administration and Supervision from the Curry School at the University of Virginia. She began her education career as an elementary teacher in Washington, D.C. and in Ohio, and she taught gifted students grades kindergarten through five in the Minneapolis area.

She has been a volunteer tutor for the Boys and Girls Club of North Minneapolis and has served on the Hennepin County Children's Mental Health Advisory Board, the Minnesota Council for Exceptional Children, and the Minnesota Council for Gifted and Talented. She currently serves as the national Gifted Children Program Coordinator for American Mensa.

Dr. Ruf lives with her husband in Minneapolis.